Russian Eyewitness Accounts of the Campaign of 1814

Russian Eyewitness Accounts of the Campaign of 1814

Compiled, Translated and Edited by
Alexander Mikaberidze

FRONTLINE BOOKS, LONDON

Russian Eyewitness Accounts of the Campaign of 1814

This edition published in 2013 by Frontline Books,
an imprint of Pen & Sword Books Ltd,
47 Church Street, Barnsley, S. Yorkshire, S70 2AS
www.frontline-books.com

ISBN: 978-1-84832-707-8

CIP data records for this title are available from the British Library

For more information on our books, please visit
www.frontline-books.com, email info@frontline-books.com
or write to us at the above address.

Printed and bound by CPI Group (UK) Ltd, Croydon, CR0 4YY

Typeset in 10/12.25 point Plantin MT by JCS Publishing Services Ltd,
www.jcs-publishing.co.uk

Contents

Illustrations

Preface

In the spring of 1814, after twenty-two years, France was once again invaded by enemy forces. Following Emperor Napoleon's defeats in Russia and Germany, the victorious Allies (Russia, Austria, Prussia and their German allies) had crossed the Rhine with an intention to put an end to a long-standing conflict with the Napoleonic regime. For the first time in a quarter of a century France had the first real taste of an experience she had so often previously meted out to her neighbours. Outnumbered on all fronts, Napoleon fought a brilliant campaign in February but none of his successes could turn the tide of war. The Allies persevered in their goal of seeing the French Empire overthrown and marched directly on to Paris.

In the afternoon of 30 March 1814, Emperor Alexander of Russia arrived on the Buttes-Chaumont and, ascending a nearby hill, surveyed the city rising in front of him in the distance. It was Paris, the city Alexander had longed to see for many years and now only hours separated him from a triumphant entry into the capital of his greatest enemy. On horseback since dawn, Alexander supervised unit movements and marked out his officers for promotions and rewards. By afternoon, the Allies had established large batteries and first few shots were fired into Paris.[*] The French commanders, realising that Paris was at the mercy of the Allies, chose to negotiate and sent an officer to the hill of Belleville, overlooking the Faubourg St. Martin, where Alexander established his command post. Nikolai Divov, a young officer in the Russian Guard artillery, saw 'a [French] negotiator arriving . . . [Our commander] escorted the negotiator to the Emperor [Alexander] who was standing, with his entire suite, not far from our battery'.[†] Alexander's aide-de-camp, Colonel Mikhail Orlov, had misgivings about this officer, who, he thought, looked more like as 'a runaway prisoner of war who lost his way in the rear of our army'.[‡] The Russian officers watched as Alexander ordered his entire suite to leave and, flanked by King Frederick William of Prussia, and Prince Karl Philipp Fürst

---

[*] For details see N. Divov, 'Po povodu rasskaza M.F. Orlova o vzyatii Parizha,' *Russkii arkhiv*, 1/1 (1878), pp. 127–8; Alexander Mikhailovskii-Danilevskii, *History of the Campaign in France in the Year 1814* (London: Smith, Elder and Co, 1840), p. 368.

[†] Divov, 'Po povodu rasskaza M.F. Orlova . . .', p. 128.

[‡] Mikhail Orlov, 'Kapitulyatsiya Parizha v 1814 godu', *Russkaya starina*, 12 (1877), p. 635.

zu Schwarzenberg, he conversed with a French negotiator, who requested the Allies to stop their attacks. Alexander responded that he would agree to an armistice only if Paris surrendered at once* and, since the officer was not empowered to accept such terms, the Russian sovereign sent his aide-de-camp Colonel Orlov to Marshal Auguste Marmont who was directing the French defences and by dawn on 31 March, the act of surrender of the French capital was signed

Early that morning, Emperor Alexander mounted Eclipse, a horse presented to him by the French ambassador six years before, and prepared for the moment of his life. He rode with his staff to King Frederick William's headquarters at Pantin and the two sovereigns then led the Allied troops into Paris. Nesselrode was struck by 'a well-dressed crowd covering boulevards. It seemed as if people gathered for a festivity, rather than to witness the entry of enemy troops'.† Alexander Mikhailovskii-Danilevskii, the famous Russian historian who escorted Emperor Alexander that day, remembered that 'a countless multitude [of people] crowded the streets, and the roofs and windows of the houses'.‡ Etienne-Denis Pasquier, who had served as Napoleon's prefect of police since 1810, recalled that 'an enormous concourse of people had wended its way since morning to every point of the road along which the strangers were to pass. The Faubourg Saint-Denis and the boulevards swarmed with them; the crowd was silent and cast down, and awaited the course of events with great anxiety'.§ Alphonse de Lamartine described streets swarming with the populace, some hoping for a riot:

[Upon the appearance of the Russian officers,] the people of the quarter of the Bastille arose in a tumult, and uttered, in sign of defiance, shouts of 'Vive Bonaparte!' Some armed men rushed out of the crowd towards an aide-de-camp of the Emperor Alexander, who was going to prepare his quarters. 'Come on, Frenchmen!' cried these desperate fellows. 'The Emperor Napoleon is coming! Let us destroy the enemy.' The people, however, were deaf to the cry. The National Guard interposed, protected the detachment, and picked up a few wounded officers. The heads of the foreign columns soon after appeared on the Boulevards.'¶

---

* According to Divov, he overheard Alexander saying in French, 'Que demain, à 6 heures du matin, la ville de Paris soit evacuee par les troupes françaises.' The negotiator responded, 'Les orders du vainqueur seront remplis.'
† Cited in Nikolai Shilder, *Imperator Alexander: ego zhizhn i tsarstvovanie* (St. Petersburg: Suvorin, 1905), III, p. 210.
‡ Alexander Mikhailovskii-Danilevskii, *Zapiski 1814 i 1815 godov* (St. Petersburg: Departament vneshnei torgovli, 1836), p. 42.
§ Etienne-Denis Pasquier, *A History of My Time: Memoirs of Chancellor Pasquier* (New York: Charles Scribner's Son, 1894), II, p. 269.
¶ Alphonse de Lamartine, *Histoire de la Restauration* (Paris, 1853), I, p. 163.

Starting around 9 a.m., the Allied columns, with colours unfurled, drums beating and music playing, began a triumphant entry into Paris. The Russian cavalry, with the Life Guard Cossack Regiment and Grand Duke Constantine at its head, led the way and Lamartine thought they represented 'barbarous war evoked from the deserts of the north to spread over the south'. Another spectator observed that the 'physiognomy of the Russian troops' indicated strongly the different nations to which they belonged. Indeed, Thomas Richard Underwood, an Englishman visiting the French capital, saw the streets thronged with

People of every description . . . inhabitants of all the north of Europe, and the Asiatic subjects of the Russian empire, from the Caspian Sea to the Wall of China, were riding about; Cossacks, with their sheep-skin jackets, sandy-coloured, shaggy beards, long lances . . . Calmucks, and different Tartar tribes, with their flat noses, little eyes, and dark reddish-brown skins; Baschkins and Tungusians of Siberia, armed with bows and arrows; Tscherkess or Circassian noblemen from the foot of Mount Caucasus, clad in complete hauberks of steel mail, perfectly bright, and conical helmets, similar in form to those worn in England in the twelfth and thirteenth centuries.*

Behind the Russian cavalry came Alexander, Frederick William and Schwarzenberg, accompanied by their generals and an enormous suite, and followed by tens of thousands of Allied soldiers.† Writing to the Russian Empress Consort Elisaveta Alekseevna, Cossack Ataman Matvei Platov informed her that 'I have no words to describe today's celebration but I humbly inform Your Majesty that never such an event had taken place in preceding centuries, and there would be hardly any to rival it in the future. There was indescribable excitement on both sides, accompanied by shouts of numerous throngs of people of Paris: 'Long Live Emperor Alexander who brought peace and prosperity to Europe!'‡ A staff captain in the Russian Imperial suite was equally awe struck by the radiance of the moment, noting 'both we and the residents of Paris took pleasure in this inexpressible joy: they because of freedom from a heavy yoke, we because of finishing a war in such a brilliant manner . . . With beautiful weather that day, streets were full of numerous people from dawn till late evening.'§ A journalist writing in the

---

* Thomas Richard Underwood, *A Narrative of Memorable Events in Paris in 1814* (London, 1828), pp. 155–6.
† *Journal des Débats*, 3 April 1814, p. 3.
‡ Platov to Empress Elizaveta Alekseevna, 2 April 1814, *Rossiiskii arkhiv* (Moscow, 1996), VII, p. 188.
§ Alexander Mikhailovskii-Danilevskii, 'O prebyvanii russkikh v Parizhe v 1814 godu', in *Russkii vestnik*, 1819, No. 9/10, p. 21.

Journal des Débats, a Royalist daily publication in Paris, described the Allied entry into Paris as 'the most amazing spectacle in the history of the world'.*

Count Louis-Victor-Léon de Rochechouart, a French émigré who served in the Russian army, noted that 'Napoleon's latest reports had represented [the Allied] army as exhausted, disorganised and reduced to inefficiency . . . [Now] this display of overwhelming force seemed to make a great impression on the Parisians. The most numerous and brilliant staff ever assembled completed the picture. Add to this, an electrified crowd, shouts from more than a hundred thousand voices, "Long live the Emperor Alexander! Long live the King of Prussia! Long live the King! Long live the Allies! Long live our Deliverers", mingled with words of command in Russian and German, the sound of carriages and horses, the tramp of infantry; the scene is indescribable.'† But not all Russian officers were enthralled by the public elation. Later that day Pavel Pushin, an officer in the Life Guard Semeyonovskii Regiment, recorded in his diary, 'Crowds of onlookers increased as we advanced into the city and all of them expressed genuine happiness, shouting "Vive Alexander! Vive King of Prussia! Vive Bourbons!" But can we really believe any of this? Just yesterday these same people were yelling "Vive Napoleon".'‡

According to the *Journal des Débats*, the Allied entry was accompanied 'everywhere by the signs of unambiguous sentiments of the inhabitants of the capital. Everywhere they spoke to the troops, they got along and have but one sentiment: hatred for their oppressors and the desire to return the legitimate authority that had been tested by the centuries and was the only worthy one of France and Europe . . . that of the princes of the house of Bourbon, this majestic august house which had brought happiness and true glory to France for centuries.'§ Some of Emperor Alexander's words and actions further intensified such sentiments. Rochechouart describes an incident, when 'a young woman contrived – how I know not – to raise herself on to one of the stirrups of the Tsar, [and] shouted frantically in his ear: "Vive l'Empereur Alexandre". The Sovereign took hold of her hands to keep her from falling, and said in his gracious manner: "Madame, cry 'Vive le Roi,' and I will cry it with you".'¶ But the majority of Parisians remained aloof to Royalist sentiments. The Duc de Fitz-James' attempts to rally a battalion of the National Guard with the cry of Vive le Roi! did nothing to change the

---

* *Journal des Débats*, 3 April 1814, p. 3.

† Similar sentiments in Pavel Pushin's diary: 'The Parisians were truly stunned by this spectacle. They were assured that only a small blundering column of our troops was marching on Paris, but now they saw a powerful army of splendid appearance in front of them.' Pavel Pushin, *Dnevnik* (Leningrad: University of Leningrad Press, 1987), p. 154.

‡ Pushin, *Dnevnik*, p. 154.

§ *Journal des Débats*, 3 April 1814, p. 3

¶ Louis-Victor-Léon de Rochechouart, *Memoirs*, p. 282.

impassive faces of its soldiers, while Sosthéne de la Rochefoucauld's effort to organise a Royalist demonstration on Place Louis XV produced a paltry group of about dozen men.* Later that day Sosthéne de la Rochefoucauld, shouting 'à bas Napoléon', led a group of Royalists to bring down Napoleon's statue on top of the column in the Place Vendôme. Despite their attempts – one of them even climbed onto the statue and 'kept slapping it on the cheeks'† – they were unable to remove it before the arrival of a patrol of the Life Guard Semeyonovskii Regiment, which Alexander sent to protect the monument.‡

The parade review ended about five o'clock in the afternoon, when Alexander retired to the house of Charles Maurice Périgord de Talleyrand, where he resided during the early period of his stay in Paris. Some of the Russian troops mounted guard, and the rest took up the quarters assigned them in the city. These were the best days for the Russian sovereign and his presence elevated European esteem of Russia to hitherto unprecedented heights. The behaviour of the Russian troops was meticulously regulated by Alexander himself, who intended to ensure and maintain Russian prestige. According to Jacob Otroshenko from the 14th Jagers, 'many Frenchmen asked us what we are going to with Paris, are we going to burn it like the French did with Moscow?'§ To allay such fears, Alexander assured the deputations of Parisians that no looting or damaging of property would be tolerated. 'I have but one enemy in France, and this enemy is the man who has deceived me in the most infamous fashion, who has abused my confidence, who has violated all his sworn pledges to me, who has carried into my dominions the most iniquitous and outrageous war. All other Frenchmen are my friends.' he declared.¶ As the tripartite government of the capital was established, the Russian General Baron Fabian Osten-Sacken was appointed military governor-general and a Russian, Austrian and Prussian commandant each had four *arrondissements* to police. The Russian troops were instructed 'to treat locals most benevolently and to overwhelm them with our generosity, rather than vengeance, and to avoid imitating French behaviour in Russia'.**

---

* Louis François Sosthènes de la Rochefoucauld Doudeauville, *Memoires* . . . (Paris: Allardin, 1837), I, pp. 45–7. Also see Gilbert Stenger, *Retour des Bourbons* (Paris, Plon-Nourrit, 1908), pp. 126–8.

† A. Mikhailovskii-Danilevskii, 'O prebyvanii russkikh v Parizhe v 1814 g.' *Russkii vestnik*, 9 (1819), pp. 13–14.

‡ I. Lazhechnikov, *Pokhodnye zapiski russkogo ofitsera* (Moscow, 1836), pp. 203–4; Jacob Otroshenko, *Zapiski generala Otroshenko (1800-1830)* (Moscow: Bratin, 2006), pp. 85–6; N. Kovalskii, 'Iz zapisok pokoinago general maiora N.P. Kovalskago', *Russkii vestnik*, 91 (1871), p. 112.

§ Otroshenko, *Zapiski* . . . , p. 85.

¶ Pasquier, *A History of My Time*, II, p. 261.

** Ilya Radozhitskii, *Pokhodnye zapiski artillerista s 1812 po 1816 g* (Moscow, 1835), III, p. 31.

Imagine what these officers felt that evening. Their diaries and memoirs reveal a sense of elation, thrill and excitement that prevented them from sleeping. Most of them probably shared the sentiments expressed by Ivan Lazhechnikov, 'What would you have said, oh the esteemed Capets, the founders of the French states, and you Henri, the father of your nation, and you, the Sun-like Louis XIV? What would you have felt, Sullys, Colberts, Turrennes, Racins, Voltaires, you, the glory of your Fatherland? What would you have said, when upon awakening from the deathly slumber, you would have heard the joyous "hurrah" of Slavs on the heights of Montmartre?'* Among the officers who could not sleep that night was Mikhailovskii-Danilevskii, who, around midnight, decided to walk in the streets and was pleased to see Parisians of all walks of life 'respecting a Russian uniform: I walked throughout Palais-Royal, stopped by the crowds of Parisians and was everywhere met with great courtesy.' As he returned home walking along deserted streets, Mikhailovskii-Danilevskii was happy to note that 'not a sound was heard in the streets of Paris, save for the call of the Russian sentries'.

Over the next few days, as the Allied army settled down, Russian officers began exploring the city all of them had heard about but very few had actually visited. In the first days of occupation, the annual salary was doubled and paid in full for three previous campaigns (1812, 1813 and 1814) at once and so eating, drinking and gambling were on the top of everyone's list. 'It is rather shameful,' wrote M. Muromtsev, a staff officer in the Russian headquarters, 'but except for the Musée Napoleon, I have seen nothing in Paris because I was preoccupied with drinking, eating and having fun.'† Food was cheap and, as another officer notes, Russian officers 'were granted large credits at shops and restaurants.'‡ Chertkov's diary shows that 'officers received 5 francs a day while staff officers – 10 francs . . . [At Palais-Royal], one could order a lunch from any six dishes and pay a moderate some of 1 franc and 50 centimes.'§ In the restaurants of Palais-Royal, the officers were 'awed by splendid rooms, beautiful furniture, and servants in opulent livery as well as fine dishes, crystals and table cloth. [We were served] exquisite dishes and wines, all served cleanly and nicely . . . Crowds of Frenchmen entered rooms to gaze at us as if we were wonders. They were surprised that we spoke French among ourselves.'¶ 'The

---

* Lazhechnikov, *Pokhodnye zapiski*, p. 189.

† Matvei Muromtsev, 'Vospominaniya', *Russkii arkhiv*, 3 (1890), p. 381. According to Lorer, during the parade review on the first day of the occupation, some officers even managed to escape from the ranks to have lunch in the Palais-Royal. Nikolai Lorer, *Zapiski dekabrista*, ed. Militsa Nechkina (Irkutsk: Vostochno-Sibirskoe knizhnoe izd-vo, 1984), p. 313.

‡ Kovalskii, 'Iz zapisok', p. 115.

§ Alexander Chertkov, 'Mon Itinéraire ou Journal de Route', in *1812-1814. Iz sobraniya Gosudarstvennogo Istoricheskogo muzeya* (Moscow: Terra, 1992), pp. 421–2.

¶ Nikolai Bronevskii, 'Iz vospominanii . . .', *Golos minuvshego*, 3 (1914), pp. 233–5.

French look at us as if we came from a different, completely unknown world,' marvelled another officer. 'They feared,' writes Mikhailovskii-Danilevskii, 'that we were Northern barbarians while Cossacks are wild and half-naked savages who skin their prisoners and cook and east small children whenever they find them in villages.' So, continues Ivan Lazhechnikov, 'our colourful uniforms, hats and plumes . . . neatness and uniformity of our clothing had a great effect on [the French] . . . They were particularly struck by the fact that some of our officers are fluent in French and speak it as easily as the French. As soon as a single French word is uttered by one of us, we are immediately surrounded by a crowd of onlookers who incessantly asking thousands of questions, many of them quite obtuse and revealing great ignorance.'* All participants recalled fondly interacting with Parisians, especially with street vendors and merchants but the presence of occupying force naturally produced frictions as well. 'It was as easy to recognise the French officers by their sombre countenances as by their uniforms,' remarks one Russian officer,

> They conducted themselves more politely towards the Russians than to the other allies, with whom they had frequent quarrels which ended in duels. The Prussians were the chief objects of their hatred, and hardly a day passed in which blood did not flow on one side or the other. The German officers, although the neighbours of the French, had more difficulty in conforming to their manners, customs, and language, than the Russians. At this time we received permission to wear plain clothes, in which we appeared in society as ordinary citizens. The Prussians and Austrians, on the contrary, continued to walk about in uniform. We may add, with perfect truth, that they did not try to adorn their triumph with modesty. The Austrians have a custom of wearing green branches in their caps and hats, which gave offence to the French, who thought they represented laurels; and hence resulted quarrels, and even murders. On the contrary, the Parisians were highly gratified by our wearing a white band round the left arm, and by our adding a white knot to our cockades. This apparently trifling circumstance turned the current of public opinion in our favour, and served as a bond of union between us.†

Nevertheless, many duels took place during the months the Russian army occupied Paris, both among Russian officers and between Russians and the French. Thus, Liprandi tells a story about a Russian officer, Bartenev, who

---

* Lazhechnikov, *Pokhodnye zapiski*, pp. 202–3.
† Mikhailovskii-Danilevskii, *History of the Campaign in France*, pp. 402. One of the places of attraction in Paris was the famous Pont d'Austerlitz, which Napoleon had built in commemoration of his great victory in December 1805. Now, in 1814, some Parisians sought to win over Alexander by erasing Imperial symbols and inscriptions on the bridge. However, as Otroshenko informs us, Emperor Alexander refused to give his consent for this, instead requesting to add just one more inscription on the bridge, noting that the Russian army crossed it in 1814. Otroshenko, *Zapiski*, pp. 87–8.

replied wittily to the French officers out to insult him personally and the Russian army in general:

> Being a lieutenant known for his bravery in the Aleksandriiskii Hussar Regiment, in 1814 in Paris he had an equally famous duel with three French officers who asked why hussars have black feathers on their hats while other Russians also have rooster's feathers, like his, but white ones. Bartenev very politely explained that it is infantry that wears the black ones and cavalry the white, and that the feathers come not from roosters but from the French eagles that they have plucked [que nous avons épluchée].'*

After months of campaigning, the Russian officers, like anyone else, were starved for female company and Paris provided them with plenty of entertainment. Palais-Royal had plenty of sporting houses and the number of ladies of the evening surprised some Russian officers. 'They walk in groups of two or three, talking and laughing loudly, making such jokes that our ears cracked . . .,' describe one officer while Ilya Radozhitskii recalled seeing these women 'seducing our youngsters with their eyes and, if they got no response, they would pinch sorely to get attention'.† Fedor Glinka writes with certain sarcasm, 'Adieu my dear and delightful enchantresses . . . you, who sparkle in the Opera, stroll graciously on the boulevards or flutter in galleries and gardens of the Palais-Royal! We will be sending you our passionate sighs from the banks of the Neva and Don. You never looked at our faces . . . A bearded Cossack and flat-faced Bashkir quickly became favourites of your hearts if they had money! You always respected the clanking sound of virtue!'‡ But these relations oftentimes led to complications and many Russians, like their Allied brethren, soon contracted venereal diseases. The young officer Kazakov was lodged at the house of the famous Parisian physician Baron Guillaume Dupuytren, who befriended him and one day took him to the Hôtel-Dieu, showing him wards full of men with syphilis and made him promise to abstain from sex.§

Reading these memoirs and diaries we see what Russian officers and soldiers experienced during the final months of the three year-long campaign

---

* I. P. Liprandi, 'Zamechaniya na "Vospominaniya" F.F. Vigeliya', *Chteniya v Imperatorskom obshchestve istorii i drevnostei rossiiskikh*, 1873, Book 1 (January–March), p. 141 (f.69).

† *Vyderzhki iz voyennykh zapisok . . .*, pp. 89–90; Radozhitskii, *Pokhodnye zapiski*, III, p. 127. For a Cossack viewpoint, see 'Na chuzhbine sto let nazad,' *Kazachii sbornik* (Paris, 1930), p. 95.

‡ F. Glinka, *Pisma russkogo ofitsera* (Moscow, 1816), part 8, p. 170.

§ Ivan Kazakov, 'Pokhod vo Frantsiyu 1812 g. Po neizdannym zapiskam praporshika leib-gvardii Semeyonovskogo polka Ivana Mikhailovicha Kazakova', *Russkaya starina* 5 (1908), p. 355.

against Napoleon, we experience their joy at winning the war over Russia's most dangerous enemy and follow them not only through the heat of battle but also delightful tours of Paris which they describe as the pleasure and entertainment capital of the world. They were thrilled by artistic treasures of the capital, fascinated by the quality of food, and struck by the freedom, one may even say frivolity, of Parisians. But they were also disillusioned by France in general. Raised by French tutors, reading French literature and often speaking French better than Russian, they had idealised this country since childhood and hoped to find an 'earthly paradise' there. And even though Paris thrilled them, many Russian officers were struck by the widespread poverty, misery and economic hardship in the rest of the country. They were surprised to find Frenchmen from all social classes rather ignorant of the world outside France, as well inconsiderate and boorish. 'The French emperor had pillaged and devastated lands all across [Europe] and yet we find the French living in poverty and misery,' observed one general in a letter.* Time and again, we see in memoirs references to grime and un-cleanliness in French towns, causing one officer to remark that 'the French have a national tendency to filthiness'.† Another officer aptly observed that 'many of our officers, who in their childhood were influenced by their foreign tutors and hoped to find a promised land in France, were sorely disappointed upon seeing widespread poverty, ignorance and despair in villages and towns.' Campaigning in the Champagne region, Pavel Pushin lamented, 'The poverty around Langres is staggering; people are deprived of most necessities . . . Houses are cold and dirty . . .' A few days later, the same officer recorded in his diary, 'A peasant's food consists of only warm water with pig's fat and crumbled bread, which they call a soup. A [French] peasant is as ignorant as a Russian one, and is as poor as our peasants in Smolensk or Vitebsk.' More importantly, to many officers, the fact that the invasion of France unfolded 'so easily' and was over in just three months told of the unpatriotic nature of Frenchmen. They compared Russian resistance to Napoleon in 1812 to the perceived French 'inaction' in 1814. This in turn led to reinforcement of the existing stereotypes of Russian superiority, i.e. dedication, loyalty, patriotism, ability to sacrifice what's dear to one's heart (i.e. Moscow) in order to win the war.

Much has been written on this famous campaign over the last two hundred years, ‡ but the Russian side of the story is oftentimes lost in the narrative

---

* Sacken to Barclay de Tolly, No. 4, 3/15 January 1814, RGVIA, f. VUA, op. 16, d. 4120, part 1, l. pp. 112–13.

† Radozhitskii, *Pokodznye zapiski*, III, 45.

‡ For an excellent operational history of the 1814 campaign see Michael V. Leggiere, *The Fall of Napoleon: The Allied Invasion of France, 1813-1814* (Cambridge: Cambridge University Press, 2007). It is indeed remarkable that while there is an extensive Russian historiography of hundreds of volumes on the Patriotic War, as the Russians call Napoleon's invasion of Russia in 1812, the campaign of 1814 still

since linguistic difficulties, administrative hurdles and political and ideological rivalries combined to create a substantial dearth of English translations of Russian account of the Napoleonic Wars. Even in Russia, historians have long concentrated on the Russian Campaign of 1812, which has been studied in minutiae detail, and have largely ignored the campaign that had finally overthrown Napoleon. Thus, *Russian Eyewitness Accounts of the Campaign of 1814* is a unique book – it is the first title to bring together letters, diaries and memoirs of Russian participants of the 1814 Campaign. It offers but a glimpse of the vibrant memoir literature that exists about this campaign but has been long inaccessible and underutilised. We do hope that this selective coverage will not detract from the overall value of the book.

The material is organised in chronological order starting with the Allied army's arrival at the borders of France. It is divided into eight chapters that contain a selection of excerpts from over two dozen memoirs and diaries, army orders and proclamations. In selecting material, we sought to include memoirs, diaries, letters and official documents to present a variety of viewpoints. These narratives are naturally subjective and occasionally imprecise but they are indispensable if we want to understand how their authors went about their normal existence and experienced the war that became the turning point in their lives. We believe that these documents show the other side of the coin: providing an unique insight on the Russian side of the war, how and why decisions were made and what Russian officers and soldiers experienced as they slowly advanced towards victory.

Every book is a result of a joint effort and I am grateful to a number of individuals for their support and assistance. Donald Graves supported my idea of an anthology of Russian memoirs and proposed it to Frontline Books. Without him, this book probably would not have been published. The publisher, Michael Leventhal, quickly saw the value of the proposal and agreed to publish not just one but three volumes of Russian memoirs, and I am very grateful for his willingness to launch this unique series. My editor Stephen Chumbley patiently waited for the delivery of the manuscript, offering support and encouragement throughout the past two years. I was able to utilise materials from over a dozen libraries across the United States and Europe, and must extend my thanks to the staff of the Green Library at Stanford, the Yale University Library, the Widener Library of Harvard University,

---

remains overlooked in Russia. The works of Alexander Mikhailovskii-Danilevskii and Modest Bogdanovich, despite being written in the first half of the nineteenth century, remain the standard accounts of this campaign in Russian. For the most recent effort at general history of the Russian army's campaigns in 1813–14, see N. Mogilevskii, *Ot Nemana do Seny: Zagranichnyi pokhod russkoi armii 1813-1814 gg.* (Moscow: Kuchkovo Pole, 2012).

the University of Chicago Library and the Russian State Library. Stephen Summerfield kindly allowed me to reproduce excerpts from his translation of Eduard von Löwenstern's memoir while Greg Gorsuch generously shared his time and knowledge to translate the memoirs of Alexander Langeron.

Last but not least, I am indebted to my family: to my sons Luka and Sergi for being perfect little boys and allowing me to carry on writing, and to my wife Anna for her constant encouragement, ceaseless aid and support for all my undertakings.

This book is dedicated to Michael V. Leggiere, the foremost modern scholar of the 1814 Campaign who has taught me much about the Napoleonic Wars. But he is more than a colleague – he is a true friend whose comradeship and support I will always cherish.

Editor's Note

Dates in original Russian documents are given in the Julian calendar, which was effective in the Russian Empire at the time. For this book, I converted dates into the Gregorian calendar and provided them in brackets. At the same times, whenever the author himself included date conversions in his memoirs, I kept them intact and they are oftentimes shown in parenthesis or separated by a dash. Russian sources often cite old measurements (sazhen, pud, versta, and so on), which I have converted to modern measurements.

The reader should not be surprised to see various numbers attached to Russian names. There were often several officers with same last names serving in the Russian army and consequently, numbers were attached to their last names to distinguish them. To distinguish between the uhlan (especially Polish) regiments in the Allied and Russian armies, I have used 'lancer' for units in the French Army and 'uhlan' for those in the Russian service.

The source for each memoir is indicated by a short title at the end of the cited text while full bibliographic details of the sources are listed at the back of the book. I tried to stay as true to the original text as possible, which entailed retaining authors' use of contemporary measurements (versta, sazhen, etc) and older names for locations.

Northern France
1814

Laon
9/10 Mar.

Craonne
7 Mar.

Soissons
Russian storming,
14 Feb.
Clash, 3 Mar.

Reims
12/13 Mar.

Château-Thierry
12 Feb.

La Ferté-sous-Jouarre
9 Feb.

Vauchamps
(Etoges)
14 Feb.

Champaubert
10 Feb.

Paris

Battle for Paris,
30 Mar.

Montmirail
11 Feb.

Bannes
25 Mar.

Fère-Champenoise
25 Mar.

Vitry-le-
François

St. Dizier
27 Jan.

Nangis (Mormant
& Valhouan)
17 Feb.

Arcis-sur-Aube
20/21 Mar.

Fontainebleau

Montereau
18 Feb.

Nogent-sur-
Seine
10 Feb.

Méry-sur-Seine
22 Feb.

Brienne
29 Jan.

Laubressel
clash, 3/4 Mar.

La Rothière
1 Feb

Nemours
Russian capture,
16 Feb.

Sens

Troyes

Bar-sur-Aube
24 Jan.;
26/27 Feb.

Chaumont

F R A N C E

B O U R G O G N E

Langres

Auxerre

Rethel

Verdun

Compiègne

Épernay

Châlons-sur-Marne

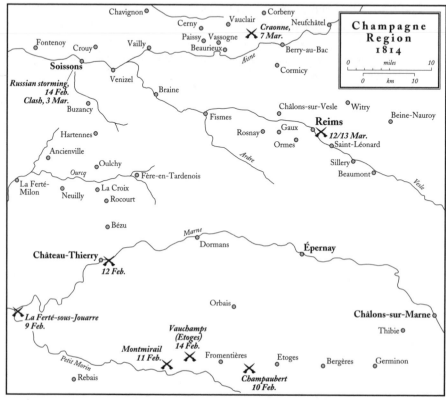

Champagne
Region
1814

Chavignon

Corbeny

Cerny

Vauclair

Neufchâtel

Fontenoy

Crouy

Vailly

Paissy

Vassogne

Craonne,
7 Mar.

Beaurieux

Berry-au-Bac

Soissons

Russian storming,
14 Feb.
Clash, 3 Mar.

Venizel

Braine

Cormicy

Buzancy

Fismes

Châlons-sur-Vesle

Witry

Beine-Nauroy

Hartennes

Rosnay

Gaux

Reims
12/13 Mar.

Ancienville

Oulchy

Ormes

Saint-Léonard

La Ferté-
Milon

Neuilly

Fère-en-Tardenois

La Croix

Rocourt

Sillery

Beaumont

Bézu

Marne

Dormans

Épernay

Château-Thierry
12 Feb.

La Ferté-sous-Jouarre
9 Feb.

Orbais

Châlons-sur-Marne

Vauchamps
(Etoges)
14 Feb.

Thibie

Montmirail
11 Feb.

Fromentières

Etoges

Bergères

Germinon

Rebais

Champaubert
10 Feb.

Chronology

1814

24 January	Battle at Bar-sur-Aube
27 January	Battle at St. Dizier
29 January	Battle at Brienne
1 February	Battle at La Rothière
9 February	Battle at La Ferté-sous-Jouarre
10 February	Battle at Nogent-sur-Seine
10 February	Battle at Champaubert
11 February	Battle at Montmirail
12 February	Battle at Château-Thierry
14 February	Battle at Vauchamps (Etoges)
14 February	Russian storming of Soissons
16 February	Russian capture of Nemours
17 February	Battle at Nangis (Mormant and Valhouan)
18 February	Battle at Montereau
22 February	Battle at Méry-sur-Seine
26/27 February	Battle at Bar-sur-Aube
3 March	Clash at Soissons
3/4 March	Clash at Laubressel
7 March	Battle at Craonne
9/10 March	Battle at Laon
12/13 March	Battle at Reims
20/21 March	Battle at Arcis-sur-Aube
25 March	Battle of La Fère-Champenoise
25 March	Battle at Bannes
30 March	Battle for Paris

1

Onwards to France!

After a string of triumphs in 1805–7, Napoleon established French hegemony over much of Europe. In 1807, he and Alexander I of Russia proclaimed an alliance of their great empires which divided the European continent into two spheres of influence. Russia pledged to join France in her struggle against Britain while France accepted Russian territorial expansion in Finland and the Danubian principalities. The treaty also provided a harsh punishment for Prussia, which was reduced to the status of a second-rate power after being stripped of almost half of its territory, forced to downsize its military and pay a heavy war indemnity. Napoleon distributed the formerly Prussian territories among his allies and created the Duchy of Warsaw which projected French interests into north-eastern Europe. At the same time, the conflict between France and Britain entered its thirteenth year and no resolution could be expected in the near future. Napoleon's military prowess secured French dominance on the Continent while Britain was protected behind the 'wooden walls' of its navy. The British government chose to fully exploit its naval supremacy to blockade the European coast, rivers and ports from the river Elbe to the port of Brest. In response, Napoleon instituted his own blockade, the Continental System, seeking to undermine the British economy by depriving it access to European markets, secure French economic dominance in Europe and promote industrial development on the Continent.

Considered by many scholars to be one of Napoleon's biggest mistakes, the Continental System ultimately failed in its aims. Napoleon did not have the ability to compel all European states to adhere to a system that was often detrimental to their economies. The Franco–Russian alliance, created at Tilsit in 1807 and reinforced at Erfurt in 1808, withered away by 1811. Russia was disgruntled by the economic losses sustained under the Continental System and concerned about Napoleon's plans for the restoration of Poland. Emperor Alexander was also alarmed by Napoleon's aggressive policy in Europe after France annexed Holland, the Hanseatic cities and the North German states. As Russia announced its decision to withdraw from the Continental System, Napoleon began preparations for war.

On 24 June 1812, Napoleon's massive army of over 450,000 men invaded Russia. His plan of forcing the Russians to fight, however, did not materialise as their armies, commanded by Mikhail Barclay de Tolly and Peter Bagration, retreated deep into the country. Compelled to follow them, the Grande Armée suffered from desertion and attrition which reduced its size to only 180,000 men by mid-August. The decisive battle at Borodino on 7 September proved to be a tactical, albeit costly, victory for the French. A week later the French occupied the abandoned city of Moscow. Yet fires soon broke out and continued until 18 September, destroying two-thirds of the city. Napoleon spent one month in the smouldering ruins of Moscow, hoping (in vain) to secure a peace with Russia. The Russian commander-in-chief Field Marshal Mikhail Kutuzov, meantime, regrouped the Russian army, encouraged popular war against the invader and formed flying detachments to threaten the enemy rear and lines of communication. On 18 October, Marshal Joachim Murat suffered a defeat on the Cherneshnya River, north of Tarutino. Hearing this news, Napoleon decided to leave Moscow before the winter arrived and commenced retreat on 19 October. Napoleon's forces dwindled to some 100,000 men, accompanied by thousands of non-combatants and an enormous train with loot. Unable to break through the Russian lines at Maloyaroslavets on 23–24 October, Napoleon returned to the devastated route to Smolensk and rapidly retreated to the west. The Russians inflicted considerable casualties on the Grand Armée in battles at Vyazma (3 November), Krasnyi (14–16 November), on the Berezina River (26–29 November) and Vilna (10 December)

The Russian Campaign had disastrous consequences for Napoleon. His military might was shattered following the loss of up to half a million men in Russia. The French cavalry was virtually wiped out and never fully recovered during the subsequent campaigns in 1813–14. Furthermore, Napoleon's allies, Austria and Prussia, exploited the moment to break their alliance with France and joined their efforts against Napoleon. The Campaign is particularly interesting for its gigantic scope, intensity and the variety of tactics employed. The war also had important effects on Russia. The Russian army became the main force in the subsequent struggle for Germany. 'The last campaign was bloody,' wrote Vasilii Norov, the young officer of the Life Guard Jager Regiment, to his father in early 1813, 'but we desire more battles in order to secure a firm and advantageous peace for our Fatherland. We have left Russia and are marching across the foreign lands but not to conquer and enslave them but to free them . . . We are marching to the West to wage war to bring about peace. Until now we fought for the peace and tranquillity of our Fatherland – from now on the struggle is for the tranquillity of Europe.'

Napoleon's defeat in Russia signalled an opportunity for other states to free themselves from French hegemony. The Sixth Coalition, involving Russia, Britain, Prussia, Sweden, Austria, and a number of German states, was formed for that purpose. Napoleon was able to raise a new army in France and defeat the Allies at Lützen (2 May) and Bautzen (20–21 May). The warring sides then declared an armistice from 4 June to 13 August during which time they both attempted to both negotiate and recover from their losses. Napoleon's intransigence in negotiations played into the hands of Austrian chancellor Klemens Wenzel *von Metternich who skilfully guided Austria from an alliance with France into the Sixth Coalition. When the hostilities resumed in late August, Napoleon scored another victory at Dresden (26–27 August) but the Allies soon seized the initiative. By avoiding direct battles with Napoleon and targeting his marshals, they gained victories at Katzbach (26 August), Kulm (29–30 August), Dennewitz (6 September) and Göhrde (16 September). The decisive battle at Leipzig in Saxony (16–19 October 1813), also called the 'Battle of the Nations', proved to be the largest of the Napoleonic wars and involved some 195,000 French and more than 350,000 Allies. In a three-day battle Napoleon suffered a defeated and was forced to retreat to France.*

The Allies were concerned about the prospects of invading France. Memories of the French levée en masse *in 1793 were still fresh and the Allies were disinclined to pay the high cost in men and materiel to invade France; besides, they still had healthy respect for the military talents of the Emperor of the French. Yet Napoleon could not bring himself to accept the Allied peace terms, offered on 8 November 1813, which would have reduced France to its so-called natural frontiers. He feared that military and political setbacks, combined with a much-reduced French state, would expose his regime to the threats of domestic opponents willing to rise against him. Napoleon's refusal left the Allies no choice but to press on, seeking to contain France and reclaim Italy, Switzerland, and the Low Countries that the French had long controlled.*

Alexander Langeron

A French émigré, Langeron had a long military career in Russia, which had its own share of ups and downs. In 1805, he experienced a humiliating defeat at Austerlitz and was disgraced to fighting the Turks in the Danubian Principalities. In 1812, he joined the main Russian army in its pursuit of the retreating French forces and, commanding a corps, took part in the battles in Germany.

If eighteen years of victory had not brought such an illustrious reputation to Napoleon before 1812, and if the greater part of his plans and military operations did not inspire such just admiration, one could possibly hazard to say that he owed his surprising success to good fortune, to the gross faults of his opponents or to circumstances that one could not divine or that one did not dare unmask, as he was shown, in these two campaigns of 1812 and 1813, to be so far below his reputation, so far below himself, that it seemed perhaps less audacious to judge it severely.

Without recounting the unpardonable faults that I have already noted in the history of 1812, faults that caused him to lose his military glory and 400,000 soldiers that had been up until then invincible; without speaking of those that had taken him to Leipzig in 1813, can one excuse him for having waited for us there? His confidence in his genius, in his talents, in a day of battle, however well founded it might have been, should he have taken battle in a position in which he had no means to vanquish nor to retreat? Can one excuse him for having, at the moment when all of his forces were necessary, left troops at Dresden, Torgau, Magdebourg, in the fortresses of the Elbe (which he could not hope to retake) numbering more than 80,000 men, including some of his best troops? He counted, so to speak, on winning the battle and pushing us back on the Elbe the next day, but even in this supposition, 10,000 men would have sufficed in Dresden and 20,000 men in the other places that were not attacked, and 50,000 men extra at Leipzig would have been no small thing.

With troops greatly inferior to those of his enemy, he placed himself in a circle, around an immense city, of which the bridges were long and narrow and offered him only a difficult retreat, and which (as we have seen) could be cut off.

He left all of his baggage in the city, without taking any precautions against the disorder that always follows a lost battle; he cared for nothing; he foresaw nothing; on the 17th he rested tranquilly, even though he could see all of our movements, and the junction of all of the armies that encircled him, in the immense plains where none of our manoeuvres were hidden from him; from the bell towers of Leipzig one could see the surrounding country for more than 50 verstas [53km].

Does one recognise there the victor of Millesimo, Lodi, Ulm, Austerlitz, Wagram? Does one recognise there the general who for eighteen years had triumphed over Europe? Or Napoleon no longer wished to recognise the talents and energy of his adversaries, of which he nevertheless had ample proof, or had an excessive confidence in his talents and his good luck blinded him; such is what any man must say who does not which to recognise, in his rise and fall, a higher cause to which one can attribute all the events of the world.

One can even add that this same Napoleon, whose genius was so precocious, who at the age of twenty-three had placed himself, as had the Grande Condé, in the ranks of the most illustrious generals, was finished at the age when other men often began their career of glory.

But if the battle of Leipzig honoured neither the foresight nor the genius of Napoleon, the enemies of France must admit that he was immortal to his troops; never had they fought so well, and, assuredly, these brave soldiers could not have been encouraged and supported by the hope of vanquishing; the generals, the officers of the army of Napoleon, had too much experience of war not too have sensed the vice and danger of their positions, even the soldiers could not ignore it. Nevertheless, not even this persuasion, nor the defection of some foreign troops who, in the midst of combat, crossed to the enemy (which naturally should have led from surprise to discouragement), not even the sight of superior forces could weaken their firmness; they fought admirably, and, if it is permissible to say so, the battle of Leipzig, completely lost by the French, earned them as much honour as did the lost battle of Bautzen for the Russians and Prussians.

It was eleven o'clock in the morning when we entered Leipzig, and at three o'clock, [Field Marshal Gebhard von] Blücher ordered us to march, with [Fabian Osten-]Sacken and myself directed to Schkeuditz. This march, which lasted into the night, was very fatiguing, especially after four days of battle during which the generals, as well as the officers and soldiers, were only able to eat very modest meals. Finding myself on the march, near the Arkhangelskii Regiment, which was one of the regiments that had suffered the most, I told the soldiers: 'My friends, we have not had time to eat, but we have other things to do.' – 'Yes, general,' a non-commissioned officer responded, 'but we are filled with glory and happiness.' [In 1815], while when we were returning from France a second time, another soldier made a remark that was not as sublime but was more pleasing. One of his comrades asked what he would do to Napoleon if we had captured him on that campaign, and he responded: 'I would quickly have released him so we could go to France a third time.' One can see they had acquired a taste for it.

We arrived to Schkeuditz too late and, the next day of 20 October, we moved on Lützen. This direction was ordered by our sovereigns; Yorck's corps alone continued his march via Freiburg. Napoleon stopped, on the evening of 19 October, at Markrandstaedt, and the next day he carried his flight toward Weissenfels. Lieutenant-General [Illarion] Vasilchikov, with the cavalry of Sacken's corps, gathered some 2,000 stragglers [traineurs] near Lützen. Yorck marched via Schlachtfeldt on Rossbach.

On 21 October, I marched on Weissenfels. The enemy had already crossed the Saale, and was bivouacking on the left bank and the skirmishers defended the bridge, where everything was prepared to burn it. I sent the 12th and 22nd Jagers to occupy the Château of Weissenfels, and to chase the enemy skirmishers from the bridge. There was a very thick fog. I exploited it to place twenty-four 12-pounders on the right bank of the Saale, which entirely dominated the left bank, and I trained these cannon on the enemy bivouacs which they had the imprudence to place on the banks; they only took two rounds before dispersing in disorder to save themselves, but they had time to set light to the bridge. By the zeal and care of the inhabitants, we constructed a bridge out of rafts, and the army crossed [at three in the afternoon].*

Nevertheless, General Yorck found himself on the flank of the enemy, which wanted to cross the Unstrut near Freiburg in multiple columns. The Prussian cavalry of Count Henckel spotted a mass of 100 officers and nearly 4,000 soldiers, most of them Austrians; these unfortunates, taken near Dresden, in August, had been walking since then in that area of Germany; they had already been in Thuringia; the fear inspired by our partisans and the capture

---

* Langeron's Note: The master carpenter who directed this work was the same man who had, in 1757, directed the building of the bridge that was raised by Frederick II before the battle of Rossbach.

of Cassel by General [Alexander] Chernyshev had led them to Leipzig, where we sent them toward the Rhine a second time; they were rescued and served as an escort for their guards, who were taken.

General Yorck reached the enemy near Freiburg, in the long and narrow pass that led to the bridge of Unstrut. The French rearguard was closed in, lost a general, a colonel, more than a thousand prisoners and left eighteen cannon in the passes, and an immense quantity of caissons, baggage, carriages, cars, handcarts, and country wagons; the road was obstructed for more than a lieue. This passage reminded me of the Berezina in 1812 and the road we followed brought memories of the road from the Berezina to the Niemen.

From Leipzig to Fulde, we found it littered with dead and dying men and horses; the Germans and the Poles, even those in the service of France, deserted in crowds and were well welcomed, but the unlucky French, objects of hatred among the local population, were massacred everywhere they strayed from the road, or thrown out of houses, and reduced to dying of hunger on the roads. Unfortunately this hatred was only too well founded [since] the stragglers committed great excesses and the Germans felt no sympathy for Napoleon's soldiers.

Everywhere we found cannons abandoned and caissons overturned; Napoleon had it written in one of his bulletins that he had only retired to Leipzig on 19 [October] because he ran out of munitions, but between Leipzig and Fulde we took or he destroyed more than a thousand full caissons [caissons chargées]. We had thought that he would dispute the long pass at Eisenbach and the forests of Thuringe, but the Bavarian general Baron Wrede, who advanced by forced marches on Frankfurt, and who could cut off the Mayence road, forced him to precipitate his retreat, or rather his flight.

General Yorck and the advance posts of General Sacken once again reached the enemy rearguard at Euroth, near Eisenbach, on 24 October, and caused him a great many losses.* The same day, General Rudzewitsch took, near

---

* Langeron's Note: On this occasion, Marshal Blücher was not content with the activity or the resolution of the Prussian cavalry; I do not know if this was wrong or with reason, but he accused it of marching slowing and letting an enemy detachment get away; I arrived to see him at his headquarters, and when he noticed me he said: 'My general, I have often told you that you have a bad cavalry, but you can say as much of mine, as it is worse still.' He could not suffer Korf, Borozdin and the two Panchulidzevs and he had good reason, as a soldier, because these men were not; he proved his discontent for the first two in a manner that was perhaps a bit frank and certainly cruel for them. While we were putting into winter quarters, at Frankfort, at a ball given by General Uvarov, some of the generals in my corps found themselves next to Blücher. The Emperor approached him and said: 'Monsieur le Marshal, you are surrounded by familiar faces.' – 'Yes, Sire,' Blücher responded pointing out Rudzevich, Emmanuel, Niedhart and myself, 'I know these men well, but I do not know those men,' he added pointing out Korf and Borozdin who were also close to him. Nevertheless he

Gotha, 2,000 prisoners. We marched via Langensalza, and on 26 October, we passed through the passes of Eisenbach.

[Unfortunately] we lost a day at Eisenbach, and this delay proved consequential: it gave time to the enemy to precipitate their retreat, and no longer pursued, they could rally their forces; but Blücher, his generals and his headquarters wished to celebrate their victory at Eisenbach, and Bacchus reigned freely at this fête. The evening of the 26th, I found all of these men too occupied with their joy to obtain what they wanted, to march the next day; they were no longer in a state to give such an order. On 28 October, we traversed Wacha, and on the 30th, we were at Fulde.

If Blücher had not lost a day at Eisenbach, and even with this delay, if he had been permitted to follow his first plan which was to never lose sight of the enemy army and to follow it as far as Frankfurt, to put it between himself and General Wrede, Frankfurt or Hanau might have been the fall of Napoleon, but in war one cannot divine nor foresee, and by a calculation that turned out to be false, but which was excusable, we believed that Napoleon, in order to evade General Wrede, would move on Wetzlar and on Coblence to cross the Rhine there.

Blücher received the order to march and from Fulde we moved on Giessen and on Siegen; soon my advance guard and Sacken's corps found themselves on the Rhine,* my pontoons arrived at the Elbe via forced marches. Blücher

---

spoke lowly enough that these men did not hear this severe truth, but the Emperor did not miss a word and remembered it only too well.

In the Russian service, where one gives for each combat recompense which, while greatly desired, loses all of its value due to widespread abuse when commanders nominate, without distinction, all of the generals, the officers d'etat major, the adjutants of their corps, etc. I had presented Korf and Borozdin along with the others: the first to the Order of Saint-Alexander; the Emperor wrote me, via Count Arakcheyev, that all that I asked for would be granted (that was before Uvarov's ball). I informed Korf, who wore the Cordon of Saint Alexander that another general had lent him. Two days later, the Emperor told me that he denied the reward – one can imagine my embarrassment and that of the messieurs involved.

At Paris, the Emperor, one day that I was in his bureau, told me: 'I am discontent with the presentation of my commanding generals and especially yours: you have asked me to reward generals that have never fought: it is fine to recommend Rudzevich and Emmanuel, but Korf and Borozdin! You treat them the same as other generals, you take the list and recommend each one without choice or distinction; I will seriously examine your suggestions.' I had nothing to say because the emperor was perfectly correct. Yet remarkably upon their return to Russia, both these generals received command of a cavalry corps and were well treated: Korf received the Cordon of Saint Alexander for some manoeuvre; I dared speak of it to the Emperor who said: 'If they are mediocre in war, they are at least excellent in training and drilling troops in peace.' The Emperor was once again correct.

* Langeron's Note: We traversed the most frightful country in Germany, the plateau of Ulrichstein, where the occupants are as savage as the country they occupy, where there isn't even a road, and where, in the Seven Years War, no troops passed. I broke my

(who had never more deserved his name of General *Velocifere*) wanted to cross the Rhine that instant, at Mulheim, before Cologne, at the very latest 13 November and be in Brussels on the 27th.*

A most untimely change in the system of war stopped us on the banks of the Rhine, and led us near Frankfurt, where we took winter quarters, near this city as well as near Freyberg and Darmstadt. Blücher took his headquarters at Hoechst, two miles from Frankfurt, Yorck at Wiesbaden, Sacken at Darmstadt and myself at Roedelheim, all near Frankfurt, and alternatively a portion of my troops were used to blockade Cassel and Mayence and cantoned around Hochheim. Count [Emmanuel] Saint Priest's corps, which had marched from Eisenbach on Cassel in Westphalia, occupied this city, from which King Jerome had trouble, for the second time, of escaping and had to leave behind a portion of his personal belongings. Count Saint Priest then occupied Dusseldorf, where he left a strong detachment, under the orders of Major-General [Dmitri] Yuzefovich, and finally took his winter quarters at Tatt and at Ehrenbreitstein, before Coblence. General [Aleksei] Sherbatov's 6th Corps joined me with the cavalry that remained with him on the left bank of the river.

Napoleon, after two bloody battles at Hanau and Frankfurt against [the Bavarian forces of] Wrede, who was gravely wounded, forced the crossing, and arrived at Mayence, which would have been impossible for him if we had not taken the wrong direction: this was a great mistake but it was not due to our army. Our sovereigns united at Frankfurt, where the Kings of Bavaria and Württemberg and all the Princes of the Confederation of the Rhine arrived to abjure the Confederation and unite with the Emperors of Russia and Austria and the King of Prussia, armed for the liberty of Germany and of the world. [From the French text in Alexander Langeron, *Mémoires*†]

Matvei Muromtsev

After the decisive victory at Leipzig, the Allied powers pursued Napoleon westwards to the French border. In November, they occupied Frankfurt am Main where they stopped for several weeks to consider what to do next. Muromtsev,

---

equipment, and destroyed my artillery horses and pontoons. At Ulrichstein, I stayed in the house of a bourgeois who naively told me that, although it was easy to see me, he had hoped that the horror of his country would spare him my visit.

* Langeron's Note: Blücher had another reason to move swiftly into Belgium: he hoped to surprise and occupy Anvers, where the enemy had no troops, and to take control of the fleet, which could then be sold to the English; he thereby hoped to gain a great deal of money; this idea was very pleasing to him, he made us a part of it by telling us in advance the share of each; mine wasn't bad.

† English translations of Langeron's memoirs have been kindly produced by Greg Gorsuch.

*who had just been promoted to a staff captain for his exploits at Leipzig, was
one of the many Russian officers who enjoyed their stay in the German city.*

[After the battle of Leipzig], our entire army proceeded to Frankfurt and all
Germans, except for the Saxons, abandoned the French cause. The Bavarians
organised our advance guard but fought the French only at Hanau. Our
forces were deployed around Frankfurt and along the Rhine, while the French
retreated onto French soil. Behind us there were still numerous fortresses
that the French held. Napoleon made a major mistake by not withdrawing
these garrisons to strengthen his army. These consisted of his best and veteran
troops and he could have been much stronger had he had their service at
hand, and he might have even gained the upper hand in war.

We stopped in Frankfurt, where all kings and princes gathered at once and
the mean headquarters of the [Allied] armies was established. We remained
here for a long time but I do not recall precisely how long. The Emperors
held lavish dinners and issued proclamations to the French . . . Before
[Imperial] dinners were held I often went out of curiosity to the dining halls,
where I had many acquaintances, to observe preparations. I noticed that a
special notch was always made in the edge of the table where King [Friedrich
I Wilhelm Karl] of Württemberg was supposed to sit so as to accommodate
his enormous stomach.

All the available intelligence, which we possessed at the time, pointed
that there was no possibility for a people's war in France. So Aide-de-camp
Mamonov and I asked for permission to march with Cossacks [across France]
to establish communications with [Arthur Wellesley, the Duke of] Wellington,
who was already on the borders of France. We were convinced that we could
easily reach southern France, where there were many Royalists. But our
request was denied.

Mamonov and I were billeted at the home of a wealthy merchant, who had
a wonderful family, including the beautiful Victorchen, who I naturally fell
in love with. . . We were accepted into the Masonic Lodge, which involved
numerous preposterous tests, oaths, etc. But back then [membership in
Masonic lodges] was very fashionable and sometimes it did have practical
uses as well: there were incidents when on the field of battle, a timely-made
Masonic sign saved a person from imminent death. [From the Russian text in
M. Muromtsev, 'Vospominaniya . . .']

Emperor Alexander I

*On 10 November 1813, at Frankfurt am Main, Alexander wrote the following
letter to the Crown Prince of Sweden, outlining main principles of the general
plan for the final campaign against Napoleon.*

Here is the plan proposed by me, and entirely approved of by the Austrian and Prussian commanders-in-chief. I hope your Royal Highness may find it equally conformable to your ideas. Offensive operations on the part of the Grand Army, between Metz and Strasburg, offer many difficulties, as we cannot leave the fortresses behind us without observation. By entering France on the side of Switzerland, we meet with incomparably fewer difficulties, that frontier not being so strongly fortified. Another advantage attending this movement, is the possibility of turning the Viceroy's left wing, and thereby forcing him to a precipitate retreat. In that case, the Austrian army of Italy may advance on Lyons, so as to form a prolongation of our line, and by means of its left wing, to connect our operations with those of the Duke of Wellington, whose headquarters are now at Oleron, Soult having retreated to Orthez. In the meantime, Field-Marshal Blücher, reinforced by the Bavarians, will form an army of observation of 100,000 men. But, without confining himself to mere observation, he may cross the Rhine near Manheim, and manoeuvre against the enemy till the Grand Army reach the field of action. All the four armies, viz.: the Grand Army, that of Italy, Blücher's, and Wellington's, will stand on one line, in the most fertile part of France. Forming the segment of a circle, the four armies will push forward; and diminishing the arc, will thus draw near its centre, that is, Paris, or to the headquarters of Napoleon.

Your Highness offered to undertake the conquest of Holland. The proposed operations, which I have submitted to you in detail, will enable you to effect your object the more easily, that they will force Napoleon to oppose the bulk of his troops to our armies on the left of the theatre of war. If your Highness will advance on Cologne and Düsseldorf, or from thence in the direction of Antwerp, you will at once separate Holland from France. In that event, should Napoleon resolve to keep possession of the fortresses, the garrisons left in them will materially diminish the effective strength of his armies. On the other hand, should the garrisons be insufficient for their defence, your Highness will have little difficulty in penetrating into Flanders, and perhaps farther. The grand object is, not to lose a moment, that we may not allow Napoleon time to form and discipline an army, and to furnish it with everything necessary; our business being to take advantage of the disorganised state of his forces. I earnestly entreat your Highness not to delay putting your army in motion in furtherance of our general plan of operations. [From the French text in *Aperçu des transactions politiques du Cabinet de Russie*]

Mikhail Barclay de Tolly

As the Allied forces moved towards the frontiers of France, General Mikhail Barclay de Tolly urged the Emperor to show caution and consider potential consequences of invading France. His letter of 9 November offers remarkable insights into the state of the Russian army on the eve of the 1814 Campaign

Your Majesty,

The enemy has been already pushed beyond the Rhine River and Germany is freeing itself from the yoke that oppressed it for so long and regaining its past freedom. The entire world follows in bewilderment these events and anticipates the outcome that will be, one may say, quite unexpected. This success is the direct result of the decisiveness and unity of the Allied Powers, of their supreme sacrifices for the common well-being . . . We must not conceal, however, that Napoleon's own mistakes in his past campaigns have also contributed to [the Allied success].

Yet, in spite of all these great successes we have gained in these campaigns, we must also admit that they have required heavy sacrifices and cost us half of our army! The vast distances that separate our troops from their reinforcements as well as their fragmentation into numerous parts greatly complicate overall command and may lead soon to the complete disorganisation of the army. There are entire regiments that have no more than 100 men. Due to the shortage of staff and junior officers even these remnants [of our regiments] cannot be brought into the necessary order. Soldiers suffer extreme deprivation in ammunition [and supplies], especially of boots, shirts and clothing. Except for the Reserve Corps that has still preserved the appearance of parade troops, and the troops in the army of the Swedish Crown Prince, who have seen less fighting than other units and in consequence have suffered less hardship, all other corps are so weakened that I have to report, with a heavy heart, to Your Imperial Majesty that in their current state these corps are quickly approaching complete collapse.

Your Imperial Majesty is well aware of the vast efforts necessary to maintain a large army in good state even in peacetime, and can only imagine the difficulties of maintaining these armies in wartime, especially when they are so far away from their borders and all the necessities; when the interests of so many powers result in incessant bickering and hampering of each other's efforts; when the commander-in-chief [of the armies] is weakened in his authority and instead of being a springboard for all operations, he in fact is unable to overcome hurdles erected in front of him at every step.

Your Majesty, armies cannot survive for long in such conditions. We are still far from accomplishing our actual goals [in this war]. Despite the brilliant success of the [1813] campaign, the freedom of Germany is far from secured. Only a peace based on unwavering commitments can ensure this. But we cannot but doubt whether Napoleon, despite being driven across the Rhine, will accept conditions we have offered him.

The state of the French borders and the character of the French people, which can be so easily aroused [to a popular revolt], are difficulties that the

Allied armies, and especially our forces, would face in satisfying their [military] needs in this [foreign] land . . . and finally the exhaustion of neighbouring powers – all these factors might in fact strengthen rather than depress Napoleon's ambitious spirit.

If the continuation of the war is unavoidable, we must take immediate measures to prepare ourselves for it. Any delays will be advantageous to the enemy while we will suffer irrecuperable losses. Yet I must inform Your Majesty that such preparations face enormous challenges. Our reserves are too far away and the closest can be expected to arrive in the next few weeks, which means the campaign would be already underway and our corps would suffer new losses in men and, by the time the reinforcements appear, they would be reduced to oblivion. This would undoubtedly occur if we do not gather all the reinforcements at one central location.

We can also easily anticipate that many of our corps would experience lack of ammunition, not because we do not have a sufficient amount of it but rather due to the difficulty, and in some cases even the impossibility, of delivering munitions to every individual unit, especially when the commander-in-chief would be unable to maintain direct communications with them and might remain unaware of specific and general plans of operations and instructions given to individual units because such dispatches circumvent him . . . Supply trains from Russia can be expected only towards the end of the campaign and even then they might not go beyond the Elbe River. If we choose to gather [ammunition] through requisitioning and then distribute it to regiments, we must either concentrate all corps in one location or grant each corps authority to do it on its own, independently of the commander-in-chief; in such a case, each corps must be assigned a separate line of communications.

Furthermore, provisioning of the army, which is one of the most important matters both in war and peace, has been so ignored and run down that we can frankly state that our current provisioning [system] is non-existent. Our Austrian allies so inadequately assist us in this matter that having used our own twenty-day supplies to meet our responsibilities to feed them while we were still in Bohemia, we still have not received any of it back and thus find ourselves without any supplies whatsoever.

Since we cannot hope for requisitioning supplies in France, we must establish our own magazines there at once. If we encounter any resistance from the Austrians, who usually demonstrate disregard for our interests, we must ensure that the armies of Your Imperial Majesty have their own lines of operation. [. . .] I will not go into details on the lack of horses in cavalry and problems that our artillery increasingly faces. It suffices to say that Count Wittgenstein's cavalry does not have even one fourth of what it had in Silesia. [From the Russian text in RGVIA f. 846, op.16, d.4122]

Proclamation of the Allied Powers

On the eve of the invasion, the Allied powers appealed to the French nation to abandon Napoleon and seek deliverance at the hands of their armies.

Frenchmen! Victory has brought the Allied Armies to your frontier. They are about to pass it. We do not make war upon France but we repel far from us the yoke which your Government wished to impose upon our respective countries, which have the same rights to independence and happiness as yours. Magistrates, landholders, cultivators, remain in your homes. The maintenance of public order, respect for private property, the most severe discipline, shall characterise the progress and the stay of the Allied Armies. They are not animated by the spirit of vengeance. They wish not to retaliate upon France the numberless calamities with which France, for the last 20 years, overwhelmed her neighbours, and the most distance countries. Other principles and other views, than those which led your armies among us, preside over the counsels of the Allied Monarchs. Their glory will consist in having put the speediest period to the misfortunes of Europe. The only conquest, which is the object of our ambition, is that of peace but at the same time a peace which shall secure to their own people, to France, and to Europe, a state of real repose. We hoped to find it before touching the soil of France. We come thither in quest of it. [From *The Examiner*, Issue No. 316, January 16, 1814]

Louis-Victor-Léon de Rochechouart

Another French émigré in the Russian service, Rochechouart was born into a prominent noble family that suffered during the Revolution but remained in France. In 1804, the sixteen-year-old Rochechouart left France and entered Russian military service. After fighting the Turks in the Danubian Principalities and the Caucasus, he served in administrative positions in the Ukraine before being appointed as an aide-de-camp to Emperor Alexander in 1810. He served on Admiral Paul Chichagov's staff in 1812 and took part in the campaign in Germany in 1813. Now, after a decade-long absence, he approached the borders of his motherland eager to restore the Bourbon monarchy.

Emperor Alexander entered Frankfurt on 20 November . . . and spent the months of November and December there, visiting Baden, Karlsruhe and Darmstadt. Emperor Alexander entrusted me with a delightful mission to Darmstadt. Sending for me to his room, the Emperor said: 'You will take this letter to the Grand Duke [Louis X] in Darmstadt, I wish to pay him a visit. I hear the Grand Duchess [Louise Caroline Henriette] is a charming hostess. I shall go as a relation. The wife [Wilhelmine Louise] of the hereditary Prince [Louis] belongs to the House of Baden, and is therefore a cousin of my Empress

Consort,* but I do not know in what degree; you will ascertain this clearly for me. I do not wish to be received as the Emperor of Russia, but as a cousin. I am going there to enjoy myself and divert my thoughts. A ceremonious reception would bore me dreadfully. I shall hold you to blame if there is one. I shall leave tomorrow for Darmstadt and shall be accompanied by my two aides-de-camp, Uvarov and Ozharovski; you will be the third. Try to arrange for a ball in the evening, and give me, beforehand, the names of the most beautiful women invited; also try to gather for me the scandalous tales about this Court. I am told there is something to glean. The Grand Duchess is a distinguished and smart woman, and she has been very beautiful. The Grand Duke is an eccentric tyrant while his son amounts to nothing [il serait fort nul]. When he was presented to Napoleon, he remained standing without saying anything. Noticing an unusual uniform, Napoleon asked him: 'Prince, what uniform is that?' 'Of my regiment, Sire,' the prince replied. 'Ah, and how many men are there in your regiment?' [Napoleon inquired] 'I do not know,' was the prince's response to which Napoleon, turning to his companion, murmured, 'Who is this great fool [grande béte]?' Well, my dear Rochechouart, that big fool is my relative. I do not want to meet him for I could not help but laugh in his face when I think of Napoleon's remark. Go and dress, and depart at once.'

Darmstadt is located six leagues [24km] from Frankfurt. I departed there [at once] and, after a two hours' ride, arrived at the Palace in great state as the Emperor wished. I had myself announced to the Grand Duke as the bearer of a letter from my Sovereign to his Royal Highness. I was at once shown into an immense room that looked more like an arsenal than a study. It was at least twenty feet high, and the walls were lined from top to bottom with weapons and armour of all kinds, from the accoutrements of the ancient Teutonic knights to the uniform of soldiers of our own day. This collection of helmets, shields, cuirasses, coats of mail, lances, swords, daggers, sabres, guns and pistols, was arranged with admirable symmetry, and furnished the room in a very curious, rare and costly manner. A magnificent bronze cannon of the largest calibre, with its caisson, completed this rich collection of armour of all ages. In the middle of the arsenal, in front of a splendid carved oak desk, covered with gilding and crimson velvet, stood a six-feet tall man of sixty-five, or seventy, years of age. His one hand rested on a superb armchair, in the other he held the letter that I had just brought. He had a handsome aristocratic face, and wore a dark blue uniform, in the style of Frederick the Great of Prussia; breeches of white kerseymere, and gaiters of black cloth,

---

* Alexander's spouse Empress Elizabeth Alexeyevna was born Princess Louise Maria Auguste of Baden. She was the third of the seven children of Charles Louis, Hereditary Prince of Baden and his wife Amelia Frederica of Hesse-Darmstadt. The youngest of these children was Wilhelmina who married Grand Duke of Hesse-Darmstadt Louis X's son.

extending to above the knee. His hair was white, and cut very close, his hands well formed; his bearing severe but refined; such was my impression of the Prince. With extremely courteous manners, he had a noble and serious, almost sad, expression, and he seemed to suffer from gout.

After having slowly read through the Emperor's letter, during which time I was looking at all this curious and warlike collection, the Prince said, in very good French, without the least accent: 'A severe attack of gout has prevented my going to Frankfurt to pay my respectful homage to the Emperor of Russia. I am grieved that this great Sovereign should come to see me first. Obeying his Imperial Majesty's wish, I will receive him as a relative; this will somewhat distress the Grand Duchess, but she will accept the order with resignation. I am sending her the kind letter you have just brought me, and you will go to her apartments, and make arrangements for tomorrow's reception. It is her domain and it entirely rests with her. It is long since I took any part in such preparations.'

Having been conducted to the apartments of the Grand Duchess by the chamberlain on duty, I was dazzled by the graceful and dignified bearing of this princess, still very beautiful, in spite of her age.* She received me most kindly, but I found it difficult to dissuade her from the idea of an official reception. I was obliged to tell her that his Imperial Majesty had ordered me to insist on this point. He was coming to Darmstadt to enjoy the pleasure of family life, of which he had so long been deprived, and not the ceremony of a court. As I withdrew, after receiving an invitation to return to dinner, I said, with the view to arouse the curiosity of the beautiful princess: 'I am charged by his Imperial Majesty to ask a host of questions with regard to the personnel of the charming Court of Darmstadt, one of the most brilliant in Germany, thanks to the august Princess who is its model, and indeed its chief ornament, uniting so many noble qualities in her person.' The soldier thus transformed into a courtier and this compliment won for me a gracious smile and the reply: 'Only a French noble could give a graceful turn to such direct flattery. I thank you, Count.' I bowed low and withdrew. The chamberlain, who had announced me, handed me over to a gentleman-usher, who had been charged to show me to my room. I strolled about the magnificent park adjoining the palace, and then returned to dress. At four o'clock I entered the large drawing-room. The Grand Duchess soon appeared, and we passed at once into the dining-room. The chamberlain introduced me to an elderly lady, and asked me to take her in to dinner. Covers were laid for twenty – the hereditary Grand Duchess, the high dignitaries of the little court, the ladies in attendance, etc. The Grand Duke always dined in his own apartments, and the Prince [Louis], his son, was travelling at this time. My neighbour was a Frenchwoman, a Canoness of Bavaria, who had been lady-in-waiting to the Grand Duchess ever since the Revolution. She said: 'You are commanded by

---

*   The Grand Duchess was fifty-two years old.

your Sovereign to obtain information with regard to the Court of Darmstadt. I have been charged to answer your inquiries. Question me.' I learned, first, that the hereditary Princess [Frederica] was the sister of the Empress Elizabeth [of Russia] and the ex-Queen of Sweden,* and was therefore the Tsar's sister-in-law, and not his cousin. I promised to inform the Emperor Alexander of this near relationship.

As my intelligent cicerone was unable entirely to satisfy my curiosity during the dinner, our conversation was continued in the drawing-room, and she put me in a position to give the Emperor, next day, most confidential information. I saw that my mission had become known among the ladies of the Court, for during the evening, in the drawing-room, I was surrounded by pretty women who, in order to attract attention and make themselves known, availed themselves of every possible pretext to talk to me about Emperor Alexander.

The following day the Emperor arrived at two o'clock. I gave him all the information I had received from the lady-in-waiting. A delightful ball followed the dinner. The Emperor charmed everyone by his amiability. Giving his arm to the Grand Duchess, as they passed through the rooms, he said: 'Are you satisfied, madame, with my young ambassador? He does have good prospects, does not he?' 'He is a very pleasant flatterer,' she replied. As we returned to Frankfurt, the Emperor expressed his satisfaction at the way in which I had discharged this pleasant duty. On such a cheerful note I finished the year 1813.

Now I come to that famous year 1814, so full of memorable events, which changed the face of Europe, by re-establishing the Bourbons on the thrones of France and Spain, while destroying an empire that appeared powerful but which was overwhelmed by the number of its enemies, in spite of the military genius of its ruler, then in all its splendour, in spite of the valour of those old regiments that for so many years had been the conquerors of Europe but were now crushed and decimated by two years of disasters unmatched in history.

On 3 January the Russian headquarters moved across the Rhine at Bale, reached Altkirch on the 13th, Vesoul on the 17th, passing by Montbeliard and Villersexel, finally arriving at Langres on the 26th. Two days later I received news of the death of my brother Louis, who was killed at Lignol, a small village not far from Bar-sur-Aube, on January 26th, at two o'clock in the morning, three days before the bloody battle of Brienne. After being separated during the campaign in Saxony, we had met briefly on the bridge over the Rhine at Bale. My brother had begged me to obtain from the Emperor a change of corps for him since he could no longer serve as the chief of staff to Count Sacken. The

---

* Frederica was the fourth of the seven children of Charles Louis, Hereditary Prince of Baden. She married King Gustav IV Adolf of Sweden in 1797 but was deposed with her spouse in 1809. They were separated in 1810 and launched divorce proceedings in 1811, completing them a year later.

Count had a great regard for him but exacted an amount of work that was beyond human capacity. His chief of staff must see everything for himself and never be satisfied with reports. At Villersexel I had an opportunity of speaking to the Emperor about this matter and I had begged him to take Louis on his staff. He promised to bring us together again and to give the necessary orders to Prince [Peter] Volkonskii.* Thus I was awaiting the fulfilment of his promise when, on the 28th, my brother's servant came into the room that I shared with Rapatel, and told me, amid his sobs, that his master was dead. Having been sent on a reconnaissance one very dark night, Louis had come upon a French grand-guard, which retreated, firing by pelotons and shouting 'Cossacks'. My poor brother had been struck by eight bullets. Taking advantage of the enemy's retreat, the Cossack who accompanied Louis placed his body in front of him across his horse and brought him back to Count Sacken's headquarters. I was deeply distressed and reproached myself for not having pressed the Emperor for the immediate fulfilment of his promise. It only remained for me to render the last honours to the companion of my childhood struggles. Not being able to leave my post, for we expected every moment the order to advance, I asked a certain person in Langres to go to Lignol and arrange for a suitable funeral for my brother, and to tell the *curé* [parish priest] that I would pay for everything as soon as possible. In the month of July I sent to the *curé* of this little parish his fees and money required to erect a gravestone with Louis' name, rank, and the date of his death.

Ever since we entered French territory Rapatel† and I had tried to promote the restoration of the Bourbons. The twenty-four years of constant wars, and, above all, the disasters of the last two years, and the continual appeal for recruits, all these causes had led to general discontent and disaffection towards Napoleon. I believe I may affirm that with the exception of government officials, the purchasers of nationalised property, and some enthusiasts for the rule of the sword, the nation was wearied, disillusioned and discouraged by so many sacrifices, and frightened at the thought of misfortunes that were about to fall upon the Country . . .

Some Royalists from Paris, including Count Alexis de Noailles, the Comte de Wall, the Comte de Virieu, and the Marquis Quinsonnas, met together at the house of the Marquis de Chalencey, where Emperor Alexander was staying. Their aim was to sound out the Emperor on his intentions with regard to the Bourbons. Before arousing any public reaction, before declaring themselves

---

* Volkonskii was chief of the Main Staff of the Russian army.

† Rapatel was a French officer who had previously served as aide-de-camp to General Jean Moreau and joined him in exile to the United States. In 1813, he followed Moreau back to Europe and was with him when the general was mortally wounded by a French cannonball. He was then accepted into Russian service and appointed to the post of an aide-de-camp to Emperor Alexander.

and inducing their friends to declare themselves, it seemed essential to have not merely the assent, but the support of the Emperor of Russia. M. de Chalencey begged us – Rapatel and I – to be present at this meeting. We drew up a memorandum on the spot that I was charged to present to the Emperor the next day. I asked for an audience, which was at once granted . . . *

Having read the memorandum, the Emperor said: 'I understand, and I approve of the steps that you and Rapatel have taken, but we are not yet sufficiently sure of victory to come to a decision. Wait for the result of the next battle, which cannot be long delayed. If fortune favours us, I will grant you the permission you ask. There is no doubt as to my feelings with regard to the family of your ancient Kings, but I cannot act without my Allies; I can only let things take their course; it is quite another thing to act alone. Meanwhile, let the French declare themselves, then many difficulties will be smoothed away.'

I communicated this reply the same evening to the Royalist meeting, which decided that we should act. [The Royalists drew up a letter to the King Louis XVIII in England, and another to the Duc de Berry.† These letters were signed and entrusted to M. Mallet, a Swiss colonel. . . .] After these letters had been sent off, we separated – some of us went to Burgundy, others to Franche-Comté, and a few remained at our headquarters . . . On 7 February we were at Troyes, where other Royalists joined us. I shall not describe military operations in detail and instead refer the reader to the work of M. de Koch.‡ I shall confine myself to the negotiations with the French Princes which were entrusted to me, on the one hand by the Emperor Alexander, and on the other by the Comte d'Artois.§

From the time of his arrival in France the Comte d'Artois found himself in a very delicate position, being in direct contact with the Austrian army, whose leaders, with the exception of Prince Schwarzenberg, were more than cold and difficult in their relations [with the Bourbons], obeying the instructions of Prince Metternich, who did not conceal his aversion to the Bourbons. So, knowing the part I had taken at the first meetings of the Royalists, Monsieur charged the Comte de Wall to give me the following letter:

'Vesoul, January 21st, 1814.

I had intended, Monsieur, to send a letter to the Emperor of Russia by the Comte de Wall, whom I sent to the Russian headquarters, but on the one hand I am so much touched, so deeply moved by the reception I have met

---

* The full text of the memorandum is in Rochechouart, *Souvenirs*, pp. 285–7.

† For their texts see Rochechouart, *Souvenirs*, pp. 288–9.

‡ See François Koch, *Mémoires pour servir à l'histoire de la campagne de 1814* (Paris, 1819).

§ The Comte d'Artois was the brother of King Louis XVI, who was deposed and executed by the revolutionaries, and of King Louis XVIII who spent more than fifteen years in exile.

with from the French people ever since I crossed the frontier, and especially here, and, on the other hand, I am so much astonished at the conduct of the Austrian General Hirsch, the commandant of this town, that I am afraid of expressing my feelings too strongly. I confine myself, therefore, to sending the Comte de Wall to you; he will explain to you in detail what has taken place, and I beg you to inform his Majesty the Emperor of Russia. . . .

Charles-Philippe.'

I delivered this letter to the Emperor, who instructed me to recommend patience to the Comte d'Artois, and, above all, to dissuade him from coming to [the Russian] headquarters, if he expressed any intention of doing so. The time had not yet come openly to take the side of the Bourbons, a course which was not equally pleasing to all the Allies. In my reply to Monsieur I thought it necessary to explain the steps we had taken before his arrival, and my position with regard to the Emperor.* This report shows the difficulties that fettered the Royalist party, how little favour was shown to them by the Allies, and, consequently, how false is the assertion, 'The Bourbons were brought back by foreign bayonets.' On the contrary, it was the French who compelled the Allied Sovereigns to recognise the rights of the Bourbon dynasty, when all their predilections inclined in another direction . . . [From the French text in Rouchechouart, *Souvenirs*]

Sergei Volkonskii

Just twenty-five years old, Volkonskii was a scion of an ancient princely family and had a successful start to his military career. Enlisting in the elite Chevalier Guard Regiment in 1805, he fought against the French in 1806–7 and the Turks in 1810–11. During the Campaign of 1812, he was already flügel adjutant to Emperor Alexander and was assigned to the Second Western Army, with which he participated in numerous battles, earning promotions and awards. In 1813, he was a duty officer in Baron Ferdinand Winzingerode's corps before being transferred to Constantine Benckendorf's flying detachment. Eventually his military career and accomplishments were eclipsed by his involvement in the Decembrist conspiracy of 1825, an attempt to achieve liberal reform by preventing the accession of Tsar Nicholas I. Following the failure of the revolt, he spent 30 years as a political exile in Siberia. He was the inspiration for the character Prince Andrei Bolkonsky in Leo Tolstoy's novel War and Peace.

Our march from Bremen to Dusseldorf, where our corps headquarters had been established, proved peaceful and I have nothing to say about it in a military sense. We advanced across friendly regions, whose population despised the French and greeted our troops not just peacefully but in

---

* Full text in Rochechouart, *Souvenirs*, pp. 291–4.

exaltation. In towns, we met not just local municipal officials but also town residents, in some places even delegations of women who gave us garlands of flowers. Upon arriving at Dusseldorf [on 6 January] we were welcomed with equal adulation. This town, located in a picturesque valley on the bank of the Rhine River, is very beautiful and its upper classes are very educated and treated us very well . . .

On 1 [14] January, orders were issued to prepare for the crossing of the Rhine River, or to be precise for the crossing of the detachment entrusted to Constantine Khristoforovich Benckendorf,* a courageous and enterprising staff officer. The means for crossing [boats], having been prepared beforehand, were placed in the river at night and, at dawn, Benckendorf, standing gallantly in the forward boat, led the crossing; infantry and cannon were transported in boats and rafts while the Cossacks, on their horses, swam next to the boats. I still vividly remember Benckendorf, sailing in front of us to what I believed to be certain death, inspiring us with his courageous behaviour. With our detachment across the river, the rest of the corps prepared to cross as well. At the start of the crossing we could see some movement on the French side but there was meagre resistance to Benckendorf's landing and our detachment soon occupied the opposite bank, while the French fell back to the fortress of Jullien . . .

> *Volkonskii did not accompany the corps beyond the Rhine since Winzingerode dispatched him to Cologne to set up a military government, take a roster of supplies that belonged to the French government and develop a supply base to support Russian operations. He spent most of January in Cologne before departing to rejoin Winzingerode.*

I found Winzingerode in Lüttich [Liège] where I resumed my responsibilities at the corps headquarters. Lüttich was the site of a major arms factory. The already produced weapons were transferred to the representative of the Dutch-Belgian provisional government for the arming of the landwehr forces in this region. We also found vast supplies of walnut gun-stocks stored inside magazines, unlike our practice of chopping down trees and using still damp timber for gun-stocks. On the corps commander's verbal order, I informed regiments that they could take as many gun-stocks as needed. The regimental commanders, naturally, fully exploited this opportunity. In addition to gun-stocks, we also found vast supplies of oak timber that was floated down the Meuse River to be used in gun carriages and the construction of fortress palisades. In addition, there was a vast flock of state-owned merino sheep. One of staff officers asked for my permission to take advantage of these supplies and I told him, 'I cannot give you official permission but I will close my eyes on any transgression if you

---

* Constantine Benckendorf was the brother of Alexander Benckendorf who commanded a flying detachment that helped liberate the Netherlands in 1813.

manage to pull it off.' Indeed, he exploited this opportunity and sold part of these resources. I mention this because I later came close to being held responsible for this transgression but they could not pin it on me (since I gave a verbal order) and I denied it. [From the Russian text in S. Volkonskii, *Zapiski* . . .]

Alexander Langeron

Langeron commanded a corps in the Army of Silesia.

We spent nine weeks in our winter quarters near Frankfurt,* although they were very tight and the wealth of the Countries had already been partially depleted by passing enemies, by the stay of a large part of the Austrian army and by that of the [Cossack] corps of [Hetman Matvei] Platov; we, never the less, still found resources. The different corps that I had under my orders were used alternately to blockade Mainz-Kastel (Cassel), across from Mainz, and

---

* Langeron's Note: In Frankfurt, I fell into disgrace with the Emperor for some time. For the battle of Leipzig, in which the corps I had commanded had fought with a success that had influenced the combat in general, I received the plaque of Saint-Alexander in diamonds and Platov and Miloradovich, (who did) very little on the first and nothing in that terrible second day, received the Order of Saint-Andrew. Miloradovich, a special favourite, was long accustomed to receiving all the graces without ever deserving one, but this was too striking not to offend his rivals (for rank, but not for glory); I complained quite strongly to the Emperor in a letter whose meaning could be interpreted in different ways; but the Emperor knew quite well the meaning of phrases and responded curtly to mine that my services had always deserved attention, and were rewarded as they deserved; however this excellent prince well understood the injustice he had committed against me and he hastened to soon amend it, because after a long time without seeing me, he admitted me to an audience with him and he seemed apologetic and said: 'Platov and Miloradovich fought before my eyes.'

Fifteen days after he had written me the response quoted above, he received deputies of Serbs and letters from Odessa that seemed to announce a new break with the Turks. They were actually incited by the intrigues of Napoleon's ambassador to Constantinople, Andréossy; there was a question of assembling an army in Bessarabia, with eyes being glanced at me and Rayevsky to command: Rayevsky was absent and sick; they made me come to Frankfurt and I spoke; I replied that I would accept, if I was given a few generals I designated: I added that we sent from Silesia, to Bennigsen, the generals that were not wanted, that the latter in having intended were even with Prince Lobonov-Rostovskii, who organised the armed reserve in Poland, and, who before I designated mine, in dealing with me as Bennigsen did to him and Bennigsen with me, and that you could imagine what I would have after three shuffles (cascades). I was allowed to take six generals of the corps I then commanded. I asked for Rudzevich, Shenshin, Count Paul Pahlen, Turchaninov and Weszelizki. But it was soon calm in Turkey, and there was no question for me about this destination, which would have greatly upset me, but I could not refuse. The Emperor decided that in case of war, the command of the troops in Bessarabia would remain with the Duc de Richelieu, who was in Odessa.

remained there almost always in bivouac, at times very hard to bear; however, the zeal, the care and activity of the corps and regiment commanders made up for everything.

The wagenburgs [fortified convoys] that I had left in Silesia arrived for me a little late, but finally they arrived; Marshal Blücher ordered for me, by requisition, the most needed materials, and my brave soldiers, who, during this short interval, enjoyed a little rest, after seventeen months of continuous marching, and the most active and bloodiest war to ever occurred, were dressed and ready to go into the field. Regimental equipment was repaired and horses provided. This is the excellent organisation of the Russian army and its perfect composition, such that after the most horrible fatigue, with just a very short time it was put in the best condition. But what chiefly deserved special attention from Marshal Blücher was to see at the end of December, the perfect state of my artillery, whose horses had suffered extremely in forced marches and horrible roads from Fulda to Giessen.

In nine weeks, everything was repaired and it was like the beginning of the campaign. I must not silence here my obligations to General [Gavril] Veselitskii and heads of companies for this preparation. I like to say it again: the Russian artillery is as perfect in its internal organisation and its material as it is distinguished by its bravery and talent. The new organisation set up by the Emperor to send exactly and successively recruits and convalescents (despite the remoteness of our national resources) was excellent in all its parts; one can judge by the way my army corps had been completed. On 8 [20] November 1813, I had 30,000 men; I had lost 18,000 in the campaign.* The corps of General Sacken, being much smaller than mine, was increased by the 6th Corps of Lieutenant-General Prince Sherbatov, part of the troops under my command. This corps (as seen) had not been at the battle of Leipzig, and had suffered little in Silesia. Thus it was fully staffed; the Tverskii Infantry and the Kinburnskii Dragoons, and four companies of artillery, Nos. 17, 18, 28 and 34, also passed to the corps of Sacken, who gave me only the 4th Regular Regiment of Cossacks of the Ukraine. These changes reduced my corps by 19,000 men, and at the beginning of this campaign, shortly after the crossing of the Rhine, I had 43,000 new men under arms.

The habitude of the war, the physical strength of the Russian soldiers, the caring leaders, also saved my troops from the fatal diseases that followed throughout the flight of the enemy, and which many of the villages in Germany were infected; almost a quarter of inhabitants of towns and villages succumbed, and at the beginning of the campaign of 1814, I had over 43,000 men, but only 800 sick, both feeble and convalescents, and I did not lose more than a

---

* Langeron's Note: Of this number, there were some patients that I had left in hospitals, but small in numbers, the rest had been killed or wounded and those few who had joined me in Frankfurt.

hundred men in hospitals. The new plan of warfare adopted by our sovereigns having driven into Switzerland by the Alsace and Franche-Comté, we stayed near Frankfurt waiting for the time to act. The corps of Yorck, reduced to 13,000 men, was brought back to 25,000; that of Sacken had as many; the two corps of mine totalled more than 90,000 men, accustomed to victories under Blücher. His army was further increased by the Prussian corps of Lieutenant-General Kleist, who had blockaded Erfurt (this corps was also 20,000 men) and finally two of the six corps that were formed by German princes. The Hessians, under the command of the Hereditary Prince of Hesse-Cassel, were destined to follow General Kleist. The troops of Cobourg, Nassau and Frankfurt, under the orders of the reigning Duke of Saxe-Coburg, would join me, but these corps were not yet trained or armed at the beginning of the campaign. [From the French text in A. Langeron, *Mémoires*]

Fabian von der Osten-Sacken

Born into the Courland nobility, Osten-Sacken had a long military career in the Russian army that began in 1766. Over four decades he had served in numerous battles against the Turks, Poles, and French. In 1799, he was captured by the French during the Russian expedition to Switzerland but soon released back home. He took part in the 1806–7 Campaign in Poland but became embroiled in a quarrel with General Levin Bennigsen and was later court-martialled for insubordination. By 1812, he was back on active service and commanded a corps in the Third Army of Observation in Volhynia. After the Grande Armée's defeat in Russia, Osten-Sacken commanded a corps in the Army of Silesia in 1813 and distinguished himself at Katzbach and Leipzig.

After writing my report No. 342 of 20 December [1 January 1814] from Rhein, the troops of Don Cossack Major-General [Akim] Karpov fought a major clash with the enemy near Mutterstadt, where they routed eight squadrons and captured 3 lieutenant-colonels, 22 officers and 198 cuirassiers and dragoons.

On 21 December [2 January] my corps proceeded to the city of Worms, where we found over 200 sick Frenchmen and over 800 muskets and some supplies. The muskets were immediately distributed to the unarmed men that were sent from reserves to the 27th Division and the 6th Corps.

On 22 December [3 January], the corps rested at Worms. The troops of Don Cossack Major-General Lukovkin overtook part of the enemy rearguard near Neustadt, where they routed it, capturing one colonel, 2 officers and 50 dragoons.

On 23 December [4 January], the corps proceed to Alzey, where Prince Biron caught up with the enemy and captured one lieutenant-colonel, 5 officers and over 100 soldiers. The Cossacks also captured sixteen ammunition boxes with new muskets, each box carrying 24 muskets that were intended to be transported from the fortress of Mainz to Metz. These weapons were also distributed among the soldiers of the 27th Division, in addition to 400 muskets taken in Mannheim.

On the 24th [5 January] the corps marched to Mannheim. The following day it proceeded to Kaiserslautern. Our advance outposts had minor skirmishes with the enemy but we still captured up to 100 soldiers while over 200 men were found at local hospitals

On the 26th [7 January], we advanced to Landstuhl and, on the 27th [8 January], arrived at Homburg. The following day, we were at Zweibrücken. During this time we captured 50 prisoners while over 200 sick soldiers were found at Zweibrücken. On the 29th [10 January], the corps rested.

On 30 December [11 January] we marched to Sarreguemines. On the 31st [12 January], the corps reached Puttelange while on January 1 [13], it was already at Faulquemont, where we rested yesterday. During this campaign, in which Marshal Marmont, retreating with some 15,000 men from the fortress of Mainz to Metz, was continually pursued by our troops. In addition to the captured French troops, we also seized 200 Dutch and German soldiers who will be returned to their respective countries. Currently, one part of my advance outposts are near Nancy while the other is at the village of Atton not far from Pont-à-Mousson.

The enemy is moving large amounts of artillery from Metz to Châlons-sur-Marne, where, as available reports suggest, his troops are also moving. Local residents are greeting us warmly and wish success to our enterprise in order to have peace. Those who escaped from Metz today assure me that the city residents were spiking [French] cannon at night which forced [the French] to deploy two sentries to each cannon. The French emperor had pillaged and devastated lands all across [Europe] and yet we find the French living in poverty and misery. [From the Russian text in RGVIA, f. VUA, op. 16, d. 4120, part1, ll. 112-113b]

Sergei Mayevskii

After enlisting in the army in 1795, Mayevskii enjoyed a successful career, rising to the rank of colonel in 1803, fighting the French in 1805–7 and the Turks in 1808–12. During Napoleon's invasion of Russia, he was a duty officer in General Peter Bagration's headquarters and distinguished himself at Borodino. His hard work and dedication was noticed and, in May 1813, Mayevskii was appointed the chef of the 13th Jager Regiment, which he led throughout the campaigns in Germany and France. In 1835, he wrote a lengthy letter to the Russian historian Alexander Mikhailovskii-Danilevskii describing his experiences of the campaign in France.

In January [1814], Winzingerode's corps, where the 13th Jager Regiment served, handed over the blockade of Hamburg to the army of General Bennigsen and was then dispatched to the main Acting Army on the Rhine. On 20 January [1 February], at Dusseldorf, we crossed the Rhine River and then proceeded to Cologne. This crossing, due to the frailty of the ice, seemed almost impossible but we still managed to build a crossing and the infantry and cavalry crossed in single file while the artillery had to be moved by hand; cannon fell through the ice on several occasions and had to be extracted by hand. [From the Russian text in RGVIA, f. VUA, op. 16, d. 3376/2]

Jacob Otroshenko

Born into the family of a retired cavalry officer, Otroshenko was turning thirty-five years old in 1814. The family was of limited means so the young man did not receive a formal education but was taught to read and write by his father, who wanted him to be a law clerk. Instead, the young Otroshenko as a private in the 7th Jager Regiment and embarked on a military career in 1800. He participated in the Campaigns of 1806–7 in Poland when he distinguished himself at Eylau, Heilsberg and Friedland, earning a golden sword for gallantry. This was followed by four years of service against the Turks in the Danubian Principalities, where he joined the 14th Jager Regiment. In 1812–13, Otroshenko took part in operations against the French, distinguishing himself at the battle of Craonne where he earned his promotion to colonel.

On 3 [15] January, Count Vorontsov's entire detachment crossed the Elbe River on the ice, which was a rather dangerous enterprise. The ice was thin and we had to spread hay and pour water to strengthen the surface. To move artillery across the river, we brought long wooden logs and made grooves for wheels inside them. Two logs were affixed to each cannon to distribute its weight more equally over the surface of the ice. We then dragged them across the river. . . Reaching Cologne, we crossed the Rhine River with the help of a flying ferry despite the heavy ice flow on the river. A flying ferry involves a raft used as a ferry and held by an anchor cable fastened upstream from the ferry site. Several lighter boats hold the anchor cable to prevent it from getting entangled on the river bottom. The ferry moves from one bank to another in an arc and it only requires turning the rudder towards the bank since the fast water flow then take the ferry across the river. The city of Cologne is ancient and vast, featuring many beautiful buildings, although its streets tend to be narrow, winding and dark due to tall buildings; besides, the streets are not well maintained. The city produces the famous eau-de-cologne that is renowned all across Europe. Among its great sights is the enormous church whose construction began some 400 years ago but it still has not been completed.* When we got out of the ferry, city residents, who had gathered on the riverbank, greeted us with cheers of 'hurrah!' [. . .] We then proceeded to Liège and Namur; the latter city is located on the river of the same name and is famous for a factory producing quality table knives. Local residents are French and incredibly rude. At the main square in Liège, we held a prayer service accompanied with an artillery salvo which damaged numerous windows. [Interestingly] those windows where owners placed a jar with water remained intact. [From the Russian text in J. Otroshenko, *Zapiski* . .]

Mikhail Kakhovskii

Son of a landowner from the province of Smolensk, Kakhovskii graduated from a cadet corps and began military service in 1805. By 1812, already twenty-four years old, he rose to the rank of colonel, having served in Poland, Finland, Sweden and the Danubian Principalities in the preceding seven years. He served with distinction during the 1812 Campaign and earned many awards for his exploits at Bautzen, Dresden and Leipzig. In 1814, he served as a staff officer in Count Wittgenstein's headquarters and maintained a fascinating diary about his wartime experiences.

1[13] January 1814, Rastatt, Duchy of Baden
Lord, please bless the start of this new year and give us peace to the world that you have created, and return us with laurels back to the embrace of our parents, relatives and friends – as soon as I woke up today this was my first prayer which I said with open heart to reach the Lord of the Heavens and Earth, may he hear it and bless us all with peace.

Yesterday, at twelve o'clock at night precisely, just as I was about to fall asleep, Brezinski came by, inviting me to go with him to celebrate the departing year and greet the new year with a bottle of champagne. However, I was already in the sweet embrace of slumber and chose not to go. This morning, as customary, I went to congratulate my comrades; I visited D'Auvray, Kikin, Count Sivers, Löwenstern, Aklucheev and finally Count Wittgenstein. Then we all went to the church, where we attended mass and prayer and listened to the priest's sermon. I wore only my uniform and got chilled due to considerable frost and wretched cold wind.

Today, the Count [Wittgenstein] held a large dinner that was attended by Prince Heinrich of Prussia and Grand Duke of Baden, who was passed by our headquarters on his way back to Karlsruhe, as well as all our generals and staff

---

* The construction of Cologne Cathedral commenced in 1248 but was halted in 1473. Work resumed in 1842 and was completed, to the original plan, in 1880. At 474ft long (with towers over 500ft tall), the cathedral is the largest Gothic church in Northern Europe.

officers serving in the main headquarters. We had a magnificent table set up in the local art gallery . . . Also today arrived Actual Chamberlain Zherebtsov, delivering to the Emperor the keys of Danzig, where the entire garrison had surrendered and everything has been captured

. . . In concluding this first day of the new year, I want to once again express my hope that this will be a successful year for me, that I will return home soon and that a general peace will be once more restored in Europe.

2[14] January, Rastatt

I spent this morning reading a book for a long time, then wrote a letter to my sister and then, around 11 o'clock in the morning, went to the Count [Wittgenstein] to present nominations [of Russians officers] to the Prussian orders for the battle of Leipzig, which he had asked me to gather together and present to the King [Frederick William of Prussia]. We dined on a cake in Tishin's apartment, whom we called a birthday boy for this occasion. Today we bound the eighth daily journal [of military operations] since our crossing of [the Russian] border a year ago. It was made in the evening and I had to pay 2 guldens and 48 kreuzers for it. I gave [my servant] another fifty [unclear what currency] to buy jacket and overcoat, but the Lord only knows if he would be able to get them since everything is very expensive. I still cannot finish reading der Dolch* and do not want to cast it aside even though there are many much better books. I twice visited Tishin today and during my last call I gulped down two glass of punch at once and then rushed back home to take care of business. I just returned from my third visit to Tishin, where I ate a bit so do not have any desire for dinner.

3[15] January, Rastatt

I woke up very early today, it was still dark, and before tea was served, I finally finished reading der Dolch, bundled all the books I have already read and then spent considerable time reading newspapers, which published a very interesting explanation Napoleon had given to the Senate of all the events and how he desired peace. The newspapers also contained the Senate's reaction and Napoleon's response in which he declare that he genuinely desires peace and is ready to make personal sacrifices to achieve it, without demanding the return of the conquered territories which had been already restored by the Allies to their rightful owners. It is rather enjoyable to see such humiliation of the proud conqueror.

Before noon the Count [Wittgenstein] travelled to Fort Louis to see if it would be possible to build a bridge which had been removed due to heavy ice flow. It has been snowing all day today.

[. . .]

---

* Kakhovskii probably refers to Carl Grosse's book *Der Dolch*.

We ate with the host who has just returned from Karlsruhe . . . The Badenese troops keep arriving and they are in very good shape. My host told me that [the former French Foreign Minister] Talleyrand has arrived to Basel to conduct negotiations and that Offenburg is supposedly chosen as the location for congress. Only Lord himself knows if this is true and how all of this will end.

I gave my carriage to Brezinski, who, together with [other officers], travelled to Baden to get pay and bathe. In the evening, [Wittgenstein] instructed me to write an order for the crossing over the Rhine and to command the Badenese in particular to treat the French well. There are already numerous complaints [about the Badenese troops] while the locals are very pleased and welcome our troops. After drinking a cup of tea, I quickly wrote a draft but do not know how well it came out so I will review and revise it early tomorrow morning when the Lord will grant me a fresher perspective . . .

4[16] January, Rastatt
I slept very poorly tonight and got up very early in the morning. Before tea was served, I revised my draft of the order [to the troops], wrote a clean copy and sent it off [to the headquarters]. I later read it out to the Count [Wittgenstein] who was very pleased with it and ordered to have the order translated into German (for the Badenese) and issued in both languages . . . Masalov has a birthday on the 7th, but since we are crossing the Rhine in two days, we decided to celebrate the day today. He arranged for a sumptuous party that was attended by numerous people. Our officers visiting Baden returned just in time to the party and we all had great fun, even acting mischievously and throwing bread and corks at each other . . . It thawed today and the bridge is again being built [over the Rhine]. The 1st Corps is scheduled to cross over tomorrow while we will advance to Haguenau the day after tomorrow. Today's newspapers announce that Lord Wellington had routed the French and captured some 10,000 prisoners so, with the Lord's help, all of this may end soon.* In the evening I again went to Masalov's quarters, where rigorous card game was underway in every corner. I drank two cups of good tea, another cup of punch and quietly slipped behind the door. Now, already undressed and in my [night] robe I am scribbling away on paper. I cannot stand noise and there is a [veritable] club [in Masalov's quarters]. Yet tomorrow we have to pack everything and get ready [for the campaign] and there is enormous amount of work to be done, not to mention to write responses to [private] letters that I have received. When will the Lord grant us peace if we are not praying or asking him for it.

5[17] January, Rastatt

---

* Probably the British victories at Nivelle and Nive in November–December 1813.

I woke with a gut-wrenching pain in stomach and cannot recall if I have ever suffered such pain before. I drank a glass of wine with Muscat nut and four cups of the strongest tea without cream, but nothing helped and I had to endure pain until lunch. In the meanwhile I had to write and twice visited the Count [Wittgenstein] . . . The Count went to bathe in Baden, where he will stay for the night. We will not be departing tomorrow since the bridge has not been completed yet and the recent thaw caused the water level to rise considerably in the river, creating new hurdles for us. Nevertheless, our 1st Corps is already crossing the river on boats while the cavalry will be moved on ferries.

Today British minister Lord [George] Cathcart arrived at the main Imperial headquarters to take part in peace negotiations, which I hope the Lord will expedite. [Wittgenstein] told me that the Emperor has already crossed the Rhine on 1[13] January. This is glorious news, considering that just one year ago the Emperor crossed the Niemen and now he is already across the Rhine. We dined at home and my hostesses treated me with some bitter preserves and liquors and prohibited me from eating anything else. Nevertheless, when I got up from the table I felt in fact fed and healthier than before. We spoke at length on various subjects . . . and I told my hosts' niece that before my departure I will steal one of her items [for remembrance]. I intend on taking a small landscape that she had knitted and that hangs in my room, but she does not know it and kept trying to guess. After lunch I returned to my writing duties, then called [other officers] to drink tea and, having sent out dispatches, we drank some punch, read newly received orders and pondered about the bliss of peaceful rural life in the company of beloved family members. We all begged the Lord to grant us peace . . . Later tonight I plan on starting to read [William] Shakespeare's tragedies . . .

6[18] January, Rastatt
This morning I was again feeling sick but my condition was not as grievous as yesterday. Before noon I visited [Fedor] d'Auvray [Wittgenstein's Chief of Staff] and then paid a visit to the Count [Wittgenstein] himself who had returned from Baden and declared that we would definitely cross the Rhine tomorrow, even if we had to use rafts to accomplish it. [Since today is the Baptism of the Lord holiday], I attended mass and joined a procession to the 'Jordan' on the river, where ceremonies were conducted with proper formalities despite heavy rain. So we returned home as wet as if we had taken a bath. Despite bad and wet weather, there were numerous spectators and the entire bridge and both riverbanks were filled with people. Later our priest, with his entire synkletos* and singers, came singing by my quarters and I

---

* In ancient Greece, a 'synkletos' was a council of the highest officials. In Russia, the word 'sinklit' was used in a figurative sense, usually ironically, to designate a full assembly of people.

had to give chervonets [10 rubles] to the singers and drink some vodka and a bottle of good old Champagne rosé wine with the priest to mark the holiday. So the lunch proved to be joyous . . .

In the evening I went to the Count to have some papers signed and asked him for permission to remain in town for another two days because I was not feeling well and, more importantly, because not all troops would be able to cross the Rhine on ferries tomorrow and I could not hope to ride a horse for now. [Many other officers] are staying with me as well and we will rejoin the troops later. The Count has just received the order to advance as quickly as possible to Luneville so we will not lag behind. We drank tea in the large hall at Brezinski's quarters, where a large crowd of people congregated. Some are still playing cards while we have just finished dinner.

7 [19] January, Rastatt

[. . .] There are many of us still remaining in town. Even those who crossed the river have returned back but cannot re-cross because both crossings are so jammed that there are fights over who gets into boat or ferry . . . Our main army expects a major battle any day now so may the Lord bless and help us for if we prevail the war will certainly end . . . At last [my companions] have learned about my theft [of a memento from the host's niece] and they long debated [how appropriate] it was but ultimately they all sided with me . . .

8 [20] January, Rastatt

[. . .] We had breakfast at Brezinski's quarters, then had a very pleasant lunch at home, took a stroll outside and went to drink tea at Brezinski's place where all officials have now congregated . . . We conversed and laughed for some time . . . then reviewed a large and beautiful map of Paris that offered great details of the city . . .

9[21] January, Rastatt

At last we have crossed the Rhine and are spending the night at Haguenau. In the morning I bade farewell to the Countess and my hosts who argued that we would have to return soon [because of problems at the crossing]. So, ignoring the Cossack who returned from the crossing and assured us that it was impossible to get across the river, we departed in company of a chaplain and others. The weather was miserable, with wet snow and wind. Upon arriving at Au [Au am Rhein], we met [our fellow officers] who had departed earlier but could not cross because the water had risen so much that it had flooded even the road; thus infantry could not cross and seven cannon and the entire train stood on the bank. So we had no other option but submit to the ineviatable and turn back. Stopping at the nearby village, we drank a bit of vodka and sent our Cossacks to attend to our chest and horses and cross the river at the first opportunity, reporting back to me. Meanwhile we returned back to [Rastatt] at one o'clock in the afternoon and our kind hosts received us with genuine delight, while many other hosts refused to take [our officers] back to the quarters . . . My host assures me that we will not be able to cross for another four days, and I find such prospects quite unappealing. There are two problems that I am facing: the Count [Wittgenstein] currently has no one with him and, second, he is already at Saverne tonight and will travel further tomorrow, so only God knows how we are going to catch up with him . . .

10[22] January, Rastatt
Waiting for the Cossack's report, I spent the entire morning till lunch at home, reading a book I borrowed from the host and a few newspapers, then walked a bit despite considerable frost. We had, as usual, an excellent and joyous lunch and when we were about to get up from the table my Cossack arrived with the news that our chest and horses had crossed the Rhine. But it was too late for us to travel today and we decided to wait till tomorrow. Instead we went to examine a local carriage maker's shop, which my host highly recommended We saw several very good carriages and [one of my companions] wanted to buy one, but the seller refused to give us for no less than 150 *chervonets* [1,500 rubles]★ . . . After drinking tea with a chaplain, we went to play bingo and I won a bit of money . . .

11 [23] January, Lauterbourg, France
Thanks to the merciful Lord, we are already beyond the Rhine and inside France. Who could have thought at the start of the war [in June 1812] or even when we entered Prussia [in early 1813] that we would actually advance so far. But the Lord directed us and all the glory belongs to him.

We got up early in the morning and, after drinking a cup of tea, prepared to depart thinking that my kind-hearted hosts were still asleep. But these decent and honourable people already stood at windows when we were getting into the carriage. We thanked them from the bottom of our hearts for hosting us, an experience that I will never forget. Despite departing early in the morning, we still found the crossing jammed with numerous carts, carriages, horses, Cossacks and God knows what else. The weather was awful, with snow and wind blowing straight into our faces. We had no shelter on the riverbank and so drank a bit of vodka and, with the Lord help, somehow managed to get our carriage and a couple of horses on to a small boat while I and [my fellow officers] hitched a ride on a large ferry. As we moved upstream to cross the river, my carriage was driven by a swift current so far downstream that it reached the opposite bank only 10 verstas [10.6km] away from the designated landing site and caught up with us only hours later. By then we walked for two

---

★ More than an officer earned in a year.

verstas [2.13km] in the worst weather possible, barely dragging our feet and wind blowing straight into our faces.

I and [three of my fellow officers] received a billet [at Lauterbourg] and visited a local tavern to eat. Most of our company departed for Haguenau while I and [two officers] decided to spend the night here since our horses arrived too late. This is the first time we are staying in France and our quarters are very poor. A small room, about three square metres in size, and even that unheated . . . I planned on drinking a bottle of champagne in the middle of the Rhine but since the carriage ended up in a different boat, we drank only after settling at our quarters, raising a couple of glasses asking the Lord for a quick and successful return. [From the Russian text in Kakhovskii, *Zapiski* . . .]

Ilya Radozhitskii

A graduate of the Imperial Military Orphanage and future major-general of artillery, the young Radozhitskii served as a lieutenant in the 3rd Light Company attached to General Alexander Langeron's corps.

While the Allied armies were advancing deeper into France, Count Langeron's corps remained near Mainz, maintaining blockade of the local fortress. I was in Frankfurt, preoccupied with my drawings.

The 1st of January! New Year! New Year! [This time around,] these are just empty words. Back at home, in our beloved Mother Russia, we usually spent the last evening of the old year in the circle of relatives or friends or with our benevolent superiors, and celebrated New Year with loud salutations to the sound of music and joyous clinking of glasses. But in this foreign land everything is quiet and dreary . . . [and] as ill luck would have it, I had not a single coin in my pockets. Oh, money, money! [The great Roman philosopher Lucius Annaeus] Seneca spoke truth when he proclaimed that in this world there is no greater wickedness than gold. Yet I am more inclined to side with Rabbi Hirsch who stated that the gold is the greatest blessing in the world . . . Alas, wise men's preaching does not buy you bread while with money, I am always fed and happy. Money can encompass all the wisdom and virtue. The question is where to find them? Their value is appreciated only when they are gone. It was with such thoughts that I soothed myself in Frankfurt, having lost any hope of going to the theatre where Mozart's glorious opera *The Magic Flute* was played. Alas, to live in Frankfurt and to be confined to a cold room filled with boredom on the very first day of a new year – I felt that this was a punishment befitting Tantalus* himself. [But] later that evening, I unexpectedly acquired one taller and, thrilled by such a luck, I hastened to the theatre.

---

* Tantalus was a Greek mythological figure, most famous for his eternal punishment in Tartarus, where he was made to stand in a pool of water beneath a fruit tree with low

[. . .]

[After a week-long] stay in Frankfurt, I learned that my artillery company was passing through the city towards Gross-Gerau. This unexpected turn of event enlivened me. I rushed to my apartment to inform my host that I was departing . . . The artillery was required to march for over 30 verstas [31.8km]. I caught up with my company on the seventh versta from the city and did not find a single officer with it. Our lieutenant-colonel stayed behind to have some fun in the city, and all the other officers stayed there as well.

On 7 [19] January I was already on the left bank of the Rhine, near the village of Nierstein located on the road from Mainz to Oppenheim. Looking out of the windows of my apartment, I enjoyed the view of the quiet flow of river that came close to bathe the walls of the house I was lodged in. Large packs of ice, like a flock of swans, drifted over the entire expanse of the river, speedily outrunning each other as if harrying to inform our enemies about the arrival of the formidable Russian forces . . . And soon the Rhine itself, after never seeing such foes except for the few prisoners of war, wails under the weight of the Russian rumble and bayonets. This time of the year, however, when everything melts, floods and gets wets, it seems that the nature itself mourns with the Rhine. Winter deprived the river of its beauty and left only the bare vineyards which like remnants of crops in harvested fields revealed its occasional vines from underneath the snow. The Oppenheim and Nierstein wines are considered among the best of the Rhenish wines and this nectar soon satisfied my thirst. So, the greatly esteemed Rhine, was there any other time that you have been saddled by the Russians!? Until now you marked the boundary of the German might and carried [the German] tribute to the conquering Gauls, knowing no other burden. Your banks, flourishing in abundance, ensured the wellbeing of their inhabitants, who cultivated juicy grapes next to your glistening waters, sang hymns of joy and amused you with their happiness. And now – only wailing and misery rein on your banks while damnations could be heard in place of blessings. Now, despite all the efforts of your lord, foreign peoples have come to cross your boisterous waters. In vain you have armed yourselves with swift current and heavy ice flow. The rumble of the Russian tsar shakes your heart and timorously you bend to our might. Weep, the Rhine, weep . . .

Below Oppenheim, where we crossed the Rhine, the river is narrower than the Vistula is at Warsaw but further downstream at Mainz, it becomes very wide, especially below the estuary of the River Main. The twelve cannon of our artillery company required two full days to cross the river on boats. The crossing was rather dangerous and had to be carried slowly and with great caution. Consequently we got both chilled and wet to the bone. Accompanying the cannon, I crossed the river several times and enjoyed the view of its banks,

---

branches, with the fruit ever eluding his grasp, and the water always receding before he could take a drink.

which, although bare, still offered very pleasant sights. The right bank was flat while the left – elevated. During the crossing we were accompanied by the 12th Division with all of its wagons that frequently hindered us. The division was tasked with blockading Mainz from the left side of the Rhine while Count Langeron led the rest of his forces to Blücher. On the third crossing, the Prince of Coburg* accompanied my cannon. I have rarely met such a handsome man and his eminent face conveyed nobility of his soul . . . Prince of Coburg, commanding the 5th German corps, was appointed to replace Langeron at Mainz but he did not have [enough] officers. Although he was given a few Prussians, he was now travelling to Count Langeron to ask for Russian officers who could train his landwehr troops.

New quarters, and worse than before. I, together with two cannon protected by jagers, deployed at the village of Ober-Olm on the left side of the Rhine, about six verstas [6.4km] away from Mainz. The remaining cannon were deployed as follows: four cannon commanded by Captain Zhemchuzhnikov were at Leubenheim, and two at Hechstheim. The troops of the 9th Corps closely blockaded the fortress [of Mainz] on all sides. Local residents assured us that Mainz would surrender soon because its garrison had no more than 8,000 men, most of them sick, many of whom were dying on a daily basis, while the healthy soldiers went over to the besieging side. We however waited for siege artillery and it seemed that we intended to capture this fortress in a proper siege.

So ten days I lived in this monotonous solitude. Days passed without any occurrences. I was alone which had some advantages. Conversing with muses, [Fridriech] Schiller, [Johann Wolfgang von] Goethe and [Jean de] La Fontaine, I did not notice the passage of time. After disorderly life in Frankfurt, one could find [different kind] of enjoyment at Ober-Olm, pleasures that were less for senses and more for cultivation of mind and heart.

On 18 [30] January I travelled to Mainz. Snow was melting and it seemed the spring was trying to make an appearance. About four verstas [4.28km] from Ober-Olm, I found a Cossack outpost deployed in the devastated village of Marienborn and another versta away from them was a French outpost. Compared to Hochheim on the opposite bank, it is difficult to get a good view of Mainz from this direction since it was all overshadowed by its fortifications. I enjoyed the view of Hochheim, observed the tower of Höchst and, peering at blue horizon, could guess the location of Frankfurt, where I had had many joys. On this side of the river, the French controlled the four closest villages, although I could not see or hear anything. What a dreary enterprise it is to maintain a blockade!

Four days later I decided to go to Hochheim where our Sub-Lieutenant Baron Ungern-Sternberg was deployed with two cannon. The village was located on the right side of Mainz, about three verstas [3.2km] away from the

---

* Prince Ferdinand Georg August of Saxe-Coburg-Gotha

fortress. Travelling along the road, I enjoyed the views of snow-covered plains and the city skyline visible on the left. The fields between the fortress and the road where I travelled were immaculately clean! The Cossacks very rarely rode along the front line. And how simple-minded the Frenchmen are. It had been already some time since we quietly took positions around the fortress and lived as if on canton-quarters. If you only they had sent a cavalry column across this field – it might not have cause much harm to us but would have produced great distress and might have gotten all the way to my guns as well! But I would have met them near the hill with jagers in close support. What a strange way of capturing a fortress – though patience! The enemy could not be seen at all. On both sides troops sit in their quarters, amuse themselves and strike up affairs until that the appearance of that all-consuming monster – the hunger. And then . . . Such were my thoughts as I approached Hochheim and heard the sound of musket fire coming from the direction of Mainz. 'It is probably skirmishing on advance posts,' I thought to myself. Probably some got bored of idleness. Having seen no bullets or cannonballs fired since the battle of Leipzig, I looked around to see if I could determine where the clash was taking place. Maybe I could go and witness it, I thought to myself. There were two cannon in front of the village. Horses were about to be taken away and a group of cannoniers had gathered around an open caisson. Not far from them stood an outpost of army soldiers, whose muskets rested on trestles near a straw hut. Several merry chaps sat around a bonfire. 'Cheers, lads!' I told them. After the usual greetings, one of the feurwerkers told me, 'Your Honour, we had a busy day today.' – 'How come!?' – 'Mikhailov has been killed and one of the limbers got damaged.' Without waiting for further explanations, I went to [Baron] Ungern who told what had happened. About 6,000 French made a sortie directly at this village and almost reached the heights of Laubenheim. They dug in inside the ruins of a monastery, deployed six cannon and, under their protective fire, advanced in thick columns of infantry and cavalry. Our troops hastily gathered some 4,000 men between Hochheim and Laubeheim. But just as [Baron] Ungern made several successful shots at the enemy columns, they stopped and retreated. Our skirmishers did not even manage to take part in the clash. The Ukrainian Cossacks captured an enemy cannon but had to relinquish it because they could not overcome the enemy cavalrymen [who came to the infantry's support]. Thus, some 6,000 Frenchmen were turned back by just two our cannon. They clearly hoped to surprise us but failed and had to beat a hasty retreat to the fortress. It would have been better, of course, if we had lured them further away and cut them from the direction of Marienborn.

[. . .]

At last, the winter almost completely disappeared. Snow turned tears that rushed in overflowing streams from the hill down the valley. All fields turned black, with occasional white scars of snow. They presented a rather depressing sight . . .

1st of February, Sunday. I went to the village church to observe religious service and the local residents attending it. Women sat dressed in blouses and white hats with flaps, so that it was impossible to distinguish married women from single girls except by looking at their faces. In the choir sat men in blue and grey coats and books in hand. The orchestra, or to be precise the pipe organ, began to play just as the priest, in white clothing, proclaimed, 'Domunis vobiscum! In secula seculorum!' The orchestra sometimes played allegro which amused the attendees. Occasionally a venerable küster,* sitting in the upper gallery, got carried away by enthusiasm and began to sing a hymn in alto, accompanied by a choir of descant and bass singers below and above him. 'Oh, what voices they have!' I told a jager officer who stood next to me, who got all red in face and bit his lip. It seemed rather strange to see a German with Latin book in hand inside a Catholic church since I got used to seeing them in simple Lutheran churches. [I wondered] if everyone understood what needed to be comprehended in this impenetrable service?

I soon received an order to depart with two guns the following day to the village of Nieder-Olm, which served as the gathering point for forces blockading Mainz. I eagerly packed my belongings and bid good-bye to the canary bird, which got used to me. If it were spring time, I would have taken her with me but the winter still held its sway, deceiving the eye with the greenery of some grass and the newly rising grain that had been sowed in the autumn.

My new quarters were with a good peasant, who was a miller and baker and had a good house. He gave me his best room . . . His joyous but unattractive daughter brought me some food. She frequently welcomed her friends, very adroit and cheeky girls, who did they best to disperse my indifference and warm up my cold heart. But their efforts proved in vain. My intellectual exercises and rather different frame of mine distracted me from their fun and play. One of the girls once dressed in a jager officer's frock-coat and appeared in front of me to introduce herself. This farce greatly entertained everyone and I must say I did not expect such deftness from a simple village girl.

On 2 [14] February, at noon, I arrived at Nieder-Olm where I was told to wait for my company. However, General Karponeko advised me to continue my route, assuming that my company could have proceeded by a shorter route to Wörrstadt. So I moved forward and indeed encountered my company at that village. After a prolonged seclusion I was thrilled to get back together with my comrades. Prince of Coburg's troops replaced the 9th Corps and we, led by Count St. Priest, hurried to rejoin the rest of our troops, who, it was said, were attempting to pull miracles [in France]. [From the Russian text in I. Radozhitskii, *Pokhodnye zapiski* . . .]

---

* A sacristan who was charged with care of the sacristy, the church and its contents.

2

The Invasion

*In early January, the Allies commenced the invasion of France with three armies –
Schwarzenberg's Army of Bohemia advancing from Switzerland, Blücher's Army
of Silesia moving from Germany toward Metz, and former French marshal turned
Swedish crown prince Jean-Baptiste Bernadotte's Army of the North advancing
into Belgium and north-western France.*

*In the wake of the devastating campaign in Germany, Napoleon sought to
assemble another army to stop the Allied invasion of France. It was a massive
challenge. Over 100,000 men were tied down in besieged fortresses beyond the
Rhine while as many more were tied down in southern France where they struggled
to contain the British and their Portuguese and Spanish allies. A sizable French
contingent was also resisting the Austrians in northern Italy and on France's Alpine
borders. By conscripting pensioners and mere boys, the famed 'les Marie-Louises',
Napoleon raised a force of almost 120,000 men which he deployed along France's
north-eastern border.*

*With his resources overstretched and armies outnumbered, Napoleon faced a
severe challenge that certainly would have shaken the composure of a less capable or
self-confident leader. Yet, the Emperor thrived in such dire circumstances. The 1814
Campaign saw the return of the younger and more energetic Napoleon – 'I have put
on my Italian boots' he famously quipped, referring to his great Italian campaigns
– who hastened his preparations for a campaign based on the strategy of the central
position that aimed at safeguarding the heart of his empire – Paris. Napoleon's task,
however, was greatly facilitated by the Allies' tensions and bickering over the outcome
of war and future prospects of Europe. The Allies' vacillation had an impact on their
military operations that were conducted disjointedly and unhurriedly. Thus, in the
opening phase of the campaign of 1814, Napoleon scored a series of victories that
regained him the respect that once made him the most feared commander in Europe.
Even though he stationed most of the newly raised army in and around Paris and
fought with as few as 40,000 men, he used the advantage of interior lines to attack
the different Allied armies in turn and push them back. He won a quick succession
of victories against his various opponents at Champaubert, Montmirail, Château-
Thierry, Vauchamps, Montereau, Craonne, and Reims. Although the French*

inflicted greater casualties than they suffered, their losses were still significant in light of limited resources at hand and the Allied manpower reserves that greatly exceeded the human and material resources of the defending nation.

Alexander Mikhailovskii-Danilevskii

Alexander Ivanovich Mikhailovskii-Danilevskii holds a distinct place in Russian historiography. An active participant in the wars against Napoleon, he went on to write influential histories that for generations shaped the Russian perceptions of this period. In addition to his many works of history, Mikhailovskii-Danilevskii also left a series of journals that he maintained on campaign, offering fascinating insights into what was transpiring in the Russian high command during the war. In 1812, Mikhailovskii-Danilevskii served as an adjutant to Field Marshal Mikhail Kutuzov who tasked him with writing reports and various memos on military operations in Russian, German and French as well as maintaining the official Journal of Military Operations. After Kutuzov's death, Emperor Alexander, who noticed this talented young official, took him into His Imperial Majesty's Suite on Quartermaster Service (the precursor to the Russian General Staff) where Mikhailovskii-Danilevskii attended the Russian emperor throughout the 1813–14 Campaigns.

At the start of every campaign, leaders usually address their armies with orders of the day which briefly explain the principles on which the upcoming campaign will be based. Such orders of the day are historical monuments which bear upon them a deep impress of the respective characters of their authors. So it seems appropriate to place here, for comparison, the order of the day issued by Napoleon to inform his army about the war with Russia [in 1812], and the order of Emperor Alexander, issued several days prior to our entrance into France [in 1814].

'Soldiers,' said Napoleon, 'Russia is carried away by fate. Her destiny must be accomplished! Can it be that she looks on us as degenerated? Are we not the same warriors who fought at Austerlitz? Let us cross the Niemen and carry the war over the Russian frontier. This war will cover the French arms with glory, and the peace we shall conclude will be solid, and will put an end to the baneful influence of Russia in the affairs of Europe.'

Let us now listen to the words of Alexander: 'Warriors! Your valour and perseverance have brought you from the Oka River to the Rhine. They will carry you farther: we are about to cross the Rhine, and to enter that country, with which we have been waging a bloody and a cruel war. Already have we saved our native country, covered it with glory, and restored freedom and independence to Europe. It remains but to crown these mighty achievements with the long-wished-for peace. May tranquillity be restored to the whole world! May every country enjoy happiness under its own independent laws and government! May religion, language, arts, sciences, and commerce flourish in every land for the general welfare of nations! This, and not the continuance of war and destruction, is our object. Our enemies, by invading the heart of our realm, wrought us much evil, but dreadful was the retribution. The Divine wrath crushed them! Let us not take example from them: inhumanity and ferocity cannot be pleasing in the eyes of a merciful God. Let us forget what they have done against us. Instead of animosity and revenge, let us approach them with the words of kind feeling, and with the outstretched hand of reconciliation.'*

The Allied armies were instructed to cross the Rhine in various places on 1 [13] January. The main army, which was commanded by the Emperor [Alexander] himself, crossed the river near Basel and our troops shouted a thundering 'Hurrah!' on a bridge across the river. The campaign in France was needed to establish a secure peace [in Europe]: besides the Emperor believed that the honour of Russia demanded that Russian banners be unfurled on top of Paris. We marched on to Vesoul, Langre, Chaumont and Bar-sur-Aube, facing no enemy resistance anywhere and occupying several regions over the next three weeks. The enemy troops were retreating everywhere and the local populace, which the prefects urged to resistance in their ostentatious appeals, were instead opening city gates to us. The papers of prefects of various departments revealed to us an order of [Jean-Pierre Bachasson de] Montalivet, the Minister of the Interior, dated 23 December 1813, which outlined what prefects were supposed to do during our invasion:

On the appearance of the enemy you are directed to leave them the soil only, without the inhabitants, as it has been done in many other countries. If it should be impossible to remove all the inhabitants, you are to leave no means untried to make at least the wealthier families quit their homes on the approach of the enemy; for those of our subjects, who shall consent to live

---

* The rest of the proclamation read: 'It is the Russian's glory to humble an armed enemy; but, once disarmed, to do good both to him and his peaceful countrymen. Such is the lesson taught us by our most holy, orthodox faith; from her divinely inspired lips we hear the command, "Love your enemies, and do good to them that hate you."

Warriors! I have the fullest confidence, that, by the moderation of your conduct in the enemy's country, you will conquer as often by generosity as by arms; and that, uniting the valour of the soldier against the armed, with the charity of the Christian towards the unarmed, you will crown your exploits by keeping stainless your well-earned reputation of a brave, and a moral people. Thus you will the sooner attain the object of our wishes, a general peace. At the same time, I am well convinced that your commanders will not hesitate to take the severest measures to prevent the possible misconduct of a few among you, from sullying, to our general grief, the good name you have hitherto so justly enjoyed.' Proclamation to the Russian Armies, RGVIA f. VUA, op. 16, d. 3376/2, l. 240.

under their authority, however temporary, must be regarded as traitors to the allegiance they have sworn. You will order the officers of every jurisdiction to remove the records. Every exertion must be made to conceal from the enemy, the documents by which they might be enabled to govern the Country, and to gain knowledge of the resources available to the supply of their troops. As to your person, you are ordered not to quit your department so long as there shall remain in it a single hamlet unoccupied by the enemy. You are to be the last to quit the department entrusted to you by His Majesty; and if it should be completely conquered, with the exception of a fortress, it is His Majesty's pleasure, that you should shut yourself up in that fortress, and that the moment circumstances permit, you should leave it, to re-enter on the exercise of your functions in governing the Department.

Proclamations which the prefects published based on this order produced no effect, however, because heavy taxes and constant military levies made Napoleon's rule intolerable to the French people.

Rain, snow, frost, and thaw retarded, but did not arrest, our troops. Though this rapidity of march was not very agreeable to some of the Allies, the Emperor, with his usual activity, continually kept pressing them to advance, often against their will. In later years, while attending him in travels and at palaces, I rarely noticed in him such a high spirit as the one he showed during the war. Having accustomed himself, from his earliest youth, to brave the inconstancy of the elements, he was commonly on horseback, and, as usual, was the best dressed of all around him. It seemed that he was not at war but at some kind of celebration. More burdensome than the bad weather was the disagreement on military operations that periodically emerged between the Allied armies. Only the presence of Alexander, who, as the head of the Coalition, tried to appease everyone, oftentimes at his own expense, to have them agree on a common course of action, made the success of a multi-national coalition possible as well as saved the armies, which, without him, would have been certainly destroyed due to discord that existed among them. Too many times, after receiving important intelligence in the middle of the night, the Emperor, sacrificing his sleep, got up and, accompanied by somebody with a lamp, walked in bad weather on mud-filled streets of villages to visit the Allied monarch or even Prince Schwarzenberg, wake them up, read the latest reports to them and discuss common measures that had to be taken. This short anecdote exemplifies what kind of difficulties the Emperor faced. In the morning of 9 [21] March, about two hours before the attack on enemy position at Arcis and when our army was already deployed in battle formation, the Emperor, as usual surrounded with his Suite, was pacing back and forth in a field. Field Marshal Barclay de Tolly was with him and, alluding to the tardiness of some of our Allies, the Emperor, among other things, said, 'These gentlemen have given me many grey hairs.' These words are particularly important because the Emperor rarely expressed what was happening deep inside his soul.

Our quarters in France were among the worst we had seen. The French houses are not built for wintertime but rather for summers and so we, accustomed to warm houses, greatly suffered from freezing rooms, especially when we had to stay at peasant houses. Imagine a large room with its back wall taken over by a fireplace where three or four wet logs were burning, giving up some heat but hardly warming up the air. The town houses are maintained in disgusting filth. We found French residents to be much less educated than the Germans. Many of our officers, who in their childhood were swayed by their foreign tutors and now hoped to find a promised land in France, were sorely disappointed upon seeing widespread poverty, ignorance and despair in villages and towns. The French walked around with downcast eyes and gloomy appearance. They did not whether they should be happy or distressed at our invasion of their country. Will we bring an end their despondency or inflict new disasters upon them? The Frenchmen, however, looked at our invasion as a temporary but unavoidable evil: even though our troops strictly maintained order and discipline, which was a subject of the Emperor's constant concern, and every violent action against the local was punished by death, it was still impossible to prevent all kinds of difficulties that the locals experienced. [From the Russian text in Alexander Mikhailovskii-Danilevskii, *Memuary 1814-1815*]

Gavriil Meshetich

In 1812, Meshetich, a young officer of the 2nd Battery Company of the 11th Artillery Brigade, saw action at some of the bloodiest battles of the campaign, distinguishing himself at Borodino where he earned a golden sword for gallantry and was cited for 'skilfully commanding cannon, causing considerable casualties among the enemy cavalry and destroying several cannons and numerous caissons'. After taking part in half a dozen battles in Germany in 1813, Meshetich brought his cannon to the banks of the Rhine and was poised to follow General St. Priest's Corps into France.

[After spending some time in Westphalia] Count St. Priest's corps marched to the Rhine River, which he reached near the city of Dusseldorf. A small French force found there destroyed all the crossings ... So our corps received orders to march to Ehrenbreitstein* in order to cross the Rhine and invade France. Koblenz was still held by the French but the corps was ordered to

---

* Ehrenbreitstein was a fortress on the mountain of the same name on the east bank of the Rhine opposite the town of Coblence (Koblenz) in the Rhineland-Palatinate. By the treaty of Lunéville, the French had to abandon the right bank of the Rhine so they dismantled Ehrenbreitstein in 1801 to prevent the enemy from utilising it.

proceed with the crossing. Thus, at midnight on New Year's Eve, a brigade of jagers under command of Major-General [Moisei] Karpenko loaded into boats, which had been previously prepared in one of the inlets, and crossed the river under the cover of darkness. Hearing the sound of rowing boats, the enemy opened a battalion fire again and when our jagers returned fire from the boats they lit up the river allowing the enemy battery to open canister fire. But just then the enemy discovered on the opposite bank our battery's cannon which opened a fierce bombardment with cannonballs and canister while several light guns, which were placed on rafts to support the jagers, also forcefully entered the fight, directing canister fire at the enemy. Upon reaching the bank, our jagers, still firing by battalions, rushed onto the riverbank shouting 'Hurrah!' and dragged their light artillery ashore. They then waited for an infantry brigade with several heavy cannon to cross the river before proceeding in dense columns towards the enemy position. By the time they reached it, they found the enemy battery abandoned and all cannon removed. The French sought shelter inside the forštate [suburb] where they held ground maintaining battalion fire and operating artillery. However, the Russian reinforcements arriving continually from the opposite bank strengthened our attack on the suburb. The attack began with a thick chain of skirmishers that was followed by columns, some of them moving around and behind the city. The enemy wavered and began removing his artillery so the Russian columns charged with a 'Hurrah!' and cleared the suburb and the rest of the city by dawn. The enemy fled abandoning all wounded and enormous hospital with the sick. [From the Russian text in G. Meshetich, 'Istoricheskie zapiski . . .']

Mikhail Petrov

Born in 1780, Petrov was seventeen years old when he enlisted for military service which continued for more than a quarter of a century and saw him take part in more than five dozen combats and battles. On the eve of the Allied invasion of France, he was a lieutenant-colonel commanding a battalion in the 1st Jager Regiment. Of sharp intellect and phenomenal memory, Petrov was tasked by his fellow officers with maintaining a campaign journal of their experiences in 1812 and this document eventually ended up on the desk of Emperor Nicholas I himself. Petrov also wrote a personal memoir that offers many fascinating insights into campaign life and the experience of battle.

Since ancient times the German nations have a tradition of greeting the New Year in public gatherings on town squares or in friendly conversations amidst a family setting, with youth dancing, old-timers singing and everyone cheering with glasses of light wine as clocks strike midnight that separate the new and old years. So it was also on the last evening of 31 December 1813 when as part of their tradition they invited us into their families and public gatherings on the right bank of the Rhine River, where our troops took up their canton-quarters.

Several days before the German New Year, our 8th Corps, commanded by Lieutenant-General Count St. Priest, arrived from Kassel after bypassing Dusseldorff and established its headquarters at the small town of Tale [?] located opposite of Koblenz on a steep tall heights where Ehrenbreitstein Fortress had been dismantled by the French in the wake of the Treaty of Lunéville [in 1801] . . .

At midnight [on 31 December] our corps was ordered to load into the already-prepared river boats in separate columns at four locations and, after crossing the Rhine to the French side, to capture the city of Koblenz. Our regiment [1st Jagers] and a German musketeer regiment comprised the second crossing column commanded by Major-General [Moisei] Karpenko. We were instructed to depart from the right bank of the Rhine by sailing down the Lahn River which joined the Rhine upstream [from Koblenz] . . . At the designated hour, I led my 1st Battalion into the row boats, which accommodated between twenty and thirty men and were manned by skilful Rhenish navigators. With a select group of my skirmishers, commanded by Staff Captain Konevtsov, in front of me, I left the estuary of the Lahn River into the fast-flowing expanse of the magnificent Rhine! Never before in my life had I felt such a higher sense of military honour as at that moment when, in actuality, not a fervent daydream, the swift current of the Rhine tamely flowed beneath the brave sons of Russia, our glorious Fatherland!

Our navigators and rowers, all Germans, worked skilfully and eagerly but without making any rattling sound of oars moving through the water, and quickly brought us to the enemy bank and the border of the French Empire! Just ten sazhens [20m] separated us from landing, when the French outposts spotted our boats and opened fire, which alerted a four-gun battery deployed in entrenchments opposite the estuary of the Lahn River; the battery made a thunderous salvo and [the battle commenced]. We moved hastily to reach the enemy bank and rushed out of the boats, organising into battalions, driving in the enemy outposts and seizing the battery together with its guns. We then spent some time in nocturnal reconnaissance and accidental encounters and clashes with the enemy, who had scattered among vineyards that lay near the former convent. At last, we drove them back . . . and rallying with other columns to form a brigade column, we moved by fast parade march with drums beating and music playing towards Koblenz which the enemy had abandoned and where the residents greeted us with wide-open gates. My 1st Battalion was at the head of this column. Because of the New Year festivities, the city was illuminated with lanterns and various lamps.

Just as the artillery and musket fire subsided and was replaced with our parade music, people residing along the city's main street, where we marched, suddenly opened doors and windows on all floors of their enormous homes on both sides of the street and, amidst cold but snowless winter night, they appeared with candles and torches in hand, shouting 'Long Live Alexander, the Saviour of Germany! Long Live his gallant warriors, heroes and benefactors, our eternal friends, hurrah, hurrah, hurrah!' [. . .] Some of them, being more daring than others, rushed into the street in front of our column and began dancing to our music, jumping back and forth, clapping their hand and swirling around, forming dancing circles and shouting as loudly as they could. On this occasion, the German soul had released all that burdened it during the nineteen-year-long French yoke that separated them from their brethren in the rest of Germany. There were some who mixed into their shouts a few Russian words, such as 'Bravo, Russko! Topra Russka!' and then erupted into obscenity-laced tirades against Napoleon. [From the Russian text in M. Petrov, 'Rasskazy . . .']

Moisei Karpenko

On 31 December 1813, Count St. Priest, a French émigré who had made a successful career in the Russian army, crossed the Rhine at Koblenz, driving out a small French detachment that defended a small local redoubt. The city residents illuminated their houses welcoming the Russians with loud acclamations. The 39-year-old Major-General Moisei Karpenko, a veteran of three campaigns against Napoleon, led the 1st Jager Regiment and commanded a brigade of the 11th Infantry Division.

The following morning Count St. Priest appointed Colonel [Mikhail] Magdenko* as Commandant of Koblenz. I ordered Magdenko to survey the entire city and he soon informed me that on the bank of the Rhine River there was a column that the French had erected bearing an inscription 'Victory over the Russian troops at Austerlitz'.† Magdenko inquired whether he should destroy the monument or not. I prohibited him from doing any damage to this column and instead to have the following words to be engraved: '*Seen and approved by us, Russian Commandant of Koblenz*.'‡ [From the Russian text in RGVIA, f. VUA, op. 16, d. 3376/2]

---

* From Mikhail Petrov's memoir: 'General Karpenko was a temporary military governor of Koblenz and was assisted by the commandant, Artillery Colonel Mikhail Semenovich Magdenko, a smart and well educated officer and hero. This man, so attentive to the glory of his Fatherland be it on the field of battle or diplomatic arena, was an indispensable assistant to Karpenko since he spoke fluent German and French languages.' Petrov, 'Rasskazy . . .', p. 252.

† In his history of the 1814 Campaign, Alexander Mikhailovskii-Danilevskii incorrectly refers to this monument being dedicated to Napoleon's campaign in Russia in 1812.

‡ Similar account is in Mikhail Petrov, 'Rasskazy . . .', p. 253.

Nikolai Lorer

A future participant in the Decembrist Uprising, Nikolai Lorer was just twenty years old when he stood on the banks of the Rhine. Born into a large noble family (of French origin) from southern Ukraine, he enrolled in the Noble Regiment of the Second Cadet Corps and began active military service in November 1812. Serving as an ensign with the Life Guard Lithuanian Regiment, he fought at Dresden, Kulm and Leipzig before seeing the land of his ancestors in January 1814.

After pleasant rest and quartering in the vicinity of Frankfurt [am-Main], the Guard Corps was ordered to march [towards France]. I bid farewell to my kind host and his family and, on a beautiful early morning our regiment departed from Offenbach, which belonged to the Princess of Isenburg;* its sympathetic residents escorted us as far as the town gates. Our path lay through Switzerland towards the Rhine. At Heidelberg I visited a young student, the son of my host in Offenbach, and gave him letters from his sisters. Since we had a day rest, I was able to visit the local castle and its famous barrel.†

We slowly moved towards the borders of France. We were supposed to cross the Rhine at Basel but suffered from terrible weather as snow and rain, combined with strong winds, greatly delayed our movements. We finally approached the banks of the Rhine. Deep snow covered its banks as a white blanket while the blue Rhine threateningly raged and rolled. Emperor Alexander himself observed our crossing. He stood near the bridge and the Guard, despite terrible weather, moved in a parade march in front of him, descended to the bridge and quickly and orderly crossed the river as if paying its respects to the famous and ancient Rhine River. We passed the city of Basel without stopping there. A French garrison was still in its citadel and we would not have escaped its guns. So we took advantage of darkness to pass by the fortress unnoticed by the garrison and, by morning, we were already at our quarters. Thus, with the crossing of the Rhine, Providence has allowed us to take revenge on a haughty enemy for [crossing] our Nieman River. The residents of the [left] bank of the Rhine do not speak French but some mixed and poor German dialect so we found it difficult to understand what they said.

I took advantage of our day break to travel to Basel to visit my relative P.P.K. [General Peter Konovnitsyn], the hero of the 1812 Campaign. He was recovering from a wound sustained during the battle of Bautzen [in May 1813]. I found him still in bed.

---

* Isenburg was a small principality located in southern present-day Hesse, in territories north and south of Frankfurt.

† The Heidelberg Tun (German: Großes Fass) is an enormous wine vat in the cellar of Heidelberg Castle, which was made in 1751 and has a capacity of approximately 220,000 litres (58,100 U.S. gallons).

'Hello, my dear (he always called me that way)! See how a French bullet had scratched me!'

'Yes, a scratch indeed!' I thought to myself, 'He almost lost his entire leg!' Later the German waters cured this great warrior and he still served the Fatherland.

In Basel I also came across the gallant Colonel Terne,* who was wounded twice in the chest during one of the battles. What a strange turn of events! I knew him back when he was still a captain, commanding a company quartered in our village in Malorossiya after the Prussian campaign of 1807.† I was then just eleven years old and he often drove me in his carriage. Now, the fate has brought us together again on the banks of the Rhine so many years later and so far from the beloved Malorossiya. He suffered from his grave wounds but he was still a young man. Nowadays, he is still alive, but an old man, his hair turned grey from age and difficult and long service.

We proceeded by forced marches into heartland provinces of France and knew nothing about Napoleon or his army. Our path lay through Champagne, towards the town of Langres. The rainy weather greatly complicated our marches. Finally we observed certain movements that indicated that we were approaching the enemy and that battle should be expected shortly. From Langres we began to make various marches and counter-marches, moving forwards and backwards, and guessing that the enemy was very close to us. [From the Russian text in N. Lorer, *Zapiski Dekabrista*]

Emperor Alexander I

On 26 January 1814, the Austrian Foreign Minister Klemens von Metternich sent a detailed memorandum on the Sixth Coalition's operations against Napoleon. After reviewing the letter, Emperor Alexander replied the same day.

To stay the operations of the armies for any but military reasons, would be to deprive ourselves of the only decisive means, from the use of which we may expect political advantages. The line of Langres, on which we now are, cannot be called a military one. Langres lies on the road along which we must march to meet the enemy and fight with him. The present movements of the Allied armies are not the beginning of a new campaign, but the consequences of measures formerly ratified, and of our very invasion of France. It never was in contemplation that the invasion should be limited to vain attempts. It constitutes a mighty warlike undertaking, having for its object to annihilate the resources of the enemy, to deprive him of the means of forming an army,

---

* Colonel Andrei Terne commanded the Vitebskii Infantry Regiment in 1812–14.
† Prussian Campaign of 1807 is the Russian term for the First Polish Campaign of 1806–7.

to weaken his power; in short, to do him all the harm it is possible to do in time of war.

I have always insisted on employing our forces in this way, and of keeping our acts in unison with military considerations.

[. . .]

It now only remains for us to carry this idea into execution with rapidity and judgment. As long as the war continues, it is impossible to affirm that the object of the coalition has been accomplished: victory must decide that. I have always steadily adhered to this principle, which may now crown our plans with success.

[. . .]

As long as a considerable part of Europe was occupied by French troops, we were obliged to proportion our demands to the amount of our force, and to express our object in general terms; as, for example, the re-establishment of Austria and the like. Such expressions do not infer the renunciation of those advantages, which Providence and our enormous sacrifices allow us to hope for. This truth is established by the example of all wars, and even by our own acts. The conditions of peace which were unofficially discussed at Frankfurt, are not those we now desire. At Freiburg we thought of other conditions than we did at Basel; and those which might have been acceptable when we were crossing the Rhine, would not have been accepted at Langres. If it is at all allowable to enlarge our demands, the principle must retain its full force so long as the war continues. The measure of its accomplishment will be regulated by prudence and state reasons; for no previous agreement between the Allies is in the slightest degree binding on them, in relation to the enemy. We have enlarged our demands in proportion to our successes; and this, of itself, proves how necessary for us it is to increase the number of the latter, that we may gain our ends with the greater certainty. A few days are not sufficient to convince us of this and therefore, we should not, by a hurried pacification, enable the enemy to escape from his present dangerous position.

[. . .]

The Allies are unanimously agreed in this, that they have no right to canvass the opinion of the French on the subject of a ruling dynasty; and still less to oppose it, whatever it may be. We are not waging war for that object; consequently it cannot become the subject of deliberation. The Allies have no desire to take such advantage of victory, as to compel the French to express that opinion; and our glory will be the greater, if, with the power in our hands, we show ourselves devoid of partiality.

We have now to agree as to the conditions on which peace should be offered to France; it being fully understood, that we reserve the right of increasing our demands, by availing ourselves of whatever success we may obtain during the course of the negotiations. I was the first to declare, that we should treat with France in the name of all Europe; and I agree that she should be allowed no voice in the fixing of frontiers, or in any arrangements whatever between the other Powers; though their nature may be communicated to her for the sake of information. All negotiations with her must relate exclusively to her future limits. If the negotiations should be spun out by delays, or should not be brought to the desired conclusion, I shall then consider it as a duty to publish to France and to Europe the conditions which were offered.

In conclusion, I must direct the attention of the Allies to the forces of the enemy, and to the necessity of crushing them, equally during the course of the negotiations, as in the event of all hope of peace having vanished. Napoleon's weakness consists in the disorder which reigns among the greater part of his troops, and in the inexperience of his new-levied recruits, who are strangers to discipline. These are the consequences of the defeats he has sustained; since which, he has not had time to re-organise his armies; but his condition is daily improving; and if we continue to delay, we shall give our enemy the means of effacing every trace of his present embarrassments.

Let us even suppose a treaty of peace to be concluded. To carry its various stipulations into effect, would require much time. How many provinces, how many fortresses, from Mantua to the Texel, would the enemy have to deliver up, and we to receive!

If, in the meantime, Napoleon were to recover his strength, and to avail himself of a thousand circumstances which might give rise to fresh discussion on so complex a subject, who can assure us that he would not tear the treaty in pieces, the instant he had caught a glimpse of success? The only security against such danger, is to be found in the destruction of the armies he is collecting, and in rendering it impossible for him to levy fresh troops. All this has no relation to a change of dynasty; but, if Providence should turn circumstances, and even Napoleon himself, into engines for the destruction of his political existence, it would neither be contrary to justice, nor to the interests of Europe. [From the French text in *Aperçu des transactions politiques du Cabinet de Russie*]

Alexander Langeron

Commanding a corps in Blücher's Army of Silesia, Langeron spent most of December blockading the fortress of Mainz.

The time having arrived for us to act offensively, General Blücher verbally advised me of his plans and his provisions for crossing the Rhine. The secret was so well kept that not only the enemy, but even the inhabitants of Frankfurt (where General Blücher came to establish his headquarters the day before departure),* had no knowledge of our next march.

---

* To maintain secrecy, he had rented, for two months, a box at the theatre.

Lieutenant-General Rudzevich, who then commanded the 10th Corps instead of Lieutenant-General Kaptzevitch, who had fallen ill, came to replace the 9th Corps Lieutenant-General Olsufiev at Cassel. I gave him three regiments of Cossacks and three of cavalry, under the command of Major-General Count Pahlen, and with the rest of my troops, I followed the corps of Yorck to cross the Rhine at Kaub.

The corps of Count St. Priest was destined to go to Koblenz, and that of General Sacken to Manheim. We marched quickly by Schwalbach and Nastätten to Kaub; we arrived there on 20 December 1813 [1 January 1814]. Our hundred pontoons were thrown down at once; there proved to be little resistance. The enemy had only small outposts along the left bank of the Rhine; they had however, across from Kaub, two cannons that fired a few shots; but Prussian jager crossed in boats, having climbed the cliffs bordering the left bank, the enemy withdrew on the route to Bingen.

The swiftness of the Rhine twice broke the bridge, which could not be completed until 21 December 1813 [2 January 1814]. The infantry of the corps of Yorck crossed in boats and on the morning of 21 December 1813 [2 January 1814], the cavalry and equipment crossed on the bridge. The corps of Yorck went by Stromberg on Kreuznach and, on the night of 21 to 22 December 1813 [2 to 3 January 1814], I also crossed the river and I moved on the route of Bingen with the 9th Corps and my cavalry reserve, under the command of Lieutenant-General Korff, who had come to join in Wetzlar, where he had his winter quarters.

I was meant to blockade and observe Mainz until the arrival of the 5th Corps of the German Duke of Coburg, which was to replace me.

General Sacken executed his crossing opposite Manheim on 20 December 1813 [1 January 1814] with great success under the eyes of the King of Prussia, who had come to Frankfurt and then continued his journey to Switzerland. The infantry of Sacken's corps crossed in boats; it won, with a loss of three hundred men, the enemy entrenchments on the left bank of the river, across from the mouth of Neckar, taking six cannons and making several prisoners. Sacken then turned on Alzey, where his outposts met those of General Yorck. Major-General Karpov with the Cossacks had on 22 December 1813 [3 January 1814] fought a brilliant battle near Mutterstadt; he crushed eight enemy squadrons, made twenty-five officers and two hundred soldiers prisoners, and the Prussian Major-General Prince Biron, with his brigade of light cavalry, took one hundred and twenty prisoners at Alzey.

On 19 [31] December, Count St. Priest gathered the 11th Infantry Division at Niederlahnstein, near the mouth of the Lahn, opposite which the enemy had a battery and where our troops were crossing the Rhine in boats assembled for some time on the Lahn. To act as a diversion, he had Major-General Kern cross the river at Vallendar, further below Koblenz with the Belozersk Regiment, the

30th Jager and one hundred Cossacks, and even lower with Major-General Pillar towards Neuwied, with the Ryazanskii Regiment, the 48th Jager and the Livonian light horse [regiment]. He gave the order to occupy Andernach and to push parties on Bonn, where there were some enemy forces. Major-General Kern had to deal with Koblenz and seize the bridge over the Moselle.

The major-generals Bistrom and Karpenkov (commander of the 1st Jager, who, seriously injured before the armistice, was only now joining my corps), with the 1st and the 33rd Jager were designated to take the enemy redoubt before Niederlahnstein and a battery of seven 12-pounders was placed on the right bank of the river to protect the crossing.

On 20 December 1813 [1 January 1814], at midnight, the troops crossed the river; the enemy just had time to fire the cannon four times. The redoubt was carried by our two brave generals, with the loss of only fifteen men, and they went in Koblenz at four in the morning, at the same time as General Kern was able to bridge the Moselle; the enemy fled at once; they took 300 prisoners, and took in the redoubt and the city seven iron cannon and a hospital with 1,100 patients; the French General Durutte managed to escape. Koblenz was instantly illuminated and the inhabitants highly manifested their joy. General Bistrom with the 33rd Jager, Isaev II's Cossacks and four cannons, was sent through the Countryside by Count St. Priest in pursuit of the enemy. In Koblenz eight cast guns were found. General Pillar, having crossed the Rhine at Neuwied also very fortunately, occupied Andernach, where the enemy, after some resistance, retired to Bonn.

Having learned that an enemy transport was on the march from Köln (Cologne) for Mainz, General Major Pillar detached Major Sukanov, of the 48th Jager Regiment, with 200 men of the regiment, twenty-five Cossacks and cannon to take it. Major Sukanov overtook it near Remagen, took it and sent it to Koblenz, but having advanced a little recklessly to Bonn, he was attacked by a corps of cavalry commanded by General Sebastiani, who came from Bonn. Major Sukanov behaved with great bravery and retired at first in good order, but the superior forces of the enemy overcame his efforts, his detachment was dispersed, he was wounded himself and taken prisoner. He lost his cannon. They were the first that the Army of Silesia lost since the beginning of the campaign.

This small failure was also the first that the army had experienced since its formation, but it was more than compensated by taking from Koblenz, seven guns, 500 prisoners and the convoy, which consisted of flour, rice, clothing and hospital materials. In these affairs, the loss of Count St. Priest was 165 men.

Beyond the Rhine near Kaub, I sent forward on the route to Bingen, my adjutant, captain of the guard, Baron Schultz, with fifty Cossacks, and followed with an advanced guard composed of the 10th, 12th, 22nd and 38th Jager, six cannons and the only regiment of Cossacks that I had with me then, all under the command of Major-General Kornilov. Baron Schultz drove the enemy from different villages that lay on the roadway, along the Rhine to Bingen, and took a few prisoners; my vanguard approached Bingen at daybreak. Bingen, like all small towns in this country, once the scene of continual wars, is surrounded by a wall, ditch, etc. The enemy had added some palisades. The Nahe river washes on the side of the city of Koblenz; it is fordable near its mouth, and there is a bridge above the road which leads to Stromberg and also Kreuznach. The causeway along the Rhine from Koblenz to Bingen is the only approach that is feasible: the Rhine is to the left, there are high, almost inaccessible mountains on the right.

The enemy General Choisy commanded in Bingen; there were eight hundred infantry and two cannons, one of which defended the bridge and the other the roadway from Koblenz and was placed on the left bank of the Nahe.

General Blücher ordered me to try to take Bingen, yet not to needlessly lose everyone, and if the enemy resisted, wait for the light cavalry of General Yorck to bypass by Kreuznach and Ingelheim.

General Kornilov sent two hundred skirmishers to feel out the city: the enemy made their advance and fired three or four cannon shots of grapeshot.

Lieutenant-General Olsufiev, who followed the advanced guard with the 9th Corps, having advanced near the skirmishers, received a bruise on the arm from shrapnel. The fire of the skirmishers lasted an hour, after which General Kornilov perceiving that the enemy had withdrawn their cannons, marched against the city with the 12th and 22nd Jager; the enemy, favoured by the position and trying to save their guns, fired a few times, but finally withdrew into the city and then to Mainz. Baron Schultz, with skirmishers reached their rearguard in the city; they fought in the streets, which left some enemy dead. We found a food store, a hospital with some hundreds of men dying and we took sixty prisoners; but with my Cossacks being tardy, the enemy had time to save their two cannons.

In this small affair, I lost only eighteen men: the Jager of the 12th and 22nd stood out, my adjutant, Captain Baron Schultz, behaved with great bravery and intelligence, as well as the officers he had under his command. I advanced my vanguard up to Gaulsheim and occupied Bingen with the rest of my troops.

On 23 December 1813 [4 January 1814], I went to Mainz to besiege it. I confided to Lieutenant-General Panchulidzev I all my light troops and directed them by Marienborn on Hechtsheim, while with the infantry and cavalry reserve, I marched on the heights of Finthen. Panchulidzev found the enemy at Marienborn and at Hechtsheim; it was (from what prisoners have said) an infantry column of seven to eight hundred Guards of Honour, cut off by the corps of General Sacken and wandering before Mainz. Panchulidzev divided his cavalry into three columns. Major-General Prince Scherbatov with the second regiment of Cossacks of the Ukraine, charged with his accustomed boldness and valour, the enemy near Hechtsheim and drove them from the village, until near Mainz. Major Leontiev with the 3rd Regular Regiment of Cossacks of the Ukraine, drove the enemy from Marienborn and continued until Bretzenheim. The fortress of Mainz produced a large fire of cannon, but without effect. My loss was thirteen men, while taking a few prisoners.

On 24 December 1813 [5 January 1814], the corps of Count St. Priest having arrived in Koblenz, I fully invested Mainz, the enemy abandoning all the surrounding villages, except Mombach and Weisenau, the villages along the left bank of Rhine, and those that I thought useless to occupy.

I entrusted the right of the blockade to St. Priest, who had his headquarters in Bodenheim, and the left to Lieutenant-General Korff, who stood in Ober Ingelheim. I took my headquarters to Oppenheim, where I wanted to build a bridge across the Rhine, but the ice prevented me for a long time. My chain of Cossacks were placed around the city, within easy reach of cannon. Lieutenant-General Rudzevich remained at first before Cassel.

I arranged my troops so that a third was in camp before the town, on the heights of Hechtsheim, of Marienborn and of Finthen and near Laubenheim and nearly a third in reserve and a third in the most distant quarters. We found all the people well disposed towards us, except government employees, many of whom left their posts and fled to France.

The garrison of Mainz was initially 21,000 men. Marshal Marmont, who commanded, marched to Metz with seven or eight thousand men, so people told me.

There remained in Mainz about 13,000 men and 2,000 men cut off by Panchulidzev who took refuge there.

The cruel disease that began to attack the French in Russia in the 1812 campaign, which since that time have never ceased in their army, and which, at Torgau, carried off in two months 16,000 men out of 25,000 that were hospitalised, also fearfully ravaged Mainz. In the first month of the siege, the garrison lost more than 3,000 men. Four thousand patients filled the hospitals; mortality was 120 to 150 men a day.

The garrison had little artillery and few old soldiers, though it counted many regiments and 700 to 800 cavalry, regimental depots or Guards of Honour assembled recently and unaccustomed to war. There was a lot of ill will among the conscripts and 400 to 500 Swiss and Dutch who deserted every day. Many Westphalian and Dutch officers deserted.

On 28 December 1813 [9 January 1814], the 9th Corps of Lieutenant-General Olsufiev, two batteries, the Mitavskii and Novorossiiskii Regiments, dragoons, the Second and the Fourth Ukraine Cossack regiments, under the orders of Lieutenant-General Borozdin, marched into France to follow General Blücher.

On 5 [17] January, the 8th Division and two batteries under the command of Lieutenant-General Kaptsevich, marched to Nancy, where General Blücher had already arrived.

On 20 January [1 February], two brigades of the 22nd Division, one from the 8th Corps, of Count St. Priest, the regiments of Kargopolskii Dragoons, Livonia Light Horse, the 2nd Ukraine Cossacks, Selivanov's Don Cossack regiment, and two batteries and a half also marched on Nancy under the command of Lieutenant-General Baron Korff and Rudzevich.

Major-General Count Pahlen stood before Cassel with a battery, the Derptskii Horse Jager Regiment, two regiments of Cossacks and Vyatskii and Vyborgskii Infantry Regiments, commanded by Major-General [Nikolai] Vasilchikov. Count Pahlen was placed under the orders of the reigning Duke of Saxe-Coburg and Coburg and Nassau troops joined him.

Major-General Morand commanded Mainz and did not seem quite sure enough of his garrison to make large sorties. He sent two or three times a few skirmishers and two to three hundred cavalry, trying to find our position, he could only suspect by the light of the fires he saw at night. On 22 January/4 February, probably having learned that my troops were reduced, he made a more serious sortie with 2,000 infantry, 600–700 cavalry and six cannon. These troops advanced towards Hechtsheim. Colonel Skobelev, commander of the Ryazanskii Regiment, who then commanded the outposts, made good dispositions and chased them back into the city with losses. They left several dead on the battlefield; my loss was twenty-eight men killed or wounded.

Meanwhile, the Prussian General Kleist had crossed the Rhine at Koblenz with his corps and was advancing by Trier on Metz. General of Cavalry Baron Winzingerode, commanding the Russian corps of the army of the Crown Prince of Sweden, also crossed the Rhine at Dusseldorf and advanced on Aix-La-Chapelle and Liège. Major-General Yuzefovich that I had left in Koblenz with the regiments of Brest, Wilmanstrand infantry, Krakow Dragoons and Kuteinikov Don Cossacks and six cannons, occupied Bonn, and then went into France with General Kleist.

Marshal Macdonald and General Sebastiani, who had 7,000–8,000 veteran troops and had little success in the order they received in Cologne to organised a conscript army, retreated precipitately on Maastricht and Namur.

The Prussian General Bülow had to gone to execute an operation in the Netherlands, as brilliant as wisely conducted; he had in two months, taken a large number of fortresses, which the Country had set up, supporting a revolution in which there was favour for the Prince of Orange, and reinforced by Dutch and English troops, he advanced towards Brussels. The progress of the Allied armies in France was as brilliant and fast and already they were approaching Paris. [From the French text in A. Langeron, *Mémoires*]

Alexander Chertkov

Before becoming a famed Russian historian, archaeologist and numismatist, Chertkov had a successful military career and, in 1814, he served as an officer in the elite Life Guard Horse Regiment. After distinguishing himself at Dresden, Kulm, and Leipzig, he now found himself on French soil.

1[13] January

We departed at six o'clock in the morning and arrived at Basel by eight o'clock. Basel is the centre of the [Swiss] canton that bears the same name. It sprawls on both sides of the Rhine but the part of the city on the opposite bank is much better built and arranged than the one on this side. Overall, neither side represents anything major but one can find anything necessary here. The city is partially built on a mountain and so the streets are narrow and winding. There is a very good pastry shop and two or three bookshops. The Rhine is not very wide here. We exchanged our paper money at the rate of 100 rubles for 7 dukats, one taller and a few minor coins. I spent the night at an inn called Kopf, where we had a very good lunch and, upon seeing Prussians, Badenese and some of our Guard troops marching by, we departed around four o'clock in the afternoon. After a six-hour march, we reached the village of Moernach by ten o'clock. Incredibly, during today's march we passed through three states, having breakfast in Baden, that is Germany, eating lunch in Switzerland and dining in France. I must also note that the Swiss do not remove their hats during lunch.

2 [14] January

We are resting at Moernach. Although we are already inside France, the locals still speak in a broken German. They are very poor and have a wretched appearance. All of them are Catholics. The ancient Alsace starts here. There was a hard frost today.

3[15] January

We departed at nine o'clock today and, after marching for seven lieues [28km] we stopped for the night at the village of Alondon [?], a small village not far from the town of Montbeliard: before the Revolution this town belonged to the king of Württemberg , it is built on the riverbank and has a castle. The residents of Alondon are all Protestants. This region does have any high mountains but is peppered with numerous hills and knolls so during the march we constantly have to move up and down; the slopes, however, are quite gentle. We already hear some French conversation – the locals communicated on a dialect that is related to the French. The region is very forested.

4 [16] January

We covered another seven lieues [28km] today and spent the night at the village [missing words] not far from Villersexel . . . the village mayor has a library which we visited since we have nothing to read.

5 [17] January

We are resting at the village. We see very few young men and even those have already been called up into the National Guard and deserted as soon as the Allied troops occupied the region. Napoleon intended to declare a mass conscription among the population but local resistance and the presence of our troops prevented him from carrying out this plan.

6 [18] January

After a two-hour march in rain and heavy winds, we finally reached the small village of Conberjon, which has been completely pillaged and devastated by [the Allied] infantry. So we had to share our quarters with the St. Petersburgskii Grenadier Regiment. The majority of residents have already fled from nearby villages.

7[19] January

We [spent the morning] resting at Conberjon. In the afternoon we proceeded to Vesoul which is the administrative centre of the Haute-Saône department. This is a rather miserable town, but at least it has two bookshops.

8 [20] January

We departed and after a two-hour march arrived at a village not far from Port-sur-Saône. Rats and mice pestered us all night long.

9 [21] January

We departed at eleven o'clock in the morning and reached the village of Arbuay, where we spent the night.

10 [22] January

Today was a severe frost. We spent the night at the village of Pierrefaites. The Champagne region starts was here. Alas, none of the homes in our village have any ovens.

11 [23] January

There was dreadful weather today: heavy snow with strong winds and severe frost. On top of these misfortunes, we had to make a nine-hour march. We stopped for the night at the village of Beze.

12 [24] January

We are resting in the same village. Overall, the French peasants are extremely poor, at least in the departments that we are passing through. Their stone homes are worthy of the proverb that 'appearances can be deceiving'. On the outside, these homes look fine, but upon entering them, you struggle to find a small spot where you can hunker down. Majority of these homes have no covered flooring and some have simple stone slabs. Rooms are filthy, and either completely lack ovens or have small iron ovens that are placed in the middle of room and produce more smoke than heat. The peasants do not even have candles and illuminate their rooms with oil lamps. Instead of shoes or boots, they were sabots [wooden shoes]. We saw some peasants, preparing to ride horses, putting on their enormous wooden shoes.

Each village is governed by a mayor. The locals tells us that these mayors are worse than seigneurs, who governed them before the Revolution, and regularly abuse and even rob them. The peasants pay very high taxes, which are even collected for individual windows and doors. To be exempt from the conscription levy, one must pay 5,000 francs.

Overall, the locals are extremely dissatisfied with their government and especially Napoleon, whom they consider the main source of all of their misfortunes . . .

13–15 [25–27] January

We are resting at the same place. I am quartered with a clockmaker called Sylvain, a very kind man who is, however, very poor. Like all of his countrymen, he is also very talkative.

16–17 [28–29] January

We changed our quarters and departed in the direction of Dijon. After a four-hour march, we entered the village of Chalmesse, located in a wooded and very mountains area. We hoped to spend the next few days at these quarters but, to everyone's disgruntlement, we departed at five o'clock the following morning [29 January] and, after passing through the town of Langres, we stopped for the night at the village of Lannes, located about two lieues [8km] from it. That day we covered nine leiues [36km] in total. Langres looks like a fortress built on top of a mountain and, if needed, can offer [considerable] resistance.

18 [30] January

Claiming to be sick, I travelled with [Lieutenant] Zhadovskii [of the Life Guard Semeyonovskii Regiment] ahead of the regiment . . . Yesterday, as we entered Langres, we marched on the ancient Roman road. [It is noteworthy] that the concepts of country [*pays*] and village [*village*] are synonymous for the French peasants. They are passionate for large cupboards – thus, even in the poorest family, where one may struggle to find even the basic necessities, there are also two or three enormous and well-built oak cupboards. Today is a thaw.

19 [31] January
We spent the night in an abandoned village.

20 January [1 February]
We departed at five o'clock in the morning and marched through Bar-sur-Aube. The regiment set up bivouacs while Zadovskii and I, completely exhausted, managed to find something resembling a small room . . . All day and night there was a battle taking place some two lieues [8km] from us.*

[After reaching Bar-sur-Seine on 5 February, Chertkov's Life Guard Horse Regiment spent the next seven days deployed at nearby villages, including Fouchéres and Clérey, that had been already pillaged and devastated by Allied troops.]

30 January [12 February]
We departed [from Clérey] at seven o'clock in the morning but soon received a counter-order and had to return. This region features wooden homes, or to be precise, what goes here for a wooden home whose walls consist of several rough logs placed on top of each other with wide gaps in between them filled with clay or limestone mixed with cut straw. The largest of these homes have only one window and many do not have any windows, together with ovens and flooring – so this is what people call la belle France! The past two days gave us taste for genuine springtime – the weather was splendid, especially this evening.

31 January [13 February]
At four o'clock in the morning, we were ordered to depart from the village. Seven hours later we entered the city of Troyes: the Grand Duke [Constantine Pavlovich] wanted to hold a military parade there but, to his great displeasure, the Emperor did not see us, which, frankly, is for the better for our troops, in their tattered uniforms and horrid horses, presented a rather pathetic sight. The city of Troyes is large but filthy and poorly built – it does not even have a main square. Its streets are narrow and winding, some homes, even two story buildings, have just one window looking out into the street.

Around one o'clock in the afternoon we reached the village of Pavillon: the Bavarian troops, not satisfied with extreme ravaging and pillaging of the poor local residents, even defiled the local church where they, without any need for it, established their bivouac. Entering the church we found straw, firewood, ashes and even pieces of raw meat. Our general [Mikhail Arsenyev] ordered soldiers to clean it at once . . . All buildings, including

---

* This was the battle at Brienne.

the stables, in Pavillon are built from limestone. [It appears that] the French peasants cannot live without their night-pots and even the poorest of them, who cannot afford bread, has one or two night-pots at home. The oats, which was given to us in this part of France, were almost completely black, though our horses eat them as well as ordinary oats. During their invasion of Russia, the French could not conceal their revulsion towards the black [rye] bread of the Russian peasants. And yet, here we are in France searching for and unable to find any white bread even in the large cities like Troyes, Langres and others. Only pains of extreme hunger could force us to eat a few bites of their extremely sour bread . . .

[After advancing to Nogent-sur-Seine in early February, Chertkov spent the next few days retreating with his regiment back to Langres as Napoleon's victories stalled the Allied offensive. Throughout the first half of March, Chertkov's regiment remained idle in the vicinity of Langres, noting: 'We spent 13 March at Frency, 14–15 March at Jevres, 16 March at Lacicourt, 17–18 March at Leuvigny. All of these villages are completely destroyed, there are very few local residents remaining and we have nothing to eat.'] [From the French text in A. Chertkov, 'Mon Itinéraire . . .']

Nikifor Kovalskii

A future major-general, Kovalskii was a young junior officer in the elite Life Guard Dragoon Regiment.

From carefree Baden our regiment advanced along the Rhine River. Every day we encountered new sights, new cities and new attire . . . Local towns greeted us like liberators from the Napoleonic tyranny, building triumphal arches, organising balls, treating us to wine, fruits, confectionary and music. This was a genuine triumphal advance! But the situation dramatically changed as soon as we crossed the French border. On 1 [14] January, after attending a grand military review at Basel, we entered Alsace. Local residents, whom Napoleonic proclamations incited against the Russians, looked at us as if we were [northern] bears. Our quarters were cold and so poorly heated with grapevine branches that we were freezing even inside homes; at midnight, we could barely warm ourselves wearing half-coats and overcoats. There was considerable scarcity of forage and food.

In the Champagne region, near Langres, [my comrade] and I were billeted to an abbot, whose name I cannot recall now. This man was so scared of us that he hid himself in a closet, where we found him only several hours later when an unpleasant odour reached us from there. The abbot turned out to be a very pleasant young man who had read too many foolish proclamations that claimed that the Russians were eating human flesh. He was startled when we spoke to him in French and could not believe for a very long time that we were in fact well-educated and well-mannered people. Soon thereafter we saw eggs, chickens and an excellent wine appear on the table . . .

Near Troyes, we stopped at the château of some old madames who were related to the Bourbons. These women usually lived in the city and came to the castle in summer time. We were forestalled here by the Cossacks, who plundered everything they could and broke furniture, windows, mirrors, forte-piano and crockery; in the cellars, they worked hard on barrels with average-quality red and white wine . . .

Our squadron was given a day of rest at this castle. One of our dragoons went for a walk in the garden and accidentally came across a small, grass-covered, opening in the wall of the castle. He prodded it with his rod to see if there was a concealed chamber where the French usually stored their bread and other supplies. However, he could not reach the bottom. He tied a rod to a long branch but even this did not help. It was obvious that there was something more here than a small safe place. He asked his friend to go inside the castle, get into the cellar and put his ear against the wall while he would tap it from the outside. This method proved to be very successful. They uncovered a concealed door and found themselves inside a crypt with a small overgrown trapdoor that the dragoon accidentally uncovered with his rod. Inside the crypt were hanging several barrels of superb wine, while next to them lay boxes with the famed *vin de la comête* of 1811 and other wines. On the walls hung cured meat. This splendid discovery caused other soldiers to search the area and they found four more crypts with chests full of silverware, antique chalices with [aristocratic] monograms, and numerous other precious items bejewelled with pearls and diamonds. Captain Stankovich, although a habitual drunkard, was also an intelligent and educated man who quickly intervened to prevent soldiers from looting and, collecting items, he took them to the madames in Troyes. As a sign of their gratitude, they offered him a silver spoon, folk and knife, but he refused. We later learned that soldiers still managed to steal some of these riches.

From Troyes our squadrons was moved to a small and beautiful town of Sezanne, where local residents offered us a rather unfavourable welcome. All the shops and the windows of homes were closed shut . . . [From the Russian text in N. Kovalskii, 'Iz zapisok . . .']

Ivan Zhirkevich

Just twenty-five years old, Zhirkevich already had the battles of Austerlitz, Heilsberg, Friedland, Smolensk, Borodino, Dresden and Leipzig behind him. A capable and conscientious officer, he commanded a light company in the 2nd Life Guard Artillery Brigade in 1813–14. His lengthy memoir contains vivid descriptions of key individuals and campaign life, including interesting insights into the social dynamics between the Russian officers during wartime.

On 1 [12] January we crossed the Rhine at Basel and entered France. Until now we had been marching through German lands and by now got so use to them that we found nothing unusual [in new territories] since we had gotten accustomed to their language and traditions. But on the second march [from the Rhine] we were startled to hear genuine French spoken all around us.

I do not remember which village it was but my company stopped there and having established its park, began to disperse to the assigned quarters. I was greeted by my host, the village mayor, who brought out his entire family which consisted largely of females since men, probably, had been conscripted. Warmly greeting them, I asked the mayor about his circumstances and requested him to deliver necessary forage and to feed my men well. He assured me on the latter account but then informed me that the village had no oats or grain and that no money could procure either of them. However, my foragers had already begun their work and one of my non-commissioned officers informed me that they had discovered a large pit dug in the cemetery and filled with a considerable amount of oats. So I [did not respond to the mayor] and instead calmly went to my quarters. Just quarter of an hour later the mayor rushed into my room shouting, 'This is robbery! Pillaging! Sacrilege!' Although I already guessed what caused his commotion, I still asked him what was happening. 'Pardon me,' he said, 'but your soldiers are digging up our dead. This is unheard of! Only barbarians are capable of this!' 'Do not get too excited,' I replied. 'We will investigate everything.' But my mayor did not want to listen to anything and began to shout louder than before, 'Robbery! Sacrilege!' I then told him everything that I had learned from the non-commissioned officer and added that we were not perpetrating any sacrilege, but rather should arrest him [the mayor] for concealing forage and spreading false information. Yet, the mayor did not listen to me and continued to shout that we were barbarians! His yelling attracted a crowd of women and children to the house and these began to shout even more than the mayor. This entire scene soon tired me out so I turned to Junker Prince Dolgorukov and, pointing to the mayor, told him, 'Take this man and shoot him behind the village!' Dolgorukov grabbed the mayor by the collar and was about to drag him out when the Frenchman turned pale and began to tremble. His wife and daughters rushed to my feet and begged me to forgive him, promising to deliver twice as much forage as I demanded. This tragicomedy, of course, soon ended but I am sure in that village it endures from generation to generation as a tradition about a 'barbaric Muscovite' who wanted to shoot the mayor . . .

[After leaving Frankfurt] a new commander was sent to the 1st Brigade of the Guard Artillery. This was Colonel [Karl Karlovich] Taube. At the beginning of the war he was still a lieutenant and adjutant to Prince Yashvil but he quickly advanced through the ranks, rising to colonel. At Borodino we had another Colonel Taube (that one was Karl Maksimovich) who was beloved and respected by all officers but unfortunately lost his leg in battle. As much as that Taube was beloved, the new Taube was despised and loathed. We referred to him only by his nickname 'Karl-is-Karl', lampooning an answer he had given to a general who asked his full name. Even before he was appointed to command us (but already after being made a colonel) he once passed in front of our brigade and our young officers greeted him with shouts 'Karl-is-Karl! Tally-ho!'

During one of our marches [General Alexey] Yermolov, who commanded the 2nd Guard Division with which my company was marching then, approached me and, dismounting his horse, walked next to me. 'Have you heard the news, my dear comrade!? You now have a new commander, and what a commander he is! A German! Karl Taube! You know what? This [damn] German will drive away all of my friends and comrades-in-arms. I do not think any of you will remain serving under him.'* I did not say anything but as soon as I reached my quarters I reported sick and no longer appeared in front of the company.

Upon his arrival, the first news that Colonel Taube received about the brigade was my report on being sick. He immediately issued the following instructions: Colonel Ladygin, who until now commanded the brigade and His Majesty's company but, upon Taube's arrival, also claimed to be sick, was immediately assigned to the 1st Company with instructions to take command only after full recovery. In response to my report, he assigned Staff Captain Prince Gorchakov II from the His Majesty's Company to my company. Taube then scheduled a review of my company for eight o'clock the following morning. This was all happening near the town of Vesoul. [By the time the review began] Ladygin had not arrived at the company yet and I did not appear at the front either. Taube travelled some twenty-five verstas [26.8km] to attend the review and went straight to the troops. He then asked Prince Gorchakov about me and inquired if he could see me. Gorchakov responded that I should not be as seriously sick as to refuse his visit. So immediately after the parade, Taube and all the officers visited me. Instead of a salutation, Taube crudely asked me, 'Are you sick, Zhirkevich?' 'Yes, I am,' was my response. 'With what?' he pressed me. So I named such an outrageous disease that everyone burst out laughing so that even I did not expect such a reaction. I was simply annoyed the tone in which Taube asked this questions as well as Taube's ludicrous idea of actually checking upon me. 'Ah, this is a sort of courteousness [ah, c'est une espèce de galanterie],' Taube

---

* Yermolov was known for his strong antipathy to foreigners, and Germans particularly. After Emperor Alexander asked once what request he might like to make as a reward for his services, Yermolov, thinking of the many influential foreigners at Alexander's court, famously replied, 'Make me a German for then I shall be able to get all I want.' Indeed, he was a nationalist of the highest degree, proudly declaring, 'The feeling of being Russian never leaves me!'

remarked and began asking questions about the company. I informed him that being sick I was not in condition to speak with him standing. He replied that since I was the host I could do however I pleased, so I invited all officers to sit down and did so myself as well. Taube alone remained standing amidst us. Seeing that I was not inviting him to sit down, he bluntly told me that after travelling on a horse for twenty-five verstas and spending two hours in cold, he would gladly partake of a glass of vodka. I gave him vodka and cheese but could not offer anything else since my cook, a common soldier, was at the review and had not cooked lunch yet. Taube drank two shots of vodka and ate more than half of the wheel of Brie cheese. He then bowed to us and left. Such was meeting that we arranged to our new commander. Who can fault him for not liking us thereafter. Yet, despite this he tried and kept on trying to find common ground with us.

As soon as Taube departed, we sat to eat lunch and during our meal I wrote and signed a report which informed Taube that I had been supposedly sick with [word omitted] illness and asked him to hasten with the appointment of my replacement to command my company while I asked to be allowed to return to Russia for treatment. I sent this report to the His Majesty's company where Taube was going to visit. In the evening I received a private letter from Sokolov, who was assigned to Taube as an adjutant in the 1st Brigade. The letter, which also contained my report, informed me that Taube chose to be lenient to me and, in addition to returning my report, he was also sending a physician to examine me and submit a written confirmation of my disease which I could use to procure a furlough. I sent my report back to Sokolov, informing him that I never asked or expected leniency from anyone except the Lord himself.

Ridicule and hounding of Taube continued for a while and three days after my report second Staff Captain Stakhovich submitted his report where he found himself incapable of serving in the artillery for the lack of proper knowledge and requested a transfer to the cavalry. I conveyed this report for Taube's attention in the brigade headquarters. A day thus passed and our comrades from other companies soon joined this enterprise. The following day I received written instructions in which Taube, very politely and without reproaching me for anything, called attention to my failure to restraint my subordinates and prevent their nuisances from reaching my superiors. This meant, he noted, that he had no other choice but to resort to the harshest measures. I was thus ordered to arrest Staff Captain Stakhovich and deliver him at once to him at the headquarters.

As soon as this letter was read, Prince Gorchakov submitted his own report asking to be transferred, due to poor health, to the infantry. Meanwhile, many officers from other companies also sent in reports requesting transfers or furloughs. Among them were Ladygin, Demidov, Sumarokov, Divov, Prince Trubetskoi and others. All of this caused Taube to lose his temper. While informing Taube about the arrival of [the arrested] Stakhovich, our brigade adjutant Timan also gave him report about Prince Gorchakov's transfer request. Taube then asked Timan, 'Well, why are you not submitting a report to get transferred somewhere?' – 'I am about to do it,' replied Timan and brought in his request as well.

[I must note also] that Jaroszewski, who had been promoted to staff-captain for the battle of Leipzig, exploited these circumstances to become intimate with Taube and soon became his right hand.

Meanwhile, we advanced towards Langres, where Yermolov, upon hearing about these events, sent an order demanding the officers from the entire brigade to come to his quarters. When they gathered, he addressed them in agitated voice, 'What are you doing? Have you gone mad? Do you want to get one of you executed? Believe me, it will happen. In fact, I assure you it will happen. What you do is nothing but a mutiny!' Hearing this, one of the officers (I do not know who exactly since I claimed to be sick and did not attend) objected, 'Mutiny involves deliberate and coordinated actions while none of us put others up to do this and have no intentions of doing it.' – 'I know that you are guided by different sentiments,' replied Yermolov. 'But I might be the only one who understands it while anyone else has the full authority to prosecute you for your actions. I'm sure if you were sentenced to execution, each of you would step forward asking to be shot first. But listen to me, my friends and comrades, stop what you are doing and come to your senses! Whose turn is it to submit a report now?' Everyone remained silent. 'I do not talk to you as a general,' Yermolov continued, 'but rather as your friend and comrade. Be forthright with me.' Korobin and Waxmuth stepped forward. 'Well then, I once again beseech you to stop. Wait a while, give me two days and then do what you want – I would not care if all of you are executed.'

Immediately after the meeting Yermolov went to [General Alexey] Arakcheyev and told him about everything. He asked him, as a man wearing the uniform of the Guard Artillery, to intervene in this affair. Arakcheyev replied that he was aware of this situation and had already advised the Emperor that Taube's appointment only exasperated the officers. But the Emperor ignored this advice and went through with the appointment, which meant that Arakcheyev, as the humble servant and executor of His Majesty's will, could do nothing but support Taube. 'However,' the Count added, 'you, Aleksei Petrovich, do have some influence. Ask for audience with the Emperor. He would not reject it and you will be able to explain circumstances to him.' Indeed, the audience was soon granted. Just as Yermolov entered [the imperial quarters], the Emperor's first words were, 'This is nothing but a mutiny!' – 'No, Your Majesty. I can pledge my word and honour that it is but frustration and discontentment.' – 'In such case, I will discharge all of them and staff this brigade with new officers,' replied the Emperor. 'It will be very difficult to replace all of these officers,' observed Yermolov. Without saying a word, the Emperor went into another room and returned back carrying a morocco-bound ledger listing officers of the Guard regiments. He opened it to the artillery brigade and began to read out names of individual officers, offering detailed observations about each of them. Once he reached the name of the last ensign, he turned to Yermolov, 'As you can see, Alexey Petrovich, I know all of these officers quite well. I would be very sorry for them but I cannot and do not want to pander to them.'

Yermolov remained silent. The Emperor walked around the room three times, then quickly approached him, laid his hand on the general's shoulder and told him, 'But here is what I am willing to do. Gather them all and inform them that I am aware of this affair, and that I desire it greatly that they withdraw their requests.' The Emperor then halted for a minute before continuing: 'Whoever does not do it can go wherever he wishes [since] I let him be.' Overwhelmed with emotion, Yermolov bowed his head and departed. When he later recounted this scene to me, Yermolov told me that the Emperor's face clearly conveyed the struggle unfolding deep inside his heart and it was visible as senses of austerity and discipline clashed with sympathy towards men who honourably fulfilled their duty in dangerous times. Even years after the event Yermolov could not remember this moment without becoming emotional.

Yermolov conveyed the Emperor's desire to the officers and everyone withdrew their requests, except for Ladygin, Demidov, Stakhovich and I. Consequently, Ladygin and I were allowed to return to Russia, Demidov – to the German water-resorts while Grand Duke Constantine Pavlovich managed to get Stakhovich transferred to the Guard horse artillery.

We buried Adjutant Timan near Troyes. He unexpectedly caught fever and died just three days later. In the absence of our priest, a Prussian chaplain conducted the funeral ceremony. Our arrangements for the Guard officers startled Prussian Guardsmen. They were especially amazed to see officers raised the coffin and carried it for more than three verstas [3.2km] to the cemetery. 'In our army, even the Field Marshal would not get such honour,' they told us, to which we replied that 'a much-loved comrade ranks higher than a field marshal'.

We reached Troyes twice [during this campaign]. On the first occasion, I was billeted in a nearby village with a priest who was at first reluctant to appear but during our lunch he rushed into the room shouting, 'Russians are plundering the church!' Although not believing him, I still followed him to the church, which we found closed. He took keys out of his pocket to open doors but first asked me, 'What do you intend to do? You are alone, while pillagers are quite a few.' 'Nothing,' I replied, turning the key and rushing inside the church. 'Get out, you brigands and robbers,' my voice thundered inside the church and I saw at once as about ten people ran headlong in front of the altar to reach windows, where they sought to escape. I caught up with one of them and gave him such a blow with a key that the back of his head cracked and began to bleed. His comrades, however, dragged him through the window. I was pleased to find that there were no Russians involved in this affair, only Bavarians. My exploit surprised the priest and, upon returning home, he told everyone about it.

In February 1814, when we advance once more to Troyes and prepared for the battle near Brienne, the company, which I still commanded despite being reported as sick, passed in front of Prince Yashvili, who had just returned from Landeck where he was treated for some sickness. Staff Captain Prince Gorchakov rode in front of the company while I was in a wagon travelling behind the company. [Upon seeing my men,] Prince Yashvili asked Prince Gorchakov,

'Do you command this company?'

'No,' replied Gorchakov, 'Colonel Ladygin does.'

'Where is Ladygin then?'

'He is sick.'

'Then you are actually in command of this company, right?'

'No,' once again objected Gorchakov, 'Staff Captain Zhirkevich is in charge.'

'Where is he then?'

'He is sick too.'

'What? What does this mean? I cannot understand this. The commander is sick, the commanding officer is sick too. Where are they now?'

'They are travelling in wagons behind the company.'

'Ah, I got it now,' Yashvili exclaimed. 'They are sick only for the duration of the march but as soon as the battle begins, they will of course show up to claim their medals. No, I will not let them fool me! Nowadays gallantry surprises no one since cowards have all died out and are no longer present in the army!'

Turning to his adjutant, Prince Yashvili then instructed him to convey an order to our brigade commander: until full recovery Ladygin and I were henceforth placed in reserve.* [From the Russian text in Ivan Zhirkevich, 'Zapiski . . .']

Alexander Mirkovich

On 14 February, in the midst of the Allied invasion of France, the young Alexander Mirkovich, a junior officer in the Life Guard Horse Regiment, celebrated his twenty-second birthday. Born into a noble family of Serbian origin, he graduated from the prestigious Page Corps in 1810 and received his baptism of fire during the 1812 Campaign.

---

* Zhirkevich noted that as the result of Yashvili's orders, he did not participate in and only witnessed the battles at Brienne and Arcis-sur-Aube.

During our campaign in France, we, for the most part, spent [nights] on bivouacs which was quite challenging in winter time; even though there was no snow, the weather was cold, damp, with strong winds. Supplies were meagre and, in a word, there were too many hardships and deprivations. Occasionally we were deployed in villages, as it happened in January when we spent three days in the village of Foucher, or in late February when we approached Langres and spent several days at quarters there. Here we saw how deprived the local population had become because of high taxes levied by its merciless ruler, and if all departments of France were in such conditions, one can only lament their wretched condition. The French peasants had to pay taxes for a window which they use to let light inside a house, for a door to enter or leave their homes, for a chimney so they do not suffocate from smoke, for fields and pastures that feed them, and for maintaining cattle. All forests are bought by the state and no one dares to use them under threat of punishment by death. The government itself sells firewood at exorbitant prices to the local population. Internal trade had all but ceased inside the state because internal tariffs had increased ten-fold. To transport tobacco from one department to another, one had to pay a fee in the amount of ½ franc per pound. And if somebody wants to buy wine, then out of 100 bottles, he has to give 36 bottles to the state. State officials, whom locals call 'rats de caves', constantly check wine cellars to ensure that no one has more wine that officially declared to the state. Heavy fines are levied on any covert sale or buying of wine. Everything is very expensive here, particularly coffee and sugar which are considered contraband. Sugar was sold for seven francs per pound while coffee for eight francs per pound. An average [French] man lives in a stone house [izba] but instead of a stove, he has a fireplace which constantly burns in winter time to provide some warmth; yet the poorly-built fireplaces mainly fill the house with smoke. A peasant's food consists of warm water with pig's fat and crumbled bread, which they call a soup. A [French] peasant is as ignorant as a Russian one, and is as poor as our peasants in Smolensk or Vitebsk. [It seems that] population has diminished significantly here since we have not seen any young single men in the villages we passed. All men between 18 and 40 years old are in the army. Those who managed to get out of conscription in previous years had been drafted in 1813 and 1814. Besides the old people and children, we had seen no one in the villages. The department prefects (who are equal to our governors) had unlimited authority in their departments and received a salary of 40–50,000 francs per year. But [in reality] their annual incomes were twice, sometimes even four times, higher. These prefects, sous-prefects and mayors sucked dry the unfortunate population. Such was the condition in which we found the French nation which had shed so much blood for its freedom that it had hoped to enjoy. It was in the heavy chains of a ravenous tyrant and moaned under his despotism. France longed to free itself from this unbearable authority. [From the Russian text in A. Mirkovich, 'Vyderzhki iz zapisok . . .']

Fedor Glinka

Born into a noble family from the province of Smolensk, Glinka graduated from the First Cadet Corps and served as an aide-de-camp to General Mikhail Miloradovich during the 1805 Campaign that ended disastrously at Austerlitz. In 1807, Glinka retired from active service and returned to his family estate, where he began to write his memoirs. In 1812, with Napoleon invading Russia, Glinka returned to the army and was appointed once again as Miloradovich's aide-de-camp, serving in this capacity for the next three years. Throughout his campaigns in Russia, Germany and France, he maintained a journal that he turned into memoirs published shortly after the end of the Napoleonic Wars. A prominent literary figure, he was involved in secret societies that led to the Decembrist Uprising in 1825.

'La belle France! The beautiful France!' – exclaim incessantly our French tutors. 'Here is a paradise on earth! Just cross the Rhine and you will find yourself in a flourishing land, amidst blissful people, vineyards on every hill and villages in every valley! Everything you look at surprises, comforts and charms. There trees are burdened with ripening fruit, fields are filled with bountiful harvests and the Countryside with joyous people. So cross the Rhine, and you will see the Country that is prosperous, abundant and populous.' This is what the French tramps claim and what the Russian people unfortunately believe! Indeed, move across the Rhine – and where is this fabulous 'votre belle France!' Where is this beautiful France? Instead, one finds utterly desolate regions, barren land, withered trees and widespread depopulation. As I look around, I see nothing but wide expanse of land, but no villages; fields are untoiled and thorns and thistles grow in cornfields!

In the cities the best buildings are barracks or hospitals. Crowds of beggars meet and escort any traveller, trying all sorts of tricks to get to his wallet. One scares you with his wounds, and the other talks about his disability, the third screams while the fourth sings. 'Here is a poor orphan!' tells you some old woman, pushing forward a little girl. 'She does not have either father or mother and only the passer-by's compassion feeds and clothes her.' She extends her pleadings for quarter of an hour before finally exclaiming, 'Now, give her a franc!'; 'Spare something for the wretched old man'; 'Something for the poor boy,' 'And what about me!' or 'Buy my flowers,' 'Sweet pies, 'Get some of my berries' and it continues on and on. That's what you hear arriving at a station. And just better to give some alms than to buy anything from a saleswoman with filthy hands and wearing rags.

It is strange that in all the places that we passed, we saw only children, old men and multitudes of women. Where is the cream of the youth? It has been claimed by Death's scythe on battlefields! The people and their prosperity has been consumed by military government. One of the things that is good here, it is great roads – marvellous roads indeed! We passed several stations without going up or down, all across a flat surface as if we were travelling on a stretched canvas; there are no carts to stop you and no bumps to throw you off. The road is clear like a current and there is, as we say, not a knot or hitch in it. This the first time in my life that I am travelling on such a marvellous road. You see mountains all around you but yet you feel none underneath you. This wonderful road is built in the form of a huge dam or rampart. Entire mountains have been cut through, hillsides removed, ditches and gullies filled and a smooth paved road or *chaussée* laid down. In some places this *chaussée* is raised as high as two, three and even four arshins [1.4m–2.8m] above the ground. Just imagine how much work it required and how many thousands of hands have been employed to accomplish such an immense undertaking! But France never had too few hands and she was blessed until these hands turned predatory, defiant and soaked in blood! [From the Russian text in F. Glinka, *Pis'ma russkogo ofitsera*]

A Russian Guardsman

For thousands of Russian soldiers, memories of the French abuses in Russia were still fresh and spurred them to seek vengeance on the French populace, grumbling when their superiors tried to restrict their behaviour.

As an example of the general feeling in the Russian army at the time they invaded France, we may mention the substance of a conversation which an officer of the Russian staff told us he had held with a private of the Russian guard on the march soon after the invasion. The soldier complained of the Emperor's proclamation desiring them to consider as enemies only those whom they met in the field. 'The French,' said he, 'came into our country, bringing hosts of Germans and Poles along with them. They plundered our properties, burnt our houses, and murdered our families; every Russian was their enemy. We have driven them out of Russia, we have followed them into Poland, into Germany, and into France; but wherever we go we are allowed to find none but friends. This,' he added, 'is very well for us guards, who know that pillage is unworthy of us; but the common soldiers and Cossacks do not understand it; they remember how their friends and relations have been treated by the French, and that remembrance lies at their hearts.' [From Archibald Alison, *Travels in France during the years 1814-1815*]

Order to the Armies, 8 January 1814

In the first days of the invasion, the Allied high command sought to curb its troops' maltreatment of the French population. This order, issued by Schwarzenberg, is just one of many similar instructions addressed to the Allied forces.

At this moment, when the army is advancing upon the French territory, I think it my duty to remind the commanders of corps of the orders which preceded that movement, and to enjoin them to redouble their zeal for the maintenance of order and discipline. They will exact the same attention, under a responsibility the most extensive, from all commanders of regiments, battalions, &c.

The troops will make the scourge of war bear as lightly as possible on the inhabitants; and on no account must they exact more than the fixed marching allowance. The conduct and exact discipline of the soldier must fulfil the solemn engagements entered into by the Allied Monarchs in their declaration to the French people; must convince them that we do not make war upon them, and that we are now in the midst of them only to conquer peace, and to enable them to participate its blessings.

The army, in uniting to its well-tried valour the most severe discipline, will fix the admiration of its own age, and of future generations.

The corps commanders must repeat to their corps the order that the most severe punishment will be inflicted on every offender, as due to the honour of the army which is entrusted to my command. They will also announce, that every inhabitant out of uniform, taken with arms in his hands, will be considered as a malefactor or assassin, and shall be judicially condemned as such, and punished with death. The town, city, or village, the inhabitants of which shall oppose any resistance, and commit any acts of hostility, shall be razed and reduced to ashes. [From the French text in No.4 Ordre du Jour, RGVIA, f. 846, op. 16, d. 4135, l. 2.]

Ivan Kazakov

As a recent graduate of the elite Page Corps, Kazakov had an idealistic vision of war and, after missing both the 1812 and 1813 Campaigns, he was eager to see some action. In June 1813, at the tender age of sixteen, he finally received his commission as an ensign in the Life Guard Semeyonovskii Regiment, which he joined on its march across Germany.

On 1 [14] January 1814 we crossed the Rhine at Basel and entered France. That same day General Sacken's corps crossed the Rhine, if I am not mistaken, at Frankfurt and the Prussian army under command of Blücher at Coblenz. It was a cold day, with freezing temperatures reaching 15 degrees. The Rhine was covered with ice and the fields were still covered with snow. After marching some 15 verstas [16km] from Bazel, the army bivouacked and I learned first-hand the difference between being on march and at war. Crossing Germany now seemed like a pleasant stroll – I very much disliked being bivouacked on snow in 15 degrees of frost. Warming near the bonfire and drinking tea, other officers frequently teased me and asked, 'Hey, Kazakov, how do you like it now? We heard you begged to be sent to war so where is it better, here or at the Page Corps?'

Austrian forces soon joined our army and the supreme command was granted, due to political considerations, to Field Marshal Count Schwarzenberg, even though our Emperor remained present at the main headquarters in the Guard Corps. As the first-rate fortress of Belfort was located on our path to Paris, it was decided to move around it and we proceed to Vesoul and Langres. A small part of the French troops that remained in front of our army quickly retreated without even firing any shots.

Two marches from Langres, I was given a mission – to deliver the sick to that city and place them at the hospital that had been established there. Anyone who had been on campaign knows quite well how unpleasant such missions are. What could I do but to obey. The sick were placed on the requisitioned transports and, after receiving the relevant papers from the regimental adjutant Panyutin, I mounted my horse and escorted the sick [to Langres] where I successfully placed them. I was then billeted to an apartment, where I spent the night and, after thanking the kind host who fed me and my horse, left the following morning to catch up with my regiment. My knowledge of the French language proved to be very useful in this mission.

The orders to the army strictly forbade any pillaging (as it usually happened in foreign lands) and troops were instructed to handle fires as carefully as possible. It was all great on paper but impossible to implement in practice: as soon as the army arrived to a place selected for a bivouac, squads were immediately dispatched for provisions, forage for horses, firewood, hay, water – which in itself is a type of pillaging – and the villages located close to an almost 100,000-strong bivouacked army were quickly devastated and plundered despite any orders. [As a rule] an officer was chosen, and an NCO and twenty-five men were selected from each company, which meant some 300 men were selected from a regiment. This [foraging] squad moved in good order to the village, where everyone scattered to find sought-for and essential items. Most local residents had fled or hidden away. So one may wonder – how could one maintain order in a village that is stretched for half a mile and, most importantly, at night time, as most foraging was usually done. Those who reached bivouacs first naturally procured everything quickly and easily, but the last comers were forced to disassemble roofs to obtain some hay and destroy entire homes to get some firewood. Can it be really expected that they would not commit some excesses and steal some unnecessary items in the process? I once witnessed how in a small and almost completely plundered village our commander-in-chief Barclay de Tolly sheltered in a small house. Once can imagine my astonishment when he hastily came out of the house and watched as soldiers removed hay and rafters from his house since neither was necessary in the winter time when it usually did not rain. When the gendarmes and Cossacks began to drive the foragers away from the roof, Barclay de Tolly laughed and ordered them to leave them alone so they did not freeze or go hungry that night. But is not this a clear-cut systematic and organised plunder and robbing which is impossible to avoid? When our army passed through Champagne and Epernay, our foragers frequently returned with barrels of wine instead of water. We saw plenty of cattle abandoned in the fields and village and thus procured plenty of meat, oftentimes slaughtering cows so beautiful that even painter's brush could not fully convey their beauty. Meanwhile those same commanders, who issued strictest orders not to burn and plunder, were calmly enjoying this wonderful beef cooked in the best of wines. Such are the inescapable consequences of war that fell heavily on the unfortunate residents on whose fields the armies are deployed for training, tactical or strategic considerations.

We advanced without any fighting until Troyes. The first battle was at Brienne, where Napoleon received education in his youth and now personally defended. The battle was neither won nor lost since both sides held on to their positions. At dusk I was against dispatched on foraging but this was my most unpleasant and unfortunate assignment. After scattering my squad and setting our meeting spot, I found myself alone with just one senior NCO. I noticed flames flickering in a nearby church and decided to go there. There was a crowd of soldiers who, as they told me, were '*cherching*'★ the place. I was infuriated by their actions and shouted, 'Get out at once! Have you forgotten that this is the Lord's house or have you become heathens?' As the torches were quickly extinguished, a voice came down, not from the heavens, but from the choir: 'Scram out of here yourself, or you will fly out of the window!' Oh, one can imagine how agreeable it was to hear such audacious words. My NCO told me, 'Your Honour, let's leave. As you can see, all of rabble of the army is here, while our men are nowhere near.'

Not far from Nogent, we heard the sound of gunfire but instead of marching there for support, we were halted and led back to our previous bivouacs. The reason for this was the news that Napoleon had defeated Blücher and forced him to retreat; that he then turned against Sacken, took him by complete surprise, then routed General Olsufiev's detachment and captured General St. Priest near Laon. Three [Allied] armies were converging on Paris, trying to coordinate their actions so they could arrive there simultaneously. But Napoleon let them approach closer and then defeated each of them separately, attacking our advance guard at Nogent which was forced to fall back and, therefore, caused our main army – consisting of the Guard and Grenadier Corps, and the Prussian and Austrian Guards – to beat a hasty retreat as well. [The French] pursued our rearguard so closely that we were not even given sufficient time to cook food and [hurriedly] retreated on the same road

---

★ From French 'chercher', to search.

back to Vesoul and Langres. The Prussians were marching with us and their soldiers [frequently] spoke with ours. The Prussians told us, '*Nach Moskau*' ['To Moscow] to which we [teasingly] replied, 'Oh no, brother, it will be *Nach Berlin* first.' We did not enjoy such good relations with the Austrians and foraging oftentimes ended in all-out brawls with them. [From the Russian text in I. Kazakov, 'Pokhod vo Frantsiyu 1812 . . .']

Mikhail Kakhovskii

After spending almost two weeks waiting to cross the Rhine, Kakhovskii and his fellow staff officers at Wittgenstein's headquarters finally found themselves in France. With the front line miles away to the west, some officers allowed themselves to indulge life in the French towns and countryside, which they oftentimes found far below their expectations.

12 [24] January, Saverne

At Haguenau we found our [staff officer] Krivskoi, who had stayed behind [when the troops advanced] and was carousing around the town for the third day in a row. Yesterday, he spent 150,000 [rubles] to buy the local theatre and had it perform only for himself, even though he does not understand a single word of German. All newly arriving officers have gathered at his quarters where we met his host, an eighty-year-old captain who had served against the [Prussian king] Frederick the Great during the Seven Years War and told us all about his exploits. We also met his young and pretty daughter, who is married to a French officer who is currently at the fortress of Magdeburg . . .

[After departing from Haguenau] we arrived at Saverne around ten o'clock in the evening . . . This town appears smaller than Haguenau but it actually has about 5,000 residents . . . Local residents speak very poorly in French and German languages so we have difficulties understanding them. The apartment that we received here was no better the one we got at Lauterbourg, and if not colder, it was certainly as cold as that one. The dinner was atrocious . . . So we bought a bottle of cognac for two francs, drank a bit of it and are now laying down on the floor, all three of us together. It is already one o'clock in the morning.

13[25] January, Sarrebourg

We endured a very cold night that was worse than the one in Lauterbourg so we frequently woke up during the night. At dawn we stoked up a small cast-iron oven but damp firewood produced such smoke that we could not get up from the floor. So with freezing temperatures outside, we had to hastily dress ourselves and open windows [to ventilate the room]. Tea was served late and, still tired from yesterday's long journey, we could not depart before ten o'clock in the morning today. We hired a guide and, asking the Lord to grant us peace, speedy return to home and better quarters (which we do not expect to happen in France), we travelled for two hours on the main road before turning, under canister fire from the fortress of Phalsbourg where a French garrison is blockaded [by our troops], to a round-about road, one may even say a path, that was laid near the fortress . . .

We arrived at Sarrebourg at eight o'clock in the evening . . . and were fortunate to receive the apartment that the Count [Wittgenstein] has stayed in . . . Today we crossed the border of Alsace and are now in Lotharingia, of ancient France, yet our host is a German . . . Our Count [Wittgenstein] is already at Nancy and only God knows where he heading next . . . [Although some officers departed during the night] I took pity on my horses and stayed, but I do intend on reaching Luneville by tomorrow afternoon. Our host gave us a few books, including some by [August Friedrich Ferdinand von] Kotzebue [August Wilhelm] Iffland, and [Johann Christoph Friedrich von] Schiller and we read them the entire evening . . .

14 [26] January, Luneville
After a good night's sleep, we departed at seven o'clock in the morning . . . Luneville is some fourteen hours away [from Sarrebourg]* and we travelled well, even though there is still a bad weather and so much snow that one might travel in a sleigh. I cannot understand why our admirers of the French sing paeans to France – there is nothing that distinguishes this land from others and which I, in fact, do not find pleasant at all. There are poor at almost every step and, despite the cold which affects them more than us, they ran after a carriage for several verstas until you are compelled to give them something. About half-way through our journey, we stopped at the town of Blamont and, without unharnessing horses, went to the best tavern to grab a quick bite. The tavern looked like one of our common cook shops [kharchevnya] and we were served a piece of boiled beef with low-quality Dijon mustard, some duck and eggs, and, for the dessert, we are given one apple each and a few almonds on a table. In addition we drank two bottles of the Bourgogne wine, which is usually served at every house because it is the cheapest wine. In the end, our talkative host made us pay nine francs for this food.

The seven hours that separate Blamont from Luneville we covered rather quickly and by five o'clock in the afternoon we were already in our quarters in the house of Count Fermont. Luneville is a large town that is known to me from the stories of our soldiers who had been captured at Austerlitz and the [Polish] campaigns of 1806–7 and had been held here in captivity . . . My apartment is in a large house and the rooms are spacious but cold since they have no ovens [but only a fireplace].

---

* The two cities are 53km from each other.

15 [27] January, Toul

At last, we have caught up with Count [Wittgenstein]. We had a rough last night because of extreme cold and got up late in the morning, dressing ourselves in front of [the blazing] fireplace. After drinking tea, we departed for Nancy . . . where we arrived at on o'clock in the afternoon. Nancy is a large and beautiful city and many say that in terms of population and size, it is second only to Paris but is as good when it comes to its location and splendour of its buildings . . . We travelled on a long and wide road that run through the suburb and entered the city through the Porte de la Constitution, proceeding along the street that bears the same name towards a large square that features fountains in each corner. In the middle of the square there is the base on which the statue of King Louis XV once stood before it was destroyed during the Revolution. This empty pedestal prompts you to ask what is it for and, upon receiving the answer, you cannot but feel revulsion for the people who could murder their legitimate ruler and destroy monuments of their ancient rulers only to slavishly obey a tyrant who sheds their blood for the sake of his personal glory.

Looking my quartermaster, we walked across most of the city before being billeted at an apartment that was located beyond the gates inscribed 'A Napoleon Grand' from where a beautiful boulevard led to a vast building of municipal government . . . Our apartment was in one of the buildings belonging to the municipal authority. We received, as usual, a small and very cold room and as the fire was stoked in the fireplace, we ordered to have lunch served at once so we could catch up with [Wittgenstein] who had left Nancy early that morning. Meanwhile, we decided to look around the city. In the morning there was a genuine Russian frost but by noon the sun came out and the day turned out to be nice . . . We spent a long time walking around the city, accompanied by crowds of poor boys who incessantly shouted 'Vive bon Roi Alexandre' and begged us for money. [My German companion] laughed and told them, 'Ah, you traitors, you should be shouting "Vive Napoleon!"' to which the boys responded by starting to yell 'Vive Napoleon l'Autrichien'. Despite the heart-wrenching sight of so many beggars and poor in the country that some proclaim as the most prosperous nation, we could not but laugh upon hearing these shouts.

In front of an Italian dealer's print shop we found a crowd of people examining the portrait of our Emperor [Alexander], yet the drawing had no resemblance to him. We entered the shop and I bought a map of France for seven francs. Overall, the prints were very expensive and six prints depicting Paul and Virginia cost twelve chervonets [120 rubles]. Returning back home in the same company [of begging boys] divested me of any desire of continuing my walk.

[After a splendid lunch] we bid farewell to our host, who mercilessly cursed Napoleon, we hit the road once again. Just as we got our of door to get into our carriage, we encountered a frightful [uzhasnaya] crowd of adult and children beggars on one side and a group of equally poor musicians on the other. We barely managed to get out of the city but even on the main road we could not find any respite from the beggars.

We arrived at Toul at seven o'clock in the evening. We are billeted in a small apartment that is cold . . . The Count is at a concert and I do not if I will see him today. We gulped down a glass of punch and now each of us sat down to write his journal . . .

16 [28] January, Houdelaincourt

This morning I met the Count and we spoke at length on various issues; he laughed that I fell so far behind and could not get to him for so long . . . We stayed at Toul until two o'clock in the afternoon and, after a splendid lunch, we left this town . . . On our way we passed through the small town of Vaucouleurs [before arriving at Houdelaincourt]. Even in the house of a common peasant, where we are currently staying, we do not find an oven and there is only a fireplace in the anteroom where the hosts are. Our room is so cold that even after bringing inside a pot filled with embers and drinking two glasses of punch we still cannot get warm. Our feet suffer from cold more inside the room than in a carriage, all because of stone walls. . . What a torture it is to sleep undressed. Oh, my dear Germany, I long for you.

17 [29] January, Joinville

I had a restless night caused by excessive cold and an uncomfortable bed. I woke up several times in the night and barely managed to awaken [my servant] Mikhail to have him serve tea. I visited the Count [Wittgenstein] and then stopped by [staff officer] Aklicheev who was very frightened by the news that the enemy had moved into our rear. But the Count had already received reports that the Prussian corps had drove the enemy back and took up position parallel to ours . . .

Our host is very talkative and unforgivingly curses Napoleon, and he seems to be genuine in his feelings since the locals have greatly suffered from the Revolution and even more so from Napoleon. Everyone here desires peace – may the Lord grant this common supplication – and remain loyal to the House of Bourbon. Their faces brighten when they hear that [Louis Antoine of France] Duke of Angoulême* is at our main headquarters. [Staff officer] Teslev assures me that we will launch an attack together with Wrede† but no disposition has been made for this. As it is, we have to sleep dressed and in our overcoats.

---

* Louis Antoine of France, Duke of Angoulême (1775–1844) was the eldest son of Charles, Comte d'Artois, and nephew of Louis XVIII.
† Wrede commanded a Bavarian corps.

18 [30] January, Joinville

We slept well and warmly but not too leisurely because we expected the alarm to be sounded at any time. In the morning I visited the Count [Wittgenstein] and spoke with at length about our current movements and the enemy deployment, as well as about continued delay of approval of our nominations to awards . . . I later wrote to Barclay [de Tolly] about our nominations as well. The Count then travelled to the advance guard. Throughout the day we heard a strong cannonade along our lines as well as those of [Prussian General] Yorck at Bar-le-Luc. The Count returned by lunch; the weather was terrible, intermittently snowy, rainy and windy . . . In the evening we received the news from Blücher that yesterday Napoleon attacked and even drove him out of Brienne but, supported by [Osten-]Sacken's corps, [Blücher] was able to beat the villain, recapture Brienne and even seize several cannon and wounded, forcing the enemy to retreat. Around 1:30 a.m., the enemy withdrew from our positions as well and tomorrow we expect to have another battle.

Today's cannonade greatly alarmed local residents who came to us seeking reassurances but their fright soon dissipated [when they saw] us staying in place. It has been said that Caulaincourt arrived at Châlons offering peace on the same conditions that we proposed during the armistice at Schweidnitz [in 1813] – but in light of our current circumstances, these proposals seem ridiculous so [Caulaincourt] was turned back. The Allied Sovereigns no longer want to negotiate with Bonaparte but rather desire to speak directly to [the French] nation. May the Lord bless our efforts to bring down this villain [Napoleon], who has enslaved humanity and shed so much blood for the sake of his own ambition. It seems decision has been to attack tomorrow . . .

19 [31] January, Wassy

Thinking of tomorrow's battle, I had uneven sleep. In the morning, I ordered to prepare horses and went to the Count who told me that during the night [General] Ilovaiskii XII launched a sudden attack on the enemy, caught him unprepared and pursued him through the town of Wassy, which has been captured by our Cossacks. This halted our scheduled offensive and the Count decided to move our headquarters to Wassy . . . Yesterday [the Prussian General] Yorck defeated the enemy yesterday and occupied Saint-Dizier, taking one cannon and numerous captured. Today, he intends on marching to Vitry[-le-Francois] and wait for [the French Marshal] Macdonald, who is marching with a corps of 20,000 men to join Napoleon; our Winzingerode is in close pursuit of [Macdonald]. So we expect to have a major battle. I must note how thrilled our hosts were to hear about these successes of our arms. M. Dessaix and his wife were almost jumping with joy . . .

[We left Joinville after lunch.] All day long the weather was dreadful, one minute there is sun, next – rain, followed by snow and terrible wind. So travelling on a horse turned out to be unbearable. . . I am billeted with an old captain of gendarmerie, whose apartment has a fireplace around which all of us have now gathered.

[P.S] I went to drink tea with the Count and listened to [Marshal] Victor's proclamation which appeals to the [French] people to take up arms and fight; yet, the locals themselves delivered it to us.

20 January [1 February], Saint-Dizier
After a splendid night, I woke up early in the morning, stoked fire in a fireplace and, with a candle in hand, woke up everyone else. Based on the Count's instructions, we will probably rest today. In the morning I prepared a list of nominations for the Prussian awards and submitted it to the Count, whom I found preparing horses to depart. He received orders to join Yorck which is why [our troops] are moving to Saint-Dizier . . . Just before lunch I received a letter from home, written on 29 November [11 December]. I do not what fool told them that I have been promoted to a general but my entire family celebrated for four days straight. May the Lord bless my precious mother for her boundless love: reading her letter I could not hold back tears and later could not eat anything. So I mounted my horse and travelled to Saint-Dizier. Yorck has recently departed in direction of Vitry, which is fortified and has to be taken by assault. I visited the Count [Wittgenstein] who does not know what we will be doing tomorrow. Today the Count ordered to announce awards for [the battle of] Dresden so I spent most of the day attending to this matter in Wassy; the printing press has not arrived yet. I am glad that two [Orders of St.] Anna have been granted. Krivskoi garnered one of them and we congratulated him over a bottle of champagne.

21 January [2 February], Saint-Dizier
We rested today. In the morning we received the news that Blücher, supported by part of Wrede's troops, defeated Napoleon yesterday, capturing forty-one cannon and several thousand prisoners. The fighting continued today as well and the enemy is in full retreat. Macdonald with just four or five thousand men, which is all that he has, is at Vitry . . .

22 January [3 February], Montier-en-Der
The night was excessively cold. We received the news that three day ago our troops captured ninety-seven cannon and about 3,000 prisoners. We have been ordered to leave Yorck at Vitry and move into the enemy's rear. [After eating an early lunch at 11 a.m.] I departed . . . It is impossible to describe what was happening on the main road today. Foot-deep mud everywhere and in some places it is even impossible to get through on a horse. I still cannot understand how I managed, with the Lord's help, to get my chest and carriage through. The weather is still dreadful so we barely dragged ourselves to the quarters. Montier-en-Der is a small town but my apartment at Madame

Pernet's home is good – of course, it is cold as usual . . . and [the ubiquitous] fireplaces will soon cause such revulsion in me that, I am afraid, I will have no desire to have one back at home. The Count [Wittgenstein] received a message from Barclay de Tolly with the news that we have captured eighty cannon and up to 6,000 enemy soldiers, that the enemy is fleeing and all of our forces are pursing him. So we are ordered to join the reserve, which is our Guard, and advance to Troyes. People says that Napoleon has been decisively defeated and there are already arrangements made to announce the Bourbon [Louis XVIII] as the king of France. May the Lord bless this undertaking, the common [French] people are thrilled by this development and eagerly await it while we look forward to entering Paris and signing peace, and pray to the Lord to see this scourge of humanity [Napoleon] annihilated once and for all.

Tomorrow we will have a long march* and will have move at least 3 lieues [12km] on the same bad road as today . . .

23 January [4 February], the village of Rosnay[-l'Hôpital]†

What a day it was! After visiting the Count in the morning, we departed and somehow dragged ourselves in the mire that reached above our knees. . . We moved for three lieues [12km] along a bad road, much worse than the one we march on yesterday, and then covered another 2 lieues [8km] to Brienne on the major road, which has been damaged by Napoleon's army. Approaching Brienne, we could see both sides of the road and fields all around us covered with corpses of the unfortunate victims of Napoleon's barbarity; the city has been burned down and plundered, as was the castle that stands on a beautiful hill overlooking the entire area. It was at this military school that Buonaparte was raised and educated upon his arrival from Corsica and it was here that lost what could be the very last battle of his life . . . General Count Wrede was stationed at the castle . . . [which] was plundered by [his] Bavarian troops. All of its magnificent collections of natural history, minerals and others are destroyed. I felt sad that I could not see them but [staff officers] Kozlov and Patton gave me a couple of seashells. The Bavarians are still deployed here and continue to plunder just as the French did in Russia. There are no quarters to occupy and it is pity to see the Bavarians, such splendid troops, behaving in such a depraved manner.

We received the news that Napoleon is rallying his defeated troops near Troyes. Blücher is already advancing on Paris and people say that a Parisian deputation has already reached our Emperor [Alexander.] We are advancing to Arcis [-sur-Aube] in order to flank the French army, which seems to be abandoning its capital. Lord, we beseech you to help us and deliver us from the road that we travelled today.

---

* Montier-en-Der is about 65km from Troyes.
† This village is about 9km north of Brienne.

24 January [5 February], Piney

Oh, these damn fireplaces and this wretched France! Our quarters are not better than bivouacs. Last night I got chilled to the bone even though I slept dressed and the fire burned in the fireplace throughout the night. I woke up early in the morning and struggled to get warm.

At first, we thought we would advance to Rameursy but the direction was changed and [Prince] Schwarzenberg ordered us to march [to Piney]. After a quick breakfast, we travelled on horse and foot, passed through Brienne . . . and left the main road, proceeding not on a road but rather across fields and swamps barely covering 6 lieues [24km] to arrive here by 6 o'clock in the evening. I do not why the Lord protects my carriage and horses, for this one march alone is worth three usual ones.

Piney is a small and lovely town but it has been ransacked by our allies . . . We are just four lieues [16km] away from Troyes and could hear a cannonade all day today. Rumours have it that the enemy has been defeated and driven back so we do not know where we are going to head tomorrow. Local villages are utterly destitute even without war, houses are small like cages. How can one even compare France to Germany!

25 January [6 February], Charmont[-sous-Barbouise] *

Yesterday we had a rough night at Piney because of the cold. But at least there we had a pleasant room and our hosts, despite being already despoiled [by our allies], were very kind people, who fed us well, offered a bed and today, while bidding farewell to them, they even expressed a wish for us to stay until peace is signed. On the other hand, here at Charmont, we ended up in a dreadful peasant hut, doors leading straight into the yard, the host having virtually nothing and all of us simply sitting in front the fireplace. And on top of it, it is so cold here that we might as well as keep sitting in front of the fire for the rest of the night.

The day began with me visiting the Count . . . after a lunch in Pirney, we moved just as we did the day before, except the weather was colder. Although it was not freezing, a strong wind was blowing and it was almost impossible to remain mounted. The 3 lieues [12km] that we marched felt like ten, and there was just one small village on the way, where we could not find any place to warm ourselves. Upon arriving at Chamont, we found no quarters . . . and spent three hours walking with a quartermaster before we lodged at the first unoccupied house. Having drunk vodka on a heavy heart and conversed around another miserable fireplace reminiscing about the beloved Fatherland, friends and relatives, I am now busy writing my journal . . . Our host, an old woman, dries her wooden shoes, which everyone wears here, and looks at me clearly startled that I can write just like [the French].

---

* This village is about 20km north of Troyes.

There is no reason for us to envy the French, who are not worthy of either praise or emulation. [From the Russian text in M. Kakhovskii, 'Zapiski . . .']

Fabian von der Osten-Sacken

After Napoleon's victory at Brienne, Blücher had fallen back to positions north of Trannes. During the next two days both sides rested their forces and Napoleon uncharacteristically remained inactive. Schwarzenberg, the Allied commander-in-chief, reinforced Blücher with two corps while the Bavarians under Wrede supported his right flank. Blücher planned his attack for the morning of 1 February. Schwarzenberg could have committed more forces to the attack, but political considerations made it inadvisable to help the Prussians to destroy Napoleon's forces. Blücher launched an assault on Napoleon's positions at La Rothière on 1 February and the battle unfolded in miserable weather, with frigid temperatures and frequent snow squalls. Napoleon managed to fight a successful defensive action for most of the day but the arrival of Wrede's corps forced him to abandon the battlefield. The battle of La Rothière was Napoleon's first defeat on French soil. Sacken, whose corps also participated in the battle, wrote this report to General Barclay de Tolly from the battlefield at La Rothière on 2 February.

Yesterday's battle at La Rothière was fought under the direct supervision of His Imperial Majesty and therefore I will only report certain details. On the right flank we had General Adjutant Vasilchikov with most of our cavalry. On his left was Lieutenant-General Olsufiev with the 9th Corps, followed by Lieutenant-General Prince Sherbatov with the 6th Corps. Farther to the left, there was Lieutenant-General Count Lieven with the 10th, 16th and 27th Divisions. He was initially reinforced by the hussars under the command of Lt. Col. Davydov and later a hussar brigade under the command of Major-General Vasilchikov. In between them stood Prince Biron with his detachment and a dragoon division under the command of Major-General Panchulidzev. Lieutenant-General Prince Sherbatov and Count Lieven directed their efforts towards the most important points during our attack on the enemy's central position at La Rothière. Major-General Nikitin commanded all of the artillery.

When all columns reached the same heights, our forces advanced and after marching for some 300 paces, [order was issued] to beat drums and play music; our men moved in fast step in complete order and, without firing, charged at the enemy and drove him back. The enemy made several attempts, even as late as 9 p.m., to reclaim La Rothière but each time he was repelled.

We captured up to thirty cannon and about 2,000 prisoners while the enemy lost up to 5,000 killed, while the number of the wounded and missing certainly reaches 15,000. Our losses are also heavy. Lieutenant-General Count Lieven, and Major-Generals Stavitskii and Kologrivov are wounded (but I have not yet received a detailed report on our losses). On this superb and memorable day, Napoleon has ceased to be the enemy of the human race; and Alexander may now say: 'I give peace to the world.' [From the Russian text in RGVIA f. 846, op.16, d. 4120/1, ll. 186–187]

Alexander Mikhailovskii-Danilevskii

Mikhailovskii-Danilevskii was a staff officer in the Russian imperial headquarters.

Upon reaching Bar-sur-Aube on 19 [31] January, we learned that Field Marshal Blücher and his Army of Silesia, after crossing the Rhine River at Mannheim, approached the Aube River and was involved in a serious action at Brienne. The Emperor decided to join the Main Army with the Army of Silesia and attack the enemy the following day.

This was the first major battle in France and therefore success or failure in it would have had powerful psychological impression on both sides. Although we had advanced deep into France, the enemy, until now, avoided pitched battles and everyone waited in great anticipation to see first-hand how strong would be the enemy's resistance within the borders of his own state. The entire morning of 20 March was spent in preparations for the battle. The Emperor reviewed the troops which were deployed in the following order: Austrians on the left flank, Russians next to them, followed by the Württembergers and, further to the right, the Bavarians who were instructed to turn the enemy's left flank. Our grenadiers and cuirassiers were kept in reserve on the road to Bar-sur-Aube while the Guard was deployed behind them. The overall command of the armies was entrusted to Field Marshal Blücher and, to avoid interfering with his command, the Emperor and King of Prussia retreated to the nearby heights at Trannes where they could observe all the movements; they remained there until evening.

Around noon, we were ordered to attack. The Allied troops, fighting in the presence of their monarchs, competed with each other in gallantry. The Russians faced the most challenging task of taking the village of La Rothière, which represented a key to the enemy position. Around 9 p.m., when it was completely dark, the French, after a furious attack, managed to seize La Rothière but were soon driven back and set the village on fire. The massive fire brightly illuminated that gloomy January night. Thus ended the battle, in which the greatest honours belonged to General Sacken, who commanded the Russian troops. In his report on this battle, he remarked, 'On this superb and memorable day, Napoleon has ceased to be the enemy of the human race; and Alexander may now say: "I give peace to the world".'

We gained a complete victory. The enemy lost over seventy guns and some 3,000 prisoners. The victory could have led to the capture of Paris if the Main Army and the Army of Silesia marched together to the French capital. Instead, relying on their numerical superiority, the two armies separated after the battle and proceed to Paris along two different routes: Field Marshal Blücher moved through Châlons while the Main Army proceeded to Troyes. The enemy's lack of troops clearly revealed itself at Brienne – France had abandoned Napoleon, who had brought her to the pinnacle of glory, at the moment when the fortune stopped smiling at him. He appealed to the nation and ordered peasants to sound the tocsin upon the appearance of the Allied troops, who were portrayed as plunderers, and destroy bridges, and demanded a popular uprising. But no one responded to his call which disappeared as if in a desert.

The following day, at nine o'clock in the morning, the Emperor, the King of Prussia and the Commander-in-Chief arrived at the castle of Brienne to discuss future plans of action. The castle and its surrounding, memorable for the childhood that Napoleon spent there, presented a picture of complete destruction. The castle contained a fine library and a room of Natural History, where a crocodile hung from the ceiling. Someone came up with the idea of cutting the ropes which held the crocodile and the fall of this massive African beast destroyed the cabinets which exhibited various shells and fossils behind glass. The laughter that accompanied this destruction of so many precious rarities was akin to the laughter of cannibals. But such events are inseparable from war. Some rooms still showed fresh traces of their residents and there was a woman's needlework on one of the tables. Here I also encountered Field Marshal Blücher, who could barely stand on his feet.

As soon the Main Army arrived at Troyes and the Army of Silesia reached the banks of the Marne River, the genius of Napoleon, which was seemingly in slumber in the beginning of the campaign, had suddenly awoke once more. With a handful of troops he appeared rapidly everywhere where he could gain upper hand and halted movements of superior Allied forces by attacking their weakest elements. He first turned against Blücher, delivering major blows at Champaubert, Montmirail, Château-Thierry and Vauchamps, and throwing him back to Châlons. This was an appropriate punishment for the carelessness with which the Prussian commander stretched out his forces over a vast area and failed to cover them with separate flying detachments. Following these victories, where the fortune had smiled for the last time on its favourite son, Napoleon moved against the Main Army and, having forced it to retreat to Langres, he hurried once more to attack Blücher who had threatened Paris. But the Main Army moved in his wake and we soon returned to the banks of the Seine River, where we took up positions for several days awaiting news from Blücher. Thus passed the month of February, full of turns of fate. The meetings of the Châtillon congress, which opened on 23 January [4 February], brought no results because the concessions that the French government was willing to make did not match the demands of the Allied Powers. But more importantly neither of the warring sides possessed a sincere desire to negotiate peace, even on the conditions that were put forth by their plenipotentiaries. [From the Russian text in A. Mikhailovskii-Danilevskii, *Zapiski* . . .]

Constantine Poltoratskii

By the autumn of 1813, Colonel Poltoratskii, who had turned thirty-one in June, had already served in five campaigns and had half a dozen battles behind him. A capable officer, he earned general's epaulettes at the battle of Konigswartha in September and the command of the 1st Brigade of the 9th Division for his exploits at Leipzig in October. He commanded this brigade during the invasion of France and fought at Briennes, La Rothière and Champaubert. The latter battle, where Poltoratskii was captured by the French, was fought on 10 February approximately 60 miles west of Paris between Napoleon's forces and Blücher's Army of Silesia. Napoleon had at first intended to strike at Schwarzenberg's Army of Bohemia but once he discovered that Blücher's forces were strung out as they pushed westward toward Paris (and that Schwarzenberg was retreating to Troyes), he changed direction in order to meet the threat from the north where Blücher stood in relative isolation south of the Marne. Napoleon's victory in this battle ushered in the Six Days campaign, during which his forces delivered several severe blows to the Allies.

Napoleon, desiring to see Olsufiev, invited him to sup with him; but as the General had difficulty in expressing himself in the French language, Napoleon sent for Poltoratskii. The following dialogue took place between them.

'How many were you in the field to-day?'

'3,690 men, and 24 guns.'

'Nonsense! that cannot be; you had, at least, 18,000 men.'

'A Russian officer does not speak nonsense. I have told the truth; besides, there are other persons from whom you can learn the same thing; then I hope you will be convinced that Russians do not lie.'

Napoleon scowled, and after a short silence said, 'If what you assert be true, it may be said to your honour, that Russians alone can fight so desperately. I would have pledged my head that you were, at least, 18,000.'

'For all that I am a prisoner.'

'What does that signify? Your Emperor has fifty of my generals prisoners, and as good as you. But, granting that I have destroyed you without great honour, as my troops fought with yours a whole day, still the consequences of this affair are important to me; and I will now tell you, that, as I have routed you today, I will annihilate Sacken to-morrow; on Thursday, the whole of Wittgenstein's advanced guard; on Friday, I will give Blücher a blow from which he will not recover, and then I hope to dictate a peace to your Alexander on the Vistula.'

'That will be rather difficult.'

Napoleon then entered critically on the subject of the late campaigns, and after running over that of 1812, ended by saying, 'Your old fox, Kutuzov, deceived me by his march on our flank.' He carried his playful humour so far, that Poltoratskii now and then disputed with him, and among other things said, that the French had burned Moscow. This expression seemed unpleasant to Napoleon, who answered: 'What! The French? That act of barbarity was the work of you Russians.'

'When you took possession of Moscow, and when all order was at end, it may be said that both the French and the Russians burned it: but I must frankly tell you that the Russians, so far from regretting the catastrophe, reflect with pride on the burning of their ancient capital, and can soon build a new one.'

Napoleon continued to grow more heated, and said, 'It was a barbarous deed, and a stain on the nation; I took Berlin, Madrid, and Vienna, and no such thing happened.'

'The Russians don't repent of it, and are delighted with the results.'

Napoleon stamped his foot, and ordered the prisoner to leave the room.

During the dialogue Marshals Berthier, Ney, Marmont, and the minister of foreign affairs, Maret, stood by in the most respectful posture. Poltoratskii was making his way, accompanied by a colonel of gendarmes, through the bivouac of the guard which encircled the house occupied by Napoleon, when he heard somebody call out, 'Where is the Russian prisoner?' It was the French General-aide-de-camp Flahaut. He very politely requested him to return to Napoleon, who, loading his prisoner with compliments, thus began his interrogatory:

'What is the strength of the Russian guards and army? Where is the Emperor and Generals?' naming many of them.

To all his questions he received one and the same answer: 'I don't know.'

'I had promised myself the pleasure,' continued Napoleon, 'of conversing with you on several matters, but your answer, "I don't know", hinders me. Why does your Emperor everywhere employ his own excellent troops, and not the Germans, whom I could annihilate in half an hour, while I have been fighting with you for a whole day?'

'You ask me about the position of our army: that is a secret. To us the will of the Emperor is sacred, send us where he may. A gallant soldier says everything that comes uppermost. Our oath to our Emperor and country forbids that.'

Here Napoleon, displaying an intercepted order from Blücher to Olsufiev, desiring him on no account to retire from Champaubert, exclaimed, 'There is your drunkard Blücher! Did he know I was here? Where I am, there are a hundred thousand more.' Poltoratskii still continuing his answers in the negative on the state of the army, was for the second time sent out of the room. Napoleon ordered him to be conveyed to Paris, and to be strictly watched. [From the Russian text in A. Mikhailovskii-Danilevskii, *Opisaniye pokhoda vo Frantsii v 1814 godu*]

Nikifor Kovalskii

A junior officer in the elite Life Guard Dragoon Regiment, Kovalskii was, with his squadron, deployed at the town of Sezanne when he learned about the Allied setback at Champaubert.

We soon received an order from General Diebitsch to send out small squads, consisting of an officer and fifteen men, to determine the location of Blücher's corps. Whe it was my turn to depart, I took with me non-commissioned officer Tarasenkov, Private Pryadko, who a very resourceful fellow, and twelve other soldiers. My guide was an old, fat French baker, who had a pigtail and overgrown sideburns. It was a moonlit night and we travelled near a large and clearly affluent village of Oye, seeing some fires burning in the distance. Approaching Champaubert, I dispatched Tarasenkov, with the [French] guide, ahead of us to see if there were any French while I remained with the remaining men about two hundred paces behind them. Less than fifteen minutes later Tarasenkov returned informing me that the baker had escaped by jumping off the horse and leaping across the fence. Not suspecting any danger, I entered the village on a narrow fenced path. I saw several men standing near a lit hut and yelled to them, 'Who are you?' The wind, however, was so strong that they could not hear my words and therefore did not respond. As I moved forward I suddenly came across fifteen fully-harnessed horses tied to a fence, a few soldiers, wearing helmets, standing next to them and another group of man sleeping on the ground. I asked them, 'Ête vous français? [Are you French?]' – 'Qui, que diable!? [Yes, who the hell is asking!?]' replied the sentry, pushing his friends. My soldier Pryadko got out his pistol and told me, 'Your Honour, allow me to shoot this Frenchman!' Just as I grabbed his hand and ordered my men to fall back, there was some commotion among the French and bullets whizzed above us. At the same time, drums beat and trumpets sounded and the entire French camp moved at this alarm. We galloped back and barely escaped from this danger.

Nearing the village of Oye, we once again came across a French picket, this time comprised of eight men. My soldiers charged and the French fled across the gardens, abandoning six fully-harnessed horses and six helmets with [horse] tails. The village was still largely asleep but [the sound of commotion] caused some infantrymen appear from houses. I ordered my men to wear the captured helmets and we safely passed through the village. At the village exit we encountered another picket and several men came out to check us but they let us through without hindrance. Thus, with the Lord's help, we escaped from possible captivity.

Several days later I was once again tasked with a reconnaissance mission but this time I was accompanied by thirty soldiers, two non-commissioned officers and one guide. As we departed, a dashing-looking Cossack officer, clearly a braggart but a pleasant companion, joined as well. He generously shared his tobacco and vodka, which delighted me since the morning was quite cold. To catch some rest, we stopped at the first peasant farm that we encountered. The [French] peasant bitterly complained to me that soldiers' visits devastated him; that all of his forage and flour had been already consumed; that his pregnant wife was about to give birth while his two little children remained unattended. Despite his complaints I sent for the [village] mayor who immediately ordered the man to provide forage for our horses and prepare something edible for us. However, we declined to eat, fearing that the food might be poisoned since locals demonstrated unambiguous enmity towards us. At that moment the peasant and the mayor became embroiled in a heated conversation which soon led to a brawl. The peasant grabbed an axe and was about to strike the mayor's head when I jostled him away. My men rushed at this thug and tied him up. I then deployed a picket next to the farm and lay down to rest. But just then Pryadko came running with the news that an enemy outpost of some twenty men appeared near the farm. With sunrise approaching, I quickly ordered that the horses be and we hastily departed from the farm. I noticed that my guide and the Cossack officer disappeared somewhere. The Cossack's batman explained to me, 'His Honour has a habit of fleeing as soon as thing become tense.'

A dragoon, who fell behind, caught up with later on the road complaining that the peasant somehow managed to free himself, dragged him from the horse, took away all of his ammunition and almost killed him with an axe. After travelling about six verstas [6.4km] [we came across] a beautiful peasant farm surrounded by tall stone walls and gates closed. I shouted to have the gates open but no one replied. My men then began banging on the gates but it was in vain – the house seemed to be abandoned. Finally, a Frenchman crawled from some place and told me that he would have gladly let us in if not for the Russian soldiers who were already inside the house and had forbidden him from opening the gates. I immediately shouted in Russian, 'Lads, open the gates!' and a minute later we were inside the farm, where we were greeted by some sixty infantrymen with muskets. These were survivors of Olsufiev's corps that had been routed [at Champaubert]. They had rallied at this farm in the hopes of some unexpected succour.

Thrilled by this encounter we organised a breakfast. The host, apparently an affluent man, brought us bread, butter, cheese and milk, and, on my request, he dispatched one of his labourers to the [village] mayor to deliver a letter in which I demanded immediate return of the horse and ammunition that had been taken from my dragoon; otherwise, I threatened to return with my squad and burn the entire village. My request was soon fulfilled.

After three hours' rest we decided to resume our journey in the direction of Sezanne, taking our host as a guide. The infantrymen keenly thanked us, calling me as their saviour and explaining that without the knowledge of the

French language and the road they would have certainly fallen into captivity. Just then we saw a squad of cavalrymen in bearskin caps moving directly on the farm. This was an excellent opportunity to distinguish ourselves. I convinced the infantrymen to take position near the gates and meet the enemy with bullets while I will charged with my troopers. 'We are thrilled to do our best, Your Honour,' responded the soldiers with one voice. After examining their muskets, they rushed out of the gates and fired at the French, killing two and wounding several. As my men charged, the Frenchmen fled and we pursued them. Unfortunately my horse took the bit in its teeth and galloped like crazy. Realising that this might lead to bad results, I turned her abruptly, barely holding myself in the saddle. The French, however, kept fleeing without looking back. It was dangerous to pursue them any further so we decided to turn back.

This farm was located about 30 verstas [31.8km] from Sezanne. For the rest of our journey, we saw many Russian soldiers, the survivors of Olsufiev's corps, coming out of ditches and brushwood to join us. In the end, there were twenty-five of them so I entered Sezanne at the head of eighty-five infantrymen . . . I went to submit my report to our squadron commander Colonel Besedin, who initially refused to believe me but I had all proofs to support my account. Finally, he told me, 'You have had quite an experience but so did I. Here was I, sitting quietly and enjoying my tea, when suddenly the doors open and four soldiers of [Napoleon] Imperial Guard, wearing their [famed] bearskin caps, entered the room one after another. I was so startled that the teacup fell from my hand. Fortunately, my sergeant appeared from behind them and announced that these men had come to surrender to us and went straight to my room without informing him. I gave a decent beating to this old fool for this scare. It is funny now but who would have wanted to be in my place?' [From the Russian text in N. Kovalskii, 'Iz zapisok . . .']

Aleksei Karpov

Despite his youth (he was turning twenty-seven in 1814), Karpov was already an experienced artillery officer, having served in several campaigns against the French. In 1814 he commanded a squad [vzvod] of two cannon in the 6th Light Artillery Company that was attached to Prince Eugene of Württemberg's corps.

On 7 [19] January, we crossed the Rhine on pontoon boats and I, with my two cannon, almost drowned in the river due to the ice floes and reached the opposite bank with great difficulty. After crossing the Rhine, we advanced at night to Strasbourg and began blockading it. We remained here until 20 January [1 February] and during this time the French made two sorties but both failed. On [date missing] January we departed from Strasbourg, entrusting the blockade to the Badenese troops and two companies of Russian heavy artillery – one commanded by Colonel Velyaminov, the other by Lieutenant-Colonel Ditterix IV. Meanwhile, we advanced without lacking any supplies, taking quarters in the following cities: Luneville, Nancy, Vaucouleurs, Bar-sur-Aube, Troyes, Méry[-sur-Seine], Pont-sur-Seine and Nogent[-sur-Seine]. Upon reaching Nogent, we encountered our retreating troops and learned that our army's advance guard, commanded by General Pahlen and consisting of some 5,000 men, had been completely routed by the enemy, losing six cannon in Colonel Markov's horse artillery and two cannon in Colonel Lipstein's battery company. Needless to say, this was a rather unpleasant meeting. We soon joined Prince Eugene of Württemberg's corps in the army of Count Wittgenstein and, the following day, we began to retreat, falling back to Méry, then to Troyes and Bar-sur-Aube, where we took up positions about five verstas [5.3km] behind the town. The French pursued us very vigorously. On 13 [25] February, we joined the Bavarian corps of General Wrede.

On 15 [27] February, we advanced against the French at Bar-sur-Aube and took up positions on the heights, leaving the town to our left while the main road to Troyes was at the bottom of the hill in front of us. The French also held the heights, the road and the town. The battle began before noon and I was deployed with my two guns separately from the rest of the company. Major-General Kostenetskii ordered me to follow him and led me in front of the entire line of our troops, where he deployed my cannon to engage six French cannon, not noticing that I was exposed from the right side where the French could engage me with another four cannon. He ordered me to hold this position until he came back. So I opened artillery fire but my two cannon could do very little against the enemy's ten guns. Furthermore, the enemy soon deployed four guns on my left flank and two Russian guns had to fight back against fourteen of the enemy's. I soon had six men killed when an enemy round hit directly on my cannon's barrel while two other cannonballs struck near the gun, killing four horses. The force of the enemy cannonball caused the gun barrel to slightly bend in the middle but since the cannon was already loaded, I still ordered it to fire which, in fact, slightly straitened the barrel and after a few more shots, it was possible to operate without any hindrance and I was able to hold my position until nightfall.* In the evening General Kostenetskii returned to us and would have been struck in the head by a cannonball if not for my timely push; still, the gust of wind threw his hat

---

* Karpov's decision was extremely dangerous since the cannon could have exploded, killing or injuring the entire crew. However, without making such a risky move, he would have been forced to abandon his position, which his superior officer had prohibited him from contemplating. Karpov clearly took such a prohibition close to heart.

to the ground. He ordered me to leave the position and rejoin my company. During this battle my entire company lost ten men killed, four wounded, twelve horses killed and wounded and two cannons damaged.

That night I advanced with a small detachment made up of the 31st* and 34th Jager Regiments to protect the right side of a small road running to Troyes. There were no enemy attacks that night and in the morning of 16 [28] February I rejoined my company. On 17–18 February [1–2 March] we marched along local roads to Troyes and in the afternoon on the 19th [3 March] we attacked the enemy on the outskirts of Troyes. Prince Eugene of Württemberg sent me with two guns to the very gates of the city with orders to break them down, but negotiations soon began and the gates were opened. During the night of 20 February [4 March] I was dispatched with the Chernigovskii and Revelskii Regiments to capture an enemy redoubt built near the road to Troyes and, although we could not accomplish it, the enemy abandoned the city by morning. For service in all of these actions I was awarded the Order of St Anna [4th class]. That same day, 20 February [4 March] we passed through Troyes and pursued the enemy towards Méry; we did not suffer major losses throughout these days.

Upon arriving at Méry, we joined Blücher's army and proceeded to Pont-sur-Seine, where Napoleon's mother had a beautiful estate which Russians inadvertently burned down; it was said that the fire was caused by the batmen of the 23rd Horse Artillery Company of Colonel Marko but this matter was never investigated properly and this palace burned for more than a week and the millions spent on building it turned into ashes. From there we marched to Nogent but soon had to fall back to Pont-sur-Seine once more. On 1 [13] March, we crossed the Seine there and proceeded to Provins. On 2 [14] March we had a small combat while two days later we were engaged in a battle near Provins, although we did not suffer serious losses.

On 9 [21] March we joined the battle near the city of Vitry, where the French hussars came very close to capturing me and my cannon. Prince Eugene of Württemberg dispatched me to occupy a nearby hill. I ordered to my crews to ascend the hill while I went ahead of them at a trot. As I reached the hilltop, I saw hussars in red uniforms and, assuming that they were Russians, I inquired which regiment they belonged to. When the officer responded 'Comment?' I realised my mistake and galloped back as soon as I could. The [French] officer dispatched four hussars to cut me off and they were already descending into the ravine where the road ran when I dug spurs into my horse spurred and rushed by them to safety. The hussars did not try to pursue me and just approached my guns, with one of them firing at me but missing.

---

* Karpov refers to the 31st Jager Regiment but he is probably making a mistake since this unit was then at the siege of Danzig. It is possible this was the 4th Jagers, which was with 34th Jagers in the 3rd Brigade of the 4th Infantry Division.

The battle of Vitry continued until nightfall and our company suffered minimal losses, but the army's loss was unknown; the French did manage to destroy several caissons belonging to Colonel Shtadin's company. On 10 [22] March, the enemy cavalry passed in front of our corps and but did not press the attack on our columns which stood in squares with artillery in between them. Still [I must admit] that the sound of charging cavalry could be rather terrifying. On 12 [24] March our entire army gathered near the city [of Vitry] at night. I was assigned to Count Pahlen's advance guard . . . [From the Russian text in A. Karpov, *Zapiski polkovnika Karpova*]

Ilya Radozhitskii

A lieutenant in the 3rd Light Company attached to Alexander Langeron's corps, Radozhitskii spent the first six weeks of 1814 in Frankfurt and at the blockade of Mainz. Now, at last, he was on the French soil advancing towards Paris . . . at least it seemed that way at first.

Late in the evening of 2 [14] February, we arrived at Alzey, located about 60 verstas [63.6km] from Mainz. Alzey is surrounded by walls and towers, features ruins of an ancient castle but everything appears as if in miniature, like Rome would have looked at its founding when Remus could [easily] jump across the city moat. Looking at these walls, I thought about those ancient times when people fought with arrows, stones, [boiling] tar, battering rams and mobile siege towers. How many transformations these ruins had witnessed! Inside Alzey, buildings are built of wood and the residents, of German Brabant origin, appeared to be rather staunch supporters of Napoleon. To lure them to his side, [Napoleon] spared them more than the Rhineland Germans. But now the plight of the local residents was miserable indeed. To collect the debt that Prussians claimed from France (about 60 million), Prince Blücher collected dreadful contributions from every village and settlement [that he encountered]. Furthermore, these villages had to satisfy the Russian troops and then save enough to survive themselves. The land seems to be fruitful but locals show no signs of industry or wellbeing.

I was billeted to a Jew but local Jews are completely different from ours in their way of life, education and entire appearance. I would not comment about their souls – everything the scions of Hebrew tribe do is based on deception and acquisition of money through the easiest means possible. In my host's cabinet, I found many French and German books, old novels and portraits of three European emperors. The locals received us well and trusted us more than they did Prussians. But we could not trust their welcome after learning about the proclamation that Napoleon issued to his peoples: [he appealed to them] to slaughter and poison us everywhere. It was said that such attempts had been made already in the corps of Baron Osten-Sacken. Our Emperor, on the other hand, issued an orders to the armies demanding treating [the civilian] populace as amicably as possible and to conquer them more with our generosity than vengeance. Quite a contrast to the French behaviour in Russia . . .

On 5 [17] February we passed by the mountain Mont-Tonnerre after which this entire province was called.* The city of Kaiserslautern was very poor but larger than Alzey. Local residents were half-Germans or Brabants, and received us very well.

The following day we had a long march of some 40 verstas [42.4km] across mountains. We passed through Landstuhl and Homburg, where houses were very decrepit. The further we advanced, the more wretched and poor residents we encountered: they wore rags covered with filth and their faces revealed emaciation. At least the area near the town of Zweibrücken was picturesque and many places were worthy of an artist's brush. We rested there and found good quarters [prepared for us]. My friend and I were billeted to a baker while our lieutenant-colonel stayed in the apartment of a widow, a certain Duchess Lewenhaupt, of Swedish ancestry.

Zweibrücken was located between the two fortresses of Saarbrücken and Bitt [Bitche?] and was bordering with Lotharingia,† where we were supposed to enter the following day.

Our detachment was commanded by Count St. Priest. Locals organised a ball in his honour and invited all officers to attend it. At 4 o'clock the following morning I was sent to Sarreguemines to prepare quarters for my company. At sunrise I was already at Blieskastel behind which I observed a telegraph tower on a mountain.‡

Under the Bourbons, French soil began at Sarreguemines. This town is located on the Saar River that separates Lotharingia from Brabant. Upon arriving here, I appeared in front of the local commander, Lt. Col. V., a rather polite Guard officer, to receive assignment of quarters. I took this document to the local municipalité that bore the symbol of the French eagle and found myself surrounded by the representatives of that very nation that had caused so much harm to all of Europe and my own Fatherland. I was left with remarkable first impressions: In German towns I got accustomed to seeing slow, mostly quiet and important-looking burgomasters, but here, on the contrary, I saw talkative, polite but sombre Frenchmen, whose swarthy

---

* Mont-Tonnerre was the name of a département of the French First Empire. It was named after the highest point in the Rhenish Palatinate, the Donnersberg.

† Lotharingia was a region comprising the Low Countries, the western Rhineland, and what is now western Switzerland. It was established in the tripartite division in 855, of the kingdom of Middle Francia, itself formed of the threefold division of the Carolingian Empire by the Treaty of Verdun in AD 843.

‡ Radozhitskii refers to the famous mechanical telegraph developed by Claude Chappe in the 1790s. Napoleon built an extensive network of such towers to maintain control over his growing empire.

faces alternately manifested all passions and moods. I thus witnessed Liberté et Égalité under the burden of unlimited despotism. Inside the meeting call, everything attracted my attention, even golden bees on blue wallpaper that covered the walls. Three mayors, all wearing glasses, fussed about assigning quarters, while other members [of the municipal authority], wearing caps and hats and smoking pipes, walking around the room. There were many other [officers] seeking quarters so I had plenty of time to observe and examine everything. Citizens, displeased with the mayors' decisions, constantly came in holding billet assignments and demanding changes to be made . . . Suddenly there appeared a swarthy and skinny but agile Frenchman, in sailor's dress, and rather brashly declared to the mayors that he was unable to maintain troops billeted to him, and that their decision were contrary to all existing laws. Seeing the mayors' firmness, he began to bang his fists on table and curse and shout at them until he was forcefully removed from the room. All of this was utterly startling to me, especially when I saw an old lady, wearing a large bonnet, shouting at the top of her lungs, chiding the mayors and ready to scratch their eyes out at the first opportunity; [she was followed] by charming dark-eyed Frenchwomen whose gentle voices beseeched the mayors [to help them] . . . Others might have been swayed by these shouts and petitions but the hard-hearted mayors, immersed in their work, neither heard or saw anything and simply continued writing billets. They appeared totally heartless. I finally obtained billets for my artillery crews and went to inspect the houses.

[After spending a few days at Sarreguemines, Radozhitskii's men pushed westwards.]

Château-Salins* turned out to be a very poor town. The local residents are completely desolate and devastated by continued misfortunes. Their behaviour reveals that they are more afraid of us than conspiring against us. It is rather strange to see a man in a ragged blue coat or a woman in a filthy dress or a begging young boy, who speak fluent French, the language that back at home is spoken only by the members of high society. Yet, here we are listening to the rabble speaking that same language. Nothing better reveals the shallowness of our [elite's] craze [for all things French].

We rarely encounter large crowds, even then we largely encounter old men, young boys and women since conscription has claimed all adult males. Beyond Sarreguemines we noticed an interesting transformation in the buildings: houses became wider, window shutters become latticed and inside the homes we found fireplaces, not ovens. The soil here appears to be rocky or clayey and thus less fertile but the local do consume good-quality wheat bread. Also, the area beyond Sarreguemines is flatter than the region between Mainz and Zweibrücken, where we had to cross mountains.

---

* Château-Salins is located about 60km west of Sarreguemines.

[At last we arrived at] Nancy which was a major commercial city, larger than Frankfurt and located on the plain that was intersected by the Meurthe River. It used to be the capital of Lotharingia but is now the main city of the department of Meurthe. It is considered one of the best cities in France and has a palace, bishopric and numerous beautiful buildings. Its streets are straight, wide and decorated with trees. The best of the city squares was named after Napoleon and featured fountains and boulevards. In the middle of it stood the bronze statue of Henry IV. Local shops are built in a particular style and present a long row of glass doors. Each home has an inscription or sign. The Polish King Stanislaw Leszczyński, who was related to Louis XV* had resided here when he lost his kingdom† and decorated the city with many beautiful buildings. This philosopher-king and his spouse were buried at the cathedral several miles from here.‡

Our troops moved by a parade march through Nancy. The French watched them with amazement in the streets. But who were these people? – Almost all of them poor. A common Frenchman is dressed worse than a Russian peasant. He wears a blue linen coat on top of his shirts and pantaloons, a cap on the head and wooden shoes, called sabots, on his feet. Such was their usual clothing.

My friend and I received quarters on the place carrée in a building that used to be a restaurant but its owner went bankrupt and died. His widow apparently still mourned him and was thus drunk. I went to see local shops and found everything too expensive; I paid five francs for a pound of sugar. Such high prices were caused not as much by war as by heavy taxes that merchants paid not only for colonial goods but everything else. All of the tobacco in France was actually produced at mills Napoleon established, and this tobacco monopoly was a profitable for him . . . since you will not find a single Frenchman who does not smoke or sniff tobacco . . . In addition, Napoleon collected taxes on doors, windows and chimneys. Such was the price the French had paid for their liberty and equality! Liberty, for which they condemned their good king. However, now Napoleon stood among them as a stork amidst frogs and devoured them as he wished.

The theatre in Nancy is as large as the one in Frankfurt but, considering circumstances, it has poorer music and wardrobe. The theatre staged the opera *La Folia* in three acts but the audience consisted of almost entirely of our officers, and even those were just a few. There were no Frenchmen, except for young boys. Almost all the boxes and seats were empty and the Cossacks

---

* Louis XV was married to Stanislaw's daughter Marie.
† Stanislaw was twice deposed from the Polish throne in the first half of the eighteenth century.
‡ Stanislaw died at the age of eighty-eight in 1766. His body was buried in the church of Notre-Dame de Bonsecours in Nancy while his bowels were placed in a cenotaph inside the church of Saint-Jacques in Lunéville.

and Prussians stood in the parterre. The opera had a pleasant music and some of its arias were charming indeed. The actors sang and played well but it was obvious that they were not in the mood for performing. And how could they be when their fatherland was perishing!? Yet they were forced to perform because the city residents refused to organise a ball. A theatre buffet resembled an open market and after each act we had to wait for more than half an hour before the curtain was raised. The French, playful and capricious by nature, then walked with their heads bowed and deeply immersed in thoughts about impending misfortunes. But the young boys were still rather talkative. After getting my seat in the first row, I would have been all alone if not for boys, in dress-coats, hands stuck inside their trousers as was the custom [in France] and hats on their heads, who approached me. They sat on the balustrade in front of me and, during intermissions, frequently asked me questions about the theatre, the city and what I liked there. Finally one of them asked me, 'Do you really think of reaching Paris?' – 'Of course, just as your troops came to Moscow.' – 'And you will burn Paris?' – 'I do not know.' – 'Please, do not burn Paris. You will be ashamed of it later . . .' The curtain rose then but I did not pay attention to the play as much as I looked at these young men, still children, who were already concerned about politics and the fate of their fatherland. It was clear how much earlier youth matured in France.

Blücher entered Nancy on 8 [20] February and was greeted by the members of the municipality and honorary citizens, who presented him with the city keys which [Blücher] immediately sent to our Emperor. We also learned that Blücher's entire Army of Silesia, having been concentrated on the road to Paris, was routed by Napoleon and that Blücher himself barely escaped French captivity; that the Prussian infantry, forming a square, had to fight its way through the enemy cavalry for some 15 verstas [16km], enduring incessant attacks . . . in six days the Army of Silesia lost some 18,000 men and 43 guns, which forced Blücher to fall back to Châlons while Napoleon turned to the main Allied army. Prince Schwarzenberg was forced to retreat to Troyes. Napoleon's rapid successes, considerable losses of the Allied armies, sicknesses that spread in the armies, devastated country that had no provisions to supply to the armies, the growing discontent of the people in the occupied regions and the corps of General Augereau, some 40,000 strong, at Lyons in our rear – all of these factors caused the Allies to offer peace terms to Napoleon. But he was so proud of his last victories that he rejected the offer with the words, 'I am closer to Vienna than to Paris.'

We expected a day of rest at Nancy but were instead ordered to advance at once to replenish losses that occurred due to Blücher's excessive haste and desire for the quick capture of Paris

On 12 [24] February we entered the city of Toul. The road occasionally would have been impassable if not for the [French] ability of raising hillocks, some as tall as 20 sazhen [40m], lined with pleasant alleyways. We encountered numerous donkeys laden with firewood, and enormous two-wheeled carts pulled by a single horse. Horses and oxen were famished all around this region. We also met numerous carts carrying the wounded from the defeated corps of the Army of Silesia. They confirmed earlier news, adding that all the generals had been captured, all the artillery had been lost and that they were retreating with just remnants of our corps. Such news obviously deprived us of any desire to march on Paris.

The city of Toul can be observed from the distance of 10 verstas [10.6km]. It is about four times smaller than Nancy and is surrounded by an earthly rampart with bastions. Given a good garrison, it could have resisted us but Napoleon left here only an invalid commandant with some 400 invalid troops, who surrendered upon the appearance of the Prussians. The fortress was garrisoned by the Spaniards who [Napoleon] had left in Nancy but they defected to our side.

I was billeted with a Royalist, or to be precise, a former grenadier of the Royal army who was discharged at the start of the Revolution. He told me detailed stories about the Revolution assuring me that it was the English who incited Prince d'Orléans* and the rabble to kill King Louis XVI and his family, hoping to exploit France's domestic turmoil to their own advantage. [The grenadier assured me that] Napoleon was mistaken in seeking to destroy Russia's power when it would have been easier to defeat the English. [He believed] that [Maximillian] Robespierre and [Honoré de] Mirabeau restored order and law which Napoleon then perfected. [He was convinced that] Napoleon's victories exalted France which was then enriched by his conquests. How saddened this veteran was to remember the gallantry and beauty of Napoleon's army on the eve of the Moscow Campaign!† His face shone when he spoke of the glorious past of the French nation which had dominated Europe for the past twenty years. The French must desire peace, he told me. Only a durable peace would revive the exhausted nation. 'Indeed,' I replied to him, 'Napoleon and his companions resemble but soap bubbles that still sparkle and float but are about to burst.'

The buildings in Toul are all old and grimy, with all shops closed. Judging from inscription on many homes, they are all for sale or rent. Streets are filled with trash and filth: untidiness seems to be a national habit [in France.] The local cathedral is noteworthy for its Gothic architecture and various stone carvings. There are very few people, but we did meet some indolent young men, who [Napoleon] should have conscripted. Judging by the large

---

* Louis Philippe Joseph, Duc d'Orléans was a member of the Orléans branch of the House of Bourbon. Influenced by the ideas of the Enlightenment, he actively supported the French Revolution, adopted the name Philippe Égalité and voted for the execution of his cousin King Louis XVI.

† The Russian Campaign of 1812.

size of individual homes and old but good furniture, we expected to find an abundance of supplies in town. But alas, only misery and scarcity greets us here. Locals resort to various means to lure a single sous from the generous pockets of Russian officers: men resorted to buffoonery while women . . . But their efforts are in vain, we are broke ourselves.

On one of the squares there was a show featuring various animals and birds. For half a franc, a beautiful, fresh, healthy-looking and young French woman explained, with her ringing voice, the names and traits of various animals. [In addition to three monkeys] she had a seal, an Alpine eagle, two eagle-owls, a rooster with horns, pheasants, bear, badger and wolf. Such is this merry family with which with this beauty freely travels even in these turbulent times and collects contributions from the conquerors of France.

[The town of Toul] also has a theatre and, judging from placards, it is playing the opera *La Fausse Magie*. But after the mirthless performance in Nancy, I have no desire to attend this show.

The village of Void [Void-Vacon] is located on the left side of the Meuse River, which is no wider than five sazhens [10m] at this location. The area is mountainous again and our quarters are paltry once more. Here I saw for the first time wooden jackboots attached to the saddle of postal courier; if a horse falls, the boots protect the rider from any harm even if he has been galloping at full speed.

The road to Ligny [Ligny-en-Barrois] is mountainous. Approaching this town, we saw vast vineyards on the slope of the mountains on our right side. Between Toul and Ligny, the soil is sandy and rocky and should not be very fertile but the local red wine is superb.

As we came from around the mountain, a pleasant view of Ligny opened to us. A river flowing through and ancient towers on battlement add rather picturesque elements to this panorama. The town gates bore inscription 'À l'Impératrice Marie Louise'. It might have been that the locals resorted to this placard in an effort to spare the town from pillaging but it was also said that the town belonged to Marshal Oudinot. The town was almost completely empty and all homes bore inscriptions 'à vendre' [for sale] and 'à louer' [for rent]; most windows had shattered glass. There was a resolute combat when Prince Sherbatov dislodged the French troops from the town. So as a precaution we were billeted two or three men per apartment. So my friend and I found ourselves assigned to the home of a ninety-year old mademoiselle* who greeted us with fear and apprehension but tried to serve us [as best as she could]. But we still did not trust this old witch.

On 15 [27] February we arrived at Saint-Dizier. The road from Ligny is a neatly-built paved road, a *chaussée*. The road, cut into the mountain slopes, surprised us with its builders' daring vision and skill of construction.

---

* Radozhitskii is using this word ironically.

Travelling along this road, our eyes feasted on many other pleasant sights that were worthy of the artist's brush.

For the third day already we encountered Prussian wagons with numerous wounded; this time [these men were coming from the battle] at Champaubert [fought on 10 February]. While we were resting, a certain person, travelling with his wife and children in a carriage from Châlons [Châlons-sur-Marne], passed by us. Upon being stopped, he produced a document, signed by Count [Alexander] Langeron, identifying him as an Englishmen. This French-Englishman told us that Châlons, where he resided, suffered greatly from the recent battle; that [the Prussian] General Yorck's attack resulted in half of the city being burned down before it surrendered; that Blücher's Army of Silesia suffered considerable losses, and that the main Allied army had retreated beyond Troyes to Chaumont. We occasionally encounter old bivouacs that suggest that we are getting closer to the front line. Rumours claim that the locals are [ambushing and] massacring the Prussians and that Blücher is shooting anyone caught with arms in hand and threatening families with exile to Siberia.

The city of Saint-Dizier is larger than Toul and stretches along the Marne. Its streets are empty and there are very few people, and even those are hiding. Inside most homes we find only women. At the apartment where I was billeted, I found three hostesses, one of whom had her husband and another her brother captured by the Russians. They fed us well but we always had misgivings that they might poison us. Local houses bear none of the signs of orderliness, cleanliness and neatness that we found in Germany. Entering the house I found three women sitting near the fireplace, with one of them reading aloud the French translation of the Russian book describing the life and exploits of Yemelyan Pugachev. For me, it was both startling and gratifying to see them doing this. I guessed that they wanted to read something to get a better idea about the Russians, whom locals are now beginning to perceive differently from what they had been told by their compatriots . . . It is said that we were surrounded by the French guerrillas so we remained constantly on guard: six of our cannon, protected by the Polotskii [Infantry] Regiment, advanced at the head; all transports moved in the middle column together with the Ryazanskii [Infantry] Regiment while another six of our guns, supported by the 33rd Jagers, stayed in the back awaiting our reserve parc.

The road to Vitry [Vitry-le-François] reminded us of Saxony in the environs of Leipzig: vast open plains dotted with groves of trees and white houses or picturesque estates. Between Ligny and Saint-Dizier, [there are] mountains, forests, sands, rocks and numerous vineyards but here we see vast grain fields grainfields and little water. On the approaches to Vitry we encountered devastated villages, empty homes without doors, windows shattered and property broken and scattered all around. The locals were all hiding in the woods and occasionally appeared in groups some distance from the road.

The ancient Gothic church of the Holy Mother adds much grandeur to the city of Vitry, which is surrounded by an earthen rampart. A Prussian garrison some 3,000 men strong is stationed here . . . The city's vast main square is filled with Prussian transports. There are numerous residents. These are local villagers who have been gathered to repair fortifications because a military depot and supply magazines have been established in the city. The city has very decent buildings.

During the night the French guerrillas roamed around the fortress intending to get inside like wolves into a sheepfold. Our one half-company was deployed outside the fortress under protection of jagers while another was with the [reserve] parc and had not arrived yet.

I got such an excellent apartment that I have never seen before: two rooms with Chinese wallpapers and opulent furniture; a spacious bed with purple canopy, antique bronze clock on a table, a fireplace with a mirror and large Venetian windows leading out into a garden. The sun shines into my rooms all day long. At lunch, I am served three excellent dishes and a bottle of superb wine. My host is a respected member of the municipal authority, whom I rarely see and, except for occasional greetings, have had no conversation as of yet. For the first time I am experiencing the pleasure of domestic life and possessions. I caught myself thinking, 'Will I ever own an apartment like that, filled with possessions chosen to my taste. If only . . . How far I am from this moment! First I must learn how to earn, then how to preserve and finally how to manage and enjoy things. It is rather pleasurable to live in an environment where our every wish is anticipated and fulfilled, where our self-esteem is constantly flattered. It is a very gratifying experience! But how long will it last? Maybe tomorrow I will be forced to sleep in rain, wind, and mud, and gnaw a coarse biscuit soaked in a dirty puddle of water! The lot of a military man is that of being patient as he struggles with every passion and experience, be it hardship and pleasure, grief and delight, a perpetual fusion of good and bad. Fortunate is he who amidst this chaos endures all these trials and emerges with unblemished heart!' Such were my thoughts as I lay on a beautiful double bed, wrapped in a satin blanket and head resting on a round satin pillow with large tassels. But the other half of my bed was vacant – I stared at it saddened, feeling emptiness in one-half of my heart.

Count St. Priest has been ordered to take command of another 10,000 Prussians who are marching behind us. Together we will comprise a corps of some 14,000 men. He is supposed to unite this entire mass of men and advance to Reims.

During our day of rest, in the morning, I took a stroll through the town and across the Marne. The beautiful stone bridge has been destroyed by an explosion that collapsed its middle arch. So a parapet was built here and a Prussian howitzer deployed on the main road behind it. Beyond the bridge there was a paved road lined with poplar trees. The road was covered with trees – about an arshin [71 cm] wide and three sazhens [6m] in circumference, with deep furrows carved by their age – that have been tumbled like proud giants who have been conquered by a mightier hand. The French axemen, acting very indifferently, were busy cutting them down and shaping poles. 'What are you doing?' I asked them, hoping to see some anguish on their faces. 'Palisades,' they coldly replied.

Upon hearing bells tolling, I rushed to the magnificent Cathedral of Notre Dame, which looked imposing on the outside. As I entered, I saw a sentry standing at the door while the entire vastness of this building was filled with straw and hay. 'What is this?' I inquired. 'A supply store!' the soldier replied . . . I pitied these immoral Frenchmen. Will we continue to emulate these charming buffoons, these courteous and polite flatterers, who, anticipating our words and thoughts, shower us with the most obsequious greetings while sharpening their daggers so at the first opportunity they can strike them straight into our hearts still bearing that same gentle smile?

Leaving the church, I went to the square. A battalion of [the Ryazanskii?] Regiment was conducting a parade or drill in a narrow space that was left in between transports. Idle Frenchmen and Prussians came from various directions to gawk at the cleanliness and beauty of the uniforms, appearance and gallantry of the Russian soldiers. The grenadier platoon was fit to be in the Guard: its men were cheerful, young and healthy . . .

A local prison houses six French villagers who had mistreated our couriers and stragglers. The order has been given to shoot them.

On 18 February [2 March] we arrived at Châlons. Once again we are in a major provincial town of the Champagne-Pouilleuse region that is so famous for its sparkling wine; yet, some people say that the best wine is actually produced in Provence. This city has once been a fortress, which can be still seen in surviving stone walls and towers. From Virty to Châlons we saw the signs of terrifying devastation everywhere. Crowds of unfortunate locals wandered in the woods or hid amidst the ruins. At the entrance to Châlons, the entire suburb had been destroyed and presented the view of homes without roofs, with straw, rags, burned timber, shattered glass, bricks and ashes scattered all around. The city walls are shattered in places and palisades are erected in front of the city gates. [Marshal] Macdonald wanted to defend this city but the Prussians, led by General Yorck, began to set the city on fire with their shells and the city residents begged Macdonald to surrender the city on condition that it would be spared. Nevertheless, the Prussians rushed in and plundered it. The residents are very poor and walk fearfully amidst the ruins, crying bitterly as they can no longer recognise their homes . . . What a miserable fate this war cast on them!

Inside the fortress walls, the city is quite large and ancient so some of the buildings appear to be on the verge of collapsing while streets are uneven and crooked. The main square houses a vast, magnificent building where municipal and departmental government as well as authorities handling military affairs reside. Four stone lions stand at the entrance to a spacious staircase . . . [while]

portraits of distinguished men, who had been born in Châlons, hang at the entrance into a large hall. Numerous rooms are filled with writing desks . . . [and] crowds of people are going back and forth everywhere . . . The best of these rooms are decorated with magnificent paintings . . . [which] are true sustenance for my eyes who have longed for it for such a long time.

Soldiers were bivouacked near the empty church in the suburbs. What a sight it was! The former place of worship now had in front of its entrance fires burning and kettles cooking meat; nearby were stored muskets while the tired soldiers were sleeping next to the church wall. Not far from them were others, with pipes in their mouth and airing their shirts over the fire or warming their backs. What a sight! How cruel a war can be!

Upon reaching the apartment I had been assigned, I found one grief-stricken monsieur and several mademoiselles and madames sitting around a large table. Glancing at my billet, an old lady quickly stood up and led me to the second floor, where I found a large apartment with many beds. 'Why are there so many beds?' I thought to myself as I came down to the ground floor. After lunch one of the ladies asked me, 'Will there be many officers in town today?' – 'You will see them yourself when you will witness the arrival of four thousand of our men.' – 'Oh, you will have a splendid spectacle then.' – 'What is it?' I inquired. 'This madame is theatre director,' responded another woman. 'and she wants to stage an opera to entertain Russian officers.' 'Oh, I see,' I replied, realising the nature of the company that I found myself in. 'So how many officers do you think will come to the theatre?' asked me against the theatre director. 'What difference does it make,' interjected monsieur. 'Just stage a cheerful opera and do not overcharge for it,' was my response as I left the room. When I came back, the hostess introduced me to a woman who had lived in Russia for fifteen years and had the honour of entertaining St. Petersburg high society in the French theatre. This lady showered me with questions about Russia but I excused myself on the grounds of fatigues and promised to talk to her after the dinner.

Tonight I had the pleasure of seeing all these individuals in their miserable theatre. There were just four musicians and about twenty in audience, with me sitting in the front row. Both plays – first *L'épreuve villageoise*, followed by *La famille d'innocens* – were poorly performed. The music was dreadful. Two actresses and one actor sang quite well, but the other roared with his hoarse bass voice. I did not expect to find such [a poor] theatre at Châlons. But it should have been expected. The French have no time for entertainment – whoever is the best, most cheerful and lively is carrying a musket in Napoleon's army.

[. . .]

[After several days spent in Châlons] we received the news that the French troops, assisted by locals, captured our Prince N. with 380 Bashkirs and 150 jagers in the town of Reims. So our corps' advance guard, consisting of the

Polotskii [Infantry] Regiment, four cannon and two squadrons of dragoons, under the command of General Emmanuel, departed to Reims . . . So farewell to pleasures, warm apartments, soft beds and delicious dishes! Good-bye beautiful women! It is time for us to return to the fields and smoky bivouacs, and perform a different kind of plays that are observed by the entire world!

And so, fires are burning, a martial spirit animates the troops amidst the ruins of devastated homes. A wild delight enlivens men around bonfires and kettles with boiling porridge. With pipes in hand, we warm ourselves near fireplaces inside burned out homes . . . Everything is permeated with war, a disastrous war! [From the Russian text in I. Radozhitskii, *Pokhodnye zapiski* . . .]

Eduard von Löwenstern

Just twenty-four years old but already a veteran of several campaigns, Löwenstern served in the Sumskii Hussar Regiment that was attached to the 1st Hussar Division commanded by Lieutenant-General Peter von Pahlen III in Wittgenstein's Russian 6th Corps. He distinguished himself on a number of occasions during the 1813 Campaign and looked forward to ending the war in Paris. But first the Rhine had to be crossed . . .

Prince Eugene of Württemberg with the 4th Division was designated to direct the crossing of the Rhine. During the night of 21 December, the [Russian] 4th Jager Regiment was to take possession of the island and Fort Louis after which the pontoon bridge could be erected. We bivouacked close to the Rhine. Count Wittgenstein, General d'Auvray, [and] Colonel Teslev spent the night in our Hussar bivouac. The night was stormy and dark; no fire dared be started; and the greatest stillness was ordered. At midnight Colonel Lützow with six companies of the [Russian] 4th Jager Regiment embarked. The Rhine was filled with ice.

Several times a strong cold wind pushed our boats back to the shore and drove them downstream. We soon lost Lützow from sight through the diligent work of the rowers and infantrymen. We waited most restlessly – everything was quiet. Only the storm was roaring, and the Rhine was driving high masses of ice with tremendous force. Tiesenhausen, who commanded his own boat, was grounded on the island; and Lützow returned after having fought in vain against wind and weather without knowing on which shore of the Rhine he found himself. At daybreak the Kremenchugskii and the 4th Jager Regiment were sent ahead again. The enemy sharpshooters pulled back from our effective fire and left the island and Fort Louis. Austrian pontonniers had finished building a bridge by midday. Our losses consisted of five dead and ten wounded. Our Cossacks immediately crossed and patrolled the roads from Strassburg to Haguenau. On 22 December, we crossed the wide old Rhine on a pontoon bridge at Fort Louis. This fort had been destroyed by the Austrians in 1794. Fort Alsace lying on the other side forms a bridgehead. I had the misfortune that my horse shied at the shaking of the bridge and fell into the water without however getting very wet, since it was very close to shore; and I fell on the piled-up ice. My comrades took this to be an evil omen. François, a lieutenant of the Sumskii [Hussar] Regiment, fell into the middle of the Rhine and was only saved with difficulty. If I am not mistaken, his horse drowned. Count Wittgenstein accompanied the cavalry himself; and after the end of a church service and singing Te Deum in Fort Alsace, we marched farther onto French soil.

In Richeveau (Roschwoog), we halted, distributed proclamations in order somewhat to calm the peasants, who met us with pale faces stamped with fear and terror. In Richeveau, we drank properly and everyone was happy to be in France. Two regiments of the Badenese light cavalry joined us here. In Sufflenheim we spent the night at a droll pastor's.

The next morning we reached Haguenau. I was sent to the post office to take control of it. We ruthlessly burned whole packets of letters, since it was much too difficult for us to look at each one individually. We stayed in the city. I lived at the *Poste des chevaux*. The depot of the [French] 18th and 23rd Dragoon Regiment was systematically plundered. Even I totally re-equipped my people. We enjoyed living in Haguenau. Whatever we wanted had to happen and to be given to us. The citizens of Haguenau, who were not secure from plundering for a moment, did their best to satisfy us. The actors here were forced into the theatre and had to play every evening. We did not spare the wine at all. The best always had to be offered, and we enjoyed it in great quantities. From Haguenau we made a forced march to Saverne (Zabern). It was unexpectedly severely cold.

In Saverne, Pahlen stayed at the post and I and Kolachevskii at an inn. We dined at a count's where three or four pretty French girls waited on us. Life was lively here. I, with a lieutenant and the 25th Jagers, was ordered to patrol as far as Baccarat; and, if possible, to find the Austrian partisan Count Mensdorff. At the same time, I was to keep an eye on [the road from] Metz to Pfalzburg, in short, to acquire as much information as I could. Since Fort Pfalzburg was strongly garrisoned, I had to go around it carefully in order not to be seen. In the dark of the night, I mounted with my Uhlans. I went along the *chaussée* as far as the hunting lodge then to the right toward the Eschburg sawmill, where a French patrol had been a few moments before. From here I went by way of Craufthal, Berlingen, Wilsberg; and at Mittelbronn, I came out on the *chaussée* again.

In Mittelbronn, I found a squadron of Olviopolskii Hussars, who were observing the fortification from here. I rested here for half an hour and hurried to reach Saarburg before daybreak. An hour after my departure, the Pfalzburg garrison used the cover of night to attack the squadron, cut down several Hussars, taking six prisoners, and drove all of the livestock into the fort. After listening to several peasants, I expected to find French in Saarburg. I approached the city with the greatest of care. When I spoke French and acted like a French patrol, they opened the gate for me. I left a lieutenant and six men behind to secure a retreat and dashed with readied lances straight to the municipality. I jumped through the window without making any noise in case any soldiers were present, to take them prisoner, but the birds had already flown the nest two hours before my arrival, Dragoons of the [French] 18th Regiment, about 300 men who had headed the direction of Metz.

Taken as a whole, it was a great coup for me to go into a city with twenty-five men, where 300 dragoons, if I had found them, could have overpowered me with the greatest of ease. I depended upon the darkness of the night, on the bravery of my Uhlans and on the swiftness of our horses. I would have certainly quickly taken several prisoners and what a triumph for me to be able to send them to the Count in the first night. I found the whole council with their red sashes assembled. The general shock was not small when they saw me come in covered with ice and snow with a loaded pistol and drawn sabre in my hand. Since I could not take any prisoners, I announced immediately a contribution of boots, horseshoes, oats, bread, and brandy. After having secured myself against any attack, I drank a cup of good coffee with rum and warmed my frozen limbs. Before sunrise I left Saarburg and went to Heming. The post master treated me with red champagne which I drank for the first time. My Uhlans imbibed so highly here that their officer and almost all of the men were drunk. Thus, I was forced to stay in Heming until evening. In the night I continued toward Blamont. An hour later an Olviopolskii Hussar came riding up with an order for me not to go to Baccarat but to go again to Saverne. I passed through Saarburg the same night. The *maire* [mayor] seeing me retreating no longer crept around like a worm but rather carried his nose much higher. Instead of coffee, they gave me brandy. Cursing, a mob surrounded my little troop and accompanied us out the gate with snowballs. It was a dark stormy night. The snowy cold and the deep snow made marching difficult. On the advice of a Hussar, I did not go around Plalzburg by way of the Eschburg sawmill occupied by enemy cavalry but headed to the left into the Vosges.

But here I was in trouble. I lost my way in the mountains and continued on without a road and path until finally no one knew where we were. My guide [*sic*] broke down from exhaustion. As long as I can remember, I have never had a more horrible night than this one. We all almost froze from the cold, and sometimes we had to slide with our horses down a cliff. The snow was slippery as ice and frozen hard. You were afraid with every step to plunge into the abyss. Only one of the uhlans' horses broke its neck during this expedition, but this otherwise misfortune was our rescue. The horse rolled into the valley and the uhlan, who had followed it and was unfastening the clock-bag, discovered a rather frozen path. With strong ropes we had made from forage cords, we lowered the other horses down and seated slid down ourselves. Here an uhlan, wanting to stop, grabbed a branch and sprained his arm. Finally arriving in the valley, we followed the path and at about ten in the morning we reached a village. Four Uhlans had frozen feet, one a sprained arm, and a horse a broken neck. I immediately had the frostbitten limbs of my people rubbed with snow and after acquiring a guide [sic], rode by way of Quatrevent to Saverne, where I arrived in the afternoon with my extremely fatigued men. Thus, ingloriously ended my expedition I had assumed and hoped to gather laurels from.

In Saverne I found everything prepared to bombard Pfalzburg. The sandbags to protect our batteries had been filled in the night, and Prince Eugene of Württemberg's infantry joined us. Pfalzburg is a regular hexagon with only two gates, one toward Saverne and the other toward Saarburg. The city consists of about three hundred houses of which the barracks, a hospital, and a depot protruded high above the ramparts. The garrison consisted of eight hundred men from the [French] 6th Light Infantry, and the 138th and 142nd Line Regiments. At the most there was one cavalry squadron in there. The commander however had forced the inhabitants to take up weapons and by turns to serve with the garrison. At morning twilight our batteries began to play. The fort did not waste a moment to answer. Since we had no siege protection but only fired from open fields, we could not do damage to the fortification. Count Pahlen wanted to frighten the fort by setting it on fire, but, as mentioned, we did not succeed. In the evening we bivouacked in Quatrevent. After we had been relieved by Prince Eugene in Saverne, we marched to Saarburg. Here the order was given that all of the houses had to be illuminated through the night.

In Heming I had the bad luck of forgetting my sabre that I only got back by chance in Blamont. In Blamont, I billeted quite badly at a schoolmaster's, who let me make a bed on a long school table next to his desk. Fortunately, a day of rest was in Luneville. My landlord, a rich Jew, did not spare on wine; and in the evening there was dancing at his place. My Jew was all for Napoleon and was immensely happy that I also did this man justice. I visited the palace of the honourable King of Poland, Stanislaus Leszcznski, who was living here in exile. Now the city had barracks for two regiments of *Grenadiers à Cheval*. A large number of our prisoners of war had been in Luneville. In Luneville we took the post and rode in a large four-seated carriage by way of St. Nicolas to Nancy. At noon we dined in *Petit Paris* [Little Paris] and left again that night. Budberg and Babst in one and I and Turnau in the other carriage. In Flavigny we crossed the Moselle and had the pleasure of seeing Budberg rolled over and over. Since no one was hurt, we did not lose our good humour and travelled on laughing, joking and drinking. In Bezelise we found the Count. I lived in the same house as the Count. Since they had already eaten supper, I had a good-tasting supper made at Budberg's. Pahlen's landlord, Monsieur

Oliver [Olivier?] entertained us with his good mood and funny songs that he, gesticulating, sang during the meal. He was a true Frenchman from the time of Louis XV. In Colombey-aux-Belles-Femmes, we requisitioned several two-wheeled carts. In the night in these comfortable conveyances, we reached miserable Maxey. Smoky steamy peasant huts were our quarters. My landlord, a miserable peasant in a blue shirt and wooden shoes, first beat his wife, then his sister during the whole night. I was forced, since seeing this fellow, to think of the frightening days of the Revolution. To fall into the hands of such a vandal was certain death.

He swore and cursed us, wished the entire Russian Army would go to hell; and since I wanted the damned devil to be reasonable, he acted insane, defied me, and used a lot of swearwords and curses I had never heard before in my life. Then I and Kolachevski and everyone took a broomstick and beat the fellow until the call to mount was blown. While we were beating him, his wife and sister sat quietly at the fireplace as if nothing were happening in the room. In Gondrecourt we ate our noon meal, went by way of St. Remy [Domrémy], the birth place of the Maid of Orleans; and at Donjeux we crossed the [Marne]. In St Remy the preacher's housekeeper gave me a pair of warm gloves. The cold, wet weather made it very difficult for us. We comforted ourselves with the hope of a marvellous coming spring and drank the best wine. We spent a day in Sery-le-Château [Cirey-sur-Blaise]. We all found Voltaire's twelve-year stay there curious.* We were shown the apartments in which this famous man had lived, his study and several little things that had belonged to him, and which were being preserved by the present owners in memory of him. The Palace of Sery-le-Château is large and has an extensive park. The members of our Regiment went by way of Doulevent. Along the way, I stayed behind to have my horse shod and arrived in Eclan [Eclaron?], where I found the entire main headquarters already dining. The owner, Monsieur Nojean, accommodated us very well. At ten o'clock in the morning, we came to Brienne. All of Europe knows this place which, though small and unassuming, has become notable because of the military school there at which Napoleon was educated. We found Brienne full of cavalry commanded by Vasilchikov and General Sacken's corps. Thus, the peaceful days were over. The enemy was very near, and at any moment the dance of death could begin anew. In the vicinity of the enemy, the inseparable companions of war returned: hunger, thirst, arduousness, exhaustion, and bivouacs. Yesterday we were indulging ourselves at Mr. Nojean's well-set table, and today we were grabbing at half-cooked potatoes; instead of champagne, we were drinking brandy.

The Saxon Army had totally ruined and commandeered Brienne. Pahlen's advance-guard was to go to Larzicourt. Through the stupidity of

---

* Voltaire lived there with his mistress the Marquise du Châtelet from 1734 to 1748.

our leader or rather through Lützow's carelessness, we missed the nearby road and made a detour by way of Lemont. We arrived late in the night in Larzicourt. Here everything was lying topsy-turvy and we were left with the sweepings. Anyone with nothing along to eat had to go hungry; and since that was my case, I wrapped myself in my coat and slept. Lanskoi with the Belorussian Hussar Regiment had come upon the enemy and been beaten. Napoleon himself with a large army was only four miles from us. Everyone was expecting a bloody battle.

Three muffled signal shots from the Brienne palace, where old Field-Marshal Blücher himself was, gave the sign to mount. Quick! A schnapps and to horse! Our patrol came upon the French on the road to Paris. I was sent to Lemont to deliver several dispatches to General Sacken and to inform him orally he dare not lose a moment in uniting with Blücher in Brienne. Immediately after my arrival, Sacken's Corps began to move. Pahlen had ordered me to be careful and not to ride the same way back but to look for him by way of Brienne. But the egg wanted to be cleverer than the hen. I took my chances; and since I heard a heavy cannonade, I did not want to miss the battle through a long detour and rode straight toward Larzicourt. How great was my surprise to be chased by six or seven *Chasseurs à Cheval,* who cut off the way to Lemont and were breathing down my neck. Without losing my nerve, I rode straight at them; shot at them with both pistols, and escaped by way of a path across a field to the road where I found General Ushakov with the Courland Dragoons.

In Brienne I met Budberg, who had been sent by Blücher. I found Count Pahlen under the strongest fire not far from the city on the heights of Perthes. The bottomless mire made a cavalry attack hardly possible. Nevertheless, our Chuguevskii Uhlans undertook several marvellous attacks, defeated the enemy, and captured four of his cannon. The cannonballs could not ricochet but instead dug into the earth. Only toward evening were we forced back toward the city, and now a lively infantry fire started to capture it. The enemy continually attacked us and bombarded Brienne with grenades and fireballs. These lit fires and part of the city burned down. The [Russian] 4th and 34th Light Infantry Regiments drove the enemy out of the city again and captured two cannon that the French had just captured from Olsufiev's Corps. Here the Sumskii Cornet Keyserling was ripped through the middle by a cannonball. We kept possession of the city that had been defended with so much blood. Pahlen rode around Brienne. The mud in the vineyards was horrible. Men and horses sank up to their necks as soon as they came a foot off of the narrow path and suffocated without rescue in the quagmire. Several of our people and especially many horses suffered this fate. The cannonballs also followed us here. Fortunately, the enemy infantry had not yet occupied the vineyards; otherwise we would have been lost. In the Palace of Brienne that we skirted from the garden side, our infantrymen did battle. The nest was stormed and taken again. In the saloons, the rooms, in the cellar, on the staircase, they fought everywhere exceedingly bitterly. Nevertheless, in the night our infantrymen had to leave the battlefield which the French immediately occupied.

Brienne burned like a torch. Many wounded suffocated in the houses and streets. Suite Colonel Count Rochechouart was thrown from his horse in the crowd and immediately suffocated in the muddy slop. Everyone scrabbled in the terrible muddy clay. The horses sank to over their knees, and only with the greatest difficulty could you work yourself out of the morass in which your horse stood half sunken. Even though we, it seems to me, had not won the battle, we did however capture several cannon and did retain the city. A French woman whom an infantry officer had married in Saverne accompanied the battle on horseback and showed extraordinary courage.

In Brienne-la-Ville we bivouacked. Everyone was so tired that no one thought of eating, even though we had fasted the whole day. Count Pahlen took over the command of the entire cavalry; and with the break of the next day, a most orderly retreat began, squadron after squadron as on the parade ground. The morass was so great that the enemy could not try anything. Nevertheless, the cannonade continued the whole day but without causing us any substantial damage. Prisoners told us that Emperor Napoleon with part of his Guard had been present at yesterday's battle. Toward noon the major part of the enemy cavalry gathered behind Brienne-le-Château. The enemy showed about sixteen cannon which followed us on the *chaussée*. The infantry went in dense columns. Count Pahlen had Vasilchikov's cavalry to the right and his own to the left of the *chaussée*. Since we lacked ammunition, we could only use seven cannon. Toward evening an Austrian general through his own carelessness came in danger of being captured. He was trotting accompanied by light cavalry along the *chaussée* straight at the enemy's advance-guard posts. Tiesenhausen pulled him back before he was lost. To all of our delight, the general thought his rescuer was a Bashkir. Imagine Tiesenhausen in costume. We bivouacked in Trannes. Our field police officer brought us a transport of champagne and provisions into camp. Once again after a long time, we could eat and drink a lot. On 19 January, we came to Eclans. Monsieur Nojean had fled and his pretty palace had been completely plundered. In Poulaines we wanted to bivouac, but the enemy did not seem willing to let us have the village. Cannon were fired and sharpshooters fired shots. We simply left the French in Poulaines and retreated back to Fuligny to bivouac. Just before our arrival, the owner of Fuligny must have still been in the palace, judging by the ladies' work standing and lying about on stretchers and an embroidery bag; but the amicable workers had disappeared.

Since all had fled, we of course played master of the house. Above all, the cellar was confiscated and found in splendid condition. The most beautiful *vin de comête** flowed in streams. Count Keller and Budberg found a large box of *Eau de Cologne de la premiére qualité.* Several French dragoons deserted to us in the night. Even though there was no lack of nice mattresses in the palace in Fuligny, and we found a quantity of silk blankets, Kovterov and Tiesenhausen got in a fight because of a pillow that ended with a formal duel in a room. The combative parties stood in their shirts with drawn sabres and hit pluckily at each other. The other ones of us threw pillows, blankets, and undergarments between the fighters. The *vacarme* [din] was without bounds and the scene was to die laughing. With immeasurable effort, we got the overheated heads apart. Here General Rudiger with his Grodnenskii Hussars and three Sumskii Squadrons, a regiment of light infantry and four cannon joined us. The day was still, foggy, and with snow flurries. We heard cannon fire in the vicinity of Brienne. In Chavange, Babst saved a pretty Spanish woman from plundering. We assumed we would be attacked here, but the French let us be. Here Pahlen also received the news about the victory won yesterday at Brienne. The Count marched by way of St. Quen, Azilliers to Lhuitre, where he stayed at a country preacher's. The sour, dissatisfied face of this man of God and the bad treatment he gave us earned him, after Pahlen had left the house, a good flogging which I and Turnau could not keep ourselves from giving him to pay him back in full.

Count Pahlen received the order to go to Plancy. The enemy had occupied Arcis-sur-Aube and burned the bridge over the Aube. Shots were fired from both shores. We fired several grenades into the city and further along the Aube after the Cossacks had been left behind. We found all of the bridges at Grand- and Petit-Viapre and Plancy destroyed. The enemy occupied the places where the bridges had been. We arrived in Plancy early in the morning. We were supposed to spend several days here. My quarters were on the market in an inn. At four in the afternoon, instead of the expected peace and quiet, alarm. Babst had taken his boots to be repaired and ran barefoot around the city. I do not know how he helped himself afterwards. He probably took the boots from the next infantryman he found. After the soldiers wantonly set the bivouacs at Plancy and Grande-Viapre on fire, we arrived in the night at Arcis. In the same night, the bridge was finished and we went to Charmont. It was bitter cold, snowing, and raining when we arrived. Ilovaiski XII with his Cossacks was here. We drove them from the palace and lay down in their warm beds.

---

* *Vin de la comête* or 'comet vintages' refers to a practice by winemakers to attribute successful vintages to the unexplained effects caused by comet. In 1811, Europeans saw a bright shining object in the sky, named the Flaugergues comet after Honoré Flaugergues who first spotted the comet in March. The comet was visible for most of the year and, in some people's minds, foretold Napoleon's defeat in Russia. But for the winegrowers, it brought good weather and excellent growing conditions, which produced a bountiful harvest. For the rest of the nineteenth century, the 1811 vintage was considered among the best and was highly sought-after.

It rained continuously the whole night and the following day. Soaked to the bone and freezing, we came to Droupt-St.-Bale in the darkness. Every bivouac means the ruin of the nearby village. May God have mercy upon the unlucky place in which soldiers arrive in the night in a rainstorm. They all pour into the village to get in a dry place as soon as possible; and then there is no discipline; no power capable of protecting that village from plundering. This unfortunate fate also befell Droupt-St. Bale.

We billeted in the palace and found the master of the house and his whole family there. All of them were filled with fear and anxiety. Most of the servants had hidden. Only the owner and his young wife did their best to satisfy us. Large fires were built in all of the fireplaces to dry out their wet guests. The beautiful furniture was covered with dripping coats and uniforms. At the meal the owner stood up to drink to the Emperor's health, slipped, and fell together with the bottle under the table. With difficulty, we pulled him out again together with the bottle into the daylight, and our wild youth was indiscreet enough to laugh loudly and to make the poor devil look ridiculous. As for me, I had boundless pity for the unfortunate family who, without support in the middle of a battlefield of the war, were being subjected to all kinds of unpleasantness. Count Pahlen left an ordnance officer with them for protection when we marched out.

Méry-sur-Seine was occupied by enemy infantry who had barricaded the streets. Our advance-guard advanced toward Méry and attacked them from two sides. The enemy left this side of the city after some resistance, crossed a stone bridge, and broke it up after them. On the other side of the Seine, houses were occupied by French sharpshooters who defended the destroyed bridge and maintained brisk gunfire throughout the whole day. This gunfire cost both sides a lot of people whose dead bodies filled the houses. In Méry, I finally received the Vladimir Order for the action of August 10 to September 16. In the night the enemy also left the part of Méry on the left side of the Seine. We immediately occupied it with infantry and sent our Cossacks in pursuit. The French knew how to plunder as well as we and had totally looted this little part of the city. The destroyed Seine bridge was rebuilt and also finished toward evening. Pahlen had a bridge built at Baudemont from pieced-together boats. We spent the night in Mazieres-la-Grand-Paroisse. In the Pontle-Château Palace of Madame Latitia, Napoleon's mother, a Hungarian Sauve [Honour] Guard was stationed that however could not prevent plundering. Count Pahlen had his infantry occupy the Etoile Forest. At La Chapelle there was a fierce infantry battle. The garden, the beautiful palace, and the shore of the Ardusson were an ideal place to view the area of the tumult covered with dead and wounded. Toward evening, the palace that had been doggedly defended was taken, and the French retreated to Nogent-sur-Seine. That beautiful Palace of La Chapelle was in a lamentable condition. The mirrors, furniture, *tableaux* [pictures], library, household instruments, busts;

everything had been smashed and shot to pieces. Unfortunately, the soldiers found syrup on the third floor. Since the barrels were smashed, the whole house was swimming in this sticky stuff. General Dechterev smashed with his own hand a bust of Voltaire, thinking that it was a French marshal. Count Pahlen with his advance-guard pushed to Nogent. The [Russian] 25th Jager and the Reval Infantry Regiment now began a dogged street battle, in which they successfully stormed the first barricade. Toward evening, the Austrian General Hardegg joined us. Reinforced by them, after the shedding of much blood, we also captured the 2nd Barricade, but the inner city, the church, etc. stayed in French hands. Here I saw young Fock von Saggad XIV lying in his own blood. The terrible butchery continued in the city until nightfall.

We lost an incredible number of men and also brave Colonel Vitoshkin of the 25th Jager Regiment. Nogent was on fire in several places. Here we received the unpleasant news that General Olsufiev together with his corps had been taken prisoner at Champaubert. Our infantry fought the whole day in the narrow streets of the city. Shots came from all the windows, the doors, from every corner. Every step, every house had to be taken by fighting. The enemy left the city in the night and blew the stone bridge into the air. Pahlen lived at the mayor's house. It was still dangerous to go out into the streets, since the enemy continued non-stop firing into the city from the other shore. Here I took a sabre blow on the right hand. Even though the wound was not very serious, it caused me immeasurable pain; also the wound healed slowly. Turnau and Kavterev got in a fight about a trifle and duelled. I was both of their seconds. A head wound that the latter took ended the dispute. In Nogent we found a quantity of the most beautiful wines: Madeira, Spanish, and French wines, Champagne *à la comête*. The common soldiers drank as much as they wanted. The common red country wine was given no notice at all, and the Hussars called it crown wine. After the plundering had continued long enough, the Count quieted things down again. Since the bridge at Nogent could not immediately be repaired, we went by way of La Chapelle to Pont-sur-Seine where we crossed the Seine on pontoons.

Not far from the little town of Villenauxe, we came upon the enemy. We took several hundred men and several officers prisoner. In St. Martin-le-Chenestron, we spent the whole night in touch with the enemy. Before daybreak we were again marching by way of Villenauxe to Fontaine-Bethon. All of the peasants had fled, but we found forage and supplies in excess. I billeted in a confectioner's shop that was well filled and instantly emptied by our officers. We only left several hundred packets of powdered [flour] untouched. We followed the retreating enemy by way of Villenauxe, St. Martin-le-Chenestron to Provins. At the bivouac in Villenauxe when I was busy building a bonfire of grape stocks, I was promoted to Captain of Cavalry for the battle at Leipzig. As a result, I had served as Staff Captain of Cavalry for one year, two months and twenty-one days.

Provins is a respectable city that I found uncommonly pleasant because of its cleanliness and pleasant location. By happy accidents, it had been almost untouched by plundering for the whole war, with the exception of a few excesses that could not be prevented as a result of the war. We stayed here for several hours and went to Maison-Rouge, where the Count stayed at a German woman's. My landlord, an old peasant, was in the best of moods. He was little bothered by the war around him. He told me: 'Go to the devil! What does your war concern me. I own nothing and therefore have nothing to lose. An old devil like I am wins some, and this war amuses me. First I see the French, then the Germans, then you funny people with your beards and sabres.'

Basically, the old fellow was right, because where there was nothing to be taken, as a rule, our people did not plunder. We passed through Nangis before sunrise and toward evening we came to Mormant, nine hours from Paris. The Grodnenskii, Sumskii Hussar and Rebrikov Cossack Regiments skirmished the whole day with the enemy cavalry on the road to Chalmes, the Chuguevskii Uhlans and Ilovaiski Cossacks on the road to Guignes. At the post in Mormant, I remounted my people on fresh horses.

The enemy advanced in the darkness in order to conquer Mormant, were however emphatically greeted with cartouches [canister] and thrown back. Count Pahlen inspected the advance-guard posts; and through deserters, we learned that Napoleon himself had been opposite us and had his main headquarters in Guignes. The infantry and supply train were prepared in the night to go back to Nangis. My old landlord prophesised misfortune for us. 'Either,' he told me, 'you will be dead tomorrow or prisoners.' Just before sunrise we began to retreat after enemy sharpshooters had pressed us heavily in the village. Markov answered the enemy artillery shot for shot as long as our flanking cavalry retreated squadron by squadron. The enemy cannonballs did us little damage. We had been retreating in this way for about an hour and a half; and it was all we could do to hold up the advancing enemy, when all at once the earth seemed to open up to spew out death and destruction from all sides. The enemy trumpeter blew to attack from all sides. And innumerable cavalry had been deployed in the lowlands and galloped at full speed toward us. Anyone offering resistance was cut down and our unimportant group immediately defeated. The French surrounded us from both sides *en carrier* [like a horserace]. Panic and fear spread. From this point, everyone only thought of himself and sought to save his life. Many pushed to the *chaussée* which soon was blocked by dismounted cannon. Colonel Markov and Rosen remained brave and defended their cannon.

The horrible horde pushed continually forwards after most of the artillerists had been cut down. The cannon were lost one by one. Soon also our Infantry Division under Helfreich was overrun. They were immediately encircled, penetrated, and captured, only General Helfreich and Fock, his Adjutant, escaped . . . Anyone who could not ride and stayed unnecessarily or fell was lost. I pressed both of my spurs into Tscherkesse's flanks and raced however I could. Everyone screamed 'Halt! Halt!' And everyone ran. To lighten their load, the Cossacks threw away their baggage. Not too far from Nangis, we ran into a squadron of Schwarzenberg Uhlans and Zeckler and Grand Duke Ferdinand Hussars [Austrians]. They were immediately attacked and badly cut up. Here and there several brave ones regrouped, what did it help? It was as if a child wanted to stop the wheels of a mill with his hands! They were ripped away in the whirlpool. You have to participate in such a melee to form a true picture of it. A daring jump over the wide ditch of the *chaussée* saved me from a sabre blow. Count Pahlen had sent me back to a Sumskii squadron; and through this stay, I came into the greatest of danger. Surrounded by enemy dragoons, surrounded and threatened from all sides, I sprang like a hare and escaped. Now the supply train, reserve and pack horses, and sutlers were overtaken. Now the slaughter really began. Each blocked the other's way and prevented him from running.

I also saw my second horse and people in the melee. I saw Kolachevskii happily escape into the vineyards. My path had already been cut off. It was high time to cry '*Pardon*'. I stopped my horse and was about to dismount submissively when next to me an Austrian woman whose hand had been severed pleaded for sympathy. The horrible faces of the dragoon with plumes of horsehair wildly hanging around and the poised broadsword of another dragoon who did not look like a *pardon*, scared me so that I, hitting my horse with both spurs, jumped over a low wall and escaped into the vineyards. My Tscherkesse had lost all four of his horseshoes through the nonsensical racing on the frozen earth and limped after the *salto mortale* over the wall. On the other side of the vineyards, I saw several enemy squadrons. I went *en carrière* to escape them. My saddle fell off and I fell into the grapevines. Luckily, I did not lose my reins; but because of the saddle and my injured hand, I could not mount. A hussar came, quickly saddled the horse and threw me up after the honest fellow had given me schnapps. This Sumskii Hussar from Taube's squadron on the same day must have either been killed or taken prisoner because I never saw him again. The French horses finally tired and the heated pursuit ended. Only in Maison-Rouge did we have peace and quiet. Here we found Count Wittgenstein and Pahlen collecting his hussars.

That night we bivouacked in Provins. The Grodnenskii and four squadrons of Sumskii Hussars joined us here. We had lost our infantry, eleven cannon, and all of the badly-mounted hussars. Several of the officers had lost their entire equipment, for example Kolachevskii and Count Keller. My people were for the present not here. At the evening meal where the Count was not present, the conversation naturally revolved around the dangers of the day that we had survived. Despite all of the bad luck, there was a lot of laughing and drinking. One fellow shoved the fault on the next, first the infantry; then this or that regiment was at fault for the general confusion. I was of the opinion that the uhlans were the first to take to their heels. General Lisanevich resented my opinion. We got so in each other's hair that he even wanted to arrest me. I did not allow that at all; and since subordination especially after a lost battle is very weak, I told the old man several very impolite things; in short, the noise in the dining hall became so loud that Count Pahlen himself came to mediate the conflict and to soothe old Lisanevich.

All of the forges were full of soldiers; and since I wanted to have my Circassian shod, I had to wait until eight o'clock in the morning before, through pleading, threatening and money, I was taken. I became aware of people running back and forth in the streets. I gave my horse to a Cossack and went into a wide street to see what was going on. I barely had gone around the corner when at the most two steps in front of me a French Dragoon officer with a bared broadsword stopped to speak with an inhabitant at a window. Without being noticed, I hurriedly went back and ran to the forge. Fortunately, my horse had been shod. I threw myself up into the saddle and hurried out of the city. Several Cossacks and Hussars were taken prisoner at the farriery. We retreated to Rogent-sur-Seine where the Duka Cuirassier Division joined us. The Emperor's main headquarters were in Rogent. You can imagine my joy when I found all of my people and horses here.

From several prisoners we had taken, we found out that we had had Napoleon himself against us in the battle at Mormant, with the cavalry of General Milhaud, of Marshal Victor, and five dragoon regiments of General Treilhard.

From here we retreated to Chartres where there was a minor battle. The auditor gave me a Turkish sabre, which, I do not know from where, he had stolen. At Merrey, we once again crossed the Seine and went along the river to Chachigny. We had barely arrived here when a heavy cannonade could be heard in the direction of Merrey. Toward evening pretty Merrey went up in flames. The French had stormed the city, but were thrown over the bridge by Sacken's Corps and set the city on fire. Many wounded and inhabitants who had hidden are said to have been horribly burned to death. We rode to join Count Wittgenstein in Villecerf and watched the enemy march on the other side of the Seine. Three light pieces fired on the *chaussée* at Troyes, were soon however driven off. At night our cavalry came to Villecerf. All of the bridges were burned. It was pitch-black; Merrey, Megrigny and another village were burning. On the other side of Seine, you heard the noise of the French marching; on this side of the river, our artillery, infantry, and cavalry were clattering. Here and there pioneers were working on the burning bridges. Several gunshots interrupted the fuming and swearing of the wagonners and soldiers on both shores of the Seine. We left Villecerf after a small detachment of soldiers had been left behind to keep the bivouac fire burning. I took a wool blanket from a noble mansion. On it in large letters was written: *des apartements de Mlle. Rosalie.* How many a pretty girl might I have covered with this blanket earlier? Not paying attention to the chamberlain's request, I threw the blanket that I very much needed over my saddle and galloped out the gate.

Early in the morning we came to Piney. Since we were not sure of anything but that at Troyes there would be a battle, we were very surprised that a day of rest should be taken in Piney. The little bit of rest did us good stead. The noble champagne since the Mormant *fatalité* had been forgotten; now the old friend came back in grace. Toward evening a courier arrived with the news: in Chatillon peace had been signed. I do not know how it happened; so much is certain that that the news of peace caused general joy. Amidst loud jubilation the goblets were emptied. Now plans were being made; the first wanted to go to Paris, the second to Italy, the third with the Extra-post straight home; the fourth wanted to marry on the Rhine, the fifth cure old sins in the waters; in short, everyone was happy to have experienced peace in one piece. Despite the supposed peace, Pahlen had sixty lancers stand by at Troyes. Their horses were in a sad condition. At Dieuville we crossed the Aube. Pahlen tried to blow up the bridge; but since it was of massive stone and we did not have powder, it was left standing. We rested for the night in Trannes, the same village, where we had been after the battle of Brienne. Not far from Trannes was a noble estate. Count Pahlen left me behind as *sauve-garde*, since the master of the house and his family had not fled. But he denied me, his protector, even a bottle of cognac and acted very coarsely and arrogantly. Only the tears and begging of his wife and children kept me from having the nest set on fire over his head. He later did not escape his fate.

Pahlen's cavalry was reinforced by Kretov's cuirassier division. At Bar-sur-Aube we came under cannon fire. Here we found Wrede with his Bavarians and several Hungarian hussar regiments. A Bavarian brigade had occupied the town. Toward evening the enemy took the place again with the bayonet. Wrede bombarded Bar with sixty cannon. Gunfire and the shouts of soldiers increased the spectacle of death. Count Pahlen sent me into the town to see what was actually happening and why the Bavarians were making this bloodcurdling noise. In Bar I saw the horrible situation up close and was witness to the most shocking atrocities.

A Bavarian battalion had been cut off in Bar and completely hacked down. Now their comrades were avenging their deaths. With fixed bayonets, the enemy was being thrown out of the temple. Shooting came from the windows and doors. My horse stumbled over the numerous corpses lying there. Grenades and fireballs were shot into the town from Wrede's and the French camps, knocking friend and foe to the ground. Everyone was screaming and shouting. The houses were being stormed. Women and old people murdered, children thrown from the second floor onto the paving and smashed. The Bavarians were avenging themselves terribly in that unfortunate town for the deaths of their strangled comrades. I was happy when I again rode out of the gate and left behind the site of all that horror and misery. We let the Bavarians burn and murder and quietly stayed in our bivouac. Early in the morning the King of Prussia, accompanied by his Princes and a considerable staff, joined us. Prisoners were brought in who stated that we had Marshal Oudinot against us, whose main quarters were in Villeville. Most of the town and the bridges were in French hands. At daybreak Wittgenstein's corps set in motion from Colombey-les-deux-Eglises. The army took up battle formation; and Pahlen with his numerous cavalry was ordered to Arsonval to come behind the enemy. Only the Pleskau Cuirassier Regiment and two or three squadrons of Luben Hussars stayed with Count Wittgenstein. Soon the cannon began to thunder and the battle had begun. After a forced march of an hour and a half, after we were already past Levigny, we were at the enemy's back. Here we would have been able to do the French incalculable damage, if a breathless adjutant of Wittgenstein's had not come racing up with orders immediately to hurry to the Army's aid.

We immediately turned around; and when we arrived at the battlefield, our help was already unnecessary. We found brave old Wittgenstein under heavy fire. In our presence, he was wounded by a musket ball. Without losing time, we took up our previous position. The French Army was already *en deroute* and the largest part had already got through the pass. Only a large group of artillery was separated from us by a deep valley. We bombarded them with our cannon. They immediately retreated down the hill in the greatest disorder; and when they saw they were cut off by our Hussars in Arsonval, they threw themselves in groups into the Aube, where they saved themselves by swimming. Many were captured. The enemy quickly retreated leaving several cannon behind. Their loss must have been very large, and our light troops daily captured scattered soldiers.

I found the order for me to go to Count Wittgenstein and take the orders for the next day highly untimely. Accompanied by the Cossack Isyumov, I road to Bar-sur-Aube. The battlefield was filled with naked corpses and wounded causing our horses to shy in the darkness. I could not ward off the thought; perhaps in a few days, you also will be lying that way – and shuddered. Not far from Bar, I met a suite officer who incorrectly assured me that the main headquarters were not in Bar but in Doulevant. The night was bitterly cold and black as pitch, the villages desolate and empty. I could find no guide to Doulevant. After seeking for a long time back and forth, I got completely lost. Thus, I decided to ride back and as good as possible to make excuses.

After this victorious battle, we felt ourselves so safe from the French that our cavalry bivouacked with unsaddled horses. Early in the morning, we came to Trannes where the Army would gather. We went by way of La Rothière to Dienville. In this little city, we found several prisoners of war imprisoned in a church and forgotten by the fleeing French. These people complained of the mistreatment they had suffered at the hands of the inhabitants of the city, and several had been killed with clubs by a mob. Count Pahlen, to set an example, had a couple of the houses of the main perpetrators, who however had escaped, razed to the ground. Our Uhlans used to carry this out did not leave one stone upon another. The brother of Marechal Moucey Duc de Conegliano, a Colonel of the Gendarmerie, and a Captain of *Chasseurs à Cheval*, who had been visiting his wife in St. Dizier, were brought in as prisoners and dealt with in the main headquarters.

On 18 February, we met the enemy in Vendeuvre, only our light cavalry and several mounted groups followed them. Several Sumskii squadrons took the city at full gallop. The enemy had retreated in the night and had gone past Pont-de-la-Guiliotiere across the Barse. It rained the whole day without stopping. It was late when we came to La Marque, a little farmstead. We all crowded in to get out of the wet, all in one room. Soaked to the skin and without anything to eat, we tormented each other, one a burden to the next, until daybreak. We marched the whole day in the rain until in the night we reached a village that had not been plundered. Since we were not to stay here, we used the short amount of time to get some provisions of food. Wine and brandy were distributed among the Hussars. In Dousche, we found a nobleman in his palace. A nicely served supper was a completely new phenomenon for us. Shots at our advance-guard posts soon drove us back to our horses. Pahlen sent strong patrols to Laubressel and other places.

When Pahlen arrived at Laubressel, the village was occupied by the enemy. The Olviopolskii Hussars and Chuguevskii Uhlans along with four cannon immediately advanced to attack the enemy in its flank. The Astrakhanskii Cuirassier Regiment was their *soutien* [support]. The Grodnenskii Hussars and all of our Cossacks with a cuirassier regiment *soutien* went through Barenton. At Thenneliere, General Rudiger found a large train of artillery that he immediately captured, but the enemy cavalry coming from St. Parc [St. Pere?] took his booty away again. Rudiger had all of the artillery horses killed and took several officers and several hundred men prisoner. General Gérard's infantry had in the meantime occupied Laubressel and kept it for several hours despite the superiority. Pahlen circled Laubressel, attacked Gérard's Cuirassier Division of Roussel that had just arrived from Spain, caused them to flee and took all of Count Gérard's equipage, who himself escaped because of the speed of his horse, after getting hit in the face by a lance. Finally, our infantry stormed the village. The enemy retreated and bombarded us anew with cannonballs. Prince Gorchakov, who was supposed to come to our aid, came creeping up with his Corps so slowly and indecisively that even though I had been sent to him three times, he nevertheless did not speed up his march.

The Yekaterinoslavskii Cuirassiers captured one cannon. The Sumskii Hussars chased courageously after the infantry, however, were stopped by a *quarre* [infantry square] and let the enemy retreat in the good of order. The Grodnenskii Hussars distinguished themselves as did Major Sadonski with two squadrons of Astrakhanskii Cuirassiers. In addition to a large number of prisoners, we also captured three cannon at St. Parc. The loss would have been greater if night had not ended the battle. The enemy retreated in the greatest disorder in the dark. Count Pahlen was so noble, that he sent Gérard back his entire equipage since the papers we found were mainly bank drafts, deeds of ownership or family documents. After finishing work, we rode to Dousche where we had a delicious supper and our tired limbs stretched out in soft beds.

In Troyes, the capital of Champagne, we united with Wrede. The outskirts and Pont-St.-Hubert were taken by storm. The French covered their retreat with a heavy cannonade. The city capitulated. The French were given an hour to leave the place. After the expiration of this period, the barricaded gates were opened; the barricades and chains removed; and we moved in with music, trumpet sounds, and flying flags. The Crown Prince of Bavaria [the future King Ludwig I], Wrede, Wittgenstein, Eugene of Württemberg and Count Pahlen had the victorious troops parade past them. I stayed back in Troyes for a while, ate in an inn at noon, bought a pair of boots which, for a lack of money, I could not pay for and remained in debt, and caught up with our cavalry on the road to Nogent. Troyes is a very respectable city with 25,000 inhabitants. The narrow streets and high roofed houses give it a drab appearance. The old noble gothic cathedral is said to be equal in age and beauty to the one in Reims.

The enemy had once again taken up positions a couple minutes from Troyes. Through an unfortunate *quid pro quo* several Cossacks met a Bavarian dragoon regiment. The darkness of the night precipitated this mistake, and many of the Bavarians were sabred before the melee could be stopped. Despite this unfortunate incident, many French were captured. Even I and Turnau caught a couple of dragoons. I gave one of them who acted shamefully a hefty blow up the side of the head. Turnau was not able to forget for a long time the outrage of my having mistreated a prisoner; and I also admit that I acted very unjustly. Turnau gave the poor devil a cloth so that he could bind up the wound from the blow.

Since we had not taken their horses, afterwards we lost them from sight. Where they were in the tumult I do not know. The Chuguevskii Uhlans also joined the battle and took forty-three booty horses which the regiment sorely needed. We spent the night in Paien [Payns] . . . The church in Paien was plundered, and Pahlen sent us there to stop this atrocity. We found a field police officer there who was intending to make off with a silver chalice. I gave him twenty blows with the flat of the broadsword at the altar and the cowardly animal took his punishment without a sound. On his knees, he begged that the incident be kept a secret and nothing said to the Count.

We went by way of Romilly to Pont-sur-Seine; that beautiful Palace of Madame Latitia, the Emperor's mother, burned down due to the carelessness of our people who totally destroyed it while plundering it. Now only black broken walls are standing as a horrid reminder of this war. My people had carried two statutes, Apollo and Venus, out of the palace as decorations for my dirty bivouac. Meat was chopped on a large oil painting on lead. The food in the bivouac was cooked with mahogany furniture, and the magnificent damask wallpapers were cut into horse blankets. We came to Nogent that, totally plundered, was in chaos. Pahlen and all of us lived in the mayor's house in the outskirts. We found wine in abundance. With Colonel Lützow, we climbed the church tower to observe the enemy's movements. Up on the dome of the church, I found the following words in Russian: 'Ensign N.N. from the Reval Infantry Regiment stormed this tower on January 30, 1814 with ten grenadiers, took 16 men and 4 officers prisoner and held out for eighteen hours against the French with his people.' According to the inhabitants, this officer had lost six men on the spiral staircase; thus, he had defended himself the whole day with four men.

Count Gérard sent his adjutant to Pahlen to thank him for the kindness of returning his equipage and especially for the important papers we had taken in Laubressel. Count Gérard also proposed ending the sharpshooter fire along the Seine, because firing from both sides the whole day could not lead to anything, was useless. Count Pahlen agreed and immediately our sharpshooters were ordered to cease firing. I was sent to meet this adjutant who came in the night along the Seine. In the mill, I blindfolded him and led him to the Count. On the way, this young man told me a lot of things and assured me that Nogent was known in France for its trade, its wealth, and its hospitality.

Now to be sure it looked lamentable. Half-starved people from the very lowest class were the only inhabitants. The adjutant dined with Pahlen. I accompanied him back after blindfolding him again. At the mill where we parted, there was a merry party. Seven or eight French officers gambled and drank with just as many of ours. The glass was passed around. Russian and French songs alternated with each other, and the greatest unity ruled among these people. We also joined the happy unity and friend and foe drank until late into the night forgetting the war. I gave my Turkish sabre to Gérard's adjutant, and thus we departed as good friends in order to thrust a sabre into each other's body or shoot a ball through our brains the next day. The wound on my hand caused me unbelievable pain when cutting the meat.

We then went to Pont-sur-Seine where we stayed for several days. The sun was beginning to shine more warmly; and even though still cold, the present spring air (27 February) enlivened all of us. The weather was nice; the roads dry; everyone breathed more freely and easily. That poor little Pont wandered, since we lacked kindling wood, piece by piece into the bivouac. Here to my unending joy, I received the golden honour sabre for bravery as a reward for Bar and Laubressel.

At St. Martin-de-Chenestron, we lazed about for several days. I was sent one night to Lisanevich. It was very dark and I met a column of enemy infantry resting on the *chaussée*. A loud *qui vive* took me aback. I turned my horse, jumped, after getting a painful blow from the butt of a musket on my knee, over a ditch. My Cossack was killed by several thrusts of bayonets. Hundreds of randomly-fired shots followed me, but I luckily escaped. Brave Count Wittgenstein left his Army here and General Rayevski took it over. We went back to Pont again, were so hotly followed that a complete pontoon bridge at Méry fell into enemy hands.

Late in the evening after a forced march, we reached great Troyes. At Premierfait, we succeeded in ambushing a battalion of the Old Guard. A large number of these *vieilles moustaches* were taken prisoner, among others the Mameluke Commander and many of his people, who our Hussars thought were Turks. We alone, except for troops from Württemberg who were active in this battle, took over 500 men of the Old Guard prisoner. The ones who escaped ran to Méry. Seldom have I seen so many handsome people together as in the church of Premierfait, where prisoners were locked for the night. On this day, our men took an immense amount of money and valuables. [From the German text in E. Löwenstern, *Denkwürdigkeiten*]

Pavel Pushin

Born into a Russian noble family from the province of Pskov, Pushin graduated from the prestigious Page Corps where he received a well-rounded education, becoming fluent in French and German and demonstrating abilities in arithmetic, geometry, algebra, history, geography and drawing. In 1802, he joined the elite Life Guard Semeyonovskii Regiment and served with this regiment throughout the Napoleonic Wars, earning promotion to captain in 1811 and colonel in 1813. Along the way he distinguished himself at Austerlitz, Borodino, Lützen, Kulm and Leipzig. On 1 November 1813, he was given command of the 2nd Battalion of the Life Guard Semeyonovskii Regiment. Starting in 1812, Pushin maintained a daily record of his campaigns in a diary which eventually covered the last three years of the Napoleonic Wars. The diary is remarkable for the immediacy of events described in it. Reading it, we can envision Pushin, tired from back and forth marching he was subjected to, sitting in his tent or on a rare occasion in a small room, and writing about his experiences and impressions under the feeble light of a candle.

1 [12] January. Thursday
At 8 a.m., I marched with my battalion* to reach the place on the main route from Lörrach to Basel where the entire corps was supposed to concentrate.

---

* Pushin commanded in the 2rd Battalion of the Life Guard Semeyonovskii Regiment.

The Badenese Guard has also arrived and joined us for the first time; like the Prussian Guard, it was also attached to our corps. Today was a hard frost, worthy of the sons of the North. Deep snow lay on the ground. By 11 a.m. our entire corps concentrated and waited for the arrival of the Emperor until 2 p.m. His Majesty personally took command of the troops and led them to Basel, which the corps passed in a ceremonial march in front of the Allied monarchs gathered on the main city square.

I do not know if the Swiss were happy to see us but can testify that, for whatever reason, they showed great curiosity upon seeing us. Like an anthill, the streets of Basel were full of people as we passed through the city. After leaving it, we made a bivouac and then moved into the quarters assigned to us. The shortest route led by Huningue, which was still in French hands and besieged by the Bavarians, so we had to make a long detour to the left. This development made the day extremely tiresome to us. We kept marching till midnight.

Having left Basel, we crossed the border of France to enter the Haute Rhine department, also known as the Old Alsace. After sixteen hours of toiling, my battalion finally reached its bivouac at Nider-Markstadt. The road on which we moved from Basel was horrendous.

2 [14] January. Friday

Day rest. We were at the distance of only 4 French miles [16.7km] from Basel; one French mile is equal to four Russian verstas.* This was the shortest route bypassing Huningue. Assuming that the French would not open fire on a common carriage travelling on the main route, I decided to travel with Captain [Gregory] Yafimovich† to Basel to better explore it since we only saw it while passing the day before. Our trip went fine and no one fired upon us. We ate *table d'hôte* in a very cold room.

The Imperial headquarters remained this town so I used this opportunity to mail some letters to St. Petersburg. I then walked in the streets of Basel and, after finding nothing outstanding there, I returned with my companion back to Nider-Markstadt [?] by 8 p.m.

3 [15] January. Saturday

We marched at 7 a.m. and after a long delay occupied quarters at Hau (Leval), a local village. I hired into my service a local boy Philipp, aged 17 or 18, who is the son of the hosts in whose house I was staying and who themselves offered his services to me. This boy seems to be very perceptive and speaks fluently in both French and German, which may be of great advantage to me in this region.

---

* One versta is equal to 1.06km or 0.66 miles, so one French mile is equal to 4.24km.
† Yafimovich was Staff Captain of the Life Guard Semeyonovskii Regiment

4 [16] January. Sunday
I departed with my battalion at 9 a.m. Our regiment marched to Rougemont [de Château] and then further on to take quarters at Lachapelle [-sous-Chaux]. The entire population speaks only a French dialect. The region is extremely poor.

5 [17] January. Monday
Today was a very tiresome day. We marched from 7 a.m. till midnight and managed to cover 14 French miles or 56 verstas [59.4km]. We finally reached the former Franche-Comté, presently known as the Haute Saône. We rested at Lure, where we found a tavern but had a dreadful meal; it is impossible to get any coffee or sugar no matter how much you are willing to pay. The locals meet us very well and wholeheartedly hate Napoleon. The corps headquarters was established at Calmoutier, while we stayed at Villeneuve [La Villeneuve-Bellenoye-et-la-Maize].

6 [18] January. Tuesday
We marched at 8 a.m. The weather and the road were terrible, a very cold wind blew and the rain poured incessantly. Because of marshy terrain in many places, we often had to move in single file [guskom], especially near Port-sur-Saone, where we crossed the Saone River. The corps headquarters moved to Surgogne, the regimental headquarters was established at Bougy. We thus moved only 7 miles (28 verstas) [29.7km] in 13 hours. I reached Bougy around 9 p.m., completely wet and chilled to the bone.

7 [19] and 8 [20] January. Wednesday and Thursday
Remained in place.

9 [21] January. Friday
Our regiment left Bougy at 10 a.m. We moved into Champagne in the Haute Marne department. The corps headquarters was set up at Fayl-Billot while we stopped at Maizières [-sur-Amance]. There are no stoves in this country, only fireplaces. The weather is dry but cold; the Russians, who are accustomed to having stoves back at home, are now freezing in homes in the Champagne.

10 [22] January. Saturday
Marched at 8 a.m. The corps headquarters was directed to Orbigny-Au-Val, while I moved with six companies to Lavernoy.

11 [23] January. Sunday
Stayed in place. One of our officers, surnamed Bock,* who, after the battle of Borodino, was considered as a coward by everyone in the regiment, remained a subject of a universal contempt.† Although very well educated, this young man was seeking an opportunity to publicly take revenge on those whom he considered his most committed abusers. While staying at Lavernoy, he chose a moment when all officers gathered for a lunch at my place. He blatantly showed up at this gathering and loudly denounced two or three of his mortal enemies whom he spotted at the meeting. This affront infuriated everyone and, in a moment, all officers without an exception moved towards him with such threatening gestures that I was convinced they would murder him on the spot. I intervened at once, moved them aside and got to Captain Bock to protect him. After quieting the officers, I demanded Captain Bock surrender his sword and told him that he was under arrest for the outrageous behaviour that he dared to commit by appearing at my gathering to cause a fight with officers whom he met 100 times a day in other places. I immediately sent him, escorted by my battalion adjutant, to the *hautpwacht* and then went in person to our General Potemkin to inform him about this incident and give him Bock's sword. I quickly realised that the general was protecting Bock but, I could not care less about him, I avoided getting into an argument of accusing or justifying Bock, and simply remarked that I could not have acted differently both out of concerns for Bock's safety and respect for the officer community. I then returned to Lavernoy, where my officers awaited me. We got back to the table and their furore gradually subsided.‡

13 [25] January. Tuesday
Remained in place. We received the order to take additional buildings for quartering so as to rest more comfortably.

14 [26] January. Wednesday
In consequence of the order received the day before, I marched with my battalion to the commune of Chézeaux. I quartered at the house of a local *curé*, a kind and charitable old man. We stayed here for a couple of days.

---

* Pushin refers to Yegor Yegorovich Bock, who served as a staff captain in the Life Guard Semeyonovskii Regiment.
† Bock's fault was that he acted cowardly in battle. Thus, I. Yakushkin remembered that during the battle of Borodino one Russian officer 'decided to pull a prank on Bock, who was a well-known coward in the Semeyonovskii Regiment: he snuck upon him from behind and threw a fistful of dirt at him. Bock was so frightened that he fell to the ground.' I. Yakushkin, *Zapiski, statii, pisma . . .*, p. 153.
‡ Bock was soon transferred as a major to the Aleksandriiskii Hussar Regiment.

16 [28] January. Friday
Bourbonne-les-Bains* is located about two miles from Chézeaux. Accompanied by several officers, I travelled there to spend a day. I cannot say anything about the curing powers of local waters but Bourbonne-les-Bains looks pitiful and we felt very uncomfortable there. This region has nothing to offer and the curé's village was a much better place so we returned there in the evening.

17 [29] January. Saturday
We finally left the vicinity of Langres where we have remained since the 10th. We marched in the direction of Chaumont for thirteen hours in atrocious weather. My battalion occupied quarters at Boulangy [Poulangy]. The poverty in this region is staggering; people are deprived of most necessities while in Champagny they are dying of thirst. Our quarters are chilly and dirty . . .

18 [30] January. Sunday
We passed through Chaumont, the administrative centre of the Haute Marne, and occupied quarters at Laharmand. After letting my regiment pass, I stayed for a while at Chaumont but found nothing interesting there, this was a rather pitiful city.

19 [31] January. Monday
We received order to bivouac at Colombey [-les-Deux-Eglises], but we had hardly deployed there when an order arrived for us to return to quarters. So we marched back for two miles to take up quarters at Meures not far from Laharmand. Would not it have been better if we were not moved at all?

20 January [1 February]. Tuesday
Our corps departed at 6 a.m. and proceeded towards Bar-sur-Aube. After passing through this town, we turned right and bivouacked around 8 p.m. Throughout this time there was a strong cannonade from the advance guard. The snow was coming down in large snowflakes and a strong wind was blowing.

21 January [2 February].Wednesday
The battle at Brienne. Our corps broke its camp at 1 a.m. at night. It proceeded towards Brienne-le-Château to form the reserves of General [Fabian] [Osten-] Sacken, who had engaged the enemy in battle. The fighting began at 8 a.m. in the morning. We did not participate in it because even without our support the enemy was completely defeated by 4 p.m. Snow and wind made our condition

---

* Bourbonne-les-Bains was known as a health resort due to its thermal springs that have been used since Roman times.

completely unbearable. Fortunately, as soon as victory became certain, we were ordered to take quarters. We marched on the road leading to Troyes and stopped at the village of Mont-Martin.

22 January [3 February]. Thursday
We hoped for a day's break at Mont-Martin when, around noon, we suddenly received an order to march. [My servant] Luka returned from Frankfurt where he left [my mistress] Elizabeth Sperl and found me at my quarters just prior to our departure from Mont-Martin. We moved hoping to bivouac but soon received order to occupy quarters. We halted at Montieramey. We were not assigned quarters and therefore occupied them on our own discretion. I got a rather deplorable quarters. The host was father of nine small children and our arrival so frightened him that I had to use various means to calm him down. We were in the department of Aube, which is no better than Haute Marne.

23 January [4 February]. Friday
Despite the horrible bed which I found at the house, I slept like a dead men because of extreme exhaustion of the previous day. I woke up on at 6 a.m. since, under orders received the day before we had to march maintaining great order to Troyes. But the indecision, typical to our commanders particularly after we entered France, showed its face once more. Another order arrived cancelling the first and we stayed at Montieramey. I decided to find new quarters where settled in a bit better conditions than in the first.

24 January [5 February]. Saturday
We left Montieramey in the morning and proceeded to Bourguignons, where we crossed the Seine River over a very narrow bridge. Here we heard the sound of cannon fire and soon received the order to halt the entire corps. We then changed our direction and marched to Troyes, that is, to the sound of the guns. The weather was nice, with some ten degrees of frost, which did not dispose us to staying at bivouacs. About half an hour after we moved in this new direction, we were ordered to turn back and had to move through Bar-sur-Seine to Polisy, where we took new quarters.

25 January [6 February]. Sunday
We marched at 7 a.m. My battalion had hardly reached Villiers-sous-Praslin when I received new orders to proceed with two companies to Praslin. There I occupied quarters with the Austrian troops. In the afternoon our entire regiment was ordered to move. It was raining heavily. We departed at 5 p.m. and, after marching for 3 miles (12 verstas) [12.8km], stopped at quarters at Vanlay around 10 p.m. I was wet to my bones and extremely annoyed by the meaningless exhaustion that we were subjected to since we, for all practical purposes, remained in the same place.

26 January [7 February]. Monday
We were forced to march hastily through Chaffois to Ville-Morugne [?], where our entire corps was supposed to concentrate to participate in the attack on Troyes. However, because the French had abandoned this town, there was no fighting and so we marched, without stopping at Ville-Morugne, towards Chapitre, which is located not far from Villiers-sous-Praslin. Thus, if I were not forced to march yesterday morning, I would not even have to move today.

27–28 January [8–9 February].Wednesday
Remained in place. Order is issued for everyone to wear a white armband on the left arm, that is, all the Allied troops had to wear it. People assure us that this is to show that we are on the side of the Bourbons.

29 January [10 February]. Thursday
We marched for 4 miles (16 verstas) [10 miles] to occupy quarters at Troyes, the administrative centre of the Aube department. I settled in the Saint Martin suburb. The city struck me as large and well-built but the circumstances, as well as large number of people concentrated there, prevented me from obtaining even most basic necessities. Besides, we were received very poorly here.

30 January [11 February]. Friday
We were already under arms and ready to march when the order arrived for to us stay put. The Imperial headquarters was located in town so I took an opportunity to pay respects to Count Arakcheyev and then spent the entire day walking in the streets. We wandered so much around Troyes that we nicknamed this period of our campaign the 'Troyens War'.⋆ In reality we could have occupied Troyes immediately after the battle at Brienne, but we outwitted ourselves and prolonged this pleasure for another ten days.

31 January [12 February]. Saturday
We marched at 6 a.m., remained on the road until 5 p.m. and halted at Maizières-la-Grande-Paroisse, where we took quarters. Here we learned that [the French] captured our entire division (Olsufiev's) with all of its generals and officers.

1–2 [13–14] February. Sunday and Monday
Now we cannot even get enough sleep. We were woken up at 1 a.m. and ordered to march to Mesgrigny, where we remained at bivouacs until 11 a.m. before we returned back to our quarters at Maizières-la-Grande-Paroisse. We found this village completely empty because all of its residents had fled

---

⋆ A play on words on the Trojan War.

during our excursion into Mesgrigny. One can imagine what a disheartening impression the sight of abandoned homes had on us. We occupied them in spite of hardship we experienced in the absence of their owners and remained there until 6 p.m. when drums began to beat and we were ordered to leave. The weather was beautiful but the darkness fell rapidly, we were tired and sleepy and not predisposed to enjoying scenery. After passing through Nogent-sur-Seine, we stopped for a rest and, after an hour, moved again, marching all night long. Finally, around 5 a.m. on the 2nd [of February], Monday, we reached La Motte [-Tilly], where we took up quarters. I dropped on the bed and slept like a dead man until noon.

3–4 [15–16] February. Tuesday and Wednesday

We remained at La Motte till 7 p.m. on Tuesday. We even began to hope that our superiors would let us have a peaceful rest but alas, suddenly an order was issued and all troops marched at once, moving through Nogent and made a rest at Romilly [-sur-Seine] when it was already dark; we soon fell asleep. This rest unexpectedly lasted until 8 a.m. on Wednesday, the 4th. A new order soon arrived which, instead of sending us to Arcis, instructed us to march once again to Nogent, where we had to take up quarters. At Nogent, I was fortunate to receive very nice quarters.

5 [17] February. Thursday

I took pleasure in staying at my quarters all day long, counting on spending the night here as well. My dinner and bed were already prepared when suddenly, around 9 p.m., the alarm was sounded. Farewell my hope for restful night. I had to bid good-bye to my warm room and march in rather nippy wind at night. Fortunately, we marched for only three quarters of a mile [0.7km] and stopped near Le Grez [?].

6 [18] February. Friday

Our entire corps moved at the same time as we did in the morning and bivouacked at Trainel.

7 [19] February. Saturday

Our corps departed at 5 a.m. and still withdrawing along the road to Troyes, it bivouacked at Prunay[-Belleville].

8 [20] February. Sunday

We departed at 3 a.m. at night, still in the same direction. Bivouacked at La Malmaison, about one mile [4.24km] away from Troyes.

9 [21] February. Monday

There are strong rumours that peace will be concluded.

10 [22] February. Tuesday
Rumours keep changing every minute. Now nobody speaks of peace, instead we are told that hostilities have resumed. Our corps departed at 5 a.m.; after reaching the suburbs of Troyes, it turned left and bivouacked at Saint-Parres-aux-Tertres, while I led my battalion to its quarters at Baires and served as an outpost.

11–12 [23–24] February. Wednesday and Thursday
The Corps broke its camp around 6 p.m. on Wednesday. I joined it and, as marching together, we reached Lusigny [-sur-Barse] in awful darkness around 9 p.m. and bivouacked there. Fortunately I found right next to our bivouac a small hut where I spent the night since it was better to stay inside than under the open sky. At 2 a.m. at night of 12 February we were ordered to march once more. The frost was quite strong. At 6 a.m. we arrived at Vendeuvre [-sur-Barse] and bivouacked there. At 5 p.m. we marched again and reached Bar-sur-Aube by midnight.

In general, our situation is highly unpleasant. We march for entire days, arrive in places late at night and then wait for hours before bonfires are set so we can warm ourselves, all of which is rather strenuous in the current cold.

13 [25] February. Friday
Our corps left Bar-sur-Aube at 7 a.m. It marched for a second time into the Haute Marne department and, at 4 p.m., bivouacked at Colombey-les-Deux-Eglises, where it had already been on 19 January. We stayed here for about two hours. After marching once more, we halted about three quarters of a mile away [0.7km] from Chaumont, where we spent the night.

14 [26] February. Saturday
We marched from 9 a.m. till 11 p.m. today. This was of course too much but the knowledge that we will have quarters instead of bivouac tonight made us ignore exhaustion. We stopped two [Russian] miles [5 miles] from Langres in the commune of Courcelles-en-Montagne.★

15 [27] February. Sunday
Day of rest.

6 [28] February. Monday
Our regiment marched at 4 a.m. It was already approaching Chaumont where the order arrived to stop and take quarters at Brottes.

[From the Russian text in P. Pushin, *Dnevnik*]

★ By now, Pushin's men had marched some 200km in nine days.

3

The Capture of Soissons

Located some 90km north-east of Paris, the city of Soissons became the site of several major clashes during the 1814 Campaign. Tracing its history back to Roman times, this fortified city held a strategically important position on the Paris–Mons road and could be used to defend the north-eastern approaches to the French capital. The fortress, however, was not well maintained and its fortifications required major upgrades while the moat was largely filled in. Although the French attempted to renovate Soissons in January 1814, they simply could not complete any major improvements before the Allied forces appeared before it. The Soissons garrison consisted of about 4,000 troops from the National Guard with eight cannon under the overall command of General Jean-Baptiste-Dominique Rusca.

The first Allied troops to arrive at Soissons belonged to Winzingerode's corps, which was tasked with intercepting French lines of communication. Departing from Namur on 6 February, Winzingerode invaded north-eastern France, capturing the fortress of Avesnes-sur-Helpes with his advance guard, led by the famed Alexander Chernyshev, on 9 February. Chernyshev dispatched several raiding parties deeper into France and on 13 February one of these detachments, led by Constantine Benckenfordd II, successfully raided the environs of Soissons. Later that day Chernyshev himself arrived with the rest of his troops and, after receiving the French refusal to surrender the fortress, he attempted to capture it on 14 February. The initial Russian attacks failed but the French counterattack resulted in the death of General Rusca, which demoralised the defenders and allowed the Russians to break into the fortress. Although General Louis Lonchamp, who replaced Rusca, managed to extricate some troops, most of the French garrison fell into Russian hands. Winzingerode, who arrived later that day, prohibited plundering and, on 15 February, attended the funeral of General Rusca who was buried with full military honours.

The Russian victory, however, proved short-lived. Napoleon's incredible Six Days campaign caused the Allied advance to falter and, on the evening of 15 February, Winzingerode received orders to evacuate Soissons and join the Army of Silesia. The following day, the Russians abandoned the city without leaving a garrison and marched to Reims. Soissons, meanwhile, was recaptured by Marshal Eduard Adolphe Casimir Mortier, who deployed here a new garrison of some 1,200 men with 20 cannon under the command of General Jean Claude Moreau.

On 24 February Blücher's Army of Silesia launched a new offensive towards Paris but suffered a serious setback at Meaux and was forced back. By early March, Napoleon ordered Marshals Marmont and Mortier to pursue Blücher while he launched a flanking manoeuvre that sought to cut off the Army of Silesia. For Blücher, the only way out was through Soissons, where Winzingerode's troops appeared on 2 March; the Prussian corps of General Friedrich von Bülow arrived from the north-east as well. Learning about Blücher's desperate situation, Winzingerode and Bülow did their best to capture the fortress of Soissons but their attacks failed throughout 2 March. The Allies then dispatched their representatives, the Prussian Captain Martens and the Russian Lieutenant-Colonel Woldemar Löwenstern who exerted psychological pressure on Moreau and compelled him to accept the capitulation, which allowed the French garrison to depart with full military honours. Just hours after the French capitulation, Blücher's weary troops poured into the city and across the Aisne River. By saving the Army of Silesia from an imminent defeat (and possibly destruction), the Allied capture of Soissons on 3 March had an important impact on the course of the 1814 Campaign. Furious at the failure of his plan to destroy Blücher's army, Napoleon demanded the immediate arrest of Moreau. Writing to his minister of war, the French Emperor raged, 'Let this wretch [Moreau] be arrested, as well as all the members of his war council; let him be impeached before a military commission composed of generals, and for God's sake act so that they may be all shot within twenty-four hours on the Place de Grève. It is time to make examples. Let the cause of the sentence be fully explained, printed, and distributed in every direction.' Moreau was fortunate that the war ended before he could be court-martialled and he was able to enjoy a peaceful retirement.

Once the Army of Silesia was safely across the Aisne River, the Allies left a strong garrison of some 12,000 men with 30 guns at Soissons. On 5–6 March the Russians were attacked by Marshals Marmont and Mortier and, even though the French managed to break into the suburbs, the Russians successfully defended the city and held on to the crossing. As the result, Napoleon had to recall his corps and proceed to Berry-au-Bac where he crossed the Aisne. On 7 March, before the start of the battle of Craonne, Blücher recalled the Russian forces from Soissons, which reclaimed by the French the very next morning.

Alexander Langeron

Langeron commanded a corps in the Army of Silesia under Blücher. According to Blücher's preliminary dispositions, Langeron was supposed to send a small force under the reigning Duke of Saxe-Coburg to blockade Mainz and march with the rest of troops to join the Army of Silesia in France.

The troops of the Duke of Coburg still not being fully organised nor equipped, I was obliged to leave him seven regiments of infantry, five of cavalry or Cossacks and thirty cannons. I entrusted this detachment to

Lieutenant-General Panchulidzev I and gave the order to Count St. Priest to march on France on 3 [15] February, with three infantry regiments of his corps and the Kievskii Dragoon Regiment. According to the orders that Marshal Blücher gave me to personally join him as soon as possible, I left 31 January [12 February], with a small detachment under the command of Major-General Count Pahlen. This detachment was composed of the Derpt Regiment, mounted jager, the second of Ukrainian Cossacks, those of Grekov XXII and four cannons from the Don.

I made forced marches via Kaiserslautern, Zweibrücken, Sarreguemines, Nancy, Toul, Saint-Dizier and Vitry, where I arrived on 11 [23] February. February 13th [25th], I marched on Arcis-sur-Aube to join the Army of Silesia at Méry, where I thought I would still find it yet, but I mostly found the banks of the Aube temporarily abandoned.

I was equally unaware of the march of Marshal Blücher and Napoleon. It was only with great luck that I wasn't discovered (it was a peasant who warned me), as I would have fallen in the midst of the enemy, with little likelihood of being able to escape. I was already at Rameri on the banks of the Aube; fortunately for me, the bridge was broken at Arcis, and the enemy worked to fix it. I sent two squadrons and some Cossacks to observe their movements, and I reported to Châlons.

On the 16th [28th], I wanted to march on Montmirail: I found at Vertus Major-General Tettenborn with four regiments of Cossacks; he told me that General Winzingerode was at Reims, General Bülow at Laon and Major-General Benckendorff occupied Épernay. General Tettenborn had been sent to the Aube to observe the movements of the enemy, as well as the Prussian partisans of Lützow and Falkenhausen.

At eight o'clock in the morning, General Tettenborn found the whole army of Napoleon near Fère-Champenoise; he was attacked by the light cavalry of the French Guard and warned me that he was retiring on Vertus and Épernay.

I was then more than two miles in front of Vertus; before supposing that Napoleon would follow General Tettenborn, I was afraid that General Benckendorff would be forced to abandon Épernay and destroy the bridge. I could not, without danger, move myself on Montmirail, where I had assumed the vanguard of the enemy was already; I knew that the bridge at Château-Thierry was destroyed and the detachment of Cossacks that General Benckendorff had sent lacked the means to repair it. My position was very critical; I decided to march through Champaubert to Épernay, and if it had been occupied by the enemy, I had no alternative but to cross the Marne by swimming near Dormans, with my cavalry, leaving my cannons and my baggage. I brought with me a huge amount, all of that of the Army of Silesia which had remained behind; a great many convoys, cut off from the Aube and having no directions, had joined my small detachment and bothered me much.

Fortunately Napoleon, too eager to follow Marshal Blücher, contented himself with pushing General Tettenborn back to Vertus and I arrived in the evening at Épernay. A huge Prussian convoy, under the command of Lieutenant-Colonel Lobenthal, consisting of a train of artillery, ammunition wagons, food, the military pay chests, in all comprised of over 300 carriages and escorted by two squadrons and two battalions of convalescents or recruits, also came to join me in Épernay, after having been at the gates of Montmirail, where it is inconceivable that it was neither seen or caught. It made eighteen leagues in twenty-four hours. The part that Napoleon had taken and the rapidity of his march show how the movements of Marshal Blücher were well calculated and useful to the general good. If Napoleon had continued to follow the Great Army, that of Silesia would have been menacing, or even occupy Paris, which only had a few defences, and if Napoleon wanting to save his capital, abandoned the Great Army, ours could quickly fall back, as it actually did. General Benckendorff, who I also found in Épernay, told me that the Generals Winzingerode and Bülow marched on Soissons to seize it again (as seen above). I determined to follow and march on the spot by Reims on Soissons.

Winzingerode and Bülow, whose corps had nearly 50,000 men, had, since the renewal of the war, been part of the army of the Crown Prince of Sweden; they had left recently for Namur and Liège, when the Prince stopped suddenly and unnecessarily (and even with the air of an intensely bad intention), and by the orders of their sovereign, they had come to open a new line of operations by the Netherlands on Laon and Soissons, through the midst of countless fortresses of Hainaut and the Ardennes, while, those of the Prince of Sweden and the reigning Duke of Saxe-Weimar, an infantry general in the Russian service, observed with the Swedish and Saxon troops.

This new line of operations would have been very hazardous, if the inhabitants of Avesnes, where there was a small detachment of regular troops, had not opened their gates to the Allies. This fortress was the only base we had to communicate with the Netherlands. Both the corps of Winzingerode and of Bülow were reunited with the Army of Silesia and brought it back to a strength of almost 100,000 men.

General Winzingerode initially moved on Soissons, that he took in a most brilliant manner (Major-General Chernishev distinguished himself and was made lieutenant-general). The French General Rusca, who commanded at Soissons, was killed, another general taken. Three thousand prisoners were taken and eighteen cannons were found. A few days later, General Winzingerode, having known the events on the Aube, left Soissons to move to Reims, approached the Main Army, and opened communications with it, but having learned of the march of Marshal Blücher and that of Napoleon, he thought it necessary to reoccupy Soissons. He concentrated with General von Bülow for this enterprise, who had just arrived in Laon, and took it a second time. It had an old enclosing wall, strong enough, and a deep moat; small palisaded redoubts had been recently built in front of each gate; eighteen cannons of various calibres adorned the walls, the garrison only consisted then of 8,000 Poles; they had too little time to defend the city, but in the circumstances that they found themselves, this was so important that the commander would have risked defending against assault even if it was hopeless to resist superior forces; he could assume that his enemies knew the weakness of his garrison; and a day later would have been useful to his party.

General Moreau commanded in the town, and although he was personally very brave, he gave in perhaps too early: desiring to save the inhabitants of Soissons the horrors of an assault, he gave up the town to capitulation, although he perhaps could hear the fire of the rearguard of the Army of Silesia engaged in Neuilly with the vanguard of Napoleon. General Winzingerode granted the garrison freedom to join his army; it was not the time to argue. This expedition was of the greatest usefulness; it is a credit to the generals who conceived and executed it. Success was never achieved in a more timely manner. General Winzingerode, as brave an officer as he was astute, rendered, on this occasion, a very essential service to the overall cause.

As soon as the French garrison was out of the city, the columns of Blücher pushed hurriedly to enter it, and if the place had been held twenty-four hours, the Army of Silesia would have been crushed and with no less than all of its artillery lost. Napoleon arrested and prosecuted General Moreau: the taking of Paris saved him.

There has been criticism, rightly, of the many mistakes of Marshal Blücher in his first move on Paris, which cost him so dearly; but in this second move forward, which was so useful, he cannot be criticised as having delayed too long in the time to withdraw to the Aisne. Napoleon did not take advantage of this fault of his enemy as skilfully as the first time. Blücher had put himself in a position so dangerous that, without the unexpected capture of Soissons, he was lost, by being left without time and unnecessary and unsuccessful attacks on Ourcq, cornered by the Aisne, a marshy river with high and steep banks that can only be crossed with difficulty.

The Army of Silesia having crossed the Aisne, the corps of Yorck, Kleist, von Sacken and my cavalry bivouacked on its right bank, at some distance from the city, where all the infantry I had with me then was placed.

It was composed of the 10th Corps, except the two regiments of Vyborgskii and Vyatkskii (standing in front of Cassel on the Rhine), the 9th Corps (reduced to less than 1,800 men after the failure at Champaubert) and two regiments of the 8th Corps, that of the Belozersk and the 48th Jager, who formed the brigade of General Kern. General Kapzewitsch, whose health did not always respond with the zeal needed to animate the service, needing a rest, Marshal Blücher appointed Lieutenant-General Rudzevich commander at Soissons.

On 21 February [5 March], the two corps of the enemy, commanded by Marshals Marmont and Mortier, who could only find our boxed-in army by the mountains which border the right bank of the Aisne, assumed that we had retired to Laon and we had left a small garrison in Soissons (although the subsequent importance of this place could be judged by our sufficient occupation), attacked at eight o'clock in the morning. They advanced on the first suburb from Paris, defended by Colonel Durnow with the 7th, 29th, 37th and 45th Jager and a battalion of the Starooskolskii.

The attack was long and sharp, and the defence as might be expected from an officer as distinguished as Colonel Durnow and the brave troops under his command. Lieutenant-General Rudzevich, and the generals Turchaninov and Shkapsky (who commanded the 8th Division in place of Major-General Pushkin, injured at Lizy) were found on the ramparts of the city, where they directed the necessary reinforcements. Colonel Magdenko, who commanded the 18-pounders of the town and the 12-pounders of mine that I had added, directed the artillery fire with great intelligence and caused the enemy many casualties. Having been pushed back at the gates of Paris, they fell upon their right at the gates of Reims, where they were received by Major-General Kern and Major Novikov, commander of the 48th Jager Regiment as at the gates of Paris and during five hours of fighting, they lost everywhere without making any progress.

About three o'clock in the afternoon, their forces had been visibly augmented and the attack became more intense. They occupied a part of the suburbs and produced, from the roofs of houses, a fire so strong that it became difficult to stay on the ramparts that were completely dominated by these roofs. Under the protection of this fire and a battery of forty cannons, they tried to take the town, but they were constantly repulsed by the 6th Corps and the brigade from the 8th. I had deployed the 9th Corps reserves in the streets and squares of the city, to bring relief where it was needed and contain the townspeople who could have given us some problems and who I had confined in their homes.

Towards evening, a grenade set fire to the city hall where I had left my wounded. It was very difficult to save them. At six o'clock the firing ceased and the enemy retreated; their loss must have been very great, because mine was 1,056 men and I had the advantage of position. I remained with General Rudzevich for most of the battle, but without taking command of which he was so worthy. This brave general and the troops under his command acquired, on this occasion, new claims to my gratitude and that of Marshal Blücher, who made them report on the events the next day.

During the attack on the city, the enemy batteries were placed along the Aisne, on the high ground near the old Celestine monastery; their fire incommoded all those who passed on the road to Laon. Under the protection of these batteries, they seemed to be trying to build a bridge over the Aisne under cover of darkness, near the abbey of Saint-Crépin; I made General

Udom march with the 9th Division that I retired from the city, the Livonia Regiment, the mounted jager, and a Cossack regiment that I had kept with me, and the enemy abandoned their project, if it had been serious.

On 22 February [6 March], at six o'clock in the morning, they made another attempt on the city, rather, I believe, to hide their march towards Fismes in the hopes of taking it. At seven o'clock, they withdrew altogether. [From the French text in A. Langeron, *Mémoires* . . .]

Sergei Volkonskii

Volkonskii was a staff officer in the headquarters of Winzingerode. After spending several days in Liège, Winzingerode's corps invaded France proper and occupied the fortress of Avesne. By early March, Volkonskii was already at the gates of Soissons.

Our corps continued the invasion of French territory and our advance guard, under [Alexander] Chernyshev, captured the fortress of Avesne [Avesne-sur-Helpe] without a fight. Our corps headquarters soon moved here. Our stay here was marked by a memorable incident. After we occupied the town, the local postmaster, Pestit, sent a letter specifying the strength of our troops to a French commander who was deployed near the town. Our outposts intercepted this letter and it was considered a criminal act. Pestit was arrested, court-martialled and sentenced to death for treason. The poor Pestit was informed of his sentence and taken to the place of execution but Winzingerode secretly instructed me to announce, once all preparations for the execution were completed, that Pestit was pardoned. The memory of this mission is still vivid in my mind and I find it consoling that I carried out an order that saved a human life . . .

After securing the fortress of Avesne, our corps resumed its advance into France and our corps headquarters soon moved to Laon, where it took up quarters at the Hôtel de la Préfecture, where we found all the necessary resources abandoned by a local prefect and had a comfortable stay without incurring any expenses.

While our corps remained in Laon, our advance guard under Chernyshev marched on the road to Soissons. Upon learning that the town and garrison were preparing for defence, Winzingerode followed the advance guard, instructing Chernyshev to approach Soissons but avoid any decisive attacks. Thus, by 1 [13] February, our advance guard approached Soissons while the rest of the corps spent the night about seven or eight verstas [7.5 or 8.5km] behind it. Despite Winzingerode's orders, Chernyshev attacked the bridgehead at dawn on 2 [14] February and found himself involved in a heated battle. Winzingerode, hearing a strong artillery cannonade at dawn, ordered the alarm to be beaten and rushed with his staff officers to the site of battle.

Upon approaching Soissons, he saw that contrary to his orders [Chernyshev] had become embroiled in a major fight and that [Chernyshev's] disposition for attack was too indefinite, unnecessary dividing his already small forces. Winzingerode severely reprimanded Chernyshev for his failure to follow orders and, turning to me, he said, 'Stay here and watch the time. If the battle does not turn to our favour within fifteen minutes, you can order the retreat on my behalf. Meanwhile, I will return to my main forces and make preparations for an attack, and unlike Chernyshev's random assault, this time success will be ensured.'

Winzingerode returned to the corps that began concentrating in the vicinity, while I stayed, empowered by the corps commander's trust, to supervise Chernyshev and his arrangements. Chernyshev, in his usual habit of claiming other's people accomplishments, stood with his suite behind a stone building that protected him from enemy fire while the fight continued in earnest. I closely monitored the course of battle, or to be precise, our assault of the bridgehead fortification. Seeing no prospects of success, I was about to order to sound the retreat when I suddenly saw one of the weakest companies of the 34th Jager Regiment climbing onto the rampart and causing great commotion among the French defenders. The capture of this section of the rampart promised to change the tide of battle and stopped me from recalling the troops. Indeed, all the bridge fortifications were soon in our hands and two guns from a horse artillery company commanded by Captain Mazaraki were moved into position there. At the same time, Lieutenant Grabigorskii, who had been assigned to this artillery company, grabbed a petard and charged, alone, petard in hand, across the bridge that connected the bridgehead with the fortress itself. He ran across the bridge, attached the petard to the fortress gates and ignited its fuse. I still cannot imagine how Grabigorskii managed to run to and from the fortress without being injured in that hail of bullets but his petard soon exploded and broke in the fortress gates. Captain Mazaraki then opened fire with his guns, smashing the gates to pieces. The entrance into the town lay completely open and the Volhynskii Uhlan Regiment, led by its gallant and intelligent Colonel and Flügel Adjutant Sukhtelen, immediately exploited this opportunity. The city was captured and the French garrison was forced to flee.

Chernyshev did not participate personally or through his instructions in these successes and I vividly remember how, after I charged with the Uhlans into the city, [Captain] Mazaraki told me, 'Well, here you are, an outsider standing shoulder-to-shoulder to us while our own commander [Chernyshev] cannot be seen anywhere.'

The confusion among the French troops resulted in the death of General [Jean-Baptiste-Dominique] Rusca, who was tasked with defending Soissons with a garrison of some 3,000 men, and who, if provided with heavy artillery, could have defended this fortified town for a long time. But the attack of the above-mentioned company [of the 34th Jagers], led, if I am not mistaken, by Captain Kuchkin, compelled Rusca to rush to the threatened sector and he was shot dead by one of our jagers. The death of the commanding general caused widespread confusion among the French and led to, as the French say, 'sauve qui peut' [a state of panic].

The honour of the capture of Soissons was assigned to Chernyshev, even though he played no role in it. The honour instead belonged to men like Kuchkin, Grabigorskii and Mazaraki, and maybe to a lesser degree to me for persistence in not calling the retreat even though the set time had expired. Chernyshev claimed the honour of the capture of Soissons as easily as he did the taking of Kassel. Kuchkin received the cross [of the Order of St. George] and I cannot recall what Mazaraki got. Grabigorskii received his St. George cross much later, only after our return from Paris. Winzingerode once met him at the palace and was surprised to see him without the St. George cross. and immediately went to the Emperor's cabinet and informed him of Grabigorskii's exploit and his right to wear a cross, which he carried out of the Imperial office [at the end of the conversation]. On the other hand, Chernyshev was promoted to lieutenant-general for no reason at all . . . As it became clear that a battle would be fought near Soissons, there were numerous intrigues among generals against Winzingerode and jealousy directed against me because I enjoyed Winzingerode's confidence. Before the battle one of the generals asked me to take with me two officers, whom I could easily to nominate for awards if they happened to be at the battlefield. I was close to this general and agreed to his request only to learn shortly thereafter that he sent these men to spy on my performance. I did not reveal that I knew of his intentions but this intrigue only compelled me to endeavour to come out triumphantly from this test. I have never been a coward in battle but on this occasion I went beyond the call of duty and thus compelled my spies to endure the test as well.

As we occupied Soissons, the town residents, hoping to gain our benevolence, shouted from windows, 'Vive l'Empereur Alexandre! Vive l'Empreur d'Austriche! Vive le Roi de Prusse!' But knowing that their deliberate enthusiasm might have resulted in our troops invading their homes, we brusquely urged residents to close all their windows and homes and protect themselves from pillaging. As I passed one of the streets, I heard yelling inside the home, dismounted and entered inside deducing that our troops probably full of activity there. So what did I see? Three soldiers got into the watchmaker's shop and were busy dismantling clocks, removing the mechanisms and stuffing clock frames into their knapsacks. The sight of a pile of clock mechanisms and the soldiers' resourcefulness in discarding what they considered useless and gathering only precious metals unwittingly caused me to erupt in laughter. I expelled soldiers from the house but allowed them to keep the loot. [From the Russian text in S. Volkonskii, *Zapiski* . . .]

1. Emperor Alexander I of Russia (by George Dawe, 1824).

2. The French retreat from Leipzig, 19 October 1813. The premature blowing-up of the bridge over the Elster River stranded thousands of French troops. Marshal Jozef Poniatowski, atop his horse, is about to plunge to his death into the river (by John Atkinson).

3. Napoleon contemplating his setbacks in Germany in 1813 (by John Atkinson).

4. The Russian Life Guard Horse Regiment passing through a German town on its way to France (by Bogdan Willewalde, late nineteenth century).

5. A mid-nineteenth century Russian painting of the battle of Montmirail, 11 February 1814 (by Mikhail Mikeshin).

6. After the battle of Montmirail (17 February 1814) Russian prisoners were marched along the Boulevard Saint Martin in Paris (early 19th century print by Etienne Jean Delecluze).

7. The battle of Bar-sur-Aube, 27 February 1814 (contemporary German print. Courtesy of the Anne S. K. Brown Military Collection).

8. The storming of Troyes by Allied troops on 3 March 1814 (contemporary German print. Courtesy of the Anne S. K. Brown Military Collection).

9. Prussians charging at the battle of Laon, 9 March 1814 (contemporary German print. Courtesy of the Anne S. K. Brown Military Collection).

10. During the battle at La Fère-Champenoise on 25 March 1814, Field Marshal Gebhard Blücher, shown in this German print valiantly leading the Allied cavalry, captured a large artillery and supply train moving to reinforce Napoleon's army (contemporary German print. Courtesy of the Anne S. K. Brown Military Collection).

11. Napoleon's victorious entry into the city of Reims after the defeat of General St. Priest's corps on 13 March 1814 (nineteenth-century gravure).

12. Field Marshal Gebhard Blücher (portrait by unknown artist, copy by Paul Ernst Gebauer, c. 1815–19).

13. General Mikhail Barclay de Tolly. Unjustly maligned for his leadership in 1812, Barclay de Tolly made a stunning comeback to lead the Russian armies to their triumph over Napoleon. After the fall of Paris, he was awarded the title of Field Marshal General (contemporary German print).

14. General Mikhail Vorontsov, who distinguished himself at the battle of Craonne (English lithograph from original painting by George Dawe, 1820s).

15. Colonel Ivan Skobelev (here shown in his general's uniform) heroically led the Ryazanskii Infantry Regiment during the battle of Reims, 12/13 March 1814 (portrait by Karl Wilhelm Bardou, 1826).

16. General Peter Wittgenstein (by George Dawe, c. 1825).

17. General Alexander Langeron (by George Dawe, c. 1825).

18. Alexander Mikhailovskii-Danilevskii, a perceptive eyewitness and talented historian of the 1814 campaign (contemporary Russian print).

19. General George Emmanuel (by George Dawe, 1821).

20. General Moisei Karpenko (by George Dawe, c. 1827).

21. Colonel Mikhail Orlov, who negotiated the capitulation of Paris on 30 March 1814.

22. General Fabian von der Osten-Sacken (by George Dawe, 1820s).

23. General Emmanuel Saint-Priest (by George Dawe, c. 1825).

24. General Ferdinand Winzingerode (by George Dawe, c. 1825).

25. The Cossack Bivouac on the Champs-Elysées in Paris, 31 March 1814 (by Alexander Sauerveid, 1814).

26. The entrance of the Allied troops into Paris on 31 March 1814. Emperor Alexander leads the procession across the Place Vendôme as the Parisians are trying to topple Napoleon's statue from the top of the column (contemporary German print).

27. King Louis XVIII's Entry into Paris in May 1814 (English print, 1814).

28. Russian troops partaking in the delights of Paris (contemporary print by Georg-Emmanuel Opitz, c. 1814).

29. Fanciful print of the Russian troops in Paris (contemporary French print).

30. A Russian officer preparing for a night on the town in Paris (contemporary French print by François Gabriel Théodore Busset de Jolimont. Courtesy of the Anne S. K. Brown Military Collection).

31. Napoleon signs his abdication at the palace of Fontainebleau on 11 April 1814 (French print, 1814. Courtesy of the Anne S. K. Brown Military Collection).

32. 'World Peace Restored' – the Allied sovereigns celebrating their victory over Napoleon (German print, c.1814. Courtesy of the Anne S. K. Brown Military Collection).

33. The medal 'For Capturing Paris 19 March 1814' was established in August 1814 to celebrate the Russian triumph over Napoleonic France. This silver medal was supposed to be given to every soldier and officer who participated in the taking of the French capital but, to avoid embarrassing the newly-restored Bourbon monarchy, Emperor Alexander postponed its distribution. The medal was ultimately dispensed in 1826 when over 150,000 men received it.

Ivan Liprandi

Ivan Petrovich Liprandi left a diverse literary legacy which also included memoirs and critical writings on the Napoleonic Wars. Born into a family of Italian origin, he began military service in 1807 and distinguished himself fighting the Swedes and Turks over the next five years. In 1812, he served in the 6th Corps and participated in virtually every major battle against the French in Russia. Promoted to staff-captain in late 1812, he took part in the 1813–14 Campaigns, serving as ober-quartermaster in Winzingerode's corps and distinguishing himself at Soissons in 1814.

Lieutenant-General Mikhailovskii-Danilevskii, in his account of the 1814 campaign in France, described the capture of Soissons based on one-sided material and, having not witnessed it first hand, he committed serious mistakes which distort historical facts. Contemporaries trusted Mikhailovskii-Danilevskii's every word and his accounts, without much criticism, have been incorporated in all subsequent works, for example the article in the [recent] *Military Encyclopedical Lexicon*. Yet, documents preserved in the archives of the General Staff should have shed a different light on this topic. Unchallenged copying of erroneous accounts distorts reality and gradually becomes part of History itself. General [Gaspard] Gourgaud justly noted (in *Campagne de 1815*) that 'l'erreur à force d'être répétée finit souvent par être prise pour la réalité', that is, an often-repeated mistake eventually is taken for truth.

I do not intent to discuss the movements of Baron Winzingerode's corps from Dusseldorf (where he crossed the Rhine) to Laon since it is not the subject of the present article and its discussion would take too much space. So I go straight to the subject.

Mikhailovskii-Danilevskii, while always portraying Baron Winzingerode as 'hesitating' and acting only under the 'direction and insistence' of Adjutant General Chernyshev, notes on page 118 of his 'Description of the Campaign in France' that 'when Winzingerode arrived at Laon, he was puzzled about which direction he should turn for faster union with the acting armies . . . Chernyshev *advised* [Liprandi's emphasis] him not to hesitate in choosing his next actions and, without wasting any minute, march to Soissons and take it by assault.' Then Chernyshev, as written by [Mikhailovskii-Danilevskii], explains the benefits of this move.

Afterwards [Mikhailovskii-Danilevskii] writes on p. 119, 'Weighing the danger of enterprise on one side, and the benefits of its successful execution on another, Winzingerode allowed [Liprandi's emphasis] Chernyshev to go to Soissons, but on the same condition as he bound him during the passage through the Rhine meaning that Chernyshev should have taken responsibility for any failure.' I do not know from which sources did this appear on the pages of History? Anyone, who knew, or, better, witnessed the gallantry of Baron Winzingerode, would be surprised to read the above-mentioned passage. Equally surprising will be this to anyone familiar with Chernyshev's intellect and agility. Is it really possible to assume that Winzingerode, widely known from his enterprise and good understanding of his responsibility as a commander of a separate corps, would start *bargaining* [Liprandi's emphasis] with his subordinate and trying to remove responsibility from his shoulders in case of a failure? Moreover, can we really believe that Chernyshev would take (and on what basis) such a serious responsibility upon himself – to assault a fortified town with a small detachment that numbered two jager regiments (19th and 40th), slightly more than 1,000 men. It is certainly more perplexing to read this because [Mikhailovskii-Danilevskii] also writes that Napoleon, on account of the great importance of Soissons, had entrusted its defence to General Rusca, one of his old companions in the Italian campaigns, who had 7,000 men under arms, and was therefore unlikely to yield the fortress without the most determined resistance. I do not even comment about the incongruity of conditions Winzingerode and Chernyshev supposedly agreed upon, but is it possible to consign such nonsense to Chernyshev? After their meeting at Avesne, the generals never met prior to Soissons to conclude such a bargain verbally, while it could not have been made in writing. So how did it find its way into the annals of History?

When discussing the capture of Soissons, our military historian makes no mention of Winzingerode, as if he not only did not participate in this action but neither he or his corps were anywhere in vicinity of the town and the entire exploit was accomplished by Chernyshev alone! Yet, this is how it took place in reality.

On 31 January [12 February], the corps made one march from Aven to Werven. The following day, 1 [13] February, it reached Laon, late that day. On 2 [14] February, at 3:00 a.m., Winzingerode marched to Soissons and, by 1:00 p.m., concentrated his troops about two verstas [2.1km] from this town. None of this shows the indecisiveness or hesitation that is usually ascribed to Winzingerode. I would not discuss what was happening in Chernyshev's advance guard since I did not witness any of it, and so I will only talk about what I personally had witnesses and participated in.

In all the movements of the corps, Winzingerode was constantly present with it; thus it was during the march from Laon to Soissons. After making a brief halt at the farm Ange-Gardien, the corps marched forward, with Winzingerode, with his staff, at the front of it. he soon reached the village of Croix, from where Soissons could be observed. Passing this village Baron Winzingerode ordered to stop the corps, which was delayed on its march, to stop on the hill some two verstas [2.1km] from the town, while he personally went to the advance guard. I, as befitted my responsibilities, went with him.

There was no shortage of cannonballs, canister, and later musket balls, fired from the walls of the town. The Baron veered to the right from the road and approached an old postal house (which Mikhailovskii-Danilevskii refers to as a station house while the *Military Encyclopaedic Dictionary* correctly identifies as a postal house) that was located about thirty sazhens [60m] from the town's gates. A rather heavy musket fire was maintained. Chernyshev approached Winzingerode, who remained mounted. I could not hear what they talked about but could see that the corps commander spoke animatedly and then suddenly turned his horse to the left and quickly moved beyond the buildings (which protected us from enemy fire) towards the road. He was initially followed by his adjutants: Baron S. G. Stroganov (now count and general adjutant), Rzhevskii (from the Pavlogradskii Hussar Regiment) and Count Gustav Armfeldt, staff captain of the General Staff. Behind them came Chief of Staff Major-General Renne, duty general Prince S. G. Volkonskii, me and a few other individuals. The enemy intensified his fire. Winzingerode continued to smoke his pipe and maintained his usually presence of mind; he encouraged two jager companies (Starkov's and Polukhin's), that were deployed on both sides of the road, to charge the town's gates and then gave some orders to the newly-arrived brigade commander Colonel M. N. Matsnev before heading back to the corps. He was followed by his entire suite, except for Prince Volkonskii who asked for permission to remain with the advance guard. After covering about half a versta [500m], Winzingerode called me up and pointed towards a small hill on the right, some fifty sazhens [100m] from the road, where he ordered to immediately deploy Colonel N. N. Antropov's battery company. The corps was already beginning to halt at the mentioned spot. The 21st Division, in columns, stood to the right of the road, while the 24th Division was to the left. I galloped to Antropov's company but could not find him (he was called up to Major-General Merlin, commander of the artillery) so commanding officer Captain Eyler led the company behind me. Antropov caught with us while we were *en route*. Observing that the gallant Colonel Melnikov and his Cossacks were moving in front of the position where the battery was supposed to deploy, I hurried to inform him about this and the Cossacks immediately moved to the left. Upon reaching its destination, the company unlimbered and opened a lively fire, at which moment I left it and returned to find the corps commander [Winzingerode] almost a versta [1.06km] ahead of the corps, near a haystack on the right side of the road. He and his suite dismounted and rested. Cannonballs and musketballs fired from the town's guns were whistling all around. Many in our convoy were wounded and some had their coats pierced by bullets. Hardly ten minutes passed after my arrival when Count Volkonskii turned up as well and, without dismounting, his first words were, 'Mon general! La ville est à vous.' This is what happened: after Winzingerode left the advance guard, the jagers whom he cheered on, found two large tree trunks and used them to break down the feeble town gates, which they occupied. During this attack no petards, which are mentioned by Mikhailovskii-Danilevskii, were employed. [Still] they might have been used prior to Winzingerode's arrival when, according to Mikhailovskii-Danilevskii, two unsuccessful assaults were made.

The chief of staff [Renne] immediately ordered me to get into the town and bring somebody from the city hall to obtain necessary information. I approached the gates just when Colonel P. P. Sukhtelen was leading his Volynskii Uhlan Regiment, at the trot, into town, so I followed him inside. There was minor skirmishing in town between jagers and the enemy, who were fleeing everywhere. I found it very difficult to accomplish my mission since not a single resident could be found. Finally one prisoner told me where the city hall was located. And it was quite far away. To gain time, I took the prisoner with me since it seemed that he could provide necessary information. I also found an opportunity to take with me one of city notables, at whose house I selected an apartment and deployed a Cossack and uhlan to guard it (to calm down the Frenchman, who was wanted some guarantee of safety for his family). They both took horses from the dismounted Cossack and uhlan and we galloped back to the corps commander. As we were passing the city gates, I encountered Chernyshev who was entering it. He was visibly discontented that I entered the town before he did or, it will be more precise to say, that I did not inform him about my mission. I do not think Chernyshev believed me when I said that 'I was told you were already in town.'

About half a versta [500m] from town, I found the corps commander who was trotting towards [the town gates]. I reported about what I had seen in town and told the Chief of Staff about my meeting with Chernysev. He immediately informed the corps commander about it and then told me not to worry about it. The corps commander found Chernyshev on the main square in front of the city hall. There was the city mayor with his friends and a few prisoners of various ranks. Winzingerode again did not dismount and, leaving the chief of staff to gather necessary information, he, accompanied by Chernyshev, left the city in direction of Paris via Villers-Cotterêts and then towards Château-Thierry. After observing the vicinity and issuing orders on the deployment of troops in case of attack, Winzingerode returned to Soissons. The Chief of Staff ordered me to review the documents of the killed General Rusca, delivered by Chernyshev. With the help of two officers of the General Staff (Count Armfeldt and A. A. Ushakov), I accomplished this rather quickly since the documents were in good order and I conveyed those that were the newest and most important to the chief of staff.

Everything in my account of the actions of Baron Winzingerode during the capture of Soissons can be confirmed by numerous witnesses. The author of 'History of the campaign in France in the year 1814' deprives Winzingerode and his entire staff of the honour of participating in this affair and credit it entirely to the commander of the advance guard alone. The decisive influence on Soissons' garrison was not so much the personal presence of

Winzingerode at the very gates of the town but the rapid appearance of his entire corps. The town could have been stormed on this side without difficulty. Had Winzingerode not moved his entire corps within cannon shot of the town, Chernyshev with his advance guard, which consisted of 1,000 men, would have hardly posed any danger to some 7,000 Frenchmen, protected behind the walls, even though these walls were dilapidated and hardly ever repaired since the fifteenth century when the Duke of Burgundy fought with the King of France over their control. Still, these walls provided the defenders with the means to prolong their resistance. If the garrison had resisted for one day longer, it would have placed Blücher's army in a most dangerous position. This would have certainly happened if Chernyshev were left alone. This is clear from Mikhailovskii-Danilevskii's own narrative as well since he refers to Chernyshev's two failed assaults, both of which occurred before the arrival of Winzingerode with his corps. Upon seeing the masses of enemy infantry already deployed at a cannon shot's distance from the city walls and a battery of artillery being deployed forward, which usually preceded an assault, the garrison realised the futility of its resistance and began to gather on the road to Paris. Of course, the death of the garrison commander, as always happens in such circumstances, could have had an important effect, particularly in 1814 when the French did not show the same energy and vigour as in previous campaigns. During this campaign we recognised the good old French [troops] only when they were led by Napoleon himself. [From the Russian text in I. Liprandi, 'Kak byl vzyat Soissons. . .']

Sergei Volkonskii

Volkonskii was a staff officer in Winzingerode's headquarters.

A day after our capture of Soissons Winzingerode received a private letter from Illarion Vasilievich Vasilchikov, who informed him of the defeat of the Russo-Prussian forces at Sezanne and Montmirail, as well as about Blücher's defeat that forced him to withdraw his troops to Châlons. In conclusion, Vasilchikov urged Winzingerode to remain cautious. We then received orders for the Russian corps to leave a Cossack outpost at Soissons and advance towards Reims separately from the Prussian corps of Bülow which had been marching to the left and parallel to us during our invasion of France. We were supposed to establish close communications through Blücher with the main Allied army.

This order was carried out at once and, crossing the Aisne River and destroying everything that could have been useful to the enemy if he were to recapture Soissons, we marched along the riverbank towards Reims. During these marches, which were quite peaceful from a military point of view, one particular aspect vividly imprinted itself in my memory – the cruel necessity of suppressing the sense of humanity in one's heart. At Soissons we captured three or four thousand men. When we left Soissons, these men had to be evacuated as well but our own troops had very scarce supplies, barely enough for three days. So we had nothing to feed these prisoners of war who were collapsing from starvation and fatigue. I still remember the bitter reproaches that they made to us as our columns marched but there was nothing we could do for them because of scarcity of supplies that barely satisfied our needs and setting aside any provisions for the prisoners would have only harmed our own men. It was a heartless but, in those circumstances, necessary decision. At last we reached the city of Reims, a prosperous town that satisfied all the supply needs of our corps.

In my capacity [as duty officer in Winzingerode's headquarters], I was tasked with arranging supply system for our troops whose number increased to 45,000 men after the detachments of Count Vorontsov and Count Stroganov joined our corps . . . During our stay at Reims I found myself amidst circumstances that later had a profound influence on my career. Count Vorontsov's intrigues against Winzingerode became so blatant and public that I thought it my responsibility to inform Winzingerode about them – this was my responsibility both as an officer and a man who felt deep personal affinity and boundless appreciation for [Winzingerode's] goodwill and trust in me. Before Count Vorontsov's detachment joined us, I received a very brusque letter from the Count who also included an unsealed letter to Winzingerode that he asked me to convey. He could have sent it sealed and I would have remained uninvolved but because the letter was unsealed I thought I had the right to see its contents. In the letter Vorontsov, in very audacious phrases, accused Winzingerode of seeking to personally insult him for reorganising combined grenadier battalions and claimed that this had been done on Winzingerode's request, even though I knew well that it was in fact Emperor Alexander's own decision. Instead of delivering the letter, I returned it to the Count explaining that I did not want to be and should not be made the bearer of such an insulting letter that was based on wrong assumptions.

I did not share the content of this letter with Winzingerode but did inform him that there were certain intrigues directed against him. His response was, 'Je ne puis croire que des gens d'honneur agissent ainsi [I cannot believe that men of honour would act in such a manner]'. Seeing his persistence in judging people based on his own honourable morals while intrigues against him rapidly escalated, I decided, without informing Winzingerode, to write directly to Prince Peter Mikhailovich Volkonskii* informing him that I wanted to leave my position and serve in line units where I could gain experience and reputation. Therefore I asked him to recall me from Winzingerode's corps

---

* Volkonskii was Chief of the Main Staff of the Russian Army.

so I could serve not as a staff but rather as a line officer. I will describe what happened to this request later in my memoirs and in the meantime want to return back to military operations.

After our prolonged stay in Reims, our corps was ordered to participate in the general advance of all the Allied armies, support [the Allied] efforts aimed at recapturing Soissons and to act depending on circumstances during this offensive.

Our corps advanced from Reims to Soissons along the Aisne but instead of following the same riverbank as before we chose to move on the opposite one while Bülow's Prussians moved to Soissons from the north. After a three-day march we approached Soissons and Bülow appeared from the opposite side, with the city effectively surrounded on all sides. After our departure, the French had reclaimed Soissons and prepared it for defence. Its commandant was the French general Moreau, who was however no relation to the famed French general who had perished at Dresden.* In spite of considerable Allied forces gathering near Soissons, the French garrison was determined to defend the town. After blockading the fortress, both Winzingerode and Bülow dispatched messengers to ask the French to surrender and, threatening to launch an assault; they pointed out the superior numbers of the Allied forces that made defending the fortress impossible. The negotiations became dragged out because of the French refusal to compromise while we became eager to take the town after receiving the news that Blücher, who as usual got carried away, suffered a setback near Meau and retreated in great disorder and closely pursued through Villers-Cotterêts towards Soissons. Thus, capturing Soissons was the only way we could ensure that Blücher would reach the opposite bank of the Aisne. Throughout the negotiations, orders were made to have music played and songs performed in our camps in the hopes that their sounds would drown out the din of distant gunfire between the retreating Blücher and his French pursuers. With every passing hour we became desperate to capture Soissons and, in order to let our negotiator [Vladimir] Löwenstern know how how grave the situation was, Winzingerode ordered me to travel as a truce-bearer into the town claiming that I was to ask Bülow not to attempt any attacks during negotiations but my true purpose was to intimate to Löwenstern that he had to negotiate the surrender of Soissons without delay, even if he had to accept the most advantageous terms for the French. The primary goal was to find the much-needed resolution to this serious situation. I was allowed into the negotiating room, where I met Löwenstern in the presence of witnesses and had to carefully allude to him what was happening outside. Löwenstern

---

* Jean Moreau, whom Napoleon exiled from France, joined the Allies in 1813 and was mortally wounded in the battle of Dresden on 27 August 1813. He died on 2 September in Louny and was buried in the Catholic Church of St. Catherine in St. Petersburg.

then successfully negotiated the surrender that granted the garrison a free and honourable passage out of the fortress. We were not concerned about the specifics of the French surrender but simply desired to have control of the fortress which was 'un point de salut' [the place of salvation]' for Blücher.

I have read once an article that credited the honour of negotiating the surrender of Soissons to the diplomatic agility of Captain or Major Martens, Bülow's adjutant. But it is a lie. The honour belongs entirely to Löwenstern. The French garrison came out with full military honours and enjoying complete freedom of action beyond the agreed-upon line of demarcation. We occupied the town at once and I was tasked with assessing all state property still present inside it. To satisfy the needs of the troops, we levied a contribution of cloth, linen and shoe material but due to circumstances we collected only a small part of it. The day after capturing Soissons, our corps crossed to the other side of the river, leaving a garrison in the town. That same day saw the arrival, in great disorder, of the Prussian and Russian troops who had been defeated at Meaux and endured a vigorous [French] pursuit during their retreat. I remember meeting [August Wilhelm Antonius Graf Neidhardt] Gneisenau★ on his entrance into the town and reporting to him that among the captured military supplies were gunpowder and munitions, which he ordered me to immediately deliver to Blücher's troops, who suffered a great shortage of ammunition. The capture of Soissons undoubtedly saved Blücher's army from complete destruction – it was retreating in disorder from Meaux and, without Soissons, it would have been pushed up against the Aisne and annihilated. The army was saved through perseverance and enterprise of Winzingerode and the skilful negotiations of Löwenstern. The junction of our corps with the Army of Silesia subordinated our commander Winzingerode to Blücher and we soon received the order to retreat together with the Army of Silesia. [From the Russian text in S. Volkonskii, *Zapiski* . . .]

★ Gneisenau was Blücher's chief of staff and their collaboration is often cited as one of the best examples of the harmonious co-operation between a commander and his chief of staff.

4

The Battle at Craonne

Frustrated by Blücher's escape at Soissons, Napoleon sought to cross the Aisne further east in order to flank the Army of Silesia. This was made possible when the French cavalry defeated a Cossack detachment and seized an intact bridge at Berry-au-Bac. Pushing forward, Napoleon received intelligence of Allied forces concentrated on a plateau at Craonne. Assuming that Blücher was still trying to retreat, Napoleon concluded that this was probably a covering force for the Army of Silesia and decided to destroy it. In fact he was facing a very strong force that included the 1st, 2nd and 3rd Prussians Corps and the Russian corps of Langeron, Osten-Sacken and Winzingerode. The battle of Craonne on 7 March did not go as either side planned. Blücher could not get all his forces into action while Napoleon did not yet appreciate how powerful his opponent was. After several hours of fighting, in which the troops of General Vorontsov particularly distinguished themselves, Blücher decided to break off the action and had the troops at Craonne fall back on the main position at Laon, about six miles to the north-west. Although Napoleon could claim a victory at Craonne since he was left in possession of the field, his army suffered heavy losses that it could not afford. After the battle both sides remained very much in the dark as to each other's actual strength and intentions. Still believing that Blücher was in retreat, Napoleon sought another opportunity to destroy part of the Army of Silesia. This led to a two-day battle at Laon where the Allies successfully repelled the French attacks and forced Napoleon to fall back.

Sergei Mayevskii

Mayevskii was the commander of the 13th Jager Regiment and, in 1835, he wrote a lengthy memo to the Russian historian Alexander Mikhailovskii-Danilevskii describing his experiences at the battle of Craonne. He later published a memoir that contains a slightly different version of the events.

It must be noted that the Allied forces, having captured Soissons on 2 [14] February and Reims at about the same time which afforded them two strongpoints, were still advancing towards Paris from various directions. Thus when we lost Reims and Soissons, the main advantages that we could have exploited fell into the enemy's hands. As a result, Blücher's army, which was already far ahead of Soissons, found itself, one can say, cut off by two main obstacles: having the Marne River and the fortress of Soissons in the rear and facing all the enemy forces that vigorously pursued it. The fate of this Army depended on the capture of Soissons, which is why Winzingerode's corps besieged it on 19 February [3 March] and after 1½ day long fighting forced it to capitulate just as the enemy's forces approached it. Thus, the enemy torrent was halted and all misfortunes that could have befallen us averted. During these events Colonel Mayevskii commanded the 13th Jager Regiment and ten combined battalions.*

After Soissons, Count Vorontsov's detachment captured, without a fight, Retel and its sizable arsenal. The enemy, still controlling Reims which was the centre of the theatre of war and thereby exploiting its central position, dispatched his main forces, together with Marshal Marmont, to Laon to threaten our rear and defeat us piecemeal. Winzingerode's corps was then deployed on the heights of Craonne.

Napoleon, proceeding to Laon with the Guard Division under the command of young Caraman, suddenly changed his direction to the left and took up position in front of Craonne, where two Cossack regiments and two squadrons of the Izumskii Hussars, under command of Lt. Col. Lashkarev, were deployed as outposts. Count Vorontsov's detachment considered this movement as a diversion and therefore limited its response to simple observing and reconnoitring. Voronstov dispatched Krasovskii to gather more information about the enemy's movement and determine his strength and purpose. Krasovskii, accompanied by Colonel Mayevskii, travelled to the front line but observed only weak enemy forces crossing at Berry-au-Bac and could not determine the purpose of the enemy movement. The enemy's advance forces moved cautiously and slowly but they nevertheless gradually covered the plain between Corbeny and Craonne. Krasovskii reported all of this to Vorontsov, who had long disputed that anything serious could be expected here, and instead remained in his position, inexorably demanding to drive the enemy back.†

---

* In his memoir, Mayevskii noted that 'up to Namur, we marched by forced marches that lasted twelve to fifteen hours. At each bivouac, locals delivered food and wine for soldiers while officers treated each other, for example, one day the officers of the 13th Jager Regiment treated their comrades from the 14th Jagers, then the following day the 14th Jagers treated the 13th'. He also observed that several days before the battle, 'me and Krasovskii each received five grenadier companies from other regiments so our regiments' strength increased to about 1,200 men and 20 officers'.

† In his memoir, Mayevskii added a few more details: 'We stood in position near Craonne [and] observed as Napoleon, having moved his entire army across the river, pushed back our Cossacks. Count [Voronstov] desired to distinguish himself with a

General Krasovskii returned to the position occupied by the enemy but as he arrived two or three vigorous enemy attacks drove our two Cossack regiments back to Corbeny while the hussars, though unable to contain the enemy's pressure, still tried to hold their ground. Fearing to lose direct contact with the army, Count Vorontsov ordered the retreat to Laon where all our forces were to be concentrated. But just as we began to withdraw, our hussars galloped headlong past us! The 13th Jager Regiment, thus, found itself on the front line – but this was a triumphant moment of the 13th Regiment!

Meanwhile, Vorontsov's detachment turned back and occupied its previous position on the slope which controlled both entrances into the village and the entire plain around it.* Silence that came down on both sides was uninterrupted by any shots or shouts. Around 8–9 o'clock in the evening, the 13th Jager Regiment descended the almost vertical slope of the mountain and occupied Craonne, where it deployed a skirmisher chain and, confident that

---

brilliant attack. Thinking that Napoleon's army was in fact just a corps, he decided to secure [the village of] Corbeny where the enemy could cut our line of communication with the army. General Krasovskii was instructed to reconnoitre the environs and prepare for battle. [Krasovskii] took me with him. But just as we reached our advance posts, our hussars mounted horses and prepared for combat. A certain Lashkarev, who commanded the hussars, pointed towards strong enemy masses deploying in the vast plain and fervently argued that he would be forced to fall back if the enemy attacked. Krasovskii conveyed his findings to Vorontsov, who, however, thought [the news about enemy's strength] had been exaggerated and remained firm in his opinion and determination to carry out his plan. The two generals soon became involved in a heated argument, with the Count demonstrating his obvious displeasure. Nevertheless, the infantry was ordered to retreat.'

* In his memoir, Mayevskii observes: '[After the initial order to retreat] we marched for just a versta when we were turned around. We encountered our hussars galloping as soon as they could along the road at the bottom of the hill. We halted on the hill that dominated the entire area. The Count was perplexed while Krasovskii argued fervently in support of his initial report. Losing patience, the Count uttered a few bitter comments . . . he still wanted to fight through to Corbeny and restore his communications with the army. Krasovskii argued that it was impossible but the Count prevailed. Late that night the Count called me and, as if to reproach Krasovskii who was also in attendance, he told me, "My dear Mayevskii, I hope that in spite of inflated difficulties, you will advance with your regiment to Corbeny. And here is your guide." I was thrilled by this opportunity but Krasovskii interfered [and told Vorontsov:] "If Your Excellency does not believe me and considers that I have warned him only out of cowardice, I must insist on being sent with this regiment." The Count tried to appease him, but now the dispute erupted between me and Krasovskii. I explained to him that he had already made his reputation while I was still making mine and [by accompanying my regiment, Krasovskii would] take this opportunity away and therefore offend me. Finally the Count and Krasovskii yielded to me and I rushed back to the regiment. However, instead of Corbeny, I occupied Craonne, which lay at the bottom of the hill where Vorontsov's corps was deployed.'

there would be no further action that night, got carried away by carelessness.*
Colonel Mayevskii decided to take a company of jagers and two squadrons of
the Rizhskii Dragoons through the woods to the clearing in order to observe
if there were any enemy forces there. But just as he had entered the defile, he
encountered the enemy who was moving with exactly the same intention – to
reconnoitre our position that was concealed by a thick band of forest.

The Russian 'Hurrah' rallied all of us together and we charged at the enemy;
a handful of enemy soldiers disappeared into the woods and the darkness of
the night.

The rest of the night went quietly but at dawn the enemy began to move
more and more of his troops into the plains. And yet, no one [on the Russian
side] still thought that there would be a major battle here.

Around 11 o'clock in the morning, Colonel Mayevskii led the same detachment on reconnaissance.† But just as he had moved 500 paces, he encountered
an enemy detachment which was led by a magnificent-looking young general
on a beautiful horse and wearing full military uniform. Once again a bayonet
charge followed the shouts of 'Hurrah' and the enemy disappeared once more.
But the enemy infantry soon appeared and opened a fierce fire which, however,
could not reach beyond the wooded plain. Colonel Mayevskii, being alone and
independent in his actions, deployed half of his squads as skirmishers and kept
the rest in reserve. Lieutenant Tovbich, who held position near the exit from
the defile, made ten charges with his company and ten times he captured and
lost the little home that served as his buttressing. At exactly five o'clock in the
afternoon, the enemy exhausted all of his efforts and used up his numerical
superiority – despite the genius and gallantry of Caraman, Ney and even
Napoleon himself, the interminable bravery of the 13th Jager Regiment and
its devotion to the Tsar, its flags and glory refused to concede even an inch of
our ground. Our units brotherly supported and replaced each other, deployed

---

* Mayevskii's memoirs: 'I was grumbling that the fate was once again depriving me
of battle and my officers shared this sentiment, despairing that they may not have to
fight without a guardian [Krasovskii]. So we indulged ourselves in childish angst and
carelessly treated each other to excellent wine. Because of importance of our position
and to get a better sense of the situation, Count Vorontsov frequently dispatched his
adjutants to see what was happening at our location, which, I have to admit, we did not
ourselves. Thus it is that arrogance and inexperience dooms many people.'

† As the years passed Mayevskii seems to have gained a better view of his failing at
this battle. In his memoir he noted, 'By eleven o'clock in the morning the French army
deployed in large masses, in our full view, on the same plain that it had occupied the
day before. We observed it rather indifferently and, to my shame, I did not reconnoitre
my surrounding area earlier. The battle did get me acquainted with it quickly though
. . . As the enemy advanced, I grabbed Cossacks and dragoons and moved on the
road through the woods. In just 100 (maybe 200) paces, I then encountered a French
general who was, of course, conducting a reconnaissance of his own.'

in formations and charged with bayonets between fifteen and twenty times. These orderly – better to say mathematically precise – movements, repulsing of enemy attacks, countercharges and replacement of units presented a rare sight to behold. All of this unfolded in front of Count Vorontsov and his entire corps and, seeming to foretell success to our arms, widespread cheers served as our reward! Colonel Mayevskii had three horses killed under him while the [13th Jager] regiment lost two staff officers, fourteen commissioned officers and up to 400 rank-and-file, but they all presented glorious examples of self-sacrifice. The remaining six officers, of whom hardly one had reached the age of twenty, took the places of their fallen comrades and fought with such valour that they caused the enemy to despair.

Unwilling to believe that they faced just a single regiment, the enemy decided to attempt a flanking manoeuvre which was facilitated by a deep ravine with thick brushwood that led directly into the rear of our corps.

This moment marked the start of the actual withdrawal of the 13th Jager Regiment.* Suffering a devastating [enemy] fire from the front, it now had to experience a similarly heavy fire from the heights that the enemy had occupied. However, the arriving companies of the 13th Jagers, as well as the entire 14th Jager Regiment, saved our unit from this dangerous situation when it had to fall back along a one narrow path that ran at the bottom of the hill and had been already intercepted by another column. 'The Tsar is with us! The Lord is with us!' shouted our gallant jagers as they charged and the enemy soldiers paid with their lives for the audacity of attempting to stop us.

Upon reaching the plateau, the 13th Jager Regiment stood in reserve to the 14th Jager Regiment, which helped our men to calmly move back. Meanwhile, the Nasheburgskii and Novaginskii Infantry Regiments, commanded by the courageous Colonel Dunaev, continued to cover the withdrawal of our troops who had been hemmed in on both sides by the enemy. Unfortunately Colonel Dunaev was [soon] wounded and his regiments could not contain the thrust of the attacking enemy, who was eager to cut the 13th Jager Regiment off from the upland that lay adjacent to the narrow passage and was intersected with ravines that the enemy used to advance from two sides.

But once again our jagers charged and gained a final victory. They advanced with bayonets and overwhelmed everything on their way. Abandoning their last hope, the enemy no longer tried their luck [in attacking us]. The 13th

---

* In his memoir, Mayevskii explained: '[Vorontsov] sent several orders for me to retreat but his messengers never got to me. Meanwhile, I could not retreat on my own, fearing losing my regiment and jeopardising my name, as well as failing to contain the enemy attack. Any rashness or hasty retreat would have deprived me of both glory and the regiment . . . [At last] I had to abandon my position . . . [Vorontsov] was initially upset at my measured retreat but, understanding the difficulties we faced, he also gave due credit to the gallantry and fearlessness of my regiment.'

Jagers quietly moved back and stood in reserve of the entire corps. Collective greetings and praise could not sooth the pain of those who mourned their heroic fallen comrades.*

On 23 February [7 March], around twelve o'clock, the enemy began to appear in a new position and since our cavalry had been sent on a flanking manoeuvre in the evening, the honour of facing the enemy fell to the Pavlogradskii Hussar Regiment, two Cossack regiment and a handful of infantry. 'The 13th and 14th Jager Regiments Advance!' – the familiar voice informed the brave warriors of the gratifying task they were about to undertake. We took position, formed into squares and opened a hellish fire [adskii ogon] along the entire frontline. A bloody battle began once more.

Count Vorontsov found himself in a critical position, lacking cavalry and facing a much superior enemy, who had already concentrated his forces on the battlefield. Vorontsov thus relied on the bravery of his troops whom he inspired through his own personal gallantry. Even though he could not stand properly due to an injury sustained to his leg on the eve of the battle, he still rushed back and forth like a spirit of war. Wherever there was the greatest danger and the most death, one saw Vorontsov! His serenity and inexplicable exultation of spirit amidst this terrible slaughter add some heavenly lustre to the earthly environment. The last [attack] effort fell to the fortunate 13th Jagers. The Count [Vorontsov] approached this regiment and like a simple battalion commander, he directed everything. Allowing the enemy to approach to just fifty paces, he shouted 'Fire!' One had to see what happened once the order was given. It seems as if Death herself had come to assist the Count and the 13th Jagers! The enemy – startled, slaughtered and humiliated – fled back while we calmly resumed our withdrawal.

We soon came across another defile that was carved by two deep ravines. We marched by battalions in echelons. The Count [Vorontsov] stayed behind with a handful of cavalrymen to cover us, and his charges, supported by the gallant Colonels Alferiev and Chechenskii, only added new laurels to his crown! We sheltered the cavalrymen, who, one may side, at times pressed with their horse tails against our chests as we slowly retreated by echelons. [. . .] Amid these difficult conditions, cannonballs, canister and shells fell like hail on us. One of the shells landed between the 13th and 14th Regiments. Somebody shouted, 'Scatter!' The 14th Jagers did it and suffered losses.† The 13th Jagers, on the other hand, firmly believed in its good fortune and maintained its orderly march and the Lord had mercy on it.

---

* Mayevskii's note in memoirs: 'The battle at Craonne put an end to the prejudice [against me] but did not eradicate jealousy. I established a firm foundation for my military reputation but grey-haired colonels often bad-mouthed me behind my back.'
† In his memoir, Mayveskii noted that the 14th Jagers lost about twenty men to this explosion.

Around seven o'clock in the evening we saw [Field Marshal] Blücher's advance guard, commanded by Adjutant General Count Stroganov. An artillery battery commanded by [officer] Czartoryski, who if I am not mistaken was [soon] killed there, opened a devastating fire on the enemy. The famed Generals Lanskoi and Ushakov then launched cavalry charges to complete the enemy's defeat, but both [generals] were mortally wounded in the process. Count Stroganov's son was also killed at the battery. The despondent father was supported by Count Vorontsov who took over overall command of the troops and finished [the battle]. The nightfall soon covered the warring sides and we fell back to Laon. [From the Russian text in RGVIA, f. VUA, op. 16, d. 3376, Part 2]

Jacob Otroshenko

After crossing the Rhine at Cologne, Otroshenko's 14th Jager Regiment advanced across Belgium to invade northern France. After the brief clash at Soissons, Otroshenko fought in the battle at Craonne, where he found himself subordinated to Colonel Sergei Mayevskii, with whom he had rather strained relations. His memoir, therefore, offers a version of events that differs from Mayevskii's.

After passing through Charleroi, we took up quarters in the vicinity of the city of Reims. At the entrance of every village, a local mayor met our troops in order to show us our quarters, a practice established by Napoleon not only in France but across all of Germany. We requested supplies to be delivered and this was immediately accomplished. The mayors never left their villages and were ready to listen to our requests. We spent no more than a week there before advancing to the fortified city of Soissons, where a French garrison was present.

On 19 February [3 March] we arrived at Soissons and, taking positions in the fields outside it, we dispatched a truce-bearer to the fortress commandant demanding his surrender and threatening to subject the city to an assault. The commandant rejected our demand. We sent skirmishers towards the city ramparts, where they were greeted with canister. But the fighting quickly ended and the commandant declared that he would surrender the city the next day, which he indeed did. The capture of this town was of great importance for us since Napoleon vigorously pursued Field Marshal Blücher who was retreating towards Soissons.

On 20 February [4 March], around eight o'clock in the morning, the garrison left the fortress. By noon, we heard gunfire coming from the road. It was [French] reinforcements arriving to support the garrison. The enemy encountered our Cossack regiments and was driven back. Soon thereafter appeared the Prussian troops who marched through Soissons, and in their wake, our detachment was ordered to left the city as well. Count [Alexander] Langeron's corps then passed through as well, leaving a garrison in the fortress.

On 21 February [5 March], we marched to Craonne and by nightfall took up quarters at a village about five verstas [5.3km] away from the town. There was a mountain on the right side of the road and local residents could be seen moving down with empty carts and moving up with various possessions. Fearing pillaging that might follow if a battle was fought [near Craonne], they were probably hiding their valuables in underground cavities.

On 22 February [6 March], around six o'clock in the morning, the 13th and 14th Jager Regiments were ordered to immediately depart their bivouacs to prevent the enemy crossing. General Krasovskii was at the detachment's headquarters and therefore Colonel Mayevskii of the 13th Jager regiment was the most senior officer. The battalions of the 13th Jagers were ready while of the 14th Jagers, only on battalion, which I commanded, was present.

Colonel Mayevskii ordered me to advance along the local road to the crossing while he led his regiment behind my column. We marched for about three and a half verstas [3.7km] before coming out onto a vast plain that resembled an isosceles triangle that was wrapped around by a river. The French organised the crossing at the tip of this triangle while we were at its bottom with the heights, covered with vineyards, behind us. The crossing was protected with numerous cannon and [we could see] many armed residents on the opposite riverbank that featured thick brushwood. Large enemy cavalry columns had already crossed the river and were on their way to Craonne, which was located to the left of us. Behind them marched infantry. Colonel Mayevskii halted his regiment on the heights and ordered me to advance with my lone battalion to the crossing, destroy it and capture the enemy batteries. This order startled me but I could not tell him that this was an impossible order because he was my enemy back then and was waiting for any opportunity to hurt me.* Yet, to obey this order, I had to march for about two verstas [2.1km] across a flat and open plain, exposing myself to devastating artillery fire from the front, local residents' musket fire from the right and cavalry attacks from the left, which would have completely destroyed my battalion. In short, the battalion was condemned to a certain and pointless death.

Nevertheless, I began making preparations for advance by conducting various manoeuvres in the hope that [time will pass] and somebody from our superiors might come. I was certain that this order would be then countermanded. I dispatched one company about 200 paces ahead of me, dispersing half of it into a skirmisher chain and keeping the other in reserve. I then changed my front to the right. It was then that I noticed General Benckendorf who was passing by my troops. I immediately ran to him, informing him of my orders

---

* Otroshenko does not specify what incident caused such bad relations between him and Mayevskii. The latter is silent about it as well.

and asked him to give me instructions how I should proceed. He listened to me and, with visible annoyance, told me, 'You must retreat in the wake of the 13th Regiment, which has turned back already.' Leaving the village where we spent the night to our left, we marched to Craonne where gunfire could be heard already. Not far from it we received an order from Count Vorontsov instructing the 13th Jager Regiment to secure the position in the vineyards close to [Craonne], dispatch one battalion to secure Craonne itself and keep the rest of the 14th Jagers on the heights behind the 13th Jager Regiment.

Around two o'clock in the afternoon fighting began in Craonne. It gradually intensified and soon involved artillery fire as well. Colonel Mayevskii committed his entire 13th Jager Regiment to the fight and held his ground until nightfall, when he retreated with a handful [of surviving] men. I was ordered to remain with my battalion to contain the enemy, whose skirmishers soon appeared. I engaged them in a firefight and then retreated as I was ordered. The darkness soon put an end to the fighting and I retreated all the way to narrow defile that was formed by a deep valley on the eastern side and the top of a deep and wide rocky ravine on the western side. There I received General Krasovskii's order to deploy my battalion in this narrow passage, at a manor located near the road running from the Soissons *chaussée* to Craonne, to establish a skirmisher chain as I found fit and spend the night there. While reconnoitring the area at night, I came across the body of a French soldier and was at a loss on how he appeared here. I was told that the French intended to seize this road but infantry battalions, which had been deployed here, met them with bayonets and drove them back into the woods to the right. The enemy harassed my skirmisher chain with occasional shots during the night but did not dare to launch a major attack. On 23 February [7 March], around nine o'clock in the morning, I noticed the enemy troops moving and ordered my Cossacks to determine which direction they were moving in. Meanwhile, musket fire broke out in the skirmisher chain and it quickly intensified. The Cossacks had to fall back due to the advance of the enemy flanquers. I received orders to hold my ground for as long as I could.

It was a sunny day. [The Russian] troops behind us were already deployed in battle formation and the rays of the sun glistened on their bayonets. My skirmishers were already fully engaged with the enemy, who kept strengthening his attacks. The Cossacks rode to the rear and puffs of smoke soon announced the arrival of the enemy artillery, which sent cannonballs to greet our columns. The enemy soon set the manor where I was staying on fire and the clouds of smoke forced me to fall back and take position above the ravines. I repelled the incessant attacks of enemy skirmishers who continually tried to turn our right flank. At that moment Count Vorontsov rode down the [skirmisher] chain and calmly observed the enemy movements, [the Russian] troops passing [orderly] by the burning estate despite the fierce fire, and the performance of our artillery. The enemy's numerical superiority and vigorous attack forced us to retreat. Skirmishers fell back to the squares while the enemy seized our previous positions and sent cavalry to attack our cavalry which moved behind our infantry. The enemy cavalry was met with canister and forced back. We had very few cavalry because General Winzingerode had dispatched most of them on a flanking manoeuvre the previous night and they had not yet returned. The enemy, on the other hand, had considerable cavalry force but location and terrain did not allow him to fully utilise it; we were thus saved by the deep, wide and rocky ravines on our flanks. After the failure of his cavalry, the enemy opened a heavy artillery fire. Our troops retreated by echelons. The French made several more cavalry charges but they were always repelled with loss.

At the start of the battle [the Russian] troops were commanded by Count Stroganov but after the death of his son, he surrendered command to Count Vorontsov. This talented general demonstrated his deep knowledge of the art of war, worthy of emulation. His composure in commanding troops and rational anticipation of the enemy's intensions represent key attributes of a great commander. Napoleon himself acknowledged that he pursued our 10,000-strong detachment with 30,000 men and still could not do anything against us. Of course, advantageous terrain facilitated our retreat but the all the credit belongs to Count Vorontsov, who managed to take advantage of circumstances.

On 25 February [9 March] we marched to Laon . . . [From the Russian text in J. Otroshenko, *Zapiski*. . .]

Ivan Ortenberg

Ivan Fedorovich Ortenberg was just twenty-one years old when he stepped onto French soil in January 1814. After training in the Noble Regiment, he enlisted in the Byelorrusskii Hussar Regiment (attached to the 2nd Cavalry Division, commanded by General Sergey Lanskoy, of the 4th Cavalry Corps, led by General Illarion Vasilchikov, in the Army of Silesia) and participated in the 1813-1814 Campaigns, finishing the war as staff rotmistr (captain).

The battle at Craone, which in its results proved to be of no value to either side, immortalised Count [Mikhail] Vorontsov's name. The French lost up to 8,000 killed and wounded, including Marshal Victor, the Duc de Bellune, and General Grouchy. On our side, some 6,000 men became casualties, and the Pavlogradskii Hussar Regiment had only 400 men surviving out of 900 that entered the battle; a greater number of generals were wounded, Ushakov was killed, [Sergey] Lanskoy was mortally wounded while a cannonball tore away Colonel Parkenson's head.

This spurious success, although granting Napoleon a pointless victory, could not satisfy his expectations. Surrounded by the dead and dying, he soon received the bitter news from Caulaincourt that the Allied representatives, gathered at the Congress of Chatillon, refused to accept any compromises and ended armistice negotiations. Staggered by such misfortune, he decided to stake his fortune once more on success of his arms.

Like a proud lion pursed by hunters, Count Vorontsov retreated, as instructed, via Chavignon to Laon. Vasilchikov's cavalry covered the retreat and, through its incessant counterattacks, it suppressed all attempts of the enemy cavalry, led by Generals Nansouty and Belliard, to disrupt the order of our march. This memorable withdrawal was like some kind of intrepid journey, full of incidents and nimble movements. Not limiting himself to simply protecting his forces, our commander [Vasilchikov] sought any opportunity to harm the enemy that continued to pursue us. So our route was marked by a series of competently-arranged skirmishes. Thus, passing by a farm surrounded by a stone wall, Vorontsov ordered the 6th Jager Regiment to take position behind it. This order prompted Vasilchikov into trying to lure the enemy cavalry under the fire of our jagers. So he hastened to retreat and Nansouty's cavalry charged after him, approaching the stone wall with its right flank. Suddenly a battalion fire began from behind the wall and farm buildings. Our soldiers fired at discretion, at almost point-blank range, inflicting heavy casualties on the French and disrupting their ranks. 'En avant! Serrez les rangs!' shouted the French officers, courageously holding their ground under fire but our hussars soon charged and routed the enemy cavalry. After this debacle, Nansouty acted more cautiously but our generals, acting more skilfully, continued to outmanoeuvre him.

To facilitate Vorontsov's retreat, Sacken sent the entire artillery of his corps to him. Major-General Nikitin deployed this artillery in two lines, separated by 60 paces from each other. The first line stood at the bottom of a hill while the second took up position on the top of the hill, where the French had to move in dense columns due to the narrow valley. As soon as they appeared, both lines of Nikitin's artillery opened fire. A terrifying cannonade continued for some twenty minutes and the French exhausted themselves in futile endeavours. They finally stopped and Vorontsov's retreat, partly to Chevregny [*Shervin'i*] and partly to Laon continued uninterrupted. At Chavignon, Vorontsov was joined by Rudzevich who arrived there from Soissons, which the French, despite their numerical inferiority to the Army of Silesia and an impending battle, immediately occupied on Napoleon's orders.

The fast-approaching darkness, the concentration of large number of troops and transports as well as the need to rest his men compelled Vorontsov to spend four hours at Chavignon. Having passed the town, the troops of Count Vorontsov, Vasilchikov and Rudzevich bivouacked on both sides of the road from Craonne to Laon. We naturally did not set up tents but were allowed to prepare porridge and soon bivouac fires illuminated our position. Our officers, smoking their pipes, stood gloomily around fires. Poignant memories of their esteemed commanders lost, and numerous friends and acquaintances killed, hung heavily above them. Suddenly a shout was heard, 'Foragers forward!' Sixty men from every regiment and horse artillery company went to their horses and deployed facing Laon. A quartermaster officer then called up officers and informed each of them which village he was assigned to forage.

At Chavignon, occupied by the headquarters, only old men, women and children remained. The foragers selected guides from among old men, who were given lamps and ordered to move, in their wooden shoes, ahead of the cavalry. They soon breathed heavily out of fatigue and loudly cursed Napoleon. Officers had instruction to gather hay, oats, cattle for meat rations, bread and vodka or wine, and then rejoin their respective regiments at the Laon position. . .

[The author spends the next two paragraphs lamenting that foraging is not discussed in military history, which prompts him to discuss it here.]

Leaving Chavigny, the forager detachment moved on the main Laon road and as it reached crossroads with local routes, regimental foraging squads turned left or right accompanied by their guides. The squad of an officer [probably Ortenberg himself], whose story I tell here, turned right from the Laon road. The night was unusually dark, weather cloudy, with occasional rain and sleet. The road passed through a broken and wooded terrain. It was impossible, and probably pointless, to send flankers to investigate various ravines and bushes. A strong wind was blowing through the forest, freezing the foragers to the bone. Covered in mud, soaked in rain and wrapped up in their coats, the foragers moved in three to the right formation, having one NCO and two privates as advance guard some 20 paces ahead of the detachment, while a rearguard of one NCO and three privates was moving at the same distance in the back. Commanding officer and the guide with a lamp were with advance guard. About four hours before dawn, the foragers heard dogs barking, a certain sign of a nearby village. Thoughts of finding warm shelter and eating a loaf of bread quickly revived everyone. In a few minutes, the barking increased and the forward flankers came across a village. Everyone stopped; the officer listened in on surroundings and studied the village street, where he saw a few houses with lights on, a sure sign of military billet.

The officer dismounted and, after studying the terrain in darkness, he deployed his detachment on a grassy field facing the road so that he could charge the enemy's flank if the enemy appeared in the village. He then ordered an NCO and a soldier to quietly enter the village, look inside the houses with lighted windows and immediately return back. The NCO was told to use firearms as a last resort only and not to surrender without firing a shot.

Obviously it was not an easy assignment. In French villages, houses rarely had windows facing the street (under Napoleon, people had to pay an additional tax on them) so to look inside the house, one had to enter the backyard, which oftentimes contain dogs whose barking could alert residents. The NCO skilfully overcame all obstacles: leaving a soldier to guard the gates, he jumped off the house, snuck into the yard of a well-lit house and crawled to the window. Looking inside, he saw two locals sitting near a fireplace where something was boiling in a kettle, two French soldiers sleeping on straw on the floor, two metal helmets with horse tails, two sabres and two sabretaches laying on a table; a cart full of knapsacks and muskets with fixed bayonets was standing in the yard.

After receiving the [NCO's] report, our commanding officer momentarily hesitated. Entering a village, already occupied by the enemy whose strength was unknown, seemed very dangerous to him, yet leaving with empty hands because of some two sleeping Frenchmen and a few muskets on a cart was also unacceptable to him. After weighing options for a few minutes, he ordered the NCO with two troopers and the guide to go to one of the homes on the edge of the village and seize and bring back its owner. Turning to the guide, the officer told him in French, 'Listen to me: you are tired, I can clear see that. I will be happy to replace you with another guide. But . . . first, here is my flask with rum. Drink as much as you need to warm yourself – then help us one more time and I will let you go home. Go to the village with my NCO and two hussars. No matter what happens you must get me one of the locals. Do not waste any time. Est-ce arrange [Agreed]?'

Against all expectations, the alcohol loosened up the taciturn guide, who kept repeating: 'Mon officier, vous serez obéi [My officer, I will obey your command]'. Then, turning to the people who assigned to accompany him, he suddenly spoke in Russian, 'Let's go, lads!'

'What a miracle! How can you speak Russian?' asked him our bewildered officer.

'I am a true Yaroslavets [from the city of Yaroslavl], Your Honour,' responded the guide in an accented Russian.

'How did you end up with the French?' – inquired the officer

'I was an NCO in the Russian army and was captured at Zurich [in 1799]. Me and other prisoners were brought here and given to locals for work and sustenance.'

'What happened to you next ?'

'Then, as today, France lacked manpower; the daughter of my master liked me, so I married her and received a house. I sinned (at these words, the guide cried) and stayed here for good. The relatives of my wife are very good people, and my wife is a very kind woman. I am very content with my life, although I have never forgotten my homeland. So I will be happy to be of service to Your Honour.'

He left with our men and returned about quarter an hour later with two locals whom the NCO saw sitting next to the fireplace. These happened to me the head of the village and his son.

'Dites moi [tell me],' the officer asked them, 'why do you have French officers in the village? How long have they been here, how large is their detachment? Do you expect any more

'Ah! Monsieur, we have only two dragoons,' responded the village head. 'Me and my son delivered provisions [to the French forces] at Craonne. We came across the battlefield and found these unfortunates, they are both wounded and half-alive.

'Are you telling me the truth? You will not be harmed if this is true, but if you lied to me, you pay dearly for this,' [our officer threatened them].

'It is all true, mon officier!'

'And what about muskets that are one the cart? And sabres inside the house?' our officer kept inquiring.

The old man seemed momentarily confounded but he quickly recovered,

'We picked them up on the battlefield . . . We need them to make horseshoes for our horses. . .'

It was clear from his response that the weapons had a completely different purpose. The French were already taking up an idea of a people's war [guerrilla war] against us and several serious incidents of this had already taken place at various points of the theatre of war. As it is known, Blücher's line of communication with Schwarzenberg was rather unreliable and that locals, led by retired soldiers and priests, often attacked our couriers and even small detachments, and that Father Potier [?] was awarded the Legion d'Honneur for leading such an enterprise.

Upon finishing his interrogation, our officer deployed two mounted sentries at every exit from the village and ordered them to let no one out. He then let the rest of troops to the village head's house, sending half of them to warm up in the neighbouring two houses and leaving the other half with the horses. He ordered the musket butts and bayonets, found in the cart, to be broken, the musket barrels damaged and the cartridges dropped into a water-filled ditch. While all of this was carried out, locals, on our officer's order, prepared ten large wagons, each pulled by three horses, full of hay, oats, chickens, geese, ducks and a few barrels of wine and vodka. The officer made the village head and his son drink a cup of both the wine and the vodka to ensure that they were not poisoned. Two cows, taken for meat rations, were tied to the last wagon. The locals had already delivered all the available bread to their army and so they could not satisfy our officer's demands in that respect. So the officer was forced to make up for this shortage in another village.

About half an hour before sunrise, everything was ready for our departure. The French were expected to resume their pursuit of the Army of Silesia and the presence of our foragers in the area between the roads to Soissons and Reims could become very dangerous. Our officer decided to move to the left side of the Soissons road, seize bread in one of the local villages and, turning to the right, to proceed to Laon.

With this intention, our foragers proceed towards the Soissons road. An NCO, two troopers and a guide were in the advance guard, followed by carriages that had four flankers on each side to supervise drivers. Then came the rest of detachment in a three-to-the-right formation, while the rearguard consisted of an NCO and two troopers.

In the first village, on the left side of the Soissons road, our officer demanded supplies of bread from a local village head.

'Mon Dieu, monsieur l'officier,' responded the village head, 'Les Russies et les Prussiens have already visited us. There is nothing else left: everything is either bought or taken by force! I swear on my honour that you will find nothing in our village.'

Because of the village's proximity to the road, on which the French army was expected to move on, our officer could not spend time searching houses and barns. So he ordered the locals to give our troops a cup of vodka and a loaf of bread, and then proceeded along the Soissons road.

In the next, much larger, village, our officer repeated his demands, but because of the closeness of enemy patrols, he chose to act very cautiously. So he came up with an idea that, most probably, saved his life as well as those of the detachment that was entrusted to him. As he began negotiating with the village head, he spoke mostly with gestures and broken French, so as to pretend that he did not know the language. Using this simple trick he oftentimes learned more than by direct interrogations.

'Mousié [sic!],' he kept repeating to the village head, 'Donnez dupin mange . . .' and so on.

About thirty locals, one of whom was a one-legged invalid, gathered near the village head's house and, listening to our officer's speech, they were sniggering and nudging each other. They all acted as if they could not understand the officer speaking.

'Eh bien, Marengo,' said the village head, turning to the invalid, 'What will you say about this?'

'Hm,' responded the invalid, making a face, 'Offrez á boire ces gredins [sic!] [Offer a drink to these morons], give them as much wine as possible, drink with them and when they disperse to the houses, then. . .'

These words sufficed to understand that a treacherous plot was under way. Our officer approached the invalid and ordered his hands tied.

'I have to do it, my friend,' he told him in fluent French, 'les grédins comme nous [morons like us] did not come here from afar to let you slaughter us. So if you want to kill us, then we have to take you to Laon and shoot you there.'

Taken aback, the village head and residents could not think of attacking us: they were unarmed and at the mercy of our detachment.

'So monsieur,' our commander told the village head, 'you have to prove to me that you were not intending to participate in this old conniver's plot. Yield to the inevitable and remember that I have sixty well-armed soldiers with me.

We need a carriage with three horses, bread and two cows. Prepare all of this by the evening, and, in the meantime, we will stay with you to rest.'

One of the locals was allowed to leave and inform the rest of the village about our officer's demands, while the rest were surrounded by our six sentries with drawn sabres. Two dismounted sentries were posted at every exit from the village and two more were sent to take up an observation post in a bell tower.

Having taken precautions against enemy attack, our foragers then ate lunch in shifts, rested a bit, fed their horses and, as the darkness descended, left the village towards Laon. They bivouacked half the way to the town and, on a foggy morning of 25 February [9 March], rejoined their division at Laon. Minutes after their arrival first shots were fired and the battle of Laon had begun. [From the Russian text in I. Ortenberg, 'Voennye vospominaniya . . .']

5

The Battle at Reims

By mid-March, the French emperor's situation was grim as ill tidings arrived from every quarter. By the terms of the Treaty of Chaumont, which the Allies adopted on 9 March, no member of the Coalition would negotiate separately with Napoleon. Although they remained divided on many war aims and other issues, Napoleon's diplomatic intransigence had facilitated agreement within the Coalition. Despite a series of earlier victories, Napoleon's army had been decimated in the bloody battles of Craonne and Laon against Blücher's forces, while the main Allied army under Schwarzenberg kept moving closer to Paris. In Bordeaux the white cockade and flag of the Bourbons appeared, and the city was surrendered to the British without a fight on 12 March. The Allies again began to consider the war won.

But Napoleon was not yet ready to quit. Searching for any bit of good news, he grasped at a timely piece of crucial intelligence. Encouraged by their recent successes, the Allies had gotten careless – on 12 March, a single Russian corps under the French émigré General Emmanuel St. Priest seized the key city of Reims, seeking to maintain communications between Blücher and Schwarzenberg. Located at the junction of major routes to Paris, Châlons and Saint-Quentin, Reims was also important symbolically as the ancient coronation site for French kings.

Napoleon immediately saw that the Russian corps (with Prussians in support) was isolated and unsupported by the Allied forces and diverted part of his army to reclaim Reims and crush the Russians. Incredibly, the head of his columns reached the town after a bruising march of twenty hours. It was near nightfall on 13 March, and St. Priest had no idea what he was facing. He initially thought to brush aside the French force confronting him but his troops were soon hustled back into the town by the stronger French forces. The ensuing battle of Reims resulted in an Allied defeat and cost the Coalition as many as 5,000 men (almost half of them killed, including St. Priest himself).

The French victory at Reims stunned the Allies who had already written off Napoleon only to see him reappear as if by magic and shatter another Allied corps. Furthermore, in one quick march Napoleon had placed himself between the Allied armies and was in a position to threaten the rear areas of both armies. For the moment, the two main Allied armies were paralysed. The question was what to do next?

Alexander Langeron

Langeron was attached to the Army of Silesia where he commanded a corps group that included St. Priest's 8th Corps as well.

As mentioned before, Count St. Priest remained with part of his troops (two infantry regiments of his corps and the Kievskii Dragoons) before Mainz on 3 [15] February. After the unfortunate fighting at Champaubert, Montmirail and Étoges, Marshal Blücher, having experienced a considerable loss of men, ordered me to recall Lieutenant-General Panchulidzev from before Mainz, and leave the Duke of Coburg some Cossacks at the outposts. Panchulidzev made forced marches to join Count St. Priest. Major-Generals Davydov and Vasilchikov, with the Vyborgskii and Vyatkskii Regiments, of the 22nd Division of the 10th Corps, and the Moskovskii Dragoons who remained before Cassel, experienced some difficulties crossing the Rhine due to ice floes, and could only come near Lieutenant-General Panchulidzev by following him closely. Count St. Priest was forced to stop at Vitry. Events that had occurred on the Aube, the retreat of the Great Army, the different marches of ours and Napoleon, the absolute cessation of communication and news, and then the order of Marshal Blücher to act according to circumstances and try to be a point of communication between the two armies, prevented him for some time from going any further. He gathered at Vitry convalescent transports, food wagons sent from Nancy to our army, one of my two pontoon companies (the other was with me), a lot of equipment of all the armies, lost or cut off and the first column of a corps of seven Prussian Landwehr battalions and recruits, under the command of Major-General Jagow, intended to reinforce the corps of Yorck and Kleist.

These different detachments brought Count St. Priest's forces to eight or nine thousand men; he then marched on Châlons and Reims, he was strong enough to compete against separate corps of the enemy, and could expect if he had been afraid of being attacked by Napoleon in open country, he would be warned by his cavalry in time to withdraw. On 22 February [6 March], he marched to Châlons, and a day later he approached Reims by Saint-Léonard. He found the city occupied by a detachment of infantry, three or four thousand National Guardsmen and eight pieces of artillery. He bombarded the suburb of Châlons and detached Major-General Emmanuel (who came with the Kievskii Dragoon Regiment, that of the Ryazanskii infantry, the 33rd Jager and two Prussian battalions) on the way from Rethel to occupy the suburb, which was done. Then the enemy, who was in Berry-au-Bac in some strength, on the road to Laon, hearing the cannonade from Reims, sent a strong detachment of cavalry to the rescue of the city. The brave General Emmanuel held the cavalry in check for a long time with his single Kievskii Regiment, which upheld on this occasion the reputation it had justly acquired throughout the war. It gave time to Count St. Priest to gather his troops and withdraw to Saint-Léonard. There he awaited the arrival of the second Prussian column and that of General Panchulidzev. They joined on 27 February [11 March] and he resolved to attack Reims the following day. Major-General Jagow was ordered to make a feint attack on the road to Soissons with the Prussians. General Pillar was to attack the enemy on that of Châlons. The Ryazanskii, Polotskii and Yeletskii Infantry Regiments, and the 1st and 33rd Jagers were intended to make the real attack on the way to Bethel, and the regiments of Kievskii Dragoons and Chernigovkii Mounted Jagers were employed to observe the road from Laon. This detachment was under the command of Lieutenant-General Panchulidzev and Major-Generals Emmanuel, Karpenkov and Bistrom. The attack succeeded completely. General Jagow and the Prussians, who had to make a feint attack, seeing the possibility of converting it into a real one, threw themselves with great bravery on the suburb of Soissons and were the first to enter the city. The attack had the same success at the gate of Rethel (called the gate of Mars).

The garrison of the city was forced to lay down their arms; there was found there regular infantry, part of the National Guard, General Lacoste and Colonel Regnier, and eight cannons were taken. The greatest order prevailed during the attack and after the taking of the town, and it only had to suffer from what could have been a fear of an assault by troops less disciplined than ours. Five hundred horsemen who remained in the city and two to three hundred infantry who wanted to escape by the road of Berry-au-Bac were completely destroyed by the cavalry of Generals Panchulidzev and Emmanuel. A colonel was made prisoner, with thirteen officers and 200 soldiers, the rest were sabered. The eight cannons were sent immediately to Châlons and then further back. If Count St. Priest had left Reims on the day of his success, to join us in Laon (something he could have done), he would have avoided a disaster that left us with so many regrets. But having learned of the failure experienced by Napoleon at Laon and of his retirement on Soissons, he thought we would follow on the road to that city and there would force him to move on Château-Thierry, and hoping to join us in Soissons, he remained in Reims to wait for news. [From the French text in Alexander Langeron, *Mémoires*]

Ilya Radozhitskii

A lieutenant in the 3rd Light Company attached to St. Priest's corps.

On 22 February [6 March] we were some 12 verstas [12.8km] away from Reims and bivouacked in the already pillaged village of Bonnome [?]. Now everything that had survived [the original plundering], except for stone walls and roof tiles, was used to stoke bonfires. Oh the misfortunes of war! You turn pleasant settlements into ruins and cemeteries! Where peaceful civilians, surrounded by their families, once enjoyed their lives without interfering into policies of ambitious men, now the thunderous rumble of cannon spreads death while frightened and vulnerable victims flee to the woods and mountains, abandoning their homes to the mercy of ravenous foreigners who bring fire and death to those who could be their best friends in peacetime.

The road from Châlons to Reims lay in a valley that appeared similar to our native steppes in the Elizavetgrad province. The soil had too much limestone in it which it unsuitable for grain but ideal for grapevines that produce a sparkling wine that has spread the name of Champagne far and wide. The grass cannot be seen anywhere yet and the fields are grey and soggy.

At six o'clock of the following morning we broke our bivouacs and marched forward. We left our trains at Sillery and advanced in battle formation towards Reims. Our advance guard, which approached the city yesterday, was greeted with cannonballs. There were no more than 6,000 of us, including Prussians.

Reims was defended by a very weak garrison commanded by General Corbineau and so Count St. Priest decided to launch an assault and capture the town. About four verstas [4.3km] from the town, we saw the tops of its bell towers and heard the sound of gunfire in our advance guard. Approaching the town to within artillery range, our troops halted behind a hill that concealed the fortress. The Count [St. Priest] examined the area to better prepare for the assault. I also decided to reconnoitre because my experiences showed that an artillery officer, more than anyone else, must examine the area in front and behind his position so he make the best judgment on how to move cannon, where to deploy them and how and where to withdraw them in case of retreat. Riding my horse on the Châlons road, I quickly ascended the hill that concealed the town and from the windmills observed the vast panorama of Reims that extended for some three verstas [3.2km] in the valley below. In between the roofs of houses, shrouded in blue-tinted smog, there were belltowers and the spires of churches. The most discernible was the great cathedral where the French kings used to be crowned: like a two-headed giant, it was overlooking and dominating all other buildings. Beyond it, I could discern other tall and beautiful buildings, the ruins of ancient triumphal arches and a Roman amphitheatre. The town was surrounded by a stone wall that dated to the age of the knights, and a deep moat. Cannon barrels could be seen protruding through embrasures while people, among whom I saw women bearing arms, crowded around them. As I travelled across the hill I inadvertently came within musket range but the [French] did not fire and allowed me to continue observing the town. Reims appeared wider than Châlons and as large as Nancy. Beyond the town, on the other side of the Vesle River, there was a rolling plain dotted with villages and adjoining to the hills covered with vineyards. I saw numerous cavalry scattered there – it was Tettenborn with our Cossacks.

Returning from the hill, I saw a dragoon officer, accompanied by a trumpeter, riding to the town as truce-bearer from Count St. Priest. His left arm was wrapped with a scarf while in his right hand he had a paper that he held above his head so it could be seen from the town walls. The officers rode to the Châlons gate and several onlookers followed him at some distance. Stopping at a pistol-shot's distance from the fortress, the trumpeter blew his trumpet but no one responded. The truce-bearer, in the hope of French coolness, moved closer and, displaying a paper, he began speaking to the [people on the town wall]. Meanwhile the number of curious onlookers from our side rapidly increased and we eagerly awaited to see what would happen next when a cannon fired on the town fall and its projectile whizzed past our ears! The truce-bearer, trumpeters and all the rest scattered at once and our troops marched towards the fortress.

The Ryazanskii regiment, with four cannon and two squadrons of dragoons, moved to the right and attacked the suburbs from the Charleville road, while the Polotskii regiment, with four Prussian howitzers, marched directly to the windmills, leaving the Châlons gate to its left. An intense firefight broke out on both sides. The Prussian howitzers did not endure for long because the French, firing from the embrasures, killed a company commander, several men and horses. The unfortunate howitzers thus became disordered and had to hastily retreat. I was ordered to advance with two licornes* and two guns to replace them. Just as I moved forward, a hare ran across the road. 'Your Honour, this is a bad omen,' the nearest cannonier told me while others began to shout and drive the hare further away from us. Old moustached artillerymen told me that we would most certainly suffer some misfortune because the hare crossed our path. 'Misfortunes will befall those who believe it,' I replied to them and began moving my cannon up to the windmills. Just then an enemy cannonball, fired from the fortress, buzzed over our heads. It did not touch us but proved to be deadly for the Prussian column that was marching behind us; it claimed more than ten men, injuring six in the legs, the rest in the head and many were simply thrown to the ground. Thus, the hare foretold death for the Prussians, not us.

My earlier reconnaissance now proved to be very useful. I deployed my cannon in such a manner as to protect them by the reverse slope and even though I saw still able to fire canister at the town walls, the enemy guns, lacking obvious targets and seeing only the ends of the barrels of my guns, the puffs of smoke rising after each shot and the heads of my cannoniers, could not cause any damage to my crews. Many of their cannonballs flew

---

* Licorne (edinorog in Russian) is the French term for a type of Russian artillery piece that combined the features of howitzers and traditional cannon. It was a muzzle-loading howitzer that had a longer barrel, giving its shells a flatter trajectory but longer range.

over our heads while some, while landing nearby, caused virtually no damage to us; I lost just one cannonier. The windmills, where my guns were deployed, suffered the most damage. To the right of us, near a stone mill, stood Count St. Priest who, exposing himself to danger, kept examining our assault through a spyglass. The attack began around 10.30 a.m. and promised to end soon when, unexpectedly, enemy reinforcements, about 3,000 cavalrymen, appeared on the road from Soissons and, moving in a dense column, hastily descended from the heights on that side of the town. The town greeted them with bells ringing. This development frustrated our attack and, around three o'clock in the afternoon, we began withdrawing in good order to the village of Sillery, on the Châlons road, in order to lure the enemy into the open field. But the French were content with our withdrawal and stopped on the heights that we previously held in front of the town.

We had to spend the night amidst the ruins of Sillery. Anything flammable was burned at our bivouacs that night. There were no residents, only occasionally we would see some old Frenchman, dressed in a blue coat, wandering wretchedly amidst the smouldering ruins. Our lads discovered a cellar with probably as many as 30,000 bottles of champagne, all of which we consumed or destroyed! There were also sixty barrels remaining. I witnessed as soldiers rolled these barrels out and, breaking the lids, cheerfully gulped down their life-giving liquid; some even cooked porridge in the champagne. We argued that because of this devastation the price of champagne would at least double in Russia and for all the wine we consumed at time of war, the French would make us pay twice over in time of peace.

Between 24 and 28 February [8–12 March], for four whole days, we remained in place. Neither the French bothered us, nor did we bother them, even though we were just eight verstas [8.5km] from each other. The Count [St. Priest] waited for the arrival of the Prussians from Châlons, intending to concentrate his forces and take the town by a formal assault. We were tasked with preparing fascines and ladders. Thus, the French did not dare to foray out of town while we avoided attacking before completing our preparations for assault.

So what do soldiers do on the eve of the battle? Some sleep, others rest or clean weapons, while most officers are busy playing cards. All of this taking place amidst smoking bivouacs, straw huts, and ruins of burned-out buildings, and representing a bewildering sight, a truly hellish image. Here, a person, isolated from the world, enjoys a full freedom of spirit and takes pleasure in the present, forgetting the past and paying no heed to the future. His emotions transcend this physical world – the closer he is to death, the more he scorns danger; the more he enjoys the sight of the smouldering ruins and the corpses of fallen enemy soldiers, and being the chief of cause of their demise, he is willing to temp fate himself and become a victim of his own ambition.

On 28 February [12 March] we were at Reims. Such are the vicissitudes of military life! Once again we found ourselves cast from misery into luxury, from the smouldering ruins into beautifully arranged rooms; instead of porridge and animal joints, we enjoy French sauces and spill champagne from our glasses! As the result of the enemy garrison's weakness and the prudent arrangements of Count St. Priest, we captured the city in a brief assault, suffering almost no losses.

Everything was prepared the day before [the assault] and we approached the city around two o'clock in the morning [on 12 March]. The first jager columns, commanded by General Bistrom, moved to the right towards the Charleville suburbs. The second column, consisting of the Polotskii regiments and my four cannon, under the command of General Pillar, proceeded to the Châlons gate. The third column, comprising of the Prussians under General von Jagow, advanced along the opposite bank of the Vesle river, along the road from Epernay. A general assault was scheduled to be launched before sunrise, around five o'clock in the morning. However, our column was delayed due to the mistake of a certain cavalry general who stumbled onto the path of the second column and whom we took for an enemy force. Peering through the darkness, our General P. [Pillar?] observed some cavalry moving in front of us and immediately ordered us to stop and open fire. Before determining that these were the Chernigovskii Dragoons, we remained uncertain [what to do] and approached the city after sunrise. By then, the French were already aware of our intentions and greeted us with artillery fire.

I quickly moved my cannon directly to the windmills, where they had previously been deployed, and was the first to return fire. I was reinforced with two heavy cannon and two Prussian howitzers. Thus, my entire battery consisted of eight guns and opened a devastating cannonade. The force of discharging cannon shook the ground and deafened us; smoke billowed all around while our projectiles struck the embrasures and flew over the town walls and the roofs of the houses. The four enemy cannon, deployed in embrasures against us, fought back very feebly. However, all our efforts were just for show since this attack, from the direction of Châlons, was just a diversion. Half an hour later we saw, to our right, jagers shouting 'Hurrah' and charging in open order directly onto the city walls. Moments later, the enemy guns fell silent and the enemy disappeared. Climbing the wall, the jagers scattered along the fortification and some of them ran in front of us. Seeing them running through the embrasures, we initially mistook them for the French and fired a few cannonballs before the running troops stopped and waved their hands. General P. then told us proudly, 'Cease fire! They are asking for mercy!' After learning that our first column had broken through into the city, General P. led us towards the Châlons gate. The soldiers charged shouting towards it but encountered an obstacle. The accursed French had brought so much earth and rubble to block the gates that we spent two hours removing it to clear the road. A ditch dug across the road also delayed the advance of our artillery. Meanwhile, some infantry officers and soldiers crawled through the breach near the gates to enter the city and scattered to look for the enemy inside homes, shops, wine cellars and stables, from where they soon returned with trophies, which belonged to them by right of conquest.

Despite our efforts we were unable to clear the Châlons gates. So I was ordered to move my cannon through the Charleville suburbs, where the city was protected by a weak wall and palisade, which the jagers broke through without resorting to ladders. In this part of the city, streets were jammed with transports. If the French had a stronger garrison and defended the town properly, we would not have seized it so easily. Our assault produced almost no casualties, the Prussians alone lost about twenty men. In the Soissons suburbs, on this side of the town, we saw several French and Prussian corpses, men who had been killed in a cavalry melee that took place here: the former were trying to escape from the town while the latter sought to prevent them. Most of the French garrison managed to depart downstream on the Vesle River, though the Prussians sabred and drowned many of the [French] lancers. We captured some 200 French wounded, including a general, and another 2,000 sick Frenchmen were found in local hospitals. We also took eight bronze cannon that were abandoned on the city walls. The [French] garrison included many armed civilians. [From the Russian text in I. Radozhitskii, *Pokhodnye zapiski . . .*]

Nikolai Golitsyn

Not yet twenty years old, Nikolai Golitsyn was a scion of an ancient Russian princely family. He graduated from the elite Page Corps in 1810 and began service in the Kievskii Dragoon Regiment, distinguishing himself in a number of battles and earning a golden sword for gallantry.

The charming banks of the Rhine, where we have spent some time already, made us forget about our prior hardships. And when we compared this tranquil life amidst vineyards and picturesque rural scenery with what we had experienced amidst our native snow during the terrifying epoch of the destruction of the French army, we could not but thank the heavens for all the grace and indulgence which it has blessed us and feel grateful that we have been born in the century which, besides the diversity of remarkable events, also offered an important lesson showing the Providence directs everything in this world and that we must venerate it, even though we often cannot comprehend its paths.

On 1 [13] January 1814, we crossed the Rhine at Caub, between Koblenz and Mainz, as picturesque a region as one can imagine. Our detachment was assigned to Count St. Priest's corps that was tasked with the blockade of Mainz. We were not particularly thrilled by this prospect since it offered us very little glory and plenty of boredom while the rest of the army was harvesting laurels of victory in the very heart of France. But nothing is certain in time of war: today you do not know how tomorrow will turn out and circumstances sometimes turn in such a way as to produce results completely different from those that you expected.

We crossed the Rhine at the same time as General Olsufiev's corps which was marching to take direct part in the events unfolding in France while we were destined to remain idle, blockading a first-class fortress which no one even intended to besiege. Such contrasting experiences produced both the feelings of joy and regret. Those who were departing for France pitied us while we envied them. But the course of war soon reversed our roles. This same General Olsufiev was captured with his entire division at Champaubert while we were among us the first to approach Paris and I was among those who endured the first shots fired from the walls of Paris on the evening of 17 [29] March.

The blockade of Mainz preoccupied us until the end of January and nothing worthy of note took place during this time. The enemy did not even try to inconvenience us with sorties. The winter, however, was quite severe by local standards and there was plenty of ice flowing on the Rhine. The war, meanwhile, continued with varying success in France. In this critical situation, Napoleon exploited all aspects of his military genius to neutralise the operations of the Allied armies commanded by Prince Schwarzenberg and Blücher, and skilfully exploiting their mistakes, he cut the communications between them. A separate corps was needed to restore these communications between the armies. Count St. Priest's corps, reinforced by a Prussian division and artillery under the command of General Jagow, was thus selected for this task.

At the end of January we lifted the blockade of Mainz and advanced via Nancy, Toul, Saint-Dizier and Vitry to Châlons, where we arrived in mid-February. We rested at St. Dizier in order to gather intelligence on the deployment of both armies. I was dispatched to Montierender to receive the necessary information at the headquarters of a Prussian corps that was located there. I would never forget this trip and the unusual adventure that I experienced. The road ran through dense forest called la forêt de Montierender which, according to local traditions, was populated by evil spirits. I was ordered to hurry but since I departed rather later after supper, I was in the midst of the forest when pitch-black darkness fell and I could not even see the road! The road, fortunately, was fairly flat and even though the ground was damp from melting snow, I galloped at full speed leaving my Cossack escort, whose exhausted nag could not keep up with my agile steed, far behind. But my horse suddenly stooped and refused to move. Raising its head, it pressed against its rear legs and trembled with its entire body and the tremor was powerful that I began feeling creeps running all across my body. I spurred him but he retreated back; I tried turning him back, instead he reared. I saw that something unusual was happening and made the sign of the cross, expecting the worst. I spent about three minutes in this grave state. I cannot describe ideas that rushed through my head but I was convinced that a bear or some other animal blocked my way and I assumed that it would attack me. But to my utter bewilderment, my horse suddenly rushed forward while I grabbed its mane so I would not fall from the saddle if he stopped. The horse galloped with remarkable swiftness for several verstas and I did not even attempt to restrain him. At last, he slowed down himself and I safely reached my destination. My Cossack also safely arrived about an hour and a half later. I began telling about my experience but no one could explain the cause for such a sudden attack of panic that seized my horse. I assume it was probably some wild beast roaming nearby that frightened my horse.

After receiving necessary information about our armies from the Prussians, I returned to Saint-Dizier the following day, and we then broke our camp and departed. In light of the positions of the Allied armies, we had to seize the town of Reims which had recently been occupied by a French garrison. As we stopped for rest at Châlons, I decided to use this opportunity to visit a local theatre and attended a relatively well-staged and played comedy *Le Sourd ou l'auberge pleine*. One rarely gets a chance to visit theatres in wartime so how could I not use this opportunity to briefly forget during the spectacle in which we were fearsome actors with swords in our hands and that France itself was our stage? Our advance guard under the command of General Emmanuel was first to depart from Châlons on the road to Reims; several days later we arrived at the village of Sillery, famous for its champagne and located eight verstas from Reims.

It was decided to set up Count St. Priest's headquarters at Sillery until Reims was taken. We began to notice hostile attitudes of local residents and armed peasants frequently attacked our officers as their travelled on missions. Thus, Prince A. M. Golitsin, officer of the main headquarters who was assigned to Count St. Priest, was saved from a very tense situation [as he was attacked by armed Frenchmen] only by the arrival of our advance guard.

The following day, 21 February under the old-style calendar [7 March], the decision was made to conduct a reconnaissance in force towards Reims. Count St. Priest did not want to use force until after all nonviolent means were exhausted in order to protect the city from the devastating consequences of a major assault. After departing early in the morning, we arrived two hours later to the city so famous for being the place where the French king had always been crowned. Nothing suggested that we would face stiff resistance and we approached the city walls without encountering anyone we could have conversed with; the cannon deployed on the walls remained silent. Count St. Priest ordered a Prussian battery deployed on a hill, at close range from the city, and then set up his tent next to it. There he wrote a proclamation to the municipal authorities of Reims, calling upon them not to resist to protect the city from the horrors of an assault. General Emmanuel and I were inside the Count's tent and the Count gave the document Emmanuel to have it immediately delivered to the city. This task was given to me but it was a difficult mission because, according to our intelligence, General Corbineau, who commanded the troops in Reims, knew quite well the full importance of this location and was determined not to accept any terms. To ensure that the proclamation reached its destination even if I was not let inside the city, I took with me a Frenchman from a nearby village who would have delivered it in my place. Preceded by a trumpeter and followed by the French peasant, I thus embarked on my journey. As I descended towards the city, I saw on the city walls numerous people who were conversing and shouting all at once so I could not understand a single word amidst such noise and commotion. My trumpeter exhausted himself blowing truce signals while I waved the proclamation above my head in order to show why I was here. But nothing helped. I did not what to do when amidst this clamour a voice suddenly shouted to me, 'Get out or you will be fired upon!' I did not want to submit to this threat without carrying out my mission so I saw called up my French companion and showed him with a gesture that he should deliver it to the people standing on the walls. But just he moved forward, fire burst out of a cannon in front of me and a cannonball flew over my head. At this signal, a general cannonade ensued and just fifteen minutes later a captain commanding the Prussian battery had his leg sheared off by a cannonball. In the wake of this failed attempt to negotiate, which only revealed the enemy's determination to fight, Count St. Priest decided to return to Sillery and ponder the next course of action. First of all, we had to reconnoitre the area to verify that we would not have to fight any additional forces beside those inside Reims. For this purpose, I was given 100 Cossacks and dragoons and instructed to conduct a reconnaissance in the direction of Fismes and Soissons. But I encountered no one there except for armed peasants, whom I was forced to subdue. Detachments sent in other directions also encountered no enemy forces. It appeared, thus, that we would have to deal only with the French garrison at Reims, which, despite its determination, could not have been strong. Yet, looking for weak spots in the fortress defences, we spent four days conducting strong reconnaissance that frequently led to fights because the enemy fired upon us with artillery and dispatched part of his garrison troops to engage us. Finally, the decision was made to storm Reims at dawn on 28 February [12 March]. The Prussians were tasked with launching a diversion at the Soissons gate which meant that during the battle, they would be separated from us by the Vesle River flowing from Sillery to Reims and around the latter town. General Emmanuel was supposed to move around the fortress and get inside it via the Berry-au-Bac gate that was the weakest spot in [the defences]. Count St. Priest (with our main force) wanted to attack other locations according to circumstances. It was agreed to leave Sillery at midnight sharp and time our marching in such a way as to be able to launch the attack at dawn. In order not to attract attention of the residents who were hostile to us, we were ordered to proceed across the fields on the right side of the road and occupy positions designated in the dispositions. Considering that our advance guard had already spent the entire week moving back and forth in the countryside between Sillery and Reims and I was well acquainted with the region, General Emmanuel ordered me to lead the first column which all other columns had to follow. The night proved to be so dark that we could barely see anything within two paces. But maintaining one's direction was not as difficult during this campaign [in France as in previous wars] and I had no fear of losing my way. An hour later we were already marching and everything was going as well as one could wish. But then Captain M., our Corps Quartermaster, approached me and asked to assume the responsibility of leading the column. I was, in fact, performing his responsibilities and therefore found it rather awkward to refuse his request. So I returned back to the General [Emmanuel] and informed him that Captain M. had asked to lead the column. Soon I noticed that we were veering to the right which meant we were moving away from our destination point. I shared my observation with Captain M. but he was convinced that we were on the right path. A short time later we made another oblique movement, then one more and by the time we veered off for the third time, we had made so many turns that even I could not figure out where we were. The column stopped and Captain M. appeared lost and unaware which direction we should take. No one could point him to the right direction because all that marching and counter-marching, which we undertook for the past three hours, made it impossible to recognise places in complete darkness. Finding ourselves in this uncertainty, we had only one option – marching ahead and hoping for the best. We soon reached a major road, which, actually, posed a major dilemma since there were supposed to be no major roads on our path. So where did it appear from? There was one possibility – that we had inadvertently passed by Reims and reached one of the roads that led from this city to Rethee or Berry-au-Bac. In such a case, we had to turn left to return back to Reims. Everyone agreed to do it but just as we made a few hundred paces in this new direction we suddenly found ourselves face to face with a detachment that was advancing directly at us. We were thunderstruck and the prospects of a battle in pitch darkness horrified us. We assumed that it was the enemy troops, who had been forewarned about our attack and hurried to abandon the city and avoid desolation that follows a full-blown assault. Our supposition seemed to have been confirmed by shouts of 'Moskal' heard on the opposite side. Orders were issued to prepare for action and the guns were unlimbered, loaded with canister and aimed at the enemy. At such moments every minute is precious because he who attacks first usually secures advantage. Our cannon were about to open fire when we heard the voice of our corps commander Count St. Priest from the supposed enemy's side. He soon galloped to see what was happening. We discovered that after leading us for four hours across the fields, Captain M. had brought us back to the road that led from Reims and Sillery where we encountered Count St. Priest who was just then departing with the reserves for Reims where he intended to take command over all of his forces that should have been gathered there by then. Thus, a minute too late and our canister would have killed our corps commander. Even after [so many years] I cannot think without shuddering about what could have happened next. As it was, we still could not recover the precious lost hours and could not reach our destination in time to launch a general assault. The Prussians were moving along a different path on the other side of the river and we could not warn them in time. Consequently, they would have launched their diversion before we even reached our positions and our plans would have been in disarray. We had no choice but to march as fast as we could even though the sun was already rising and we had been marching all though the night. The sound of the tocsin soon informed us that the Prussians had been spotted. Cannon fire soon followed and we had no doubt that the Prussians were engaged in a heated battle. General Emmanuel immediately advanced with his cavalry moving at the trot while we hastily moved around the town. We reached the valley with the road to Berry-au-Bac just as an enemy battalion of some 500 men, with about as many cavalrymen, was coming out of the city. This battalion fought gallantly and despite our repeated attacks, none of our seven squadrons managed to break it. With artillery still far behind us, the enemy battalion managed to get away from us. But at least we were able to pursue the enemy cavalry which we drove into the Vesle River and completely destroyed. Meanwhile, the Prussian feint in fact resulted in the capture of the city and this fortuitous turn of events compensated for our nocturnal wanderings. [From the Russian text in N. Golitsyn, *Ofitserskie zapiski* . . .]

Mikhail Petrov

Petrov commanded the 1st Battalion of the 1st Jager Regiment.

During the storming of Reims . . . I was among those who charged through the city gates that had been smashed in by our battery guns. Some of the garrison was killed or captured but most of it managed to escape from the fortress and fight their way through Major-General Panchulidzev's cavalry detachment towards Soissons . . .

Once everything settled and we secured the city, our corps commander [St. Priest] ordered us to beat the 'all-clear and rally' signal to put an end to sacking and the regiments, compelled to give up what belonged to them by the right of assault, rallied and deployed in formations on squares and internal esplanades in front of those places where they stormed the city. After reviewing these storming units, the corps commander announced his complete gratitude to the troops and ordered the regiments into quarters inside the town and in nearby villages, without dividing into companies and instead billeting many men into large houses. He then dispatched his advance guard, consisting of dragoons and mounted jagers, along the Soissons road to Fismes, where it took up position with advance outposts, under command of Panchulidzev, that spread insufficiently to the left (towards Paris) in the direction of the town of Fère [en-Tardenois].

My battalion was given thirteen homes. My apartment was on the cathedral square, almost opposite the entrance into this magnificent example of Gothic architecture where the French monarchs, except for Bonaparte, had traditionally been crowned. I shared my apartment with my favourite officer, Lieutenant Gotovtsev.

Our host was a young and handsome merchant who had a charming brunette wife. They naturally greeted us with the required politeness, but with their faces betraying fear and hearts filled with hatred. Before the storming our columns concentrated neat the great château at Sillery, which possessed vast reserves of the champagne so famous in Russia, but we launched the assault without tasting it. So now Gotovtsev began making arrangements for breakfast as vigorously as famished man could do. Our hosts, claiming that they had been already plundered even though their home bore no signs of it, served us with a veritable salad of acerbic excuses and only made promises to help us find something edible. Indeed, they soon served us meagre breadcrumbs on an untidily-laid table. Seeing no signs that our lads had ever visited this home and perceiving the hosts' shameless prevarication from our requests (when we were entitled to them by the rights of assault), I became so disgusted with their food that I refused to eat it and instead went to explore the left side of the town . . . In vain did Gotovtsev, whose entire body yearned for food, assured me that it would take us just a few minutes to devour the hosts' meagre breakfast that could satisfy our hunger for at least an hour. I refused and followed an inexplicable desire to see what was happening outside. Coming out to the porch, I looked the marvellous entrance to the cathedral, which stood just thirty paces from me and asked the host, who was keen on bidding goodbye to us, if he could find the doorkeeper to this cathedral so we could take a look inside it. He [brusquely] replied that the doorkeeper was most probably lying dead somewhere and therefore he could not be of any help. I stopped worrying about him and moved to the left side, ordering two of my sentries to follow me at a distance.

As we walked some 200 paces from the apartment and passed two blocks to reach another square, we heard wailing and shouting coming from nearby homes. Sending one of my sentries to quickly bring half of my entire battalion guard and reserve, we rushed to help people who were being plundered after an order prohibiting it had been issued. Running from one home to another, Gotovtsev and I saved victims from the hands of marauders, especially the Prussian landwehr from General Jagow's division, who were burning with intense hatred against the French for their pillaging of the [Prussian] kingdom. The arrival of my jagers from the battalion reserves greatly facilitated our dangerous toils amidst crowds of renegades. But in one of the home that we endeavoured to save, I almost killed Lieutenant Gotovtsev. Rushing into the house of a tailor, I saw a Prussian landwehr kicking an old Frenchman on the floor and attempting to stab the rest of his family that was hiding in a corner; he was demanding money, shouting [in broken French] 'Donnez[-moi de] l'argent.' As I grabbed his musket, I accidentally pulled the trigger and fired the weapon, with the bullet tearing the collar of Gotovtsev's coat. Turning around and seeing him still standing amidst the smoke, I could hardly believe my eyes that he was still alive . . .

After putting an end to the plundering in this part of the town . . . Gotovtsev and I decided to return to our apartment, instructing the local residents to have a few men follow me so they knew where I was staying, promising to arrive at once if they needed me. So eight young men followed us and when I gave orders to a non-commissioned officer of my battalion duty service to double patrols in that part of the city, some of these men rushed inside the house of my host. As I returned to the apartment, I told Gotovtsev, 'My dear friend, now that we have done a good deed, we can have a pleasant dinner without our hosts' reproaches, so please ask them to serve us whatever meagre provisions they have.' Gotovtsev asked the host about dinner, telling him it did not matter what it would comprise. But the host earnestly beseeched us to wait for half an hour so he could serve us appropriately. In vain did I assure him that we would be content with the simplest meal, he insisted on us having a proper dinner. Indeed, half an hour later a small table was set with plentiful and delicious dishes and drinks. Our host and hostess treated us generously, accompanying each dish with genuine compliments. This was the most delicious dinner I have ever eaten in my life . . . After the dinner and coffee, my host informed me that the townsfolk, whom I had saved, found the doorkeeper in some underground crypt on the other side of the town and the cathedral was thus open for us . . . [From the Russian text in M. Petrov, 'Rasskazy . . .']

Ilya Radozhitskii

After the seemingly effortless capture of Reims, Radozhitskii led his company into the city and was soon thrilled to learn that his skilful direction of his artillery battery earned him the nomination to the Order of St. Anna, Second Class.

Entering the city, we found streets empty as all the residents, expecting imminent pillaging and murder, had hidden themselves in cellars and lumber-rooms. We naturally could not ensure that none of the victorious troops entered homes and shops to claim whatever was to their liking. Several Frenchmen later complained to me about this but I only shrugged and told them that I could do nothing since such was the reality of war.

All our infantry concentrated in the city square, where I brought my cannon. The streets were soon crowded with our troops. Clamour, movement and joy was everywhere. Everyone congratulated each other with the successful turn of events. At last, the city residents appeared as well and the victors began to disperse to their billets. The Prussians were moved to the nearby villages.

In the afternoon I went for a stroll around the city. I saw a member of the municipal government, accompanied by the beating of a Russian drum, walking in the streets and reading Count St. Priest's proclamation at street junctions. The French men, wearing blue coats and wooden shoes, and women in bonnets gathered there to listen to announcements. They were ordered to immediately surrender all weapons and any remaining French troops. 'We are all prisoners of war, including our women!' shouted one of the Frenchman.

The town of Reims is quite large, and its buildings are tall and well built. The front of the [famed] Cathedral, built in Gothic architecture, is decorated with exquisite and skilful carvings that resemble lace. On the main square there is the statue of [King] Henry IV, with a pool and fountains around it. The square is surrounded with three- and four-storey buildings, without columns or frontons . . . There are numerous shops and market stalls but that day they were all closed. At the corners of buildings and street junctions, there were proclamations calling upon the French people to arms and resistance; some of these posters claimed that the Allied had been defeated and for their complete defeat, every Frenchman had to take up arms. There were also prints with the news of the defeat of our 9th Corps . . . which infuriated me and I took it down. A Frenchman, who passed by at that moment, noticed my action and said laughingly, 'Misérable Napoléon!' [From the Russian text in I. Radozhitskii, *Pokhodnye zapiski...*]

Alexander Langeron

Langeron commanded a corps in the Army of Silesia and exercised authority over St. Priest's forces as well.

Napoleon had planned to march on the Aube by Épernay and Châlons when, having learned of the occupation of Reims by Count St. Priest, he resolved to surprise and reoccupy a position that was necessary to cut anew the communications between our two armies. Therefore he quickly moved by Fismes. Count St. Priest was so unprepared for this movement that he took no precautions on the side where he didn't think that the enemy's attack would come from; he only pushed a small reconnaissance towards Fismes and put the excessively large Prussian cantonment on the same road by which Napoleon surprised him.

At ten o'clock, General Jagow warned him of marching enemy, but Count St. Priest believed that the troops we discovered were those of Marmont's corps, which, after being defeated at Laon (which we had learned of at Reims), could have been cut off from the army and sought to withdraw to Reims, that he was ignorant of having been taken. He sallied out with all his forces to fight. He was soon undeceived; 8,000 French cavalry, against which Count St. Priest could only send 700, advanced across the vast plains surrounding Reims. The Prussian battalions were surrounded and taken while leaving their camps. Others retreated into the city, and Napoleon himself soon appeared, with his whole army. He put a huge battery on the heights between Champigny and Ormes, and deployed with it all his infantry. His cavalry tried to cross the Vesle at the ford, but was prevented by the fire of our skirmishers. Count St. Priest, seeing then, but too late, what he had to deal with, felt the need to withdraw. He ordered his troops of the second and third line to recross Reims as soon as possible and directed to the road of Laon, transport convoys and march immediately to Châlons, and he stood in front of the town near Tinqueux and Sainte-Geneviève to cover the retreat with his cavalry and the regiments of Ryazanskii, 1st and 33rd Jagers. At four o'clock, St. Priest was mortally wounded by shrapnel that shattered his right shoulder. He fell unconscious, and at the same time a part of the French cavalry, composed of cuirassiers and Guards of Honour, entered the suburb of Soissons behind him and cut him off from the city, where his cavalry and the 1st and 33rd Jager Regiments had already withdrawn, by his orders, to man the ramparts and banks of the Vesle. He would have fallen into the hands of the enemy without the heroic devotion of his adjutant, Lieutenant Volkov, of the Life Guard Semenovskii Regiment and his orderly, Lieutenant Avilov, of the Cossack regiment of Kuteinikov VIII; these two brave officers, assisted by some other lower-ranking orderlies, snatched him in the middle of the enemy's skirmishers and carried him more than 500 yards to the first battalion of the Ryazanskii Regiment, which occupied the village of Tinqueux to ensure the right flank of the troops who had withdrawn. The second battalion of the same regiment occupied the city gate.

The Vesle River is very swampy and presented difficulties for Count St. Priest to cross; but on the other hand, the enemy's cavalry occupied the suburb we also had to cross, and our troops, repulsed by such superior troops, leaving the city or filling the streets, were in a bit of a mess, inevitable in such an unexpected retrograde movement. Already Timaseev's artillery company of had lost a cannon, and he himself was mortally wounded [and died shortly after]. The Prussians had lost eleven cannons. The position of the Ryazanskii Regiment was very critical, it must save its general and enter the city. This admirable regiment and its commander, Colonel Skobelev (given command), complimented one another. The regiment had nearly 500 men in each battalion, Colonel Skobelev formed a square of two companies, in the middle of which he moved Count St. Priest, and with the other two companies of the 2nd Battalion, threw himself with fixed bayonets on the enemy's cavalry, who, surprised by this unexpected attack, trapped in the streets of the suburb, unable to find an exit to the right, where canals and reservoirs for the mills make the passage impracticable, struck through the gate by two pieces of cannon, and the fire of the 2nd Battalion of the Ryazanskii Regiment which also advanced then with the bayonet, was largely destroyed, both men and horses. More than 500 men perished, no prisoners were taken. The Ryazanskii [Infantry] Regiment, which, as all the troops that Count St. Priest commanded loved this general, avenged his death.

The French cavalry was composed largely of these unfortunate Guards of Honour, formed from young people from distinguished families, who Napoleon had taken as hostages against them and obtain, without charge, by violent means seven or eight thousand more horsemen. It was, in truth, a detestable cavalry, but as individuals, despite being sacrificed and used everywhere poorly, they showed the personal bravery which distinguished the French nation. The suburb had been cleared and Count St. Priest was brought to Berry-au-Bac and the next day at Laon.

Lieutenant-General Panchulidzev took command. General Bistrom with a battalion of jager and a Prussian battalion defended the gate of Soissons; the 30th Jager Regiment and the regiment of Polotsk, the other gates and walls; Generals Karpenkov and Emmanuel, with the 1st Jager Regiment and the cavalry defended the banks of the Vesle. The night came on and encouraged retreat and the defence of the town; however, the fire lasted until nine o'clock in the evening; at midnight, all our troops abandoned the city and joined the rest of the corps at Berry-au-Bac on 2 [14] March; the 3rd [15th], Lieutenant-General Panchulidzev came to Laon, where he met our army. In this unfortunate case and the two happier ones that preceded it, our loss was nearly 3,000 men killed, wounded or taken, 600 Russians and the rest Prussians. We lost twelve cannons.

Generals Emmanuel, Bistrom, Karpenkov and Jagow particularly distinguished themselves, as well as the regiments of Kiev, of Chernigov, of Ryazan, the 1st and 33rd Jager and Prussian Landwehr battalions; in the successes as well as in the reverses all these troops showed the greatest courage and the most intrepid firmness. Count St. Priest died on 17 [29] March at Laon; few generals that die in battle were regretted more and merited it more by their peers and subordinates. He offered a model of the social and military virtues; despite his high rank he was allowed to display his talents, he had only one fault, but it cost him his life. The sovereign whom he had the honour of serving, honoured his tomb with tears. Marshal Blücher also felt strongly that loss which increased our regret that Count St. Priest (and the unfortunate Prince Bagration, who died of his wounds shortly after the battle of Borodino and carrying to the tomb the sad feeling for the loss of Russia) did not lived long enough to see his last moments softened by the happy revolution, the day after his death, replacing on the throne its rightful owners. I gave the command of the 8th Corps to Lieutenant-General Rudzevich. [From the French text in Alexander Langeron, *Mémoires*]

Nikolai Golitsyn

With the capture of this important location, St. Priest succeeded in establishing direct communications between the two armies. Confident that there was no attack forthcoming, St. Priest decided to stay at Reims and deployed his troops in quarters. The following day, a Te Deum was scheduled to celebrate our victory. But immediately after the service, at eleven o'clock in the morning, we were astonished to hear gunfire near the gates of Reims. In moments, everyone mounted horses and rushed to see why there was gunfire at such close proximity. Upon arriving at the Soissons gates we learned that an enemy detachment, consisting of several squadrons and two cannon, had conducted a reconnaissance and finding our infantry near the city gates, fired several rounds and quickly fell back. A prisoner, captured by our flanquers, revealed that Napoleon himself was near the city. It was clear that the day would not end without some major occurrence and indeed at 4 o'clock in the afternoon we saw vast forces of enemy cavalry and infantry appearing from behind the hill, preceded by numerous artillery that speedily deployed its guns and opened a deafening cannonade. We vigorously defended Reims, especially near the bridge over the Vesle where we found ourselves in a fierce combat far outnumbered by the enemy; one cannot imagine anything bloodier and more terrible than that clash. In the midst of this battle our corps commander suffered a mortal wound to his shoulder and was forced to leave his command just when his presence was needed the most. Fortunately as the result of competent direction by General Emmanuel, who took over the command, as well as the successful attack carried out by the Ryazanskii Infantry Regiment under the leadership of its gallant Colonel Skobelev in the enemy rear, our circumstances improved and we held on to Reims throughout the day and night even though we faced Napoleon himself and were far fewer in numbers. The following day we retreated to Berry-au-Bac (the enemy did not pursue us) and joined the army of Field Marshal Blücher who was at Laon. Count St. Priest was slowly transported to Laon where he passed away two weeks later. On his death bed he had at least some consolation in seeing his service recognised and rewarded as the Emperor [Alexander] granted him the Order of St. George of second class for the capture of Reims. [From the Russian text in N. Golitsyn, *Ofitserskie zapiski* . . .]

Ilya Radozhitskii

With his company quartered in Reims, Radozhitskii looked forward to having some entertainment and rest. Alas, the events turned out quite to the contrary.

The day after the capture of Reims, Count St. Priest came up with the dazzling idea of gathering all Russian forces outside the city, between the roads to Charleville and Neufchatel [Neufchatel-sur-Aisne?] where they were deployed in a large square to hold a Te Deum service to celebrate our victory. After the parade and ceremonial procession, regiments dispersed back to their quarters in the city suburbs and only the Ryazanskii [Infantry] Regiment marched to the city square, where it took up guard duty. Meanwhile, I joined Captain Zhemchuzhnikov and Pioneer Captain Belusovich to attend a mass at the [great] cathedral church. We marvelled at the vastness of the church, where an entire brigade could have been easily deployed, and its ornamented architecture. A long sequence of columns separated the central part of the cathedral from walls and in between the columns, in front of the altar, was an elevated spot where a royal throne stood during coronation ceremony. Near that altar place sat eminent but gloomy monks holding silver trumpets which they periodically blew to produce a weird and muffled sound. The altar itself was simple and open. Examining the interior of this magnificent cathedral, I took pleasure in gazing at the large painting depicting the Crucifixion . . . The French also showed us a marble tombstone that was covered with skilfully carved depictions of the hunting of wild lions . . . The French assured us that the cathedral was more than one thousand years old.* [Alas] its interior decoration suffered greatly during the Revolution . . .

[As we indulged ourselves,] Count St. Priest, accompanied by Lieutenant-Colonel Malinovskii, entered the cathedral; Malinovskii departed a minute later while St. Priest stayed and conversed with a few madames sitting on chairs in front of the altar. Several minutes later the Count called Captain Zhemchuzhnikov, who received some instructions and left. Belusovich and I went closer to the altar that was surrounded by numerous women in black dresses and bonnets, holding prayer books . . . Just as I sat down to observe the mass and listen to the dull singing of the monks . . . Malinovskii returned and whispered something into Count St. Priest's ear. The Count sent him back again and, leaning on a chair, he continued conversing with a woman. Eventually I was called and ordered to move out my cannon. I was startled by this order and could not understand what was happening, and thought that something clandestine was taking place . . .

As I came out of the cathedral, I saw [widespread] confusion in the streets as soldiers rushed back and forth. Oh, I thought to myself, the French must be somewhere close. And indeed they were – at the gates of the city. I was a duty officer in my company that day and ordered my feldwebel† to immediately gather all our men and horses at the parc, which was located outside the city, on the hill slope near the Soissons gate, so the French could see our guns only after they approached this suburb. Meanwhile, I rushed to my apartment where

---

* The original church was indeed established in the fifth century but the great cathedral was built in the thirteenth century.

† Feldwebel was a rank of non-commissioned officer.

I found my friend Baron von Schlippenbach. Our young and obliging hostess had prepared a splendid lunch for us and the table was covered with bottles of champagne and delicious dishes that tempted all of our senses. It was spell-binding sight but our thoughts were about the enemy and, fearing that we might be poisoned, we hastily left the apartment, ordering our batman to grab a few pies and bottles of wine for the road. I rushed to the artillery parc. There was a terrible commotion beyond the gates where the jagers, deployed in front of our parc, were already firing on the enemy cavalry that was advancing towards the suburbs. General Bistrom ordered four guns moved forward but our artillery crews, well fed by their kind hosts, were still making preparations. This only foretold more bad news for us. None of our officers could be seen anywhere. I rushed back into the city and encountered Baron von Schlippenbach, who was leading his two cannon, in full readiness, out of the city. Just as he climbed the hill in front of the parc, he encountered a French cavalry column but managed to halt it with his first few shots. Captain Zhemchuzhnikov, with four guns, moved to the left on the Epernay road, while I, with another four cannon, moved directly on the middle road in between the two main roads. I was accompanied by our company commander, Lieutenant-Colonel Timofeev.

Upon realising that their intention to catch us by surprise had failed, the French began to withdraw and a general battle line emerged. On the Soissons road, the Ryazanskii Regiment and the Prussian howitzers drove the French back; in front of them were scattered jagers while two squadrons of Leib-Hussars and Leib-Dragoons, with a squadron of Prussians, formed a separate detachment under the command of General Albrecht and moved in between my cannon. To the left, on a hill, there were two battalions of the Prussian infantry and Schlippenbach with two guns. The French continued to fall back but our troops did not pursue them too far and halted about three verstas [3.2km] from the city; the flanquers from both side, meanwhile, continued to harass each other.

At that moment the forces of our corps were dispersed along every road around the city and acted with inexplicable casualness . . . Hearsay claimed that we were facing Marshal Marmont, with some 15,000 men, who had strict orders from Napoleon to take the city at all costs. But we only laughed at this gossip.

It was already three o'clock in the afternoon and our troops remained calmly in their positions near the city. The enemy had many cavalry. [Suddenly] we saw puffs of smoke from artillery discharges rising in the hills far ahead of the enemy line. These were the two unfortunate Prussian battalions with their howitzers who had been quartered in the village of Rosnay after our capture of Reims, and were now entirely captured by the French. In addition, the French seized three more battalions near the city itself, and only half a battalion managed to reach my guns. It was only then that we perceived the French intentions. We were very lucky that our regiments, instead of being scattered at their quarters in various villages, were gathered that morning for the Te Deum service. It was said that the city mayor had secretly communicated our disposition to Marmont and that he had been already arrested and kept under strict guard to be executed [after the battle]. If we had been a bit more careless, the French would have routed us in piecemeal as we remained scattered in villages. This incident demonstrates how dangerous it to take up quarters in proximity to the enemy force. Of course, this was done to take better care of soldiers in the bad time of the year but this chariness proved to be detrimental to us.

The French made limited manoeuvres. Their entire cavalry moved against our left flank, leaving the Soissons road almost completely empty. Artillery was silent on both sides. Taking advantage of the free time, I went to examine our deployment. The weakness of our position on this side of the city suggested that either we were not intending on holding our positions for long or that the French did not want to attempt any major attacks in this direction. The majority of our troops was on the other side of the city. Count St. Priest and his suite were on the right flank, near the Prussian artillery. Arriving there, I heard as a hussar, dispatched by Count Wittgenstein, asked instructions from Count St. Priest, who told him, 'Be patient, lad. I will call you when everything settles down.'

Meanwhile, the Count noticed the enemy cavalry moving to our left flank and decided to go there in person. Driven by curiosity, I followed him as well, and enjoyed the sight of French *chasseurs à cheval*, in their bearskin caps, [skilfully] evaded our Cossacks, whom they lured back into ambushes and captured. As I returned [to my cannon] I noticed a vast multitude of troops appearing on the road from Soissons and thought it might be some troops from Blücher's [Army of Silesia], which was at Laon, marching to support us. Both sides began to move and I rushed to my post.

Stillness is usually followed by a tempest. And so we were, almost snoozing and talking about our quarters, when suddenly at four o'clock in the afternoon, we were rudely awakened. On the Soissons road first appeared a cavalry column that charged the Ryazanskii Regiment, which stood on our right flank and was closest to us. The soldiers of the Ryazanskii Regiment, commanded by their gallant commander Colonel Skobelev, twice very successfully repelled enemy attacks, maintaining battalion fire and supported by our batteries. Then this vast mass of cavalry rushed to our left flank while its position was taken by an eight-gun battery that, swiftly moving forward, treated us to a shower of cannonballs and explosive shells. The enemy battery kept increasing in size and soon numbered thirty cannon. Meanwhile, my four guns, deployed in the centre [of our position] were joined by six Prussian howitzers. A terrible artillery duel then commenced, spreading death and destruction all around. Shells kept exploding with hellish shrieks around us – one of the splinters flew just inches from my head while another wounded [our company commander] Lieutenant-Colonel

Timofeev in the leg. He was carried away from the battery and [some of] our cannoniers lost their nerve. So I dismounted and encouraged them, personally aiming cannon. Unable to endure the enemy fire any longer, the Prussian howitzers soon left their position and our entire line began to fall back hastily while the left flank had been overwhelmed. A half-battalion of the Prussians, standing to the left of my cannon, also prepared to leave when I told their officer, 'Courage, Kameraden! Französisch kaputt!' He shook his head while his soldiers, evading enemy projectiles, turned left and marched off without a command. Soon thereafter the two Guard cavalry squadrons, from General Albrecht's detachment, also passed through my battery, leaving just flanquers who were hard pressed by the enemy troops. Even when the French cavalry crossed the stream in front of my battery and menacingly approached my guns, I still remained in position, intending to use my four cannon to cover the retreat of the remaining troops in the city. At last, Captain Zhemchuzhnikov arrived and told me that it was time to leave this position. I turned around and saw, on my left flank, some infantry charging towards the Soissons gate. The French cavalry was very close and, to avoid being captured, I immediately moved my guns towards the gates, where everyone was rushing. To the left of me, coming from the suburbs, were the Prussian howitzers that the French were about to overtake. Anticipated a terrible misfortune if I allowed the Prussian artillery to anticipate me to the city, I rushed forward, grabbed the reins of the lead horse of the first howitzer and, raising my sabre, I shouted, 'Halt! Der Teufel!' The howitzers stopped and I immediately moved my cannon across the bridge. If I had not done this, my battery would have been captured by the French, who were already attacking the Prussian gun crews. Thus, all that remained behind, including the entire Prussian artillery, my caisson and one cannon, which was deployed with skirmishers, were lost to the French. I myself barely managed to get across the bridge into the city: shouts, pushing and shoving, musket fires, bullets whizzing and sabres of red and green Frenchmen – I have never experienced such confusion, chaos or danger . . . Our Count [St. Priest] was also barely saved – he was mortally wounded in the beginning of the enemy attack when a cannonball sheared off his shoulder. His injury was the reason for or disordered retreat. Just as the French reached the bridge, General Bistrom ordered the city gates closed and, defending its approaches with his jagers, he prevented the enemy from entering the city.

As I moved my cannon along a large street, I heard some commotion behind me. Our dragoons, with sabres unsheathed, galloped down the street shouting 'They are here! They are here!' and so frightened us all that we rushed headlong out of the city and scattered across fields into various directions . . . Some went on the road to Laon, others towards Rethel and few to Châlons. I, with seven guns, was among those who proceeded to Châlons after noticing that the Polotskii Regiment was left to defend the Châlons gate. As the proverb states, the fear has big eyes for the panic in the city was caused by a trifling incident. Amidst the confusion a single French cavalryman happened to pass through the gates and founded himself amidst our dragoons. At first he covered himself with a cloak and quietly rode with them until someone noticed him. Our dragoons attacked him but he fought back and the leading dragoons, hearing the noise and thinking that the French had broken into the city, caused the alarm.

As darkness fell, I noticed that there were few of our troops retreating on the Châlons road and so decided to turn back and move through the Charleville suburbs, where most of our troops sought to escape. The gates on this side of the city were protected by the jagers and four guns from our company. I was the only officer accompanying seven guns that moved to the Laon road where we encountered a cavalry outpost on the left and two Prussians battalions resting in a vale on the right. Further to the left, towards the river, there was an open area while enemy bonfires could be seen in the distance. The artillery fire died down at the nightfall but occasional musket shots could still be heard. Observing enemy bonfires to my left, I was concerned about a possible enemy cavalry attack and cautiously moved forward with my guns. The Prussians told me that many Russians had marched on the road to Berry-au-Bac. I soon encountered the brigade of Prince Gurielov who sent the Rylskii [Infantry] Regiment to protect me. Seeing no one in front of me and fearing French captivity, I mistook [our] dragoon outposts for the enemy. But my apprehension was not unfounded. Just as I approached the village of Saint-Thierry, I heard musket fire in my rear, which forced me to stop. Soon we heard shouts 'The French! The French!' and everyone began running once more. Indeed, just as I feared, the French cavalry had crossed a rivulet, occupied the road and attack the infantry, killing many idling Prussians and capturing their three howitzers. Our infantrymen greeted the enemy with a volley [, halting its attack]. Thus, for the second time around, I successfully escaped with my cannon.

I struggled to imagine the confusion that reigned inside the city. When the French repaired a bridge at the village of Saint-Brice [Saint-Brice-Courcelles], they got their lancers across the river under cover of darkness and made an unexpected attack on our troops defending the Laon gate; they killed many of them and broke into the city, which caused our jagers and the Polotskii [Infantry] Regiment to retreat along the Châlons road. Thus the French seized Reims from the [north] and captured everyone who had not left the city by then; among these were Captain Zhemchuzhnikov and Lieutenant Katomin of our company. I was also unaware of the whereabouts of our wounded [company commander].

Meanwhile various transports, cavalry and infantry began to pass by me so I ordered my crews to move faster. Shouts and noise amidst pitch-black night only further heightened our sense of terror. After moving for most of the night, we caught a brief rest around a bonfire where many of our scattered troops gathered, and joined a small detachment, commanded by General Panchulidzev, that arrived at Berry-au-Bac . . . where we found the outposts of the Prussian corps of General Yorck. Exhausted by our experiences, we halted here and slept for three hours. By dawn I was joined by Lieutenant Baron von Schlippenbach with four cannon. I replenished my ammunition from a reserve parc. The following day, General Panchulidzev greeted me sympathetically and thanked me for saving our guns, expressing his sorrow for the losses we have suffered. At the end, he offered me a glass of a very good champagne.

Thus ended this unfortunate battle at Reims. Count St. Priest soon died of his wound. We lost about 3,000 captured, another 1,000 killed and about twice as many wounded. The Prussians suffered most of these losses, including the loss of ten guns and howitzers against just one of ours. The survivors of this defeated corps scattered along the roads to Châlons and Rethel.

[As we moved forward on 14 March,] some of our scattered units continually rejoined us, including a battery company (led by Captain Vyrubachev) that delivered our wounded [company commander] Lieutenant-Colonel Timofeev. To escape the French, the company made a long march through Witry [Witry-lés-Reims], Bourgogne and Neufchatel-sur-Aisne to reach Berry-au-Bac. By now, Timofeev was suffering from a burning fever and he was transported to Laon. With Captain Zhemchuzhnikov in French captivity, I found myself commanding the entire company . . .

We spent the night in a barn . . . I had saved some fifteen bottles of champagne and enjoyed them with my surviving companions in a jovial conversation that made us forget our recent misfortune. And of course we could not but remember the incident with the hare that crossed our road on the eve of our capture of Reims. We frequently shrugged our shoulders when discussing various events and incidents of the yesterday's battle. Were we in position to judge the mistakes of our generals and analyse strategic considerations? We cannot see beyond our own limited range, and who does not commit mistakes once in a while? [From the Russian text in I. Radozhitskii, *Pokhodnye zapiski* . . .]

George Emmanuel

Of Serbian origin, Emmanuel was born in the Banat region of the Austrian Empire and served in the Serbian and Austrian armies before entering Russian service in 1797. He distinguished himself during the 1806–7 Campaign against the French, which earned him command of the Kievskii Dragoon Regiment. In 1812, he commanded a cavalry brigade in the 4th Reserve Cavalry Corps and served with distinction during the Russian Campaign, earning promotion to major-general. The following year, he commanded the advance guard of Langeron's corps during the campaign in Germany.

When the corps of Adjutant General Count St. Priest left the blockade of the fortress of Mainz, where I commanded all forward outposts, the Kievskii Dragoon Regiment, entrusted to my command, was assigned to His Excellency [Count St. Priest]. No noteworthy events took place between the [corps'] departure from Mainz on 3 [15] February 1814 and [its] arrival at the town of Châlons. Upon arriving at Châlons, Adjutant General Count St. Priest entrusted me with the command of a detachment consisting of the Polotskii Infantry and Kievskii Dragoon Regiments, with four cannon of Lt. Col. Timofeyev's [4th] Light Company. He instructed me to proceed towards the town of Reims because the rumours claimed that this town, which had been captured by our Cossacks, was reclaimed by the French troops and that Napoleon himself was present there. Consequently Adjutant General Count St. Priest commanded me to conduct reconnaissance.

I departed with the above mentioned detachment from Châlons on 19 February [3 March] and, moving in the direction of Reims, was already half way to St. Petites-Loges when I encountered a crowd of armed men attacking a Cossack detachment that had been dispatched here under command of Lieutenant Prince Golitsyn of His Imperial Majesty's Suite on the Quartermaster Service.* I immediately sent two squads [vzvod] of the Kievskii Dragoon Regiment against these rebels and almost all of them were captured and dispatched under strict escort to the corps commander. Since Châlons was about 10 French miles† away from Reims, I decided to stop about two miles away from the town, near the village of Sillery, where my detachment camped for the night, intending to conduct reconnaissance the following morning. On 20 February [4 March], I took only one squadron of the Kievskii Dragoon Regiment and two cannon and marched towards the town of Reims. At first impression, the city seemed to be poorly defended since there were no outposts or guards even as close as half a versta [500m] away from the town, which only confirmed that the town garrison was very weak and lacked cavalry. However, several artillery rounds fired in my direction also revealed that the town indeed possessed some artillery. I immediately reported my finding to Count St. Priest and then returned myself to Sillery. The detachment of the Prussian General von Jagow, consisting of 4,000 infantry and a considerable number of guns, soon joined our corps and Count St. Priest decided to attack Reims. With this in mind, he arrived with the corps in the vicinity of the village of Sillery on 22 February [6 March]. On the 23rd, the corps advanced towards Reims. Based on his own observations and reports on the weakness of enemy forces there, the corps commander supposed that the city, defended by such a weak garrison, would surrender without resistance in order to avoid an

---

* Prince M. M. Golitsyn was assigned to the 8th Corps.
† A French mile was equal to 4.4km or 4.17 Russian verstas.

assault. Therefore he dispatched Staff Captain Prince [Nikolai] Golitsyn of the Kievskii Dragoon Regiment, who was assigned to me, as a truce envoy to convey our peaceful intentions to the townsfolk and promise to maintain order and peace in the town. Yet, the town's response was firing canister shot at our truce-bearer. Upon seeing this, Count St. Priest gave the order to launch an attack but it had hardly begun when numerous cavalry appeared from the direction of Berry-au-Bac and soon arrived at the town. Count St. Priest decided not to proceed with the attack since it was assumed that further [enemy] reinforcements could arrive from the same direction. Instead, he chose to withdraw to Sillery and wait for the arrival of Lieutenant-General Panchulidzev with 5,000 infantry, 12 battery guns and the Chernigovskii Horse Jager Regiment, which had been left at the fortress of Mainz. General Panchulidzev arrived on the 27th [11 March] and preparations were immediately made for an assault on Reims.

By the dawn of 28 February [12 March], the following disposition was made: General von Jagow, with the Prussian troops, would make a diversion from the Reims road across the Vesle River while Count St. priest would command the assault. I, with the Chernigovskii Horse Jager and Kievskii Dragoon regiments, was to proceed along the road to Berry-au-Bac to cut off any [enemy] forces that tried to escape from the town. All of this was successfully accomplished. With the above mentioned regiments, I charged an [enemy] columns of some 500–600 men that departed from the town and completed annihilated and destroyed it [istreblena i unichtozhena]; whoever was not captured, drowned in the Vesle River. Meanwhile, our infantry broke from all directions into the town, where it captured ten cannon and several hundred prisoners. This successful assault, which established our communications with Field Marshal Blücher's army, cost us very few losses and lasted no more than an hour.

The following day, 1 [13] March, our entire corps concentrated near the town and performed a Te Deum ceremony. After this celebration, just as our regiments prepared to depart to their assigned quarters, we received reports on the enemy approaching from the town of Fismes. I immediately went with Count St. Priest to reconnoitre and we indeed observed the enemy advancing in large numbers, with the cavalry alone numbering up to 8,000. This entire mass of cavalry, with a considerable number of cannon, moved at once across all points and attacked us with utmost swiftness and vigour by the evening. Count St. Priest was quickly wounded at the start of this attack. Our weak corps was in no position to contain the enemy's superior forces led by Napoleon himself, and was thus hard pressed during the crossing over the Vesle River. The enemy attacked in so remarkably swift a manner so that each of us had to seek salvation for himself. Such a disorder in such crucial circumstances would have certainly brought destruction to the corps if not for the battalion of the Ryazanskii Infantry Regiment, which amidst this disarray maintained the order, composure and martial spirit that are hallmarks of firm and intrepid warriors. It alone managed to contain the enemy cavalry's swift and almost irrepressible onslaught. Amidst the most terrible disorder and confusion, ignoring all dangers and following the word of command, this battalion halted and redeployed while I shouted that they alone could save the entire corps. The thrashing and furious mass [of enemy cavalry] then crashed into this battalion, which repelled the attack with enormous losses but nevertheless gained time for all our cannon and other transports to get out of the town. Darkness soon fell but the fighting was not over yet, though order was slowly restored [among our troops]. I ordered Major-General Bistrom to defend this position [the crossing] with the same forces, reinforced with the Yeletskii Infantry Regiment that was dispatched by Major-General Karpenko. I then went to seek out Lieutenant-General Panchulidzev and other generals to discuss what to do next. I found them already gathered behind the town. General Panchulidzev had not yet recovered from a fainting spell that he had suffered earlier that morning (as the enemy attacked the town, he passed out and fell from his horse) and announced that even though he was the most senior officer after the corps commander, he could not accept the command of the corps. Thus, I took over the corps. At the council of war we decided to defend the town until morning and if no reinforcements arrived from General Yorck's corps, we would then retreat to Berry-au-Bac. But the enemy soon forded the Vesle river and began moving around the town of Reims. So we convened another council of war and decided to abandon the town and retreat. Consequently, I dispatched a non-commissioned officer of the Kievskii Dragoon Regiment to General Bistrom ordering him to abandon the town and retreat as carefully as possible. Meanwhile I myself travelled along the road to Berry-au-Bac. My NCO could not find General Bistrom, who had departed earlier leaving an excellent non-commissioned officer of the 33rd Jager Regiment with 200 of the best soldiers selected from various regiments to defend the town to the last possible moment, and if unable to break out, to surrender to the enemy. My NCO found these gallant warriors, who stayed behind to sacrifice themselves, encouraging each other, dividing their remaining cartridges and taking all possible precautions to defend the town entrusted to them. They carefully withdrew from this dangerous position and were fortunate to avoid all dangers as they moved amidst the enemy under the cover of darkness, with their own prudence and the Providence guiding them safely back to their regiments. Napoleon himself entered the town of Reims only after this band departed from it at around 2 o'clock in the morning following my NCO's order to leave this treacherous post. Thus are two most admirable and exceptional exploits of the battalion of the Ryazanskii Infantry Regiment and the valiant men gathered from various regiments, and I find no words to express my admiration to such glorious deeds that brought immortal glory to these heroes. [From the Russian text in RGVIA, f. VUA, d. 3376/2]

Ivan Skobelev

Born into an underprivileged family, Skobelev, who lost his father at an early age, faced an uphill struggle from early on. He received no formal education but, possessing an inquisitive mind and natural talents, he still managed to educate himself. Enlisting in the army at the age of fifteen, he dedicated the rest of his life to military service, slowly rising through the ranks. He took part in campaigns against the French in 1806–7, the Swedes in 1808–9 and the Turks in 1810–11, earning promotions and awards for gallantry. In 1812, he was appointed as a staff officer to the main headquarters of the Russian army and distinguished himself at Borodino, Tarutino and Krasnyi, earning promotion to colonel and appointment to the elite Life Guard Lithuanian Regiment. After another successful campaign in 1813, he was appointed commander of the Ryazanskii Infantry Regiment which he led during the Allied invasion of France. The battle of Reims solidified his reputation as a capable and fearless commander and earned him further awards. After victory in France, his military career spanned another thirty-five years, culminating in his promotion to a general of infantry in 1843.

On 28 February [12 March] 1814, at 3 o'clock in the morning, our entire corps was already battle ready and according to the disposition, each of its detachments advanced towards the walls of the town. Around 5 o'clock, the signal was given for the assault. 'Hurrah!' – and the Russians were in Reims. The French abandoned it after firing barely one hundred shots from cannon and as many from small arms. Our cavalry pursued the fleeing enemy, but part of our infantry, as it rushed into the town through the wall, observed in the midst of confusion inherent in such circumstances that some French soldiers were still entrenched in homes and fired from the windows. This allowed some our infantrymen to indulge in some freedom, namely, to profit from the property of ordinary townsfolk. The town residents did not remain quietly in their homes: confusion increased everywhere and shooting continued on the streets and partly inside buildings, spreading fear. The cry of humanity finally reached the gentle and noble heart of Count St. Priest. This general rode to my regiment, which, after entering Reims though the town gates from the direction of Rethel, was deployed motionless in platoon column [vzvodnaya kolona] awaiting further orders.

'M. Skobelev, put an end to this impudence that is so harmful to the honour of our arms, and become a benefactor of this city!' Such were the words of the Count as he passed by me.

Fully sharing the sincere grief of this fatherly commander, I designated the nearest house as my headquarters and rallying point, and not wasting a minute, dispersed my entire regiment in small detachments under command of reliable officers and even non-commissioned officers. These troops were ordered to detain anyone found with plundered items and bring them all to me. A few hours later our angel of peace, the kind Count [St. Priest] soothed the fears of peaceful residents and entrusted the Ryazanskii Regiment, which so despised vile greed and followed the voice of command, the mission of restoring complete peace in the town and appeasing its residents. Every item from my quarters was returned to its present owner and the general security was achieved – and the joyous smiles of gratitude replaced fear on the faces of the citizens.

As peace and order were restored, I, as the newly appointed commandant of Reims, had to receive the town's deputation which came to me with the expression of thanks and an invitation to dinner the following day. In the evening order was given for the corps to prepare for the church service to thank the Lord for the successful resolution of the attack.

On 1 [13] March, at 8 o'clock in the morning, all the troops (except for six Prussian battalions that after the assault moved to the Soissons road) came out into the open plain [outside the town], attended the Te Deum ceremony and dispersed for a temporary respite into the villages in the vicinity of Reims. On request of the authorities of Reims, my regiment remained inside the town and carried on its guard duty. The staff and commissioned officers, as well as lower ranks, were given double portions, and we all hoped to have a pleasant and cheerful time. Alas, it all turned out quite differently.

At the beginning of the 11th hour I returned with my entire regiment to the town square surrounding the Reims church [of Saint-Rémi] so famous for being the site where the king of Frances were crowned. The Count [St. Priest] listened to divine service inside it. Unaware of the number of posts I could not calculate how many guard outposts I had to deploy. The mayor of the city, preoccupied with preparations for the impending feast, could not come to me soon enough. Major N of the Rylskii Infantry Regiment, the elderly duty officer in charge of the guard, was engaged in a friendly conversation over breakfast with the owner of the house where he was staying. So while waiting for one or the other, I was compelled to order my soldiers to place their weapons on racks and wonder around freely.

About 11.30, a Prussian cavalryman rode into the square and, asking for the senior officer, he informed me that General von Jagow was routed and that the Prussian battalions, encamped on the road to Soissons and not expecting the enemy, were washing their clothes in the river, having left behind their equipment, and were consequently either cut to pieces or captured upon the sudden appearance of the French cavalry; only those few who were on guard duty [the Prussian officer informed me] managed to escape and were retreating with their general without any hope of salvation. I rushed with this unpleasant news to the church and informed Count St. Priest, who responded that this alarm was probably the result of the French partisans who had come from Epernay and that neither the French army, nor the corps deployed near Soissons, which was occupied by the Allied forces, could be expected to appear here. If the guerrillas, and [St. Priest] was certain it was them, managed to attack without artillery that could not be moved through the woods, and exploit General von Jagow's mistake, then it was the Prussian general who should be held responsible. Just as I returned with this answer, another [Prussian] bearer of sorrowful news told me that the large French forces pursuing the Prussians could take the city unless immediate measures were taken, and that the enemy was just half a mile from the forštate [suburb] and that our cannon deployed there would soon become their prey.

Wasting time on further questioning seemed inappropriate, and therefore, sending a messenger to Count St. Priest, I immediately commanded, 'To arms! Run! Load your weapons!' A few minutes later I was already beyond the gates, and in few more minutes – beyond the forštate. General von Jagow was retreating in a square and his soldiers, even though only half of them were in uniform and the rest were in shirts, some even barefoot, fought like lions. They were chased by three to four thousand cavalry, some of which were bustling about our guns – from Lieutenant-Colonel Timofeyev's company – deployed beyond the forštate. My appearance alleviated the enemy's onslaught on von Jagow while the skirmishers dispatched towards the windmill forced the enemy to fall back and ride away without looking back.

Having deployed one of the battalions of my regiment in a square and leaving the other at various points in the forštate, I advanced straight at the enemy desiring to demonstrate that we were sufficiently strong. The General [von Jagow] was on his horse but riding without a saddle, but this did not deprive him of the appearance inherent to a hero. As he passed me, he unleashed a torrent of the vilest cursing; although I do not speak German, I still understood at least that it was not directed against me. The relative safety in which he now found himself could not remove expressions of grief from his face nor comforted his broken heart: he had just lost half of his bravest warriors. 'May the Lord comfort your grieving soul,' I thought to myself. 'However, it is still unforgivable to let the French guerrillas, lacking cannon, to gain an upper hand on you like this!' But before I could even finish that thought, a shot from the enemy's guns delivered a three-pound greeting.

I was furious! I bemoaned the lack of means to return this favour and standing demurely, I sent a messenger to inform Count St. Priest that up to five thousand cavalry and two guns deployed on the edge of the woods were clearly not led by a guerrilla. The Count arrived at once. The misfortune of General von Jagow lay heavily on his soul and he clearly did not know whom we were facing or how these unexpected visitors appeared here; he certainly could not envisage that the Allied troops had abandoned Soissons without informing him of such an important turn of event, which as events later revealed, was precisely the case.

Having a cavalry screen before him, the enemy stood quietly and his guns fell silent. It was the vanguard that decided to constrain its actions in anticipation of the army. And yet our circumstances also gradually improved as troops began returning from the nearby villages. Major-General Emmanuel was first to arrive with the Kievskii Dragoons Regiment, and deployed it in a mixed screen. The soldiers on town guard duty, numbering some 600 men, were deployed as skirmishers and placed under my command. The 1st Battalion of my regiment was ordered to take the manor (it was either a village or some kind of factory building – I cannot recall it for sure) located about two verstas [2.1km] from the city on the bank of the Vesle River while the 3rd Battalion still remained in reserve in the suburb. By then other regiments had arrived as well and they all took up defensive positions. We only lacked accurate information on whom Fate chose to confront us and whether we should launch offensive operations or not. The Count commanded a prisoner brought to him and moments later a Cossack officer from his convoy brought him a Frenchman captured in the outposts. I do not know whether the Frenchman was instructed to say so or was just plain stupid but we became convinced, based on testimony of this oddball, that we faced not Napoleon himself but rather [his Marshal] Marmont, and thus assumed that the enemy had no more than 12,000 men, instead of the actual 70,000, and remained full of hope to cut him to pieces.

Our corps had about 14,000 experienced men under arms and Count St. Priest naturally was not afraid of Marmont and never considered retreating, which, considering circumstances, was the only thing he should have done. Consequence, all of our orders were completely inappropriate to the dreadful circumstances we faced . . . It is not a subordinate's task to judge his superior's mistake and my heart is unable to pass judgment on the actions of the Count [St. Priest] whom we all adored so much; besides, even on his deathbed he did not admit his mistakes. Nevertheless, our troops soon gathered, a general disposition was made and each unit occupied the spot assigned to it. It was still quiet. Riding with Prince Golitsyn of the Quartermaster Service along the right flank of our skirmisher screen, which was placed under my command, we noticed that [the enemy] columns standing in the groves doubled in size and that the number of cannon greatly increased and that new cavalry forces appeared on the right side of the road, that is against our left flank. The enemy soon opened artillery fire against our right flank and our cannon immediately returned fire. The Count, demonstrating his famous fearlessness, moved around the skirmisher chain and, approaching my post, he appeared certain of impending victory, jokingly commenting to me, 'Skobelev, I am sure you would not give up the post so crucial to our position before I do Reims!' 'Where else would you want me to retreat in that case?' I inquired. "True,' replied the Count with a smile, '[if I give up Reims,] you would have only way out . . . into heaven. But there would no retreating [today]!' And with these words he galloped away.

Soon thereafter Major-General Bistrom II, the commander of the 33rd Jager Regiment, arrived with a formal order for my battalion not to abandon the current position and informing me that, if necessary and depending on the actions of the enemy, the Count would personally issue new orders for me. Just as the general conveyed the order to me, the French batteries concealed in the woods opened a terrifying fire. The cavalry launched an attack on our left flank and the enemy forces revealed up to 20,000 men in that direction. Our skirmishers were instantly cut to pieces, except for 160 men who were close to my battalion and joined it. Suddenly everything had changed. Our troops were driven back and cannon were abandoned during the withdrawal through the forštate. Everyone was rushing back, putting obstacles to each other at every step and in less than fifteen minutes there were none of our troops left in front of the city except for my battalion of the Ryazanskii Regiment and the few surviving skirmishers.

The danger was obvious as the only way to salvation lay through the forštate already occupied by the enemy while I was separated by the wide Vesle River from the road along which our forces began to move an hour later. There was still no [enemy] infantry against me so I had to defend against the cavalry. Major-General Bistrom II, entirely surprised by such disarray, galloped away to rescue his retreating regiment and the hope for the Lord's help was my sole sustenance. Forming square, I had barely issued the necessary orders regarding successful loading of muskets by skirmishers who were intentionally placed inside the square when a formidable mass of cavalry charged at me. Some inexperienced soldiers, especially those from other regiments who had barely escaped death earlier, became disorganised and began to groan, but this disarray was quickly corrected. I strictly ordered, on pain of death, to observe silence and not to shoot without my order. After letting the French approach within sufficient range, I regaled them with unhurried but precise battalion fire. These successful volleys met my expectations quite well. The [enemy] cavalry was, I assume, newly raised and inexperienced. The sight of some hundred men shot to the ground prevented the others from carrying on and, with our fire intensifying, they quickly saw that we were far from showing any mercy to them. So they wavered, halted and thus allowed us to kill a few dozen more of them before they finally circled left and away. Taking advantage of this moment, I marched at a brisk pace towards the forštate and the thought that if I was destined to die, I would at least perish one sazhen closer to Mother Russia, was the sole consolation at these desperate moments! After letting their cavalrymen through, four guns of the enemy horse artillery opened canister fire at me, which would not have stopped me but would have certainly devastated my ranks if not for the enemy's decision to launch new [cavalry] attacks which after surviving the initial charge now seemed like child's play to me. I repelled another and then another attack, but the canister fire caused considerable losses: more than fifty of my comrades perished with honour while the forštate was still one versta [1.06km] away from me. Some of my best officers tried, carefully and with utmost discretion, to point out to me that since the point, where we were retreating, was already occupied by the enemy, we could avoid certain death and save our men for the Fatherland by surrendering to the enemy. While my heart could not accept this, I found it also rather coldblooded and unjust to condemn some 700 men to certain death. My heart was filled with grievous sorrow and I confess that I had begun to waver. At this moment, Lieutenant Volkov of the Life Guard Semeyonovskii Regiment and a Cossack officer brought on a common soldier's overcoat the mortally wounded Count St. Priest, who, seeing the critical situation of the Ryazanskii Battalion, forgot about his own condition and ignored the fact that he was surrounded everywhere by the enemy. Instead, as he later observed, he admired his guard battalion's* 'training exercise with gunpowder' and remained on this side of the town, attended by the above-mentioned officers whose noble deeds and exemplary intrepidity is above all praise. No sooner had this sorrowful procession entered the square that a new [enemy] attack commenced! But, with the Lord's help, this attack, like previous charges and two more assaults that followed, was repelled with great success. 'Save my honour, my dear Skobelev!' the Count told me. 'I do not want to hide from you that my honour will be compromised if I am captured. And despising death, even if I could not earlier, I would have learned from our gallant Ryazanskii warriors.'

My heart was bleeding. 'Your Excellency,' I answered. 'Nothing will part with our honour, neither the impending death nor even the destruction of the world itself! I swear for myself and all my comrades that the enemy will lay hands on you only after the very last one among us, who have decided to sacrifice ourselves for you, has perished with glory that the Lord and our duty present to us!' Turning to my companions, I then said, 'Repeat the oath, my friends! Let's pray fervently to the Lord so he may show his innumerable favours on the loyal subjects of the Russian Tsar; may He infuse our hearts with new strength, and courage, and may He raise our spirit and mind above the perils that surround us! Until now we have shown how the Russians fight, let's now show how they die!'

Shakos flew off the heads and everyone crossed themselves, shouting 'We swear!' Repelling two more attacks, we approached the forštate. The pursuing enemy forces then left us alone, either because of the rapidly-approaching darkness or the assumption that we would be dealt with by the [enemy] forces ahead of us. Napoleon had already moved his main forces across the pontoon bridges that were set up at two, if I am not mistaken, spots on the Vesle River. The enemy troops that blocked the gates of Reims turned their complete attention to the city, not expecting to see a handful of fierce Muscovites, whom they did not notice amidst the din of the fighting, suddenly appearing in their rear. Without wasting a moment, I left the Count in the care of the

---

* Skobelev's comment: 'This is how St. Priest referred to the Ryazanskii regiment after the battle at Mainz on 28 January [9 February] 1814'.

gallant Major Rodovskii and a squad of soldiers, and, after discharging a volley, charged with the remaining troops in a bayonet attack. Struck by the suddenness of this charge, the enemy abandoned his cannon next to our guns in the forštate and fled headlong in different directions. Some of them jumped into the river separating the city from the forštate while those who dared to resist us were all slaughtered.

Meanwhile, the 3rd Battalion of my regiment, which was kept in the reserve and held on to the city, continued to fire from the city walls; it was supported by the Kievskii Dragoon Regiment under command of General Emmanuel. The general order had by now collapsed inside our corps and despite the efforts of our quartermaster officers to preserve people, only few retreated organised in regiments. Emanuel saw that if he left the city without gaining time for all of the parts of the corps to get away to a safe distance, they would all become certain victims of the enemy.

Meanwhile it was believed that I and my 1st Battalion had already fallen into captivity. Before darkness fell, some of our troops saw my desperate circumstances and bid farewell to me. But, worst of all, there was no news about the corps commander. Everyone was overcome with despondency and only Emmanuel, whose fearless spirit rose above perilous circumstances, acted as the genuine hero exposing himself to numerous perils and hovering above them like an eagle as he sought to contribute for the common cause.

I owe it to my strong breast and voice, whose value I fully appreciated only at that moment, that my Ryazanskii comrades, who stayed in the city and did not recognise us in darkness, kept firing from the walls, did not slaughter all of my conquering comrades. A bullet hitting my spur and a severe contusion to my left hand amplified my shouts that were finally heard and recognised. The shooting stopped, gates were unlocked and we were saved! Count St. Priest was immediately put into the carriage, and gallant Emanuel, praising the bravery of the Ryazanskii soldiers and ordering me to defend the town for at another hour, marched away in the wake of the corps. About five minutes later, a resident of the town– a middle-aged and noble-looking man whom I had previously met in Count St. Priest's quarters – ran up to me with the news that the French had already entered the town through the Châlons gate and, if I did not hurry to leave, my regiment would be completed destroyed. It was inappropriate to challenge the truth of it all and besides I was not defending a fortress: my goal was to protect the retreating forces, the last of whom by now should have been at what cowards call a 'dignified distance'. Therefore, I ordered Captain Honsburg, commanding the 3rd Battalion, to gather as many skirmishers as he could from the town walls and proceed towards Berry-au-Bac while I moved forward with the 1st Battalion and a handful of men from the 3rd Battalion. The kind Frenchman shook my hand and told me that he considered himself fortunate for having had a chance to offer such timely assistance to the Russians since he considered them fighting this war on behalf of the rightful king. He led us through the narrow streets, begging us to remain quiet. Everything around us was silent. We were approaching the gate when suddenly we clearly heard the clatter of the French troops marching on the main street. The weather was warm but I felt a chill spreading through my entire body. Fear of being ambushed was amplified by the darkness of night, drizzling rain and deathly gloom. For five minutes we stood motionless like grave stones, but the clutter soon died away. Our guide informed us that we could no longer escape through the gates since the French must have captured them. We turned in another direction and after wandering for another quarter of an hour, finally came to a postern gate in the town wall. After opening it, our guide embraced me and wished us good luck; he explained how we should proceed and, declaring that anyone serving under Count St. Priest was dear to his heart, he quickly ran to the 3rd Battalion, which soon encountered our saviour and equally owes its escape to this man. It is a pity that I am still unaware of this heavenly messenger's name!

Leaving town, we walked across the field towards the road. Men often fell down but they did so silently. We soon heard human voices: these were the enemy's mounted patrols – the sentries at the gate called out to them. The road ran from the gate and was therefore not far, but prudence demanded that we continued our march through the field. We probably moved more than six miles before everything became quiet and only the voice of singing man could be heard in the distance. This voice got louder from time to time and finally it was possible to distinguish that it was a Russian song. We all breathed freely now and gave thanks, with our hearts, to the Lord for our miraculous salvation. But before proceeding further in our narrative of this campaign, it is necessary to mention where this Russian voice, which thrilled us so much, came from.

At the beginning of the battle my batman Golikov departed on a rather languid horse with some vodka and snacks sent to me by the mayor of the town. I could not care for neither drink nor food at that moment so Golikov simply waiting for me to work up an appetite. Half an hour before the battle, I ordered him, as a [militarily] useless person, to go to supply train. He was saddened to hear this order and . . . stayed with me. A few minutes later, upon seeing him next to me once more, I repeated what I considered to be rather beneficial advice for him but he flatly refused to obey, declaring that he would die for me; he thus stayed. The first two attacks, as the soldiers later testified, he endured bravely, but after the last charge, upon hearing grumbling among soldiers and some declaring that death was imminent, our gallant man decided, as they say, to bail out and left the square. Unfortunately, he did this just as the third enemy attack was underway with terrible cries and odds were clearly not in our favour. Golikov's horse, as I mentioned above, was rather languid – he himself lacked spurs and a whip while his Bucephalus simply ignored blows with the bridle-rein. Considering such haste, he was, of course, just short distance away from our square when two Frenchmen, either of their own accord or ordered to, charged at him, probably thinking that he might be a senior officer seeking to save his life for future laurels. In vain did our knight tried to shake off his companion's lethargy and unconcern for danger: despite the rider's best efforts, the horse simply remained unresponsive. This, however, did not prevent Golikov taking tactical precautions: he turned the horse towards the riverbank and just as his pursuers reached him, he jumped over the animal's head into the river, sustaining two light sabre cuts in the back, which was protected by a leather sack with my breakfast . . . After firing a couple of pistol shots and wounding Golikov, the French turned back while [Golikov's] horse, with his usual apathy, continued to graze calmly in the field. A few moments later we reached this spot and my soldiers, seeing a horse without a rider and its saddle covered with remnants of the breakfast, assumed that Golikov had perished and wished eternal memory to the zealous servant. But this was not the end of him. Removing his coat and holding on to the remnants of the above-mentioned breakfast, Golikov safely swam across the river, drank the vodka and wine in the surviving bottles, reached the main road and, laying under a tree, he indulged himself in a hero's slumber. After waking up at midnight and finding himself in pitch darkness, and, above all, unaware in which direction to go, he decided that the best thing in this perilous circumstances was to sing a song out of grief. This peculiar development in fact helped us because we reached the main road before we could have dared to, and without this mellifluous sign, who know how long we would have roamed in the fields in search of the main road.

In conclusion, I must note that my account does, without a doubt, suffer from some shortcomings and errors, especially with respect to other parts of our corps and the movements of Napoleon's army. My constraints are too narrow to discuss either of them. I cannot recall without sorrow the Count, who met his unfortunate fate here. To the chagrin of everyone who knew him and valued his talents, he passed away sixteen days after the battle at Reims. The details of what transpired on 1 [12] March should not be expected from me: I only described what I have heard and witnessed.

It was still dark when we arrived at Berry-au-Bac on 2 [14] March. I immediately reported to the Prussian General von Yorck, who commanded Blücher's vanguard. This great commander spoke to me in Russian. After receiving from him an order to proceed to Laon and approaching my battalion deployed on the river bank, I was thrilled to see that the survivors of the 3rd Battalion had arrived from Reims and joined us.

The sun rose soon. I saw my courageous friends and officers and soldiers all rushed to greet me. Tears of joy flowed on everyone's faces and we all remembered with great emotion how we astonishingly escaped from such perilous circumstances. 'Kneel, my friends!' I told them. 'First of all let us thank the Lord, who had shown us his mercy. Those who survived the 1st of March no longer belong to themselves, but rather became an integral part of Providence itself!' Only those do not shed tears during their prayers to the King of the Kings who have traversed from cradle to grave along the road strewn with rose petals. But we had just barely survived through thickets of prickly thorns and, therefore, it was not surprising that sobbing frequently interrupted my speech. We had no chaplains so I said the prayer, and as I finished, a pure joy rustled in the air. Warriors embraced each other, struggling to believe in their lucky break. Sharing this joy with each and all of them, I was, no doubt, overjoyed but also completely exhausted. For thirty-six hours I remained without sleep and food – and for twenty of these hours I ceaselessly fought with all of my body and soul; besides, I felt incredible pain from the blow to my left hand. Our supply train was further ahead but my comrades pulled out their coveted provisions out of their knapsacks and prepared an excellent breakfast, sweetened with a bottle of nice champagne. With the Prussian vanguard vigilantly watched over us, I then decided to give my men some rest and, after enjoying it myself, embarked on a further journey in painful but much better condition. [From the Russian text in I. Skobelev, *Rasskazy russkogo invalida*]

Moisei Karpenko

In 1839, after reading Alexander Mikhailovskii-Danilevskii's history of the Allied invasion of France in 1814, Karpenko wrote a lengthy letter to correct some of inaccuracies he had found in the historian's narrative. His letter directly contradicts Emmanuel's above-mentioned memoir in discussion of the aftermath of St. Priest's injury.

Skobelev, commanding the Ryazanskii Infantry Regiment, was first to endure the violent attack of the enemy cavalry. The Prussian General Jagow failed to live up to his responsibilities and perished with many of his men. I do not want to criticise the dead but must note that Jagow and Lieutenant-General Emmanuel bear the brunt of responsibility for the enemy's sudden attack on us because, under Count St. Priest's disposition, our troops had already moved to nearby villages while neither Emmanuel nor Jagow informed us of the enemy's appearance. When the first alarm was sounded, Colonel Skobelev rallied his Ryazanskii Regiment and drove twelve cannon by hand outside the city, where he deployed them on positions chosen by Count St. Priest and was first to clash with the much stronger enemy. Eternal glory and honour to this hero, whose actions saved survivors of the 8th Corps. Forming a square with his men, he protected the mortally wounded Count St. Priest. I was positioned with four regiments on the right side of the town and at the most critical moment, the Ryazansk grenadiers brought St. Priest on stretcher. Already drained and depleted, Count St. Priest ordered me to 'rally the remnants of the corps and proceed to Laon to join the rest of our forces, because Lieutenant-General Panchulidzev refused from taking over command due to ill health.' Such were the words that the Count addressed directly to me. I assigned a company of jagers and, placing him in carriage, send him along the road to Laon. Lieutenant-General Emmanuel, whom Your Excellency [Mikhailovskii-Danilevskii] mentions in this context, was in fact not present and none of us knew at that moment where he and his troops were located. Thus, contrary to your description, I must note that it was not Emmanuel who took over responsibilities after [the injury of] Count St. Priest but rather it was me. By eleven o'clock in the evening I was joined by Colonel Skobelev, who brought four cannon and [the remnants of] his regiment. The following day, Major-General Bistrom also joined us. Emmanuel, on the other hand, was missing until we joined the rest of the army. [From the Russian text in RGVIA, f. VUA, op. 16, d. 3376/2]

6

Onwards to Paris

After Napoleon's victory at Reims, the Allies vacillated about their next moves but their hand was forced by Napoleon's offensive. The French Emperor chose to exploit his success at Reims by moving further eastward with a striking force and linking up with the French garrisons near the Rhine that were blockaded by the Allies. This, combined with the growing partisan activity in the eastern part of France, would sever the supply lines of the Allied armies. However, before this bold strategic move could be undertaken, Napoleon decided to first target Schwarzenberg's Army of Bohemia that had got dangerously close to Paris. Napoleon again left Marshals Marmont and Mortier to watch Blücher in the north, and marched south with the remaining forces aiming at the rear of the Army of Bohemia. Upon learning about the French movement, Schwarzenberg turned his forces back and began moving eastward immediately. But on 20 March, the Austrian commander, receiving updated intelligence, uncharacteristically decided to halt his retreat and go over to the offensive, which Napoleon did not expect. In the ensuing battle at Arcis-sur-Aube the Allies proved victorious primarily because Napoleon underestimated them. To recover his position, Napoleon then resorted to his earlier plan of marching eastward and linking up with the garrisons and partisans to cut the Allied supply lines. This was a bold course indeed and Napoleon thought it was the best one currently available.

On 23 March, he outlined his plan in a short letter to his wife Marie-Louise, which was, however, intercepted by the Allied cavalry. The letter offered crucial intelligence on Napoleon's plans, his intentionst, and even his initial line of march and allowed the Allies to shift their attention to the French capital, where, as additional captured dispatches revealed, the political situation was very unstable. Napoleon's ministers spoke of the alarming extent of Royalist and other subversive activity, as well as of the weak defences of the city. Emperor Alexander quickly realised the importance of this information and insisted that the Allied armies should march immediately on Paris. On 25 March, the Allies scored an important victory at La Fère-Champenoise and marched unhindered to the French capital.

Alexander Mikhailovskii-Danilevskii

Staff officer in the Russian Imperial headquarters.

We had no news from Field Marshal Blücher for over a week. Finally, on 2 [14] March, we received the news of his victory at Laon and the Main Army decided to resume offensive operations, moving to Arcis. It was here that Napoleon and Alexander encountered each other on the battlefield for the last time, and the former, having exhausted all his efforts, was forced to retreat. He became convinced of impossibility of resisting the forces of Emperor Alexander and decided, as a last resort to save himself from destruction, to attempt one of his boldest movements, which however not only failed to produce any success but instead put an end to his reign that was full of astonishing deeds. This movement brought us to Paris and therefore deserves a detailed explanation, particularly since it has not been done in any of the works that have been published until now, while I have received details about it from one of the generals who attended the council of war at Sommepy

Based on observations made during the battle at Arcis-sur-Aube and intelligence provided by our light detachments, we realised that Napoleon was retreating in the direction of Vitry. Having dispatched Marshal Ney to occupy this city, which was held by Allied troops, he crossed the Marne River and proceeded to St. Dizier, with intention of falling upon the communications of the Allies and forcing them to retreat to Chamons and beyond. Based on this news, Prince Schwarzenberg made a decision to follow Napoleon with his entire army and join Blücher who was located at Châlons; Blücher was informed to immediately march in direction of Vitry. The Main Army marched towards the village of Sommepy around nine o'clock in the evening. By 1 a.m. we made camp in the village of Dampierre, where we received enemy dispatches that had been intercepted by our troops. On being opened in presence of Princes Schwarzenberg and Volkonskii and State Secretary Count Nesselrode, these dispatches revealed, among other documents, the following letter written with Napoleon's own hand to his consort Marie-Louise: 'My love, I have been all these days constantly on horseback. On the 20th I took Arcis on the Aube. The same evening the enemy attacked me near that town, but I beat them: they had four thousand men killed. The next day the enemy marched in the direction of Brienne and Bar-sur-Aube, and I resolved, in order to draw them away from Paris, to lead my army to the Marne, and to approach the fortresses. This evening I shall be at St. Dizier. Farewell, my love, give a kiss to our son.'

This letter, which presented the events of Arcis in a prejudiced manner, clearly revealed Napoleon's plan of action and his desire to gather the garrisons of various fortresses and move the theatre of war closer to France's frontiers. After this letter was read Prince Volkonskii proposed that after uniting with Blücher, only a strong corps should be sent after Napoleon, while the united armies should take the nearest road to Paris, where they would be in five days, and have it in their hands before Napoleon could know anything about it. Prince Schwarzenberg thought this idea too bold, and raised concerns about our lines of communication. Prince Volkonskii responded that we should not be concerned about it since the army had reserve parks, pontoons and supplies for ten days and, in case of failure, lines of communication could be established through Flanders. The Field Marshal replied that he would not venture on such an enterprise without the consent of the Emperor Alexander and the King of Prussia.

At two o'clock in the morning of 12 [24] March, we left Dampierre for Sommepy, where we made a second halt. The intercepted letters were here laid before his Majesty by Prince Schwarzenberg, who on retiring told [Prince Volkonskii] that the Emperor retained his former opinion, which was to unite with Blücher at Vitry, and following Napoleon with the combined armies, attack him wherever they should find him. He then mounted his horse and rode off while the Emperor desired to call a meeting with his generals: Count Barclay de Tolly, Prince Volkonskii and Generals Diebitch and Toll. Informing them about the content of Napoleon's letter to Marie-Louise, he inquired, 'What is your idea, gentlemen?' Count Barclay de Tolly thought it would be best to follow Napoleon and attack him. General Diebitch proposed that while the united armies were engaged in following Napoleon, the Prussian General Bülow, who was at Soissons, should make a dash for Paris. To this Prince Volkonskii replied as follows: 'It is well known that there are in Paris 40,000 National Guard and fragments of various regiments, and that in addition to these, at a short distance from the capital are the two corps of Marmont and Mortier. All these troops together form a total of 90,000 men, consequently we cannot expect that Bülow with his 30,000 will attack an enemy so greatly superior to him in numbers. I may add, that if we follow Napoleon, we must leave a powerful rearguard to repulse the attack of these two marshals. Taking these circumstances into consideration, I am inclined to think that it would be the best plan first to unite with the Silesian army, and then to detach against Napoleon a numerous body of cavalry and some regiments of infantry, with instructions everywhere to prepare accommodation for the Emperor, that it may be believed we are following with the whole army. We ought then to march straight to Paris through Fère-Champenoise, and Blücher through Etoges, maintaining uninterrupted communications between the two armies. Following this route, we must attack Marshals Marmont and Mortier wherever we meet them. We shall beat them, because we are stronger than they, and each day will place two marches between us and Napoleon.'

This plan being approved, the Emperor, wishing to communicate his plans to Prince Schwarzenberg, called for his horse and rode off towards Vitry, where he found him together with the King of Prussia. He invited them to dismount, and then explained to them Prince Volkonskii's opinion, which the King and the Prince at once approved. There, in the field, they signed orders to Blücher to march to Etoges; the troops were told to halt wherever the new orders reached them while General Winzingerode was sent with 10,000 cavalry, one jager regiment and two light detachments towards St. Dizier. To further deceive the enemy, the Emperor suggested setting up a camp at Vitry. The plan of marching on Paris had to be kept in complete secrecy for some time and I will never forget as General Toll, after leaving the council of war at Sommepy, whispered in my ear, 'We are marching on Paris but, for God's sake, do not tell this to anybody!' This same general was first to inform me about the decision to abandon Moscow at the village of Fili [in 1812]. [From the Russian text in Alexander Mikhailovskii-Danilevskii, *Zapiski*. . .]

Ilya Radozhitskii

After surviving the battle of Reims, the gallant Radozhitskii marched with his artillery company northwards to join the Army of Silesia that concentrated at Laon.

In the evening of 4 [16] March we were informed that we were coming under the control of the Army of Silesia and that Blücher had decided to review us. So we made preparations for a parade. The town of Laon, located on a hill, can be seen from far away. As we approached it, we encountered numerous signs of a vicious battle that had recently taken place there: corpses of men and horses, cannonballs, rags, damaged transports, straw and finally an entire burned village came into view.

Upon reaching the town we had such a long respite that my men managed to catch a solid nap while I went to examine the town. Laon, as previously mentioned, is located on a steep hill that overlooks a vast plain with small villages. It could have been made into a major fortress but the French neglected it. Blücher exploited this to capture the town and entrench himself so strongly that even Napoleon, despite his best efforts, could not dislodge him. The town is surrounded by a stone wall with towers that have almost completely collapsed. In the spring this area probably offers many picturesque views . . . but now everywhere you look, there is nothing but dreadful sights. The suburbs are so devastated and plundered that only stone walls remain standing; even roofs have been dismantled. Furthermore, trash of various sorts, mixed with human filth, mud and billowing smoke all served as reminders of a fierce battle waged here. [. . .] Laon is not a large town and its buildings are quite outdated and covered in age-old grime; the local church looks more like a Chinese pavilion than a cathedral. The overcrowded streets, where numerous soldiers, horses, carriages and transports all struggled for space, served as a reminder that Blücher's headquarters was established in the town. Occasionally we saw local residents, stripped naked, emaciated and hungry, wandering around to gather rags, fragments of weapons or barely moving horses who had been abandoned [by troops] by the wayside. Sometimes, we could see old women moving like ghosts amidst the ruins, wearing nothing but rags, disfigured by their misfortunes and starving to death. Laying their hands on their chest, they gazed at the enemy troops passing by as if beseeching them to spare their devastated city that had already been turned into ashes and rubble. Only the younger and prettier girls remained upbeat and always smiled – their circumstances were much more fortunate, although one can hardly call what they had to endure good fortune . . .

Blücher cancelled the parade claiming ill health so we were moved across the narrows around the city and past the entire corps of Count Langeron that was bivouacked near the devastated villages. However, our guides got confused and mistakenly brought us into such defiles, covered with brushwood, that we barely got out of there and took a position beyond Laon, on the road to the village of Coucy [. . .] Just as we prepared to settle down, the entire village was pulled to pieces by soldiers in just a few minutes: these troops dismantled fences, roofs, walls, in short everything that was wooden, and, like ants carrying heavy burdens, they dragged their bounty back to the bivouacs. The flocks of sheep that the residents left behind were all captured [and slaughtered].

The weather was nice – larks began to sing and the sun shone brightly. But we lacked provisions and struggle to find meat and straw, while only few biscuits had remained. The live in bivouacs is akin to a gypsy life, sometimes it is joyous and at other times it is full of grief. . .

At six o'clock in the morning on 6 [18] March, the forces of Blücher's [Army of Silesia], consisting of the [Russian] corps of Count Langeron, Baron Osten-Sacken, General Winzingerode and the Prussian corps of Yorck, Kleist and Bülow – no more than 45,000 men in total – broke its camps and advanced. General Winzingerode, with 8,000 men, was in the advance guard. Upon departure the troops set fire to their bivouacs and the billowing smoke, the plain covered with corpses and various debris, the sight of locals wandering in rags amidst ruins and the troops departing in columns represented an astonishing sight of the calamities of war that would have overwhelmed any observer.

Passing by one of the ruins I witnessed a very poignant scene. An old woman, exhausted and mourning, lay dying on the pile of stones of a collapsed wall. A younger Frenchwoman, pale as death, deeply mourned her, bitterly crying, embracing and kissing the old woman. Nearby stood an old and drained man in rags who also loudly grieved the woman. They did not hear the clamour of the troops passing by and did not even notice curious onlookers who stopped by fleetingly and left. I also stopped and stepped over the doorway. The Frenchman, as if awakened from slumber, shouted at me, 'Barbare! Achève notre malheur! . . . C'en est fait! [You, barbarian, come and finish our misfortune! Everything is over!]' This dreadful shout from an unarmed man could not frighten me but it awoke such deep compassion in my heart that seeking to do something to alleviate their suffering I quickly took the last of my money out of my pocket and put it in the poor man's hand . . . His eyes, gazing directly at me, became moistened with tears . . . and I departed, long to be haunted by the visions of this heartbreaking scene.

General Rudzevich was appointed to replace Count St. Priest as our corps commander. We veered left from the main road and stopped for the night at the village of Royancourt that was sixteen verstas [17km] away from Laon and eight verstas [8.5km] from Berry-au-Bac.

At eight o'clock the following morning we resumed our march towards the village of Corbeny. At Berry-au-Bac, I saw Blücher's entire army for the first time: the whole area was covered with troops. Count Langeron's corps stooped near Berry-au-Bac while the rest of the troops began crossing the river on the pontoon bridges or across the fords. The French had destroyed the bridge and their outposts withdrew towards Reims. Bülow's corps departed at Corbeny towards Soissons while Yorck's corps left at Berry-au-Bac in the direction of Château-Thierry while Kleist proceeded to La Ferté Sous Jouarre . . . Count Chernyshev once again occupied Reims while the French partly retreated towards Soissons. The Prussians led our advance while Count Langeron's corps remained in reserve.

After crossing the river at Berry-au-Bac, we turned right and proceeded along the left bank of the river towards the village of Fismes. We halted about six verstas [6.4km] from it and dispatched foragers to nearby villages. . . Woe to the unfortunate residents! Our foraging continued for twenty-four hours. The foragers of Colonel Magdenko's battery company returned with forty horses while our men brought back ten. Instead of issuing any provisions, Blücher ordered entire villages to be assigned to each regiment and artillery brigade. So whoever arrived first could claim more of anything. The success of foraging thus depended on how industrious its officer was. Infantrymen never shied away from marching further away and usually uncovered provisions in cellars, wells and under heaps of trash, where the locals usually concealed their possessions. This was a terrible misfortune was unavoidable in the ongoing ruthless national [zhestokaya natsionalnaya] war – while in quarters our troops endured guerrilla attacks and the locals, suffering from devastation and pillaging, soon became active participants in this war, taking up arms and attacking us. In this region the war almost reached the extremes we witnessed in Russia.

Count Langeron's corps marched through Fismes on the way to Reims . . . We made a ceremonial march through Reims. All streets, squares and houses were filled with spectators, most of them women . . . They faced conveyed a range of emotions: old women appeared frightened, younger ones joyous, while [some] men were hiding behind women or gazed from behind corners. Some residents in coats and gloomy faces occasionally moved back and forth while the children danced to our regimental music. Some residents recognised their roomers and greeted them . . .

Our cavalry deployed at Sillery while we went with the infantry to Saint-Leonard . . . Bonfires soon illuminated bivouacs and smoke billowed towards the heavens.

On 12 [24] March we advanced towards Châlons. This movement seemed inexplicable to many of us. Some argued that Napoleon had moved all of his forces to Saint-Dizier in the rear of the main Allied army and that we were rushing to join it; others claimed that General Wrede and the Prince of Württemberg had routed two French corps marching from Châlons and that we were in fact pursuing Napoleon and intending to cut him off from Paris; finally, there were also those who opined that the Austrians were already in full retreat after their Emperor Francis had reconciled with Napoleon and left the army for Vienna. I could not figure out which of these claims was true and so waited to see how things turned.

About one and a half verstas [1.6km] away from Châlons, our corps bivouacked at the village of Recy on the Marne River. The following day we made a ceremonial march through Châlons and across the Marne and then turned to the main road to Paris. Generals Winzingerode and Count Vorontsov continued to follow Napoleon. Meanwhile our Emperor had made the decision to march directly on Paris and the main Allied army was already on its way there while Napoleon wandered around in its rear.

At the village of Chaintrix [Chaintrix-Bierges?] the cavalry commanded by Baron Korf and the 8th Corps moved left across the fields. We soon saw smoke billowing in the distance – this was Korf attacking the French. The rest of our corps proceeded on the main road. We were in the process of converging with the main Allied army when we stumbled upon two enemy corps, under Marmont and Mortier. The former had just reached the town of Vertus, where he discovered the advance guard of our main army, which defeated him and drove him back to Sezanne . . . By nightfall we halted amidst a vast plain at Montmirail. The fields were covered with corpses of horses that had been killed in the earlier battle . . . From here we marched through the day and most of night along the main road to Paris and covered almost 35 verstas [37.3km]. It was clear that we were in a rush to get to Paris before Napoleon did.

'We are advancing on Paris!' the generals proclaimed, adding, 'Moscow will be avenged! We will overthrow the usurper from the throne that he had seized. we will free France from this tyrannical despot!' The blissful thought of us advancing on Paris cheered up the troops . . . The main road to Paris, on which we marched, was a paved road but it was a very bad condition as if someone had intentionally dug up large stones to complicate movements. The magnificent poplar trees that lined the road on both sides were cut down in places and lay like vanquished giants by the wayside. We occasionally stumbled on stripped carcasses of horses and tattered remains of shakos and knapsacks. [From the Russian text in I. Radozhitskii, Pokhodnye zapiski...]

Ivan Kazakov

[After the French victories in early February] we beat a hasty retreat, not to say ran, from Napoleon. Upon arriving at Langres, everyone thought that we would cross over the Rhine. But after spending the night at Langres, we were instead moved to the right while facing Napoleon on the *chaussée* was a strong cavalry detachment under command of General Winzingerode who was supposed to continue retreating to Basel on the Rhine. After leaving the *chaussée* at Langres, our army proceeded by forces marches, in two columns, along a new route through the Champagne towards Meaux and Paris. Napoleon fell for this ruse – he made two marches pursuing Winzingerode towards the Rhine while we made two lengthy marches towards Paris. Such a risky flanking manoeuvre was, of course, conceived not by Schwarzenberg but the Emperor [Alexander] himself and his Chief of Staff Diebitsch. Orders to the army forbade leaving any stragglers and there were indeed none left behind. We faced no troops and only at La Fère-Champenoise did we encounter some 6,000 fresh conscripts under the command of Marshal Soult. Our cavalry, comprising our advance guard, quickly charged at them but they deployed in square and repelled our Cossacks. The French then began to retreat. Our army, moving in two columns, was stretched for more than ten verstas [10.6km]. So orders were issues to move forward cavalry regiments that were at the head of the columns and, as they arrived, they were sent at a trot into a charge. But neither succeeded. The enemy repelled these cavalry charges and continued retreating in good order until the arrival of artillery, whose canister fire disordered their square. The French retreat then turned into a rout as our cavalry pursued, cut and slashed, and captured numerous prisoners before halting at dusk being exhausted after a forced march. The army, meanwhile, reached La Fère-Champenoise only [late] in the evening. After passing through Meaux, where we left a corps to hold off Napoleon, who realising his inability to not only contain but even catch up to our army, turned for Fontainebleau. Sacken and Blücher also converged on Paris and, by 29 March, we halted near Paris on the following positions: the Guard Corps near Belleville and on the *chaussée* near the village of Pantin; the Grenadier Corps – to the left, at Buttes Chaumont; Sacken in front of the canal de l'Ourcq, while Blücher was near Montmartre. [From the Russian text in I. Kazakov, 'Pokhod vo Frantsiyu . . .']

Aleksei Karpov

Karpov commanded a section of two cannon in the 6th Light Artillery Company that was attached to Prince Eugene of Württemberg's corps.

The battle [at La Fère-Champenoise] began at nine o'clock in the morning on 13 [25] March. Marmont took the heights located in front of us and, deploying his artillery there, he disordered our entire frontline, with some of our cuirassier regiments becoming so disordered that they retreated in confusion to the rear. However, our other units managed to flank the enemy and forced him to abandon this position. Marmont then withdrew to another position where he repelled our attacks but seeing the numerical superiority of our army he began to fall back. During this withdrawal he lost his artillery, caissons and trains. I was attached to the infantry which naturally could not keep up with the rapidly retreating enemy, so I was soon moving with the dragoons and uhlans. Together with this cavalry, I advanced forward and engaged the enemy with cannonballs and canister. However, due to the complete exhaustion of my men and horses, as well as the need to replenish my caissons with ammunition captured from the enemy, I halted my troops on a hill, where I was joined by Colonel Markov with his four guns, whose [crews] and horses were fatigued as well. We remained at this location for about an hour. We soon heard gunfire on our flank and observed two columns of French infantry [from the divisions of General Pacthod and Amé] and about 100 cuirassiers. These columns advanced directly at us and few of our Cossacks were riding around them. I galloped towards the Cossacks, who informed me what was happening. Returning back to my position, I prepared my men to meet the enemy. With neither our infantry nor cavalry present, I ordered to open [artillery] fire at the enemy, who was formed in square and returned fire in battalion volleys as well as with two cannon. Hearing this gunfire, Emperor [Alexander] and the Prussian King [Frederick William] rode out with a small cavalry escort and dispatched orders to turn back several cavalry regiments. Meanwhile, we fired canister and spread disorder in many enemy squares. Soon several regiments of our cavalry and infantry arrived, as well as ten cannon of our company and four guns of Colonel Lipstein, while the rest of our infantry could be seen moving not far behind them. The French could no longer defend themselves but they refused to surrender. The Emperor [Alexander] dispatched a colonel [Rapatel] from his suite [to offer surrender to the French] but he was almost immediately killed. At last, we destroyed the last of the French cannon. The Emperor then ordered his [cavalry] escort to charge, and the officers who accompanied them rushed forward. The Emperor himself passed by my cannon, reigning in his horse and looking back to see if there was anyone from his suite who could stop him from this reckless enterprise. After virtually stomping on the same spot for some time, he moved about fifteen paces in front of my cannon when a member of his suite fortunately approached [asking him not to endanger himself] and the Emperor halted. He moved back slightly but the colonel urged him to stop once more, 'Your Majesty, your life is too precious, please halt.' The charge, meanwhile, ended with the attacking side repelled by [the enemy] musket fire and rushing back headlong. The Emperor again sent a messenger offering [the French] to surrender, promising them his benevolence. The [few] French cuirassiers, who accompanied the infantry, turned their horses and left. When one of the [infantry] columns surrendered its arms, it was attacked by our newly arriving cuirassiers [of the Chevalier Guard Regiment]. Many unarmed Frenchmen were slaughtered or wounded. Meanwhile, the other column, where the General [Pacthod] was present with his wife and young son, who was wounded by canister, continued to hold their ground. Finally, on the general's orders, the front ranks began to drop their weapons. Just at that moment, Colonel Markov, who was recklessly gallant, rushed with two guns and broke into the square. All the French troops then threw down their weapons and surrendered. Upon observing this, the Emperor promoted Markov to major-general. The French general's wife was invited to dine with the Emperor that evening, receiving 10,000 rubles and a carriage, and travelled with her husband and son to Bohemia. All the prisoners were sent there as well.

For this battle I received the cross of Pour Le Mérite from the Prussian king while my Sovereign gave me nothing. Yet, after the war the sycophants sang the praises of the meaningless attack that the Emperor had launched [in this battle.] None of them dared to write the truth because in our days it is impossible to speak the truth, not to mention to write it. Besides, almost all sycophants are generously rewarded while the truth might earn you exile and hard labour in Siberia or some other remote location, where humanity is oppressed and men are treated worse than criminals. But I can testify to what had transpired in front of me: upon seeing two enemy infantry squares and about 100 cuirassiers halted and hesitating what to do next, the Emperor ordered his escort, about 100 Black Sea and 100 Life Guard Cossacks, to attack these squares. The sight of the Cossacks charging impelled over 100 various officers, who accompanied the Emperor, to rush forward as well. Among these officers was the Emperor himself, who was on the right side but rode at the slowest gallop [samym malenkim galopom], looking back to see if there was someone who could keep him from this extraordinary gallantry. It was then that a staff officer, who rode slightly behind him, grabbed him by the hand and told him 'Your Majesty, your life is too precious, please halt.' The Emperor stopped and quickly turned his horse back, returning to his earlier position instead of moving forward. Thus was the gallantry that everyone so praises . . . [From the Russian text in A. Karpov, *Zapiski*...]

Eduard von Löwenstern

A junior officer in the Sumskii Hussar Regiment which was attached to the Russian 6th Corps.

Through a letter captured by General Tettenborn's Cossacks, we acquired the news that Emperor Napoleon was going across the Marne to operate at our backs and was removing the artillery from Paris by this manoeuvre. This meant that we were closer to Paris than the French. Toward ten o'clock in the morning in Soude-St.-Croix, we came upon the corps of Marshals Mortier and Marmont. The Chuguevskii Uhlans immediately defeated the cuirassier regiment with great losses; and in Soude-Notre-Dame, we took prisoner a large number of light cavalry who had stayed in the village too long. On the plains of Sommesous, we were met with such terrible cannon fire that we had not heard since the battle of Leipzig, preventing the Sumskii and Grodnenskii [regiments] from advancing; but they quickly overthrew the cavalry and that horrid battery had to leave its position at Sommesous. Count Pahlen with all of his hussars followed in order to intercept the troops at Lenharree as fast as possible. The retreating enemy was being heavily pressed; and before they could reach Lenharree, we took five of their cannon. General Rudiger with the Sumskii and Grodnenskii Hussars and the Cuirassier Brigade Staal drove the enemy cavalry totally from the battlefield. March 13th was in every respect an unforgettable day for me. Marmont's infantry formed into a large square when we reached them, and here was shown what brave soldiers can do if they work together. The square had the cavalry and artillery in the middle. We swarmed around this column from all sides shooting grenades and firing cannonballs into the thick mass. The Bavarian Ambassador's Chevalier Schilling,* who also belonged to our headquarters for the past few days, was struck on the knee by the Count's horse so that he fell to the ground like a ball. Lieutenant Rohde of the Sumskii Regiment, because he ventured too far ahead, received several sabre blows to the head and was taken prisoner. We attacked the column several times and by the time we had passed La Fère-Champenoise and Connantre, we had already captured two generals, many officers, and soldiers and a lot of cannon. The enemy slowly moved through Connantre toward La-Fère-Champenoise. Many dismounted cannon were left in the villages and inns. Count Pahlen and Prince Adam of Württemberg† pursued the French. Behind us, or rather more to the right, we heard at a distance of a lieue a terrible cannonade. Immediately, the thronging French screamed: 'Vive l'Empereur!' Their cavalry that had been between the infantry columns formed up, advanced at the trot, and dared to attack. But that is exactly what our hussars wanted. General Sesslavin with the Sumskii [Hussar] Regiment attacked them in the flank and drove them back with heavy losses. The French had thought that Napoleon would come to their aid, that it was his cannon heard in the distance. It was however Emperor

---

* Probably Heinrich Ludwig Christoph Baron Schilling von Cannstadt, born 1789 in Reval, who later was ambassador to China.

† Duke Adam of Württemberg (1792–1847) was the son of Duke Louis of Württemberg and the nephew of Russian Empress Maria Feodorovna (Emperor Alexander's mother). He commanded the cavalry in the 4th (Württemberg) Corps in 1814.

Alexander, who had cut off Pacthod's division and completely routed it. We attacked Marshals Mortier and Marmont several times, causing them great casualties; but we were unable to break through despite all efforts. The path the brave French column took was covered with dead and wounded.

While the Emperor was routing Pacthod's division, the cavalry of the Crown Prince and of Prince Adam von Württemberg and Count Pahlen pursued the enemy which was heading toward Linth. Our few cannon – since the Emperor had had most of them sent to him – shot cartouche [canister] into the thickly-bunched [French]. When it finally was completely dark, we stopped. The enemy column slowly continued its march. We cheered and rejoiced about our decisive victory. The results of the battle were splendid: eight generals, seventy-two cannon and over 10,000 prisoners were in our hands.

It is remarkable that only the cavalry and light artillery took part on the battle of La Fère-Champenoise. Fifteen thousand horses, more or less, were used to win this magnificent victory. Every Frenchman who took part in the battle of La Fère-Champenoise can and has to be proud of it and has won the greatest right to call himself a brave soldier. Even though they lost the battle, this infantry nevertheless decorated itself with fame. I love the Russian soldier and grant him in every way his personal bravery; but I am, freely said, convinced that the Russians would not have been defeated in this way. Here was no fear of the rod, menial fear that suffocated the young recruit's bravery in the bud. Here was no hope of rich booty. It was *point d'honneur*, love of the fatherland, and the pride of a brave soldier who would rather die with honour under the blows of his enemy than give up as long as several of them stayed together. These might be the reasons for the French infantry not losing its composure. [From the German text in E. Löwenstern, *Denkwürdigkeiten*]

Louis-Victor-Léon de Rochechouart

In the middle of January Napoleon and the Allies agreed to a conference at Chatillon-sur-Seine with the object of negotiating a peace. After long debates, preliminary conditions were agreed upon and the peace appeared to be forthcoming. It only remained for Napoleon to ratify it. Rochechouart recalled how many of his Royalist friends were upset by such a turn of events. Among them was Carlo Pozzo di Borgo, a Corsican with a long-standing rivalry with Napoleon. Rochechouart recalled that Pozzo 'came to inform us that peace had been signed and he had seen the ratification of the Allied Powers; but, suddenly rising and striking the table with his fist, he said with all his Italian fire: "No, gentlemen, it is not all ended, the Corsican has not signed." The expression "the Corsican", thrown out so unexpectedly, amused us greatly, coming as it did from another Corsican.' Pozzo was correct and Napoleon refused to ratify the terms accepted by his envoy. The fate of Europe would have to be resolve on the battlefield . . .

After the negotiations at Chatillon had been broken off, the Emperor Alexander, wearied with the delays of the Generalissimo Prince Schwarzenberg, resolved on a more vigorous campaign. A whole week was spent in a series of successes and checks, marches and counter-marches. At last the armies met at Arcis-sur-Aube. Severe fighting took place. Napoleon, having sustained enormous losses, withdrew to Vitry-le-François. The Russian army followed him. The combat was renewed with varying fortune. Suddenly Napoleon effected a manoeuvre that has been differently criticised, blamed by many, approved by a few. The actual result was to bring about the fall of the great leader within a few days. The manoeuvre involved marching into the rear of the Allied armies in order to cut off their communications. Napoleon hoped that they would follow him and thus be drawn away from Paris. The Allied armies divided; two Russian and Prussian corps remained to watch Napoleon, while the rest of the army, under the Emperor and the King of Prussia, and the Army of Silesia, as it was called, under Field-Marshal Blücher, marched directly on Paris, driving before them the corps of Marshal Marmont, Due de Raguse, and of Marshal Mortier, Due de Trevise. In this sudden and rapid movement the Emperor of Austria became separated from his allies, an apparently unimportant incident, which deprived Napoleon of the protection of his father-in-law, and of Prince Metternich, at a very critical moment for himself and his dynasty.

Napoleon, aided by the valour and devotion of his troops, carried out the most skilful manoeuvres and passed from point to point with bewildering rapidity. But nothing could avert his ruin. All the writers of that day throw blame on such and such a manoeuvre, such and such a decision; on the inaction, incapacity or faintheartedness of such and such a general. Undoubtedly the Marshals of the Empire did not possess the military genius of Napoleon; they were very brave, but too accustomed to receiving their master's orders, and acting without initiative. Napoleon's manoeuvre was therefore dangerous; it separated him from the generals under him, and thus deprived them of the inspiration of his genius and of his eagle glance that saw at once the advantage to be derived from the enemy's position. Moreover, every victory hastened his downfall by the price it cost. France no longer provided recruits; the old army, the veterans who had conquered on all the battlefields of Europe, lay dead amid the Russian ice and snow. If the greatest general of modern times was deceived in his calculations, the reason is that there comes a day when human power and wisdom are of no account. Let men call it destiny, fate, or invent some other name, what can they do against the will of Him who moves the heaven and the earth?

On 25 March we met a French column at La Fère-Champenoise. I will give the narrative in the words of M. Koch,* adding a few details, as I took part in this fierce encounter:

---

* See François Koch, *Mémoires pour servir à l'histoire de la campagne de 1814* (Paris, 1819).

The column, whose appearance caused so much astonishment and alarm to the Allies, was formed of the Pacthod and Amey divisions that had reached Bergeres on the 24th, General Pacthod, in haste to join Marshals Marmont and Mortier, had sent an orderly officer to Marshal Mortier, and, without waiting for his return, began to march on Vitry at daybreak. Arriving at the outskirts of Villeseneux at ten o'clock in the morning, he received a message to remain at Bergeres (where he was supposed to be) until further orders. This division, which escorted a large convoy of supplies and munitions, had been marching during part of the night; the horses were dropping down with fatigue. General Pacthod, believing he was out of danger, thought there would be time to rest at Villeseneux. But he had scarcely settled down there when he was attacked by General Korf, who was following the road from Châlons to Etoges. General Pacthod at once formed his troops: the right supported by the village, the left covered by an immense square, the convoy in the rear.

M. de Beauchamp* gives further details:

The convoy was in itself of extreme importance, as is evident from the number of troops accompanying it. It was observed by [Field] Marshal Blücher's cavalry. The Field Marshal at once detached the cavalry generals, Korf and Vasilchikov, to attack it. At the sight of the enemy, the column and convoy fell back on Fère-Champenoise at the very moment when the cavalry of the main Russian army reached this point by the road from Vitry. On receiving news of this encounter, Prince Schwarzenberg had hastily recalled part of the cavalry from the pursuit of Mortier and Marmont; at the same time the Emperor Alexander ordered the Russian artillery of his Guard to advance. Pursued and attacked on all sides by troops under the immediate command of the Sovereigns, the French column formed in several squares, and prepared to make the most heroic resistance; it was composed entirely of young soldiers and National Guards, but nothing could intimidate these novices in warfare. The squares continued to fire and retreat, braving the cavalry charges, rejecting the repeated Russian summons to a truce, refusing to lay down their arms. In vain did Colonel Rapatel, a distinguished officer, the same who had received the dying message of his former chief, General Moreau, advance alone to bring to an end the useless struggle. 'My friends! My fellow-countrymen!' the Colonel called to them, 'Cease fighting! You have won enough honour! The Emperor Alexander will restore you to liberty.' Scarcely had he spoken these words than he fell, struck by two bullets, and died, honoured by the army and by the Emperor, to whom he was aide-de-camp.

Artillery alone could conquer this handful of brave men struggling against a whole army. The batteries opened fire, breaking through the squares; simultaneous charges completed the work, carrying death and disorder into

---

* See Alphonse de Beauchamp, *Histoire des campagnes de 1814 et de 1815, ou histoire politique et militaire des deux invasions de la France, de l'entreprise de Buonaparte au mois de mars, de la chute totale de sa paissance, et de la double restauration du trône, jusqu'à la seconde paix de Paris, includivement* (Paris: Le Normant, 1817).

them; it was necessary to surrender. Generals Pacthod and Amey, five brigadier generals, twelve cannon, 4,800 infantry and the entire convoy fell into the power of the Allied armies.

The following are the details which I will add to these two narratives: On the first appearance of the French column there was, in fact, a moment of bewilderment in the Allied army. To what corps did it belong! What was the cavalry that appeared on the right? We were in the midst of an immense plain. the Artillery of the Guard received orders to advance, when suddenly we saw the distant cavalry charge the column, which at once formed the infantry in squares and opened a vigorous fire of artillery. There was no longer any doubt; the column belonged to the French army; orders were given to the Russian artillery to attack, and the whole of the cavalry also began to advance. Rapatel, believing that two of his brothers were with the opposing forces from information received from some prisoners taken that morning, went forward to assure himself of the fact, and to persuade the column to yield to such superior numbers. What became of him? I did not know. The order to charge having been given to the cavalry, our staff had no time to move aside to let them pass; we were compelled, under pain of being crushed, to follow the torrent. In two minutes the Emperor Alexander and the King of Prussia found themselves in the midst of the enemy column, borne along by a cavalry charge of 16,000 Russians, Prussians and Austrians, cuirassiers, dragoons, hussars and Cossacks. Never again shall I see such a melee. I can scarcely relate it, the confusion was so great, the incidents so many and strange; it was all over in less time than it takes to write it.

In an instant, the column of 9,000 men lost some 4,000 dead or wounded, lying on the road they had taken in the hope of reaching a wood not far away, where they would have been protected from the cavalry attacks and the incessant firing of thirty cannon. This column, as I say, was escorting a large convoy of supplies and munitions for the French Grande Armée; from afar it seemed much stronger than it really was, and this is the reason that such powerful forces were sent against it. The wagons were drawn up in the centre with the carriages, notably those of General Pacthod, who was the commander-in-chief. Their defence was heroic, and the more praiseworthy as the troops were conscripts or mobilised National Guards, hastily gathered together; only the artillery was served by old soldiers recently come from Spain.

At the moment when I found myself in the midst of the principal square, together with the Emperor of Russia, the King of Prussia and the officers of their numerous staff, carried away by the charge of the hussars and Cossacks of the Guard, I saw a French officer near me, struggling with some Cossacks, who were trying to kill him in spite of his cries and protests. 'Take me to my brother; I have a brother in the Russian Army.' 'What is your brother's name?' I asked. 'Rapatel,' was the reply. I threw myself between him and the Cossacks, ordering them to leave him alone. I said: 'Your brother is my comrade. Come so I may have the pleasure of taking you to him.' I had scarcely spoken, when Brozine, one of my colleagues, came running to me and said: 'Oh! Rochechouart! What a misfortune! The Emperor has just heard of the death of poor Rapatel; he has sent me to look for his body.' Could there be a more pathetic scene? The poor prisoner miraculously escaped from the massacre of his troop only learn of the death of his brother at the very moment when he was looking forward to receiving help and consolation from him. Tears ran down his face, which was still black with the smoke from the powder. I grasped his hands, saying: 'You are my prisoner; you will not leave your brother's comrade.' I obtained a riderless horse for him, and asked him, 'Have you any belongings that can be saved?' He answered, amid his sobs, 'As I was a commandant of artillery in Pacthod's division, all I possess is in a caisson.' I set out with him to find this caisson, which we found still intact; the Cossacks had pillaged the carriages, but had left the artillery and the caissons alone.

The five captured [French] generals got into General Pacthod's carriage, which the Emperor had just given back to him. He had also returned to these generals their swords, saying: 'Gentlemen, when you can use them so well you ought never to be separated from them.'

Just as we were setting out for Fère-Champenoise we found hidden under the carriage a charming little girl of eight or nine, who was weeping bitterly. General Pacthod asked her how she came to be there. She pointed to her father, a mobilised National Guardsman whose body had been cut in two by a cannonball. 'I followed him,' she added, 'so that I might not be alone in the house. My mother is dead; I do not know if I have any other relatives. After my father was killed, I slipped under the carriage to avoid cannonballs.' General Pacthod placed her up on the box of his carriage, saying, 'Little one, if all this ends well, and soon, I will take care of you.' He kept his word; being unmarried, he had the poor orphan brought up in a good school. In 1824, I was one day dining with him [and saw her]: she had grown tall and very pretty. I believe she married the nephew of her benefactor, and General Pacthod left her a part of his fortune.

In the evening I presented [the captured] Captain Rapatel to the Emperor, who, as usual, was most kind. He expressed great regret at the death of Rapatel's brother, whom he valued highly, and asked captain about his plans. 'I beg Your Majesty to set me free, but, at the same time, I beg that you will allow me to wait for a favourable moment to enjoy it. I will remain with my brother's comrade and friend, M. de Rochechouart, who has promised to be a brother to me in his stead.' 'Be it so,' said the Emperor. 'When peace is signed, if you would like to fill the post of aide-de-camp that I gave to your poor brother, it will rest entirely with you; you are in good hands until then.'

So I took Captain Rapatel with me. I had already Armand de Polignac, who had been charged by the Comte d'Artois to accompany Emperor Alexander in order to take advantage of every opportunity of speaking to him. Two days later another Frenchman serving in the Russian Army, the Marquis de Montpezat (formerly a captain on the staff of the Duc de Richelieu at Odessa) arrived from the blockade of Hamburg and begged me to add him to my companions. The gravity of events prevented his receiving any reply to the dispatches he carried. As we were so near Paris, he naturally wished to be at the Allied headquarters at the moment when everything was to be decided; he shared my carriage with Rapatel. My suite was further increased by a young French non-commissioned officer, named Boutet, who had been saved on the battlefield of Tarutino in Russia in [mid-October] 1812* by the Lieutenant-Colonel of the [Life Guard] Cossack Regiment, who had picked him up when he was seriously wounded and had his wounds dressed. This young man wrote in a very beautiful hand and he suggested that I should keep him with me and make use of his [writing] services, at least until our entry into Paris. He retained a grateful recollection of the Cossack colonel without whose help he would have died at Tarutino, but he thought that presently I could be of more assistance to him. Later, he became aide-de-camp to Armand de Polignac. [From the French text in L. Rochechouart, *Souvenirs*]

Eduard von Löwenstern

Napoleon with his entire army, in the meantime, was coming toward our rear, had occupied St. Dizer, Bar-le-Duc and Toul, reconnoitred to Nancy and Metz and frightened all of our reservists, wounded and recovering soldiers following the Army. Emperor Francis would have almost been taken prisoner in Bar-le-Duc, and we were completely cut off from communicating with the Rhine. Nevertheless, Emperor Alexander did not let himself be led astray and marched straight toward Paris, while Winzingerode had to amuse the French Emperor in the Champagne with 8,000 horse.

We spent the night in Connantre with Grand Duke Constantine. I had the pleasure here of speaking with General Potapov, whom I had not seen during the entire war. Early in the morning, we came to Sezanne. Pahlen stopped at the house of a Pole who was living here. By force, Budberg and I took several bottles of rum from the Sarmatian which he had the audacity to refuse us. We went through Coulomuniers to where the Emperor's headquarters were supposed to go and spent the night in the Palace of Pommeuse. We went around Crécy. Here, as is well known, the Black Prince, Edward of England, used cannon for the first time. In Trilport, we found the large stone Marne Bridge destroyed. Until two pontoon bridges had been built, we remained

---

* The battle of Tarutino or Vinkovo took place on 18 October 1812 when the Russian army surprised the Grande Armée's advance guard under the command of Murat.

in the place. I saw Grand Duke Constantine in a street. Since I was less than dressed according to regulations, I hid in a low pigsty. Upon entering I saw someone standing very uncomfortably there and soon recognise Count Hochberg. I inquired what remarkable happenstance had brought him here. He could not lie and confessed, though reluctantly, that he also wanted to avoid Grand Duke Constantine. I was happy to be in such good company and instead of pigs to have found a reigning Count. If I were Count Hochberg, Commanding General of the Baden troops, I think, I would not avoid anyone this way. I found [my brother] Woldemar not too far from Meaux. He was galloping on a superb English sorrel along the *chaussées*. At that time, I did not know that brave brother who was so good in every way very well or not at all. It was pleasant to be together with him. In his company, I quite felt the superiority he had over me; and I was never so monosyllabic and awkward as when I was with him. By nature dumb, I had little trust in myself. In order not to commit a stupidity in Woldemar's presence, I was silent. Only later did I totally lose this incomprehensible compulsion in the presence of a brother. Woldemar met me with so much friendliness and love that he received not only my complete trust but also my boundless friendship. Even up to the present, he has a great ascendance over me. It was not however this adverse feeling that it used to be, but rather esteem for his heart, understanding and courage. If I could prove my devotion to him, I would gladly sacrifice everything for him except my honour. We stayed until late in the night on the *chaussée* not far from Claye and bivouacked in Noisy-le-Sec. We found a lot of champagne in the mayor's house that kept us cheerful the whole night. We had received orders to bind white cloths around our left arms as a field sign of the artillery. The mayor's trunks provided us with a quantity of batiste handkerchiefs which we took immediately to decorate our arms. Early on 18 March we headed straight for Paris. Our Corps had taken the heights of Belleville and the village of La Villette. The 5th Infantry Division went to Romainville, and Count Pahlen followed with his cavalry. We took Romainville and pushed the enemy back to Belleville. Here in the extreme terrain, a terrible infantry battle took place in the countless orchards and vineyards. The enemy used the trenches on the heights, several earthworks thrown up near Belleville, from where they could bombard us heavily with their cannon. [From the German text in E. Löwenstern, *Denkwürdigkeiten*]

7

The Battle for Paris

By noon on 30 March 1814, after several days of marching, Emperor Alexander of Russia had arrived on the Buttes-Chaumont and, ascending a nearby hill, surveyed the city rising in front of him in the distance. It was Paris, the city Alexander longed to see for many years and now only hours separated him from a triumphant entry into the capital of his greatest enemy.

Paris was defended by the battered corps of Marshals Marmont and Mortier. The Allies had decided to make their attack to the north of Paris, with the aim of taking the heights of Montmartre, which would have offered them the dominant position in the city. Far outnumbering the French defenders, the Allied troops began their attack on a broad front and quickly got tangled up in a series of uncoordinated assaults on the northern faubourgs. The fighting continued all day and was desperate and bloody, especially around the faubourg of Pantin. By nightfall the French had prevented the Allied forces from getting into Paris proper but it was clear that the fate of the city had already been sealed. During the night Marmont and Mortier accepted the Coalition parleys and began negotiations to surrender the city. They agreed on terms at two in the morning on 31 March. The French army was allowed to evacuate and retreat intact before the Allies entered the city later the same day.

Eduard von Löwenstern

A junior officer in the Sumskii Hussar Regiment which was attached to the Russian 6th Corps.

For the first time on the heights of Belleville, I saw Paris. I am incapable of describing the feelings that we all felt upon seeing that great imperial city. There was that proud Paris in an incalculable amphitheatre at our feet. There the domes of the countless churches, the Cathedral of Notre Dame, the Louvre, the Tuileries, the Hôtel Invalides. How the palaces gleamed in the morning sun breaking through a heavy fog! I forgot the cannonballs hitting near us and only had thoughts for illimitable Paris, whose laws had been ruling Europe for a decade. I was proud to be one of the brave ones who, with sabre in hand, covered with blood and dust, in powder smoke, had blazed a trail from the shores of the Volga to Montmartre and now were ready to take by storm the residence of the greatest military leader. If a mine had exploded next to me, I would nevertheless have gazed at Paris. Who could think about death today? In Belleville, we had to fight for every step. We learned from prisoners that in Paris with the approach of the Allies neither a general march order had been sounded nor the storm bells rung. Empress Marie-Louise, the King of Rome, and all of the ministers had left the city. Since we were of no use to the infantry in the gardens of Bellville, we went through Montreuil and Vincennes, leaving them behind, and took several National Guardsmen prisoner. These poor devils, cobblers and glove makers, were mostly poorly clothed and armed with guns of various calibres. They cried bitter tears, pointed out their houses in the outskirts of St. Antoine and despaired leaving their wives and children and, as they believed, in the future having to live from trapping sable in Siberia. Twenty cannon were rolled out at the Porte-du-Trone and immediately thundered boldly at us. The Sumskii Hussars and the Chuguevskii Uhlans, with Major Isyumov of the Uhlans at their head, rushed in and captured fourteen of them without resistance. Young people from the *école polytechnique* were manning the pieces standing there without any cover. Most were still children of about fifteen, some begging *pardon* with tears in their eyes, others holding tightly to the cannon and rather ready to die than leave their positions. Toward evening, we heard a loud hurrah along the whole line – Montmartre had been taken by storm. King Joseph of Spain and the city capitulated. Woldemar [Löwenstern], I, and Budberg rode to Montmartre. From here you can see a large part of Paris. The fog that had jealously covered us and most everything had disappeared, and a pleasant evening hid nothing from us. In Belleville, the horror of the battle reached its height. Stacks of dead and wounded covered the streets. Russian soldiers plundered the houses and choked each other over the booty. A French officer lying there with a smashed foot asked me if Paris had been taken. When I told him yes, loudly sighing, he wrapped himself in his coat and died. We spent the night in Noisy-le-Sec. [From the German text in Löwenstern, *Denkwürdigkeiten*]

Nikolai Golitsyn

After surviving the battle at Reims, Golitsyn, who served in the Kievskii Dragoon Regiment, was charged with conducting reconnaissance for Count Langeron's corps as it advanced to Paris.

The short-lived successes that Napoleon gained during this campaign only further boosted his ambition and caused him to make new demands at a congress convened at the town of Chatillon. Thus, all of these accomplishments soon contributed to his downfall and even the capture of Reims, which opened a way for him to advance through Vitry to St. Dizier to threaten our lines of communication, turned against him as it opened our road to Paris.

At Laon, it was decided that General Emmanuel would take commander of the advance guard of Count Langeron's corps. It was there that we also learned that Emperor Alexander decided to advance directly on Paris as soon as he became convinced that Napoleon had decided to move into the rear of our armies.

From Laon we advanced on the shortest route to Epernay in order to reach the main Paris road that ran through Château-Thierry and Meaux. I was given sixty Cossacks and forty dragoons to reconnoitre the countryside and ascertain enemy forces. With these men I cleared the path to our detachments all the way to Dormans, without encountering any enemy troops. Along the way we captured the town of Epernay, famous for its champagne. And so for the first time the warriors in Russian uniforms visited local wine cellars and numerous devotees of this wine eagerly emptied glasses to cheer the success of our arms. We soon resumed our advance, still encountering no resistance. On 14 [26] March we reached Etoges, where General Emmanuel received an order to take a company of pioneers, the Arkhangelogorodskii and Staroingermandlandskii Infantry Regiments, the Kievskii Dragoon Regiment, a Cossack regiment and twenty-four cannon, and proceed to Trilport, near Meaux, in order to build a bridge over the Marne River. A brigade of Prussian infantry, commanded by General Horn, was supposed to march there along a different road and support us if needed. This was an important mission and it had to be accomplished swiftly. The distance was long and General Emmanuel decided to depart at once. To protect his left flank, he dispatched me with a cavalry detachment to Rebais to reconnoitre the entire countryside between this town and Trilport, where I was supposed to rejoin him. It was while staying at Rebais that I learned about the victory that the Russian Guard scored at La Fére-Champenoise and immediately informed the General [Emmanuel] about it. I then calmly resumed my advance. Local residents hid from view upon seeing my Cossacks and acted peacefully, without attempting any resistance as it happened around Reims. Upon arriving at Trilport I saw that the bridge had been already completed despite the enemy's attempt to foil it and that part of our troops were already on the opposite bank of the Marne.

Marching from Etoges to Trilport, General Emmanuel conducted a reconnaissance near La Ferté Sous-Jouarre, located on the Marne, and discovered large enemy forces there. He calculated that taking advantage of the river's twists and turns, he could actually beat these forces to Trilport, where he left a small detachment to divert the enemy's attention while he proceeded by forced marches to the spot where the bridge had to be built. At Trilport, he found a brigade of enemy infantry defending the crossing.

Batteries were quickly set up and our troops began building a bridge which, despite the enemy's canister fire, was constructed with such remarkable swiftness that it bewildered the Prussian brigade that arrived just in time to witness this exploit. While the bridge was constructed, a battalion of the Arkhangelogorodskii Regiment crossed the river on boats that were discovered by chance at Trilport. The enemy met this battalion with canister but the Russian bayonet overthrew everything it encountered in its path. Once the bridge was built, our infantry and the Prussian brigade quickly moved across the river and pursued the enemy to Meaux. Just then I arrived at Trilport and also hastily moved my small detachment to the opposite bank. I soon overtook our infantry and, encountering a detachment of enemy cavalry, pursued it to the very gates of Meaux. As I turned back, I found myself in the rear of the French infantry and, as it was already late in the evening, I exploited the cover of darkness to charge in between the enemy battalion with shouts of victory that astounded the enemy who was unprepared for our sudden appearance amidst their ranks. All of this happened to quickly that the French infantry fired only a few shots and only when I was already far away from them.

The swift and successful completion of the bridge over the Marne was very important for subsequent events since a day later Field Marshal Blücher's Army of Silesia used it to cross over the Marne and advance to Paris; everyone knows how precious every minute was back then because Napoleon almost managed to come back to defend Paris, and who knows what would have happened in that case? We spent the night of 16 [28] March in front of Meaux, disturbed only by the sound of explosion of a gunpowder magazine that the enemy ignited.

On 16 [28] March we resumed our march to Paris, which was located just 18 verstas [19.2km] away. As before I had 100 cavalrymen and reconnoitred to the left and right without finding any enemy forces. The following day we were instructed to resume our advance but the order also specified to avoid any hostilities until two o'clock in the afternoon. It seemed that we expected a word on the surrender of Paris and wanted to show that we desired to avoid unnecessary bloodshed. Unfortunately that very day, while moving through one of the villages, my detachment was attacked by the locals who fired from behind fences and hedges and killed several of my Cossacks. So I was compelled to use violence to end violence which, in turn cost the lives of some of these misguided locals. General Yorck, who passed that village in the evening, noticed the signs of the recent firefight and ordered the culprits who dared to violate the order to avoid hostilities before two o'clock to be found. But once details of what had transpired became known, everyone agreed that I could not have acted otherwise.

I soon received an order to get to the town of Gonesse, located about eight verstas [8.5km] from Paris on the right side of the main road, and inform local authorities that General Yorck's corps would bivouac in the vicinity later that evening. Locals were required to provide provisions, firewood and hay for 40,000 men. I went at once to Gonesse, which lay not far from the main road and was, it was said, famous for its simpleminded residents. I left an officer with half of my detachment to observe the region and took the rest of the men with me. Our descent from the mountain could be observed from afar and this sight, so new to the locals, attracted almost the entire populace so that I had to enter the town in between two rows of onlookers. I noticed that their faces showed more signs of apprehension than curiosity and asked the crowd to show me how to find the mayor, adding that I was instructed to inform him that a Prussian corps would be bivouacked nearby later that evening; that the town had to provide supplies since the Russian Emperor had forbidden, on the pain of the most severe punishment, his soldiers to enter homes under any pretext; that we were here to bring peace to them, and that the Allied armies would, in all probability, depart the following day towards Paris. This speech – so novel and almost inconceivable for most of my listeners – resulted in a storm of questions, to which I responded curtly since I could not waste time, and insisted on being shown to the town hall. There I found the mayor and his assistants and informed them of what they were required to provide, remembering to stress that property rights would be strictly upheld. They seemed willing to satisfy our demands and promised to do everything requested of them. As I prepared to depart, these kind people asked me to write my name in their municipal book and were surprised to hear that I was not a Frenchmen or son of some émigré and that a 'Cossack' could speak their language so fluently. Once everything was settled, I was sent off, one may say, triumphantly. The inhabitants of Gonesse struck me as very kind people and maybe that is why Parisians call them simpleminded. I must admit that in the wake of my experiences in the morning I thought that I would find at least barricades in the streets of Gonesse. I even gave the necessary orders to both parts of my detachments, and the one that stayed behind was supposed, upon the first sound of gunfire, to appear on the mountain in order to frighten the locals. Fortunately, none of this proved to be necessary and everything worked out for the best. In 1822, while visiting Paris, I was curious enough to visit Gonesse once more and found the same mayor who greeted me in 1814. Even under Napoleon he was an ardent Bourbon supporter in his heart and thus had no difficulty in retaining his position when the regime changed.

I rejoined the officer whom I left on the main road and we continued our journey. Paris soon unfurled itself in front of us. At the junction of the roads from Soissons and Meaux, my Cossacks stopped a carriage travelling to Paris. Knowing their predisposition towards looting, I spurred my horse and galloped to the carriage, arriving just in time to calm down several female passengers who were in tears after being frightened by the sudden appearance of Cossacks. I reassured them in French and ordered them to be let go while they showered me with gratitude. These travellers were completely unaware that we were so close to Paris and were already preparing to enter it. I asked them to convey this good news to the Parisians. The male passengers gave me their visiting cards and offered their services in Paris, asking me to visit them so they could express their appreciation for my help. The carriage soon departed and my comforted Parisian ladies waved their handkerchiefs to express their joy that so quickly replaced their terror.

I soon witnessed a different scene as well. My cavalry's advance forced several [enemy] skirmishers to come out into the open and the Cossacks quickly surrounded and captured them. Meanwhile, Emperor Alexander advanced with the main army along the main road to Paris and, not expecting to see any of our troops so far ahead, he sent an officer to inquire which corps we belonged. His Imperial Majesty was unaware yet about our successful crossing of the Marne River. At the same time General Emmanuel appeared with his entire advance guard and carried out a very successful diversion, attacking the flank of the enemy forces that our main army was about to engage. Emperor Alexander witnessed this manoeuvre and sent a message of benevolence to our general. We spent the night of 18 [30] March near the village of Aubervilliers, in front of Paris. Even though I desperately needed some rest, I could not close my eyes all through the night. I could not believe that it was all happening in reality, that we are indeed at the very gates of Paris . . . the city whose name alone evokes so many thing; that after months of camp life filled with dangers, alarms and deprivations, we were about to indulge ourselves to all the pleasures of this new Babylon. But suddenly a disturbing thought flashed in my mind – that upon approaching Moscow the French flattered themselves with similar dreams only to find them crushed [when the city burned down]. My dreams quickly dissipated into worries and I tried to reassure myself, 'The French are not Russians. They are incapable of sacrificing their capital that is more important to them than anything else. Besides, we are not French either and, unlike their attempt to enslave our Fatherland, we do not intend on conquering France.' These various thoughts kept me awake all night long. Early next morning everyone was dressed in sharp uniforms expecting that the gates of Paris would be soon open and we would triumphantly enter the city. Alas, the capture of the French capital was not destined to happen without one last effort on the part of the Allies.

On 18 [30] March, at dawn, we approached Montmartre and our infantry became engaged in a firefight with the French troops defending La Villette and the suburbs of Paris. From the heights of Montmartre the enemy showered us with cannonballs. On the left flank, where the Imperial headquarters was located, there was a fierce and resolute battle, especially on the Butte Chaumont. However, by two o'clock in the afternoon we captured all the heights on this side and only Montmartre continued to resist us. It appeared that we would have to make considerable efforts to capture it. Around three o'clock in the afternoon Count Langeron received His Majesty's order to seize this height at any cost and to dispatch General Emmanuel with 2,000 cavalry to Neuilly to move around Paris and threaten the enemy defences at the gates of l'Etoile that led to the Champs-Elysées. We were concerned that Montmartre, which maintained [artillery] fire incessantly throughout the morning, would offer most resolute resistance which did not require much effort in light of the steep slopes and the numerous fences and hedges that this hill was peppered with. General Rudzevich, who was given the task of capturing this position, deployed his columns for assault and bid us farewell as a man about to face certain death. In the subsequent assault, to our surprise, the enemy fired only a few artillery salvos before our troops captured Montmartre in little more time than it would have taken to climb that mountain. From that moment Paris was ours.

Meanwhile, before this attack was successfully completed, we set off to carry out our orders and I, accompanied by my cavalrymen, once again moved at the head [of the column]. When we reached the alley leading to Neuilly, bullets began to whizz past our ears – several men, hiding behind a barricade erected on a bridge at the end of the alley, fired on us. Since even a small number of soldiers, sitting behind a barricade, could cause considerable harm, I ordered my dragoons to dismount and attack. In a rapid assault, they cleared the barricade and dispersed about thirty men who defended it. These were retired soldiers of the Imperial Guard who lived in Neuilly. One of my officers and several soldiers were wounded in this clash. General Emmanuel, meanwhile, arrived with his detachment and directed his artillery at the enemy troops defending the l'Etoile gates, showering them with cannonballs. An enemy messenger soon appeared and informed us that the capitulation of Paris had been negotiated and signed. Indeed, soon thereafter we received official notification of this. It was around six o'clock in the evening.

We spent the night of 19 [31] March at Neuilly, filled with the sense of enthusiasm that this conquest arouse in all of us. At the start of the day we occupied Boulogne after passing through the Bois de Boulogne which sadly did not justify my expectations. We encountered no resistance and, although we were told that the bridge at St. Cloud had been mined, we crossed it without any difficulty and went to see the magnificent palace that had not been yet closed. We found [Empress] Marie-Louise's apartments still open and did not miss an opportunity to play on an instrument that had been accustomed to producing music beneath the gentle fingers of the French empress. Yet now the rough and gunpowder-blackened hands of warriors, who had emerged from the depths of Russia and overcame numerous dangers and battles, filled the halls of this palace with the sounds of 'God Save the King' in honour of our benevolent and adored Monarch. Oh, these were marvellous moments for the Russian heart! We felt fully compensated for all the dangers and deprivations that we had overcome to enjoy this incredible moment. That same day the Allied sovereigns, at the head of the Russian columns, made a triumphant entry into Paris. [From the Russian text in Golitsyn, *Ofitserskie zapiski* . . .]

Pavel Pushin

Pushin commanded a battalion of the Life Guard Semeyonovskii Regiment.

18 [30] March. Wednesday
The Battle at Montmartre. Our corps marched at 7 a.m. in the direction of Belleville, which was already attacked by the 3rd Corps. The battle began almost simultaneously with our departure. The French fought courageously at Belleville but were forced to submit to our superior numbers and our corps, except for the Prussians, whose Guard remained in the reserves and, despite fighting like lions at Panten [?], its troops took no part in today's battle since the 3rd Corps, which we were reinforcing, did not waiver even for a minute in its confidence of victory and required no assistance. Belleville was captured; our centre, that is the position between Belleville and Montmartre, also operated successfully. The Emperor [Alexander] and the King of Prussia, as well as the entire General Staff soon arrived and took up position on the Belleville heights from where they had a clear view of the entire battlefield. We all were extremely nervous, our hearts were pounding as the moment of the surrender of Paris approached; [meantime] General [Osten-] Sacken with his corps was still one day's march behind us in order to oppose Napoleon who, having heard about our offensive on Paris, moved by forced marches to attack us from the rear. [Everyone] was concerned that he would arrive before the [French] capital was in our hands, which would have produced God knows what kind of results. During the day the Emperor [Alexander] received several negotiators and at the moment when it seemed that he was losing patience with all these negotiations, an adjutant arrived with a report that Count Langeron's corps had occupied the heights of Montmartre. Indeed, shortly before 4 p.m., we saw Count Langeron's advance guard, under the command of [Lieutenant-] General [Alexander] Rudzevich, deploying in attack columns, take Montmartre by storm, which was the last position still defended by the French. We saw how the French fled and sent their messenger with an offer of surrender. The Emperor, gleaming with happiness, mounted his horse and congratulated us with the capture of Paris. A thundering 'hurrah' spread along our ranks. We marched past Their Majesties [Alexander and King Frederick William III], passed Belleville, and bivouacked [in the field] with our left wing anchored on Belleville. Many Parisian women visited our camps that evening. [From the Russian text in Pushin, *Dnevnik. . .*]

S. Khomutov

A staff officer in the Russian imperial headquarters.

17 [29] March [Tuesday]

The main headquarters was moved to the village of Claye, about four miles outside Paris. General Toll conducted a reconnaissance together with the Emperor [Alexander] and Prince Schwarzenberg, and we then spent the night about two miles away from Paris, at the village of Bondy. At Claye I witnessed a very touching scene: Polignac, who owned the village of Claye, met Gibson, his childhood friend; the Revolution separated these friends but the war now returned them to their homeland and reconnected them here.

18 [30 March, Wednesday]

Early in the morning, I travelled with General Toll to the battlefield. Marshal Marmont's corps occupied a very strong position just outside Paris and resolutely defended it. It was attacked from every direction and a fierce battle continued for almost six hours. We lost many troops, including our gallant officers Knorring and Lutinskii. Finally, around 2 p.m., we occupied the heights of Belleville which swung the battle in our favour. The enemy fled and Paris now lay exposed in front of us. It is impossible to describe what we felt at this sight. I was standing next to Count Miloradovich, who exclaimed, 'Here is the capital of the entire world. I will treat it in my own manner.' He then ordered several bombs to be fired into the city. We then travelled to the very gates of the city but our troops received the order to halt. The Emperor was soon approached by a [French] negotiator who announced that the French army is retreating and Paris surrenders itself to the victors. [The act of] capitulation was signed and, forgetting ourselves out of sheer happiness, we all began embracing and congratulating each other, pointing to Paris and thanking God. Leaving Count Miloradovich, I went to find Toll, who was not with the Emperor, so I looked for him after the capitulation was agreed on. Ascending one of the heights, I saw him travelling in my direction while His Imperial Majesty [Alexander] and Barclay de Tolly approached me from opposite directions. His Majesty, seeing the latter, exclaimed, 'My congratulations to Field Marshal Mikhail Bogdanovich!' The Emperor [later] announced many other awards and, satisfied, happy and crowned with immortal glory, we travelled to spend the night at Bondy. [From the Russian text in S. Khomutov, 'Iz dnevnika svitskago ofitsera']

Mikhail Orlov

Just twenty-six years old, Colonel Mikhail Orlov had already made a brilliant career. An illegitimate son of the influential General en Chef Count Fedor Orlov, he was fortunate to have been recognised by his father and used his family connections to advance. After distinguishing himself at Austerlitz, he earned praise for his gallantry at Heilsberg and Friedland in 1807 and served with distinction during the Campaign of 1812 in Russia. Appointed flügel-adjutant to Emperor Alexander, he earned his promotion to colonel in 1813.

It was easy to conclude from the current military situation that Napoleon, having been defeated at Laon and Arcis, was much weaker than any of the two Allied armies converging on Paris. Controlling interior lines, he had a perfect opportunity to concentrate all of his troops against one of his enemies, and he did try to exploit this advantage several times. But all of his attempts proved futile and only further revealed the material weakness of his forces. In this almost desperate situation he turned to his last resort which was induced not so much by common sense as by incredible impudence. And so, exposing Paris, which was entrusted to the corps of Marmont and Mortier that were supposed to follow in his wake, Napoleon crossed the River Aube in the middle of the day right in front of Prince Schwarzenberg's entire army deployed in battle formation, and marched in the direction of the border fortress on the Rhine. With his impertinent strategic movement he hoped to force the enemy to fall back, which he had failed to achieve, despite repeated attempts, through his ferocious and tumultuous tactics.

However, the enchantment [that Napoleon held over us] had been already broken and this ploy was so obvious that it deceived no one. The Allies followed him to Vitry to maintain communications between the two armies but then suddenly turned around and quickly advanced to Paris. They destroyed or drove back any corps they encountered on their way and threatened not only the enemy lines of communication, which [Napoleon] had himself exposed, but the capital, and the centre of his authority, itself. On 17 [29] March, our advance guard under command of General [Nikolai] Rayevskii, occupied the forest near Bondy and the main headquarters of the Russian Emperor was set up in the village; in the meantime, the left wing marched on Charenton and Vincennes while Blücher advanced on Bourge. In the rear, General Winzingerode, with a strong force of cavalry, moved in the wake of Napoleon while General [Fabian Osten-]Sacken occupied Meaux, ready to either assist the main army in its attack on Paris or fight Napoleon if he decided to hurry back to defend his capital. This general movement on Paris proved to be the turning point of the campaign, [success] from now on seemed inevitable and all consequences from this movement were expected to unfold to our advantage. Napoleon, who during his stay in Vilna told General [Alexander] Balashov that he goes to war like to a hunt and can afford wasting 300,000 men each year, did not have two Parises in his empire so he could gamble on them and loose.

At dawn on 18 [30] March, we all mounted horses and gathered in the yard of the castle at Bondy and awaited when the Emperor would assume the supreme command of the decisive battle for Paris. The gunfire had already began and our columns were already moving when a French officer, whose name I forget, was brought to us. He declared that he was the negotiator, but he was probably a runaway prisoner of war who lost his way in the rear of our army. He was immediately brought to the Emperor who wanted to question him personally and announce his will. During these negotiations which continued for almost three quarters of hour, Adjutant General [Fedor] Uvarov, while conversing to me, told me that Count [Karl] Nesselrode was instructed to start negotiations on the surrender of Paris at the first opportunity. I observed that it was necessary to create such an opportunity and for that purpose it would useful to attach to him a military person who would have authority to announce the ceasefire wherever he found it necessary. Uvarov agreed with my opinion, went inside the castle and a few minutes later I was called into His Imperial Majesty's cabinet.

The Emperor's status was extraordinary at that time. He spoke eminently and highly every time he had to defend pan-European interests but was always humble and calm in affairs involving him personally or his own glory. In reality, the future of the world defended on him, yet he called himself merely a tormented instrument of Providence. His political conversations bore imprints of both these sentiments. He combined confidence in victory with concern, almost fatherly anxiety, about the fate of his vanquished enemy. With the first words he uttered, I understood these dual sentiments and perceived that the day would end with decisive actions that would lead to the conclusion of an even-handed capitulation. Upon my arrival, the Emperor quickly and clearly outlined intelligence he had received about the enemy's state of affairs, added his own observations and then concluded his speech with these memorable words,

> Go on, I grant you the authority to announce a ceasefire wherever you find it necessary. In order to prevent and put an end to all future adversities, I grant you, with the promise not to hold you accountable, the authority to stop even the most decisive attacks, even if they are about to deliver a complete victory to us. Paris, deprived of its scattered defenders and its great man, will be in no position to resist us. I am firmly convinced in this. It pleases the Lord, who has given me strength and victory, that I utilise them only to secure peace and tranquillity in Europe. If we can secure peace without shedding blood, so be it. If not, we will have to concede to the necessity and fight because whether freely or by force, through a battle or parade march, on the ruins or in palaces, Europe must spend this night in Paris.

I was destined to represent this Europe, desiring to spend the night in Paris: the triumphant entry of the Allies took place no later than the following day. Such was the Emperor's mood when he let us go. I went with a French officer, accompanied by two trumpeters. We galloped towards the village of Pantin, which was occupied by a Russian infantry brigade. The fight had already begun there; all columns were on march and a general musket fire was underway along the entire front line.

Approaching the forward outposts, I immediately ordered the ceasefire from our side and told the trumpeters to blow their trumpets. At that moment, the French officer, who came with me, went to [the French] troops and also managed to stop their fire. After achieving this first success, we followed our negotiator and approached the enemy at thirty or forty paces. The negotiator went to the French and, after a short conversation, he disappeared among them. We were still standing and wondering whether our attempt would be successful, when violent shouts, accompanied by volleys, announced, without any warning, the resumption of hostilities. At that moment about twenty *chasseurs à cheval*, taking advantage of the fact that we were far removed from our troops, charged at me and Colonel Dyakov, who accompanied me. I barely managed to draw my sabre and parry blows while Dyakov, whose horse [the French] seized by the harness, defended himself with a whip. All of this happened in an instant but we managed to escape with [the French] at our heels. As we approached the village [Pantin], our troops advanced and the *chasseurs* were all captured. They were all drunk and, as we concluded, were inspired by not by a natural but this artificial ardour. Thus ended our first attempts to open negotiations. Many other attempts followed it but they all, albeit in varying circumstances, shared the fate. Yet, the battle continued and the blood flowed, reinforcements were arriving to the battlefield and cannonballs began to fall in some very populous parts of the city.

[. . .]

The Allied efforts and the enemy resistance caused many casualties before we seized the village of Bellevile and St. Chaumont hill. We managed to accomplish this only by 4 p.m., after eight hours of fighting. At the moment when the Emperor was reviewing the Guard intending to commit it against the enemy, a genuine envoy finally arrived and requested the start of negotiations. The Emperor immediately called me and instructed me to converse with the [French] officer. Our conversation was brief: he had no authority to negotiate and simply requested that the attack to be suspended. This would have meant delaying our victory, and potentially letting it slip out of our hands. So his request was rejected and I was instructed to travel with him back to the Duke of Ragusa [Marshal Marmont] who commanded [the French troops] fighting us.

And so we galloped at full speed, through canister and musket fire, both endangering our lives to meet death at the hand of either enemy or friends. The first man I encountered in the front line of the enemy's troops was Marshal Marmont himself. He stood with his sword drawn, encouraging his worn-out battalions with his actions and voice. He had a firm and warlike appearance but the poignant expression on his face also revealed the anxiety of a statesman who bore a vast burden. This responsibility hanged heavily on him and it seems that he was already anticipating that he would become a target for attacks and a victim of wounded national pride. The threat was extremely high and each minute was precious. The duke's words were short and firm, his determination complete and earnest. Upon seeing me, he approached me at once and addressed me bluntly, 'I am the Duke of Ragusa; who are you?'

'Colonel Orlov, flügel-adjutant to His Majesty the Emperor of Russia, who desires to save Paris for France and the world.'

'That is my only wish and hope as well; we have otherwise nothing left for it but to die on the spot. What are your conditions?'

'Hostilities to be suspended; the French troops to retire within the gates; plenipotentiaries to be instantly appointed to make arrangements for the surrender of Paris.'

'Agreed. The Duke of Treviso [Marshal Mortier] and I will go to the barrier of Pantin for that purpose.'

It is decided then. Let's cease firing along the entire front line. Good bye.

After riding for some distance, I returned to the Duke and told him, 'Of course you understand that your troops are to evacuate the position of Montmartre?' He thought for a minute and then replied, 'That is fair, Montmartre is outside the gates.' At that moment, shouts of 'Vive l'Empereur, Vive le Grand Napoleon!' spread along the entire French line and from the sight of these gallant warriors, it was clear that this cry, incited by the Marshal himself, spoke more about their eagerness to fight than their delight on impending end to hostilities. This was a truly magnificent sight. The struggle has ended but their loyalty had survived fully intact.

Our troops stood some 200 paces away from there. [We could see and hear] drums beating, officers running through the ranks and a small number of the most committed soldiers still determinedly firing at the enemy. I will never forget the comical disgruntlement of one Russian grenadier whom I had forbidden to fire and ordered to return to his company. He gave me a look full of reproach and, pointing to a French skirmisher whom he probably already considered a personal foe, he told me in almost pleading voice, 'Your Honour, allow me just to have a shot at that fellow!' I naturally did not let his revenge or fury reign freely and, returning to his company, he grumbled against what he called my ambiguous injustice.

Not far from there I found the Emperor and the Prussian king, dismounted, on a hill. Here, the Emperor personally deployed His Imperial Majesty's Guard battery company of twenty-four guns. The Prussian king thanked our officers for a splendid attack that they carried out earlier as they charged from the village of Pantin into flank and rear of the French batteries on St. Chaumont hill. Everyone eagerly awaited the news I carried. I hardly finished my account when the Emperor called up Count Nesselrode and gave him instructions, which he drafted earlier together with the Prussian king and Prince Schwarzenberg. The commission was organised at once and it consisted of Count Nesselrode and me. Prince Schwarzenberg also attached to us his adjutant Colonel Parr, while Nesselrode was accompanied by Captain Peterson, a Russian born in Lifland who had served as a *kamerger* at the Russian court but entered military service out of sheer patriotism at the very beginning of war.

We immediately went to the barrier of Pantin, where we found the Duke of Ragusa with his entire staff. He greeted us outside the barrier. The French troops had already retreated inside the city and were deployed in lines along long palisades that were built on both sides of the entrance that was protected by tambour of several guns. It was five o'clock in the evening. The gunfire completely ceased on the French side but not on the side of Blücher, who had not received the news of the armistice yet and continued to fire. The Duke of Treviso was informed [about negotiations] but had not yet arrived. Marmont proposed that they should ride on to meet him by the road. We accepted this offer and travelled along the line of palisades in the direction of the barrier of La Villete. I had an opportunity to observe what was happening in this part of the city: the French quickly and orderly occupied their weak bastions; soldiers stood along the palisades, resting on their muskets. Several radiating corners were set up to flank long *courtines* [walls] that were completely exposed. New uniforms, which we had not encountered on the battlefield, indicated the presence of the National Guard. However, there were few people behind the troops, and in some places none at all; no shouts could be heard, or movements or unusual preparations could be seen. In short, this was a composed, well thought-through defence, arranged in purely military fashion, without strong enthusiasm on the part of the people, or any revolutionary improvisations on the part of commanders. It was very important for us to observe these assuaging signs.

Upon arriving at the barrier of La Villete, we found the Duke of Treviso who was preparing to meet us. After a short conversation between the two Marshals, we entered some sort of tavern where negotiations began. It must be noted that throughout entire negotiations, anguish did not disappear from Mortier's face even for a moment. He expressed his assent to his comrade's words or disapprobation of our demands by nods. Conversation was maintained only by the Duke of Ragusa, who discussed all details. The marshals probably had agreed earlier on how they would act. The Duke of Ragusa assumed a political role while the Duke of Treviso continued to act in a purely military capacity: withdrawing of troops from the city and directing columns.

The Allies had won the battle and their superiority in numbers and positions was so obvious that the very thought of military resistance was impracticable. And so, we had to turn this undeniable advantage to our benefit. We had to use the capture of Paris as the first step towards general peace, and, with this in mind, we had to destroy, suppress as many troops that were at Napoleon's disposal as it was possible . . .

Count Nesselrode opened negotiations by proposing that Paris should capitulate with all the troops it contained. The Marshals indignantly rejected this offer. They appealed to their long service and to the numerous battles in which they had covered themselves in glory, and declared that they would rather perish under the ruins of Paris than sign such a condition. In vain did we brought up various arguments to shake their resolution, such as the saving of the capital, and their responsibility, if the consequence of their obstinacy should be the storming of Paris; futile were efforts to explain the need to use moral and physical pressure to compel Napoleon to accept peace since otherwise he would never willingly agree to it. The latter observation, which had to be made very cautiously, had, like all our efforts, no effect. The Marshals were not thinking of the future but were concerned to protect their honour in the present. They remained unwavering in their determination. Suddenly, in the midst of heated discussion, the occasional musket fire on the extreme right flank [of the Allied armies] rapidly increased and was replaced by intense skirmishing. We found ourselves in a very awkward position and the [Marshals] could accuse us of treachery. Fortunately, the firefight was quickly over and, as complete silence descended, we learned that Count Langeron, who was unaware of the armistice, had captured the heights of Montmartre. After receiving the news he ceased the attacks and informed the French on the cessation of hostilities.

This turn of events, unforeseen by either side, could have shaken [men of] less hardened valour than the two distinguished Marshals and, causing them to despair, would have compelled them to accept our conditions. But the Marshals continued to refuse our conditions. Count Nesselrode, seeing them inflexible, found it necessary to return to His Majesty to request new powers and permission to move negotiations to St. Chaumont Hill. And so we left, accompanied by a French general, as I recall it was Lapointe, whom the Marshals entrusted the fate of the army and city. He was to bring the ultimatum of the Allied sovereigns. At the same time he was entrusted with a letter addressed by Napoleon to Prince Schwarzenberg. This letter sought to convince the Field Marshal that Napoleon had opened direct negotiations with his father-in-law the Emperor of Austria, that they had agreed upon all articles and that it would be prudent of the Austrian general to suspend the attack on Paris at once. The Prince gave the letter to the sovereigns who decidedly rejected it. After a brief council, which we all attended, the decision was made to renounce our intention to force the Marshals to surrender but to continue negotiations in the same spirit, that is, with intention to suppress Napoleon's militaristic spirit by limiting resources that were at his disposal. Therefore, the ultimatum was not issued and we returned to the barrier of La Villette to resume negotiations. It was around 7 p.m. when the Allied commissioners met the French marshals at the same place.

After a brief preamble in which he praised the magnanimity of the Allied sovereigns, Count Nesselrode informed the Marshals that they might retire with the troops belonging to their corps from Paris, but only by the roads which the Allied sovereigns should appoint. In essence, this was a slightly revised version of the earlier condition. The Marshals conversed in a corner of the room and the Duke of Ragusa soon returned, telling us that Paris was not, and could not be, surrounded, and since the roads were open, their troops might retire as they chose. Still, he asked Count Nesselrode to better explain the condition and specify which road the French could march on. By the road to Bretagne was the answer, but as soon as we said that the Marshal informed us that he could not continue negotiations on such conditions. He told us that the real route of retreat was evident and still open to him; that if he were to defend Paris inch by inch, nothing could hinder him from crossing the Seine to the Faubourg-St. Germain, and retreating on Fontainebleau, the road to which was open. Therefore, we should not seek to obtain something, that cannot be seized by military superiority, through negotiations that are contrary to the old soldiers' honour. He gradually became animated and concluded with these words, 'Fortune has favoured you, your success is certain and I can envision that the consequences of this victory would be profound; be at once magnanimous and moderate, and do not push your demands to extremity. The counsel of magnanimity is often better than the counsel of power.'

All of us knew well the truth of the Marshal's words. If we were in his place, any one of us would have said the same words and referred to the same reasons. But we acted based on instructions that we were given. Once again, our mission was to constrain Napoleon, the titan of war [ispoln bitv] and to break his sword that had been hardened in a thousand and one battles. But to accomplish this, we had to divide, scatter and crush his forces, destroy any means of resistance and to leave him standing alone and naked, with all of the egoism of his genius and glory, facing the masses whose authority he refused to acknowledge and whom he despised for so long – in front of Europe, which rejected him out of foresight, and in front of France, which rejected him out of sheer exhaustion. This was the goal that we so eagerly pursued, contrary to our martial sympathies that made us respect the unwavering sensitivity of the Marshals. We sought to secure peace and ensure humanity's future, and our goal certainly did not entail vanity and desire to belittle our vanquished enemy. At that time our intention was not understood and when the Duke of Ragusa, in the turn of events, had to resort to it at Essonnes,* it was too late. His deep conviction turned, in the eyes of the Frenchmen, into a treachery, which later became a source of his many sufferings and hardships.

[After the Marshals rejected our conditions] another round of arguments and responses began, with conditions put forth more resolutely and new, even

---

*   After retreating from Paris, Marmont had his headquarters at Essonnes, where he made his decision to surrender his corps to the Allies.

stronger, objections raised. Finally, after long debates and clamour, the Duke of Treviso decided to leave us. The responsibility that lay on his shoulders, he told us, was so great that he could no longer stay and had to return to his troops to start preparing the defences of Paris. As for negotiations, he entrusted them to his comrade, whose decision he would accept.

This decision was final. Marshal Marmont kept firmly to his purpose and refused our proposals. Such determination only added to his honour since he already had, after 2 p.m., the permission of King Joseph to negotiate not only the surrender of Paris but even of the army still deployed there. And so both sides stood their ground and negotiations produced no results. It was already eight o'clock in evening, the night was drawing on, and the capitulation was not yet concluded. I told Count Nesselrode that the Marshals were in a more advantageous position since we could no longer attack Paris at night while the darkness would enable the French troops to retire by whatever road they chose. Marshal Mortier probably left us purposely to arrange this withdrawal and tomorrow at dawn we would find Paris abandoned and both Marshals on the way to join Napoleon. I concluded that we had to reach an improvised capitulation or attempt to get the requested conditions by ending negotiations. I suggested staying as a hostage in Paris until the termination of the armistice. Count Nesselrode agreed. He immediately interrupted the negotiations and, leaving me as a hostage to Marshal Marmont, he gave him his word of honour that no attacks would be made on Paris until I return to the Russian advance outposts. As our men travelled to our camp, I followed Marshal Marmont into Paris, where we entered just minutes after [negotiations ended]. We travelled slowly on horses, in deep silence and darkness. Only the sound of our horses clattering could be heard in the distance, and occasionally a few anxious and nervously curious faces appeared in windows, which quickly opened and closed. Streets were empty and it seemed that the incalculable residents of Paris all fled from the city; they seemed to be in a state of disbelief. And we, in whose hands the fate of so many people was thrust, looked like a small patrol making a round in the streets of the abandoned city. Each of us was deep in thought and I cannot recall what was said at that time, not even a single word. Once Marshal Marmont called up one of his adjutants and quietly gave him some order. The Adjutant departed and a few minutes later we heard the sound of cannons moving in the neighbouring street. This sound continued throughout my journey and its direction confirmed my suspicion that both marshals wanted to prevent Paris from facing any adversity, which would have been inevitably if they continued to fight; at the same time, unwilling to be forced into eccentric [ekstsentricheskii] retreat that would have deprived them of opportunity to join Napoleon, they decided to leave the town and maintain their lines of communication. Later I learned that my supposition was completely true.

We finally arrived at [Marmont's] house which presented a complete reverse to the streets of Paris. The hotel was illuminated from top to bottom and numerous people, eagerly awaiting our arrival, gathered there. When we entered the Marshal's dining room, all these people rushed towards us, but then dispersed into groups engrossed in very animated conversations. These conversations discussed the events of the day in thousands of details. The marshal instructed his adjutant to take care of me and then disappeared with a few persons inside his office.

[. . .]

[Holding conversations with French officers, Orlov noticed that people kept coming to Marmont's quarters and among the visitors were many prominent men.]

Throughout the evening [virtually] all the distinguished men of France, who had stayed in Paris, made their appearance and among them was Prince Talleyrand. Very few of these men approached me for they were preoccupied with the dangers of the present and the uncertainty of their future, all of them burdened with the seriousness of circumstances and the burden of tremendous responsibility. They faces bore the stamp of concern and fear. All of this was revealed in the hastiness with which they came in and departed. None of them stayed to converse and all of them seemed to be more or less dissatisfied with the Narshal's decisions.

[. . .] Upon arriving Talleyrand went directly to the Marshal's office, proceeding through the hall with the same calm and detached look that he is so famous for. He stayed there for quite a while and, coming out of the office, he stopped for a moment to stay a few word to the crowd of people. Everyone rushed to learn what he had said and he had exploited this moment to quietly approach me. 'Monsieur, please lay at the feet of the Emperor [Alexander] the most profound respects which the Prince of Benevento [Talleyrand] feels towards him.' 'The Prince,' I replied in a low voice, 'be assured that I shall not forget to lay this blank cheque before His Majesty.' A faint, almost unnoticeable smile quickly appeared on the Prince's face and, probably content that he was well understood, he left without showing that he understood me, and without adding anything to his first phrase, which was both quite formal but full of significant meaning. Several men overheard the Prince's words but could not hear my response. They gathered around me saying, 'Has Talleyrand gone mad? What does this blank cheque mean that he is sending to the Russian Emperor?'

Just at that moment there was a commotion in the room caused by the appearance of Napoleon's aide-de-camp, Lieutenant-General Alexander de Girardin. It seemed as if everyone felt the presence of the great man himself. Everyone's faces turned more serious and all those, who just a minute ago was ready to sign a peace treaty, now assume a proud warlike appearance. Conversations turned into whispering and those who approached me earlier now became lost in the crowd. It was eleven o'clock in the evening, so we went to dine. I found myself seated next to Girardin and we quickly recognised each other from our meeting in Vilna in 1812. Girardin was a very intelligent man who expressed himself with remarkable openness and eloquence. But he now found himself in an awkward situation where he tried in vain to stop the adversity from happening. Yet, circumstances were extreme and he could not do anything where even Napoleon's genius had failed.

Orlov then recounts the story of Girardin's difficult task. The French officer had to convince Parisian authorities to hold out till Napoleon's arrival, and, for this purpose, had to convey the lying assertion of Napoleon's having entered into negotiations with Austria, and of the speedy conclusion of a separate peace with that power. Furthermore, Girardin was, on one hand, to excite the troops and the inhabitants of Paris to prolong the defence, while on other hand he also had verbal orders to blow up the powder magazine on the plain of Grenelle, which could have caused widespread destruction. When he revealed such an order, the officer in charge of the powder, Colonel Lescaur, demanded a written order, which Girardin could not to give him, so Lescaur refused to destroy the magazine. Orlov then includes his recollections of conversations he had during the dinner at Marmont's quarters.

Meanwhile, no progress was achieved in the negotiations. After the departure of our commissioners, all communication between the sides ceased and I was completely unaware of our cabinet's intentions. I was just a hostage, had no official capacity and could not do or decide anything. I began to get concerned when I was finally informed of the arrival of Count Parr. He brought be a letter from Count Nesselrode, which gave me authority to complete negotiations for the surrender of Paris. It was already two o'clock in the morning. Here is an exact copy of the letter:

To Colonel Orlov,
     His Imperial Majesty, in agreement with Field Marshal Prince Schwarzenberg, finds it more advantageous to the Allied armies not to insist on the condition that has been earlier put forth for the surrender of Paris. But the Allies retain the right to pursuit the French army along the route that it chooses to retreat on. Thus, you are authorized, together with Colonel Count Parr, to conclude the convention on the surrender and occupation of Paris on conditions we had agreed upon with Duke of Treviso and Ragusa before my departure.
     Please accept, kind sir, the assurance of my highest respect.
     [Signed]: Count Nesselrode
     Bondy, 18 (30) March 1814

This letter removed all obstacles. After informing Count Parr of the letter's content, I informed Marshal Marmont that we were ready to prepare and sign the capitulation of Paris. The Duke of Ragusa arrived and, sitting in his dining room in front of all who were present there, we drafted articles of the surrender. Not a single disagreement or impediment occurred in this process. The treaty was written on a simple postal letter and written entirely by me. Count Parr, holding onto my shoulder, watched and expressed his consent as I wrote. Within a quarter of an hour everything was ready. I gave the marshal the drafted treaty which contained the following:

Capitulation of Paris

Article 1
The French forces under the command of Marshals Dukes of Treviso and Ragusa, will evacuate Paris by seven o'clock in the morning of 19 [31] March.

Article 2
They shall take with them all the appurtenances of their corps.

Article 3
Hostilities shall not recommence until two hours after the evacuation of the city, that is to say, on the 31st of March, at nine o'clock in the morning.
Article 4
All the arsenals, military establishments, workshops, and magazines, shall be left in the same state they were previous to the present capitulation being proposed.

Article 5
The infantry and cavalry National Guards will be separated from the troops of the line, and at the pleasure of the Allies, will be either disbanded, or employed as before,

Article 6
The corps of the municipal gendarmerie shall, in every respect, share the fate of the National Guard.

Article 7
The wounded and stragglers found in the city, after ten o'clock in the morning, will be considered as prisoners of war.

Article 8
The city of Paris is consigned to the generosity of the Allied monarchs.

Marshal Marmont took the paper and read it with an anxious expression on his face. It seemed he wanted to find something in our conditions that would serve as a cause for quarrel. But his face soon calmed down and he read all the articles out loud in a clear voice, with an appearance that seemed to have requested comments and counsel from his numerous listeners. Everyone remained silent, and no one uttered a world. He then gave me the paper and told me that he had nothing to say against the treaty, its format or articles and therefore expressed his complete acceptance of it. At the same time he instructed Colonel [Charles Nicolas] Fabvier and [Charles Marie] Denys to sign it together with us. We immediately signed the paper and made a copy which was given to Marshal Marmont.

We then had to organise a deputation that would greet the Emperor [Alexander]. I observed to the Marshal that the capitulation has resolved all military affairs but I avoided civil affairs of Paris with an intention to give the municipal authorities the right and opportunity to negotiate on their own with the Allied sovereigns, who, on their side, would have a chance to show their magnanimous intentions to the residents of Paris. [I explained] that the deputation could freely announce its intentions and I took responsibility to see them honoured; that trust is honourable for both those who show and who are shown it; and that I took it upon myself to prepare the eighth article of the capitulation which reflected His Majesty's order to avert any humiliation of Paris – to give the keys of the city to some foreign museum. The Marshal shook my hand and soon everyone was in commotion to select a deputation.

The day was beginning to dawn when the delegation was finally ready to travel. I mounted my horse and led the delegates to Bondy through our bivouacs that represented a huge mass of bonfires around which our soldiers, already rested, were cleaning their weapons and preparing to celebrate the final act of the terrible struggle that had just ended. Arriving at the headquarters, I led the delegates into the main hall of the castle and ordered to inform Count Nesselrode about their arrival. Nesselrode soon appeared and I went directly to the Emperor, who greeted me laying in his bed, 'Well, what news have you brought me?' – 'The capitulation of Paris,' responded I. His Majesty, having read it through, folded the paper and put it under his pillow. He then told me, 'Come, give me a kiss. I congratulate you on adding your name to such a great event.' He minutely questioned me about the evening I spent as a hostage and he showed a lively interest when I told him about Prince Talleyrand. 'As yet this is but an anecdote,' he told me. 'But it may become history.' [From the French text in RGVIA f. 846, op.16, d. 4134]

Nikolai Divov

Divov served as an ensign in the Life Guard Artillery Brigade of His Imperial Highness Grand Duke Mikhail Pavlovich.

On 18 [30] March 1814, our battery, commanded by Colonel Taube, was dispatched by A. Yermolov to occupy the Chaumont heights and open fire on the city of Paris. This order was issued at 3 p.m. As we arrived, a battalion of French troops fired at us but then quickly retreated which allowed us to occupy the above-mentioned heights. On the order of Colonel Taube, we opened fire from twelve (and not twenty-four as M. F. Orlov claims) guns in the direction of the city of Paris. Hardly half an hour passed before a [French] negotiator arrived requesting us to stop the bombardment since the city of Paris was surrendering. Colonel Taube escorted the negotiator to the Emperor [Alexander] who was standing, with his entire suite, not far from our battery. Colonel Taube received the Order of St. George (3rd class) directly from the hands of the Emperor.

The Emperor, the King of Prussia, Grand Duke Constantine Pavlovich, Field Marshal Prince Schwarzenberg and the Emperor's entire suite then moved to our battery. Stopping by my two guns, the Emperor ordered me to remove my entire artillery crew. He then stayed there with the Prussian king, Prince Schwarzenberg and a French negotiator. I do not know what they discussed but, as he was sending back the negotiator, we heard the Emperor say in French, 'Que demain, à 6 heures du matin, la ville de Paris soit evacuee par les troupes françaises.' The negotiator responded, 'Les orders du vainqueur seront remplis.' Afterwards the Emperor, still standing at the same spot, summoned Flügel Adjutant Colonel M. F. Orlov and told him in French, probably so that Prince Schwarzenberg could understand him: 'Orloff, allez dire de ma part au maréchal Barclay de Tolly de faire cesser le feu, sur toute la ligne.' Hearing these words, Prince Schwarzenberg asked the Emperor, 'Est ce que Barclay est maréchal?' – 'Oui, il l'est depuit ce moment.'

These unforgettable moment were particularly soothing to us: we heard the Emperor thanking us for our efforts and suffering during the last three years [of campaigning] and congratulated us with the peace and our [expected] entrance into Paris tomorrow morning. [From the Russian text in N. Divov, 'Po povodu. . .']

Sergei Mayevskii

Mayevskii's 13th Jager Regiment was in the front line during the battle of Paris, occupying one of the suburbs and suffering considerable losses in the process. As the battle died down in the evening, Mayevskii decided to travel closer to the city.

Curiosity was the main factor in my decision but I also intended on conducting reconnaissance for [my regiment] was among the lead troops and I had to determine the most advantageous places for our assault. The Cossacks preceded us and were already wandering through the suburbs. At one place I saw a large crowd of Frenchmen gathered around the body of a woman who had lost her life in a despicable manner and her body revealed sign of ravaging by the Cossacks. [General Krasovskii] and I quickly departed from that place and went towards the city gates, where some French were coming out to observe the Russians. A Polish officer approached us and, after several questions, he observed, 'Monsieurs, tonight we are comrade in arms, but tomorrow we will be enemies by the very same reason.' But he proved to be mistaken for later he was the first to meet me in Warsaw and we became very good friends.

When it came to pillaging, the Prussians proved to be good students of their French tutors – they had already managed to plunder the suburbs, where they broke into cellars and smashed barrels and, no longer drinking, were now walking up to their knees in wine. For a long time we obeyed [Emperor] Alexander's order to be compassionate but temptations soon overpowered fear: our men went to fetch firewood and returned with barrels of wine. My share included a barrel with about 1,000 bottles of champagne. I distributed them in my regiment and enjoyed myself as well, thinking that this indulgence would quickly end with the start of a new day. In the morning we were ordered to prepare for the triumphant entry into Paris but our soldiers were more than half-drunk so it took us much effort to assemble them and get them in formation . . . [As we waited to enter the city] a woman appeared with two beautiful daughters. She looked at us fearfully and could not believe for a while that we were indeed Russians. The common people are thus being deceived similarly everywhere and imagine enemy as cyclops and cannibals. I remembered how upon our arrival in Hungary, the owner of the house where we were billeted hid his children thinking that we would eat them alive! [From the Russian text in S. Mayevskii, 'Istoriya. . .']

Louis-Victor-Léon de Rochechouart

On 17 [29] March there was fighting at the gates of Paris along an immense front. The main Russian Army and the so-called Army of Silesia formed an effective force of at least 150,000 men. To these the French could only oppose some 25–30,000 men, who were already disheartened by the recent defeats. They were under the command of Marshals Marmont and Mortier but the generals did not agree and would not act in concert. There was also a third leader, Joseph Bonaparte, invested with the title of Lieutenant-General of the Empire. Thus, the confusion was great and the capture of Paris inevitable . . .

The Allied army marched on Paris in the form of a semicircle; only the route to Orléans was open, and along this route Empress Marie-Louise, her son, [imperial] ministers, the Council of Regency, and Prince Joseph Bonaparte, retired. They took up their residence at Blois, thus leaving the capital without government, and a prey to all the elements of intrigue that were within it.

On 29 March, the [Russian] headquarters passed the night at Bondy. On the 30th, as we were crossing Pantin, I sang to my comrades 'Que Pantin serait content, etc. etc.' A grocer, standing at his shop door, was watching us pass.

He called out, 'Look, here are Cossacks singing our old song.' During the day the Pres-Saint-Gervais, the Buttes-Chaumont and Belleville were occupied after a vigorous resistance and many casualties on both sides.

Around 2 o'clock in the afternoon Emperor Alexander arrived on the Buttes-Chaumont, whence he could observe Paris. We could hear a terrible musket fire and incessant discharges of powerful artillery in the direction of Montmartre and Vincennes. At this solemn moment the Emperor dismounted in order to get a better view of the impressive scene. He asked me to point out the principal buildings. His face soon became sombre, he ceased to question me, and remained engrossed in deep thought. Of what was he thinking? God only knows. He seemed no longer to hear the cannon or the fusillade or the murmur of the great city at our feet. I withdrew discreetly, and I, too, gave myself up to strange reflections.

The Emperor was soon aroused from his dream by the arrival of a messenger with a flag of truce, brought by Count Nesselrode.

The Emperor, the King of Prussia, the generals and ministers present, assembled for the council of war. At the end of a quarter of an hour the Emperor signed to me to come forward. 'Go and find the Comte de Langeron; he should be at the foot of Montmartre; tell him that I have just granted an immediate suspension of hostilities. Consequently, let him give orders to cease firing at once, and that no soldier shall attempt to enter Paris even if the barriers should have been captured. I shall hold him personally responsible. Go, as quickly as you can.'

I set off at a gallop, but what a terrible and perilous mission it was! In order to take the shortest route I had to pass through narrow streets where furious fighting was still going on. From every house, transformed, as it were, into a fort, there came a murderous fusillade; at every step, cannon, on one side or the other, enfiladed the streets, the roads and byway. I said to myself: 'I shall never reach my destination through this hail of balls and bullets. I shall be killed ten times over.' Fortunately, and by some miracle, I came through without a scratch. I fastened a white handkerchief to the end of my sword, and all the way as I went I waved my flag, and shouted in Russian, French, and German: 'Cease fire, by order of the Emperor. My friends, do not fire any more, there is a suspension of arms. I am going to announce it to the whole line.' They mostly listened to me, except in some places where the struggle was too fierce, or the noise too great for me to be heard. At last, after exceptional dangers, I found M. de Langeron at Montmartre. I repeated to him, word for word, the instructions of the Emperor. He immediately gave orders to cease fire, laid down some rigorous measures, and forbade, under pain of death, that anyone, no matter who, should leave the ranks or enter Paris. The advance guard of his division was already occupying the barriers Rochechouart, des Martyrs, Blanche and de Clichy. Two hours later firing had ceased along the whole line, and I returned to inform the Emperor that his orders had been carried out.

He said: 'You have done well, you have lost no time.' Several days later the Emperor rewarded me for this perilous mission, making me a Commander of the Order of St. Vladimir, with the following note: 'In recognition of your conduct in the battle for Paris, 18/30 March 1814.'

The Emperor made his way back to Bondy, where his presence was needed for negotiations that were prolonged far into the night. Armand de Polignac, Montpezat, Rapatel, Boutet and I took the road towards Belleville, where we were to have supper and spend the night. As we followed the boulevards outside the barriers of La Villette and Pantin, we entered into conversation with many of the inhabitants, who were terrified at the thought of the morrow. Some of these wretches even told us, 'Let us come with you to the suburbs where there will wholesale plunder.' Wherever we could we distributed the proclamation of the King.*

As night fell we left the barriers and entered Belleville, where everything was still in confusion; there had been street fighting during the day, but, strange to say, no [major] damage had been done, either by the French or the Allies . . .

We ordered supper at one of the more prosperous inns of the suburb. The landlord, with his wife and children, his cook and cash-box, had taken refuge in Paris, leaving the head waiter, a wide-awake fellow, in charge of the establishment, with two assistant cooks. They began cooking dinner and were not lacking provisions for it . . . There were many of us, all Frenchmen: the Comte de Lambert, whose division occupied Belleville, and the Baron de Damas, had joined us as well. The waiter, hearing us all talking French, without a word of Russian, could not conceal his astonishment. Folding his arms, he said: 'Oh come! For Cossacks, you chatter away fast enough in French, and the best French, too!' We answered with a merry peal of laughter, and Boutet gravely remarked: 'You need not wonder at that, waiter, we learned French when we were put out to nurse.' Towards eleven o'clock my companions and I went to the house where we were billeted, a pretty country residence belonging to a major merchant in the Marais. The gardener, who was caretaker, had been threatened with having to billet Cossacks, and was delighted to receive an aide-de-camp of the Emperor [of Russia]. [From the French in Rochechouart, *Souvenirs*]

---

* See Rochechouart, *Souvenirs*, pp. 322–4

8

The Short Sojourn in France

On 31 March 1814, the Allied armies made a triumphant entry into Paris where they remained for the next month and a half. This stay in Europe's greatest city left a profound impression on many of the Russian officers who struggled to convey the full range of their emotions in their diaries and memoirs. 'To describe Paris is akin to attempting to build new pyramids of Egypt,' wrote one of them.

Alexander Mikhailovskii-Danilevskii

Mikhailovskii-Danilevskii served in the Russian Imperial headquarters where he had a perfect opportunity to observe the Allied leadership at this moment of great triumph.

At dawn on a beautiful morning on 19 [31] March, the generals and officers of His Majesty's suite began to descend into the broad court before the castle of Bondy. Meeting each other they shook hands but remained silent. Around 6 a.m. the deputies of the municipality of Paris arrived in their state carriages; they were in such a panic that could they barely speak. They were followed by a man on horseback, whose appearance was well known to us all – it was Caulaincourt, sent by Napoleon with an offer to accept the peace.* The soldier of the Life Guard Preobrazhenskii Regiment, who was standing sentry, told him he must dismount, and the French Minister was obliged to comply. On seeing the officers assembled in the court, he took off his hat, and with eyes downcast passed by us. While the Emperor was informed of his arrival, I was asked to engage him in conversation so I requested him to walk into the castle. I must confess here that it was not without a feeling of satisfaction that I beheld the humiliation of this upstart, who, notwithstanding his sincere attachment to Emperor Alexander and his persevering efforts to dissuade Napoleon from the war with Russia, had set no bounds to his overbearing pride while he was [the French] ambassador to St. Petersburg. The Emperor passed more than an

---

* Peace terms that the Allies offered at Chatillon.

hour with him and, judging from [Caulaincourt's] troubled air on leaving the audience chamber, we concluded that his offers had been rejected. Precisely at eight o'clock, the Emperor mounted his horse named Mars. On the road he encountered the King of Prussia, and a little way further on, the [Russian] Guard. No pen is able to describe the enthusiasm with which he was hailed by the Guard soldiers. Some three verstas [3.2km] from the city appeared the Parisians, all asking one question, 'Where is Emperor Alexander?'

The numerous edifices of Paris gradually came fully into view. Some of our officers had rode into town early in the morning with orders of different kinds, and on their return increased by their accounts our general excitement to get to the capital. All were burning with impatience to enter a city which had so long assumed the right of giving law to the world in matters of taste, fashion and enlightenment; in which were unrivalled treasures of art and science; which contained all the intricate pleasures of life; where laws were issued for nations and chains were made to enslave them; and from where armies marched to every corner of Europe. In short, the city was considered the capital of the world. To crown their two years' series of victories, nothing was wanting to the Russians but the triumphant possession of Paris. Until that moment, it was impossible to enjoy the fruits of so many bloody battles and victories gained in the last two years. Every step, which separated us from the city, prevented us from fully embracing the feeling of satisfaction that Russia was avenged. But another minute and the mighty Empire, which had extended from the Baltic Sea to the Tagus River, shaken to its very foundations, and tottering to its fall, would have crumbled. The fall of great powers is akin to the death of great men: it leaves a certain emptiness in this world and questions immediately arise of who would take the place of the man who just passed away?

At nine o'clock in the morning we reached the suburbs of Paris. The Guard Light Cavalry Division moved first, with the Leib-Cossacks at its head; the Emperor was some distance behind it, surrounded by a brilliant suite and followed first by the grenadiers, then Guard infantry, cuirassiers and several battalions of Austrians, Prussians and Badenese. The morning was beautiful and the air was becoming clearer and crisper with every passing hour. A countless multitude crowded the streets, and the roofs and windows of the houses. At first it seemed as if the inhabitants were still under the influence of fear, for their acclamations were not general. Their puzzlement continued for a few minutes, during which they kept continually asking us and one another, 'Where is the Emperor?' 'There he is, there is Alexander,' exclaimed they. 'How graciously he nods to us; with what kindness he speaks with us!' The French, who had pictured to themselves the Russians as half-wild men, worn out by long campaigns, speaking a language altogether unknown to them, and dressed in a wild, outlandish fashion, could hardly believe their eyes, when they saw the smart Russian uniforms, the glittering arms, the joyous expression of our men, their healthy countenances, and the kind deportment of the officers. Our officers' sharp repartees in the French language completed their astonishment. 'You are not Russians,' they said to us, 'you are surely émigrés.' A short time, however, served to convince them of the contrary, and the news of the incredible accomplishments of the conquerors flew from mouth to mouth. The praises of the Russians knew no bounds; the women from the windows and balconies welcomed us, by waving their white handkerchiefs and from one end of Paris the cry of 'Long live Alexander! Long live the Russians!' was uttered by a million voices.

In the meantime, we passed through the suburbs of Montmartre, and turned off to the right along the Boulevards, where the festive crowd soon became prodigious. Indeed, it was hardly possible to make one's way on horseback: the inhabitants kept constantly stopping our horses, and launching out in praise of Alexander, they rarely alluded to the other Allies; very rarely could one hear the shots of 'Vive Francis!' or 'Vive Frederick!' Emboldened by the affability of Emperor [Alexander], they began to wish for a change of government and to proclaim the Bourbons; white cockades appeared in the hats, and white handkerchiefs in the air; many people, gathering around His Majesty, requesting that he would remain in France. 'Reign over us,' said they, 'or give us a Monarch like yourself.'

Passing in front of rows of magnificent buildings and monuments, erected to perpetuate the glory of French arms, we finally reached the Champs-Elysées, where the Emperor halted and reviewed the troops which marched past him. The Parisians rushed here from every quarter, lured by the novelty of this spectacle. The French women requested us to dismount and allow them to stand on our saddles, in order to have a better view of the Emperor. The march was opened by the Austrians. In spite of their utmost efforts, the gendarmes could not contain the people and the curious Parisians crowded the ranks of Austrians troops. But the moment the Russian grenadiers and Guard infantrymen appeared, the French were so struck with their truly military appearance, that they did not require to be told to clear the way: all at once, as if by a secret unanimous consent, they retired far beyond the line traced for the spectators. They gazed, with silent admiration, on the Guard and grenadiers, and acknowledged that their army, even at the most brilliant epoch of the French Empire, was never in such order as were these two corps after three immortal campaigns.

The review ended about five o'clock in the afternoon, when His Majesty [Alexander] retired to the house of M. Talleyrand, where he resided during the early period of his stay in Paris. A part of the troops mounted guard, and the rest took up the quarters assigned them in the town. At that moment the mob [chern'] began to insult the monuments which had been erected in honour of the previous ruler of the French. But the majority of the inhabitants still seemed lost in wonder, as if not believing what they saw with their eyes, and kept asking each other if it were really true that their conquerors were enlightened and compassionate. Is it possible, they asked, that Alexander can limit his triumph to securing the happiness of the country he has subdued? Evening at length came to give that repose which was equally necessary to the victors and the vanquished; the streets were gradually thinned of their crowds, and a general stillness ensued which was the more sensible, that during the course of the preceding days every breast had been agitated by various hopes and wishes which had been crowned by the most fortunate events. All we saw and felt was so fully equal to our expectations, that the consummation of our happiness was perfect. We were left powerless out of happiness.

I could not sleep that night. Around midnight I went into the street; there was no one there. Near the house where the Emperor had taken up residence, was posted a battalion of the Life Guard Preobrazhenskii Regiment, while His Majesty's company occupied the yard. All lights were extinguished. No light could be seen in the Tuilleries Palace either. This ancient edifice, which served as the palace for the Bourbons, the assembly place of the republican governments and later the palace of the ruler of the wealthiest countries of Europe – but a building which Emperor Alexander did not deem worthy of his stay – was guarded by a Russian sentry post. Amidst the silence of midnight, I reached Palais-Royal, where all parties, that reigned over France in the last twenty-five years, had first tested their powers. In the gardens and galleries I could see thousands of Parisians, carried away by various passions and thoughts. Some looked up into the sky and sighed heavily, but most gathered around various speakers. Some of them praised the Bourbons, under whose royal sceptre their ancestors lived for centuries; others extolled their past victories [under Napoleon] and thought it prudent to do nothing drastic while awaiting for the arrival of the Emperor at the head of his army. What I saw here gave me first and real understanding of revolutionary events and people's gatherings. Despite the diversity of their opinions, they all respected a Russian uniform: I walked throughout Palais-Royal, stopped by the crowds of Parisians and was everywhere met with great courtesy. I then went to a coffee house and barely managed to take a seat when the locals began to drink a toast to the Russian officer's health. Finally, walking along deserted streets, I returned home. So perfectly were the rules of discipline observed by our army, that no disorder was reported, although over 50,000 foreign troops passed the night in the city. Not a sound was heard in the streets save for the call of the Russian sentries. [From the Russian text in A. Mikhailovskii-Danilevskii, 'Vkhod rossiiskoi armii . . .']

S. Khomutov

Khomutov was a staff officer in the Russian imperial headquarters who maintained a daily journal of his campaign experiences.

19 [31 March, Thursday]
Members of the Senate and other officials arrived in Bondy from Paris. The Emperor met them very kindly. They assured us that the Parisians hated Napoleon's tyranny and awaited us eagerly. At 10 a.m. the Emperor mounted his horse and travelled to Paris, escorted by a large suite which also included me. Our entire Guard, Grenadier Corps, three cuirassier divisions, part of the artillery, Prussian guard, Austrian grenadiers, Bavarian corps, Württemberg corps and Badenese guard stood in parade formation at the city gates which were closed. As soon as His Imperial Majesty approached, the gates opened and music thundered from every direction. Several cavalry squadrons and the Guard Cossacks opened the parade, followed by the Emperor, the Prussian king and Prince Schwarzenberg. People crowded around us, expressing great joy. Everyone rushed to the Emperor's feet, kissed his clothes, even his horse. [People] incessantly stopped us and called Russians as their saviours, yelling 'Vive Emperor Alexander! Vive King of Prussia! Vive Louis XVIII! Vive Bourbons! Vive Peace!'

The Emperor stopped on the Champs-Elysèes and all our troops marched in front of him, which continued for over four hours. Crowds surrounded His Majesty and we had to use force to push them back. After the parade, the Emperor travelled to the palace of the Prince of Benevento [Talleyrand], where he settled in, although the Elysèe Bourbon was prepared for him. We all felt that we were experiencing a beautiful dream. It seemed that anyone who witnessed the entry of the Russian Emperor into the capital of France has nothing else to wish in this life. [From the Russian text in S. Khomutov, 'Iz dnevnika svitskago ofitsera']

Nikolai Bronevskii

A graduate of the Grodno Cadet Corps, Bronevskii began his military career in the North Caucasus, where he fought against local mountaineers. In 1814, he served as a staff officer in Blücher's Army of Silesia.

On 19 [31] March 1814, Emperor Alexander Pavlovich, accompanied by the Prussian King, made a triumphant entry in Paris. I want to share some of my impressions of what I had seen and heard that day . . . There were enormous crowds of people everywhere. Not only houses, but even trees were full of people. I had a hot-tempered horse that kicked at the smallest touch. Although I warned anyone getting too close to me [that my horse might kick], due to the density of the crowd, it was impossible to avoid my horse being touched. Yet I was astonished by the calmness of my Circassian [horse]: he stood quietly and silently, without paying attention to anyone around him. Finally, I heard the thunder of music. People rushed forward, all eyes fixed on the conquerors, cries 'Vive Alexander!' reaching to the skies. I stood among the French as if among our good old Russian citizens. Next to me and my horse stood a family of three: a chubby gentleman in the National Guard's uniform, his pretty and pleasant wife and their beautiful daughter. Suddenly I heard the madame's request to allow her and her daughter to sit on my horse so they could better see the ceremony. I explained to her that my horse was rather unsteady and might hurt them. The lady, caressing my horse on the head, kissed him and said: 'He is a good horse and will let me sit on him so we could see this celebration in its entire splendour.' Imagine my bewilderment when my Circassian continued to stand very quietly and calmly as I helped the lady and her daughter to climb onto the saddle; I then supported the madame while the daughter held on to her father. They were so grateful to me that they gave me their address and the gentleman later proved to be very helpful to me during our stay in Paris. I cannot fully describe the solemn procession [of the Allied entrance into Paris.] [Sadly], I could not see the passing of our Guard. . . The French were surprised at its order and discipline as well as its composure. The cries of 'Vive Alexander!' continued uninterrupted.

As the troops passed, the crowds dispersed. Our generals went to dine at some of the best restaurants, including at M. Veraux [restaurant] at Palais-Royal. [We were awed] by its splendid rooms, beautiful furniture, and servants in opulent livery as well as fine dishes, crystals and table cloth. [We were served] exquisite dishes and wines, all served cleanly and nicely. We paid handsomely. Crowds of Frenchmen entered the rooms to gaze at us as if we were marvels. They were surprised that we spoke French among ourselves. Our generals paid for the food and were surprised how cheap it was. We then returned to the camp. From the evening of the 18th [30 March], our camps turned into bazaars. In an instant, anything one could desire was brought there; there was hardly any bargaining and sellers took whatever money was offered. Of course, everything seemed inexpensive to us. And where else can you find such an abundance of oranges, lemons, apples, fresh grapes, various candies, wines in full and half bottles, porter, liqueurs, different pirogues, patties, oysters, cheese, rolls, in a word, you could have found anything you had ever desired.

The following day, we saw carriages with women arriving at our camp; they moved freely around the camp. If our officers, who could speak the French, approached them, they talked to them tenderly and treated them to oranges. Our officers then generously brought out scarves full of oranges, apples, sweets and gave them to women. Acquaintances were made within an hour. We were allowed to go to the city, but were required to wear our uniforms, maintain cleanliness and be always courteous and kind [to locals]. Soldiers were prohibited to leave camps alone. In short, we felt as if we were in Moscow, St. Petersburg or some other nice provincial town. All passers-by bowed to us and we replied to them with same courtesies. We visited churches, prayed to God and everyone looked at us with wonder. In theatres, most of the seats were occupied by our officers . . . [From the Russian in N. Bronevskii, 'Iz vospominanii']

Declaration of His Majesty the Emperor of Russia

The armies of the Allied Powers have occupied the capital of France. The Allied Sovereigns receive favourably the wish of the French nation. They declare, that if the conditions of Peace ought to contain stronger guarantees when the question was to bind down the ambition of Buonaparte, they may be more favourable, when, by a return to a wise government, France herself offers the assurance of this repose. The Sovereigns proclaim in consequence, that they will no more treat with Napoleon Buonaparte, nor with any of his family; that they respect the integrity of ancient France, as it existed under its legitimate Kings: they may even do more, because they profess it as a principle, that, for the happiness of Europe, France must be great and strong. That they will recognise and guarantee the Constitution which France shall adopt. They, therefore, invite the Senate to name immediately a Provisional Government, which may provide for the wants of the Administration and prepare the constitution which shall suit the French people. The intentions which I have just expressed, are common to all the Allied Powers.

(Signed) Alexander.

Paris, March 31, three o'clock in the afternoon.

[From *Cobbett's Political Register*, 1814]

Nikifor Kovalskii

In 1814 Kovalskii was a young junior officer in the elite Life Guard Dragoon Regiment.

On 19 [31] March, at dawn, the [Russian Imperial] Guard received orders to prepare for a ceremonial entry into Paris. Our generals, staff and junior officers were ordered to wear laurel wreaths on their helmets and a white scarf with ribbon on the left arm. The parade began at nine o'clock in the morning. First marched the Leib-Cossacks, followed by Emperor [Alexander] and the Prussian King who were accompanied by a vast suite. Then came the Guard in the following order: Life Guard Hussar, Life Guard Uhlan, Life Guard Dragoon, Life Guard Horse and Chevalier Guard regiments, followed by the Guard infantry (accompanied by music), the Preobrazhenskii, Semeyonovskii, Izmailovskii, Life Guard Jager and Finlyandskii regiments. At the end of the columns came our artillery. The weather was fine and the

Parisians greeted us as amiably as it was possible; standing at windows and balconies, women threw white cockades. The parade continued for a very long time so that the Guard light division reached the Champs-Elysées no earlier than five o'clock in the afternoon. Once there, our men dismounted awaiting further instructions on billeting. At seven o'clock we were led past the Place de Vendôme, where a large crowd had gathered around the famous bronze column and tried to pull down Napoleon's statue. However, upon hearing this our Emperor [Alexander] ordered the French to be stopped and the statue was covered with a sheet; nevertheless, the following day it was pulled down anyway.

After crossing the Seine, we went to the Rue de Grenelle, where we were billeted in the barracks belonging to the [French] Guard dragoons of Empress Marie-Louise. The building turned out to be excellent and, most importantly, spacious enough to accommodate our three regiments, though many of our men were missing. Instead of plank-beds as there are in our barracks, we found beds with mattresses stuffed with horsehair, flannel blankets and two pillows. The stables were immaculately clean. In the vast yard there were two fountains in marble-lined pools. Our officers were billeted in a separate building.

We were starving and decided to leave the barracks and eat at the nearest tavern. We knocked on the door – the cantinier and servers were startled to see Russian uniforms and they were even more astonished when we politely asked, in French, to have something to eat. The tavern owner, who was a woman, came down to look at these transmarine creatures. At the end of the dinner we had another comic scene. The tavern-keeper initially refused to take our money but we made her take a few francs, so she changed her tune and invited us to stop by frequently.

As we came out of the tavern, Baron S. noticed a magnificent building nearby. He called the doorman (I still remember his name, M. Dubois) and asked him if it was possible for us to take quarters in this house. Dubois, whether out of fear or kindness, told us it was possible and this is how we found much better housing compared to simple barracks. The house, or to be precise, the palace was decorated in the old style and belonged to a certain marquis of ancient pedigree, who, as Dubois told us, still had the guillotine that cut off King Louis XVI's head. For our bedroom we chose a vast round-shaped green room where the light fell only through a round window in the ceiling. In the morning, Dubois served us coffee and, at noon, he treated us to a splendid breakfast and, after we gave him twenty francs, he quickly got acquainted with our habits.

I ordered a new full-dress uniform, which was made with remarkable swiftness, and went to the Palais-Royal, where, among other things, they were already selling Russian epaulettes, sabres and even awards and orders. The crosses [of the Order of] St. George, which were probably French-produced fakes, featured an English-style horse which seemed to suggest that merchants expected the Russian army in Paris and prepared their wares beforehand so they could charge three-times higher prices for them. Our officer Bazilevskii paid 120 francs for the St. George.

When I returned to the yard of our barracks, there were already some 50 female traders with pies, cigars, nuts and various minutiae. Soldiers joked and flirted with them and only God knows on what language or dialect they were communicating; thus, they called woman who sold alcohol *lagutka* after the French word *la goutte*. That same day I learned that Yurko (from the Ukraine), well known in our squadron as a drunkard, went in search of a tavern and came across a pharmacy. There he frightened an apothecary with his fierce black-dyed moustache and somehow sniffed out a bottle with [medical] alcohol, which he emptied while snacking on an onion bulb and left contently rubbing his stomach. The dumbfounded apothecary soon came running to our barracks, assuring us that he bore no responsibility for the imminent death of our comrade but Yurko did not even blink [v us sebe ne dul].

There was also another memorable incident. One evening we were drinking tea at Colonel Prince Khilkov's apartment. The prince was in a bad mood because his valet, Semyen, left that morning without permission and had not returned yet. At last, the valet appeared, clearly drunk and in high spirits. He was a handsome-looking dark-haired man, wearing a hussar dolman and tight pants. When Khilkov began to berate him, the valet responded, 'Your Excellency, what could I do? I was buying oranges when two French officers approached me, murmuring something to their noses. One of them pushed me and I pushed him back. We quickly brawled and two other officers approached us, put me forcibly into a carriage and took me to the bois de Boulogne. I thought they intended to shoot me there and feared for my life. But once we arrived, they shoved a pistol into my hand, gave another pistol to the other officer, measured the distance and told us to shoot each other. I fired and shot my opponent's cap while his bullets tore a button off my dolman. The officers then rushed to embrace me, shouting "Bravo Russe!" and took me to a tavern where they treated me to the Champagne wine.' This incident eventually reached the Emperor's ear as well. Because the duels between Russian and French officers occurred very frequently, orders were issued to allow us to wear civilian dress, which included dress-coat and frock-coat.

On 20 March [1 April], we rented a box (for 130 francs) at the Grand Opera and went to dine at Verry's [restaurant]* in the Palais-Royal. As we were finishing eating, a Cossack staff officer approached us and, explaining that he could not speak French, asked us to order for shchi [cabbage soup], a piglet sautéed in sour cream, etc. But since there were no such dishes in the menu, he requested wine and calmly began to smoke his pipe. Upon seeing this, the

---

* Verry's was one of the most famous restaurants in Paris, renowned for its carte du jour that featured upwards of 300 dishes.

waiters began to fuss around and Verry himself came down to beg the Cossack to stop smoking since high-end restaurants did not allow it. The Cossacks modestly extinguished his pipe, put it in his pocket and then got out his money pouch that was overflowing with Napoléon d'or [gold coins]. Unfastening it he dropped, as if by chance, about ten gold coins that rolled down the floor. 'This is for the servants,' he said without turning his head and left.

In the evening we went to the Grand Opera that was packed with people. There was unbelievable crush of the people. Amidst this overcrowding, someone tore off General [Mikhail] Miloradovich's epaulette while we only just reached our box. Upon learning that instead of the announced play *Triomphe de Trajan* the actors would be performing *La Vestale*, the French began to shout and bang loudly with their feet. At last a certain man appeared on the scene and announced that the change of plays took place at the personal desire of their majesties Emperor Alexander and the Prussian king. The public calmed down for a minute and then erupted into a thunderous shout, 'A bas l'aigle! A bas l'aigle!' In response a black sheet was lowered over Napoleon's [personal] box and covered the Imperial eagle; similarly, a sheet was thrown over another eagle that was above the stage. Soon Emperor Alexander and King Frederick William entered the box and the public greeted them with loud applause. Women threw white cockades into the parterre that were immediately seized upon and fixed to hats. There was incredible excitement in the air and it only increased when the then-famous singer [name unclear] sang,

> Vive Guillaume,
> Vive ce Roi vaillant!
> De son royaume
> Il sauve les enfants,
> Par la victoire
> Il nous donne la paix,
> et conte gloire
> Par les nombreux bienfaits
>
> Vive Alexandre!
> Vive ce roi des rois!
> Sans rien pretendre,
> Sans nous dicter des loix,
> Ce prince Auguste
> A le triple renom
> D'étre heroes, d'étre juste
> Et de nous rendre des Bourbons

The Emperor and the Prussian king cried out in excitement while thunderous shouts of 'Hurrah!' did not cease for a moment.

The next day, on the Emperor's order, the following allowance money was set according to rank: ensigns – 3 francs; lieutenant – 4; staff captain – 5;

captain – 6; colonel -10. Lunch cost us very little money and we enjoyed large credit at trade stalls and shops. Officers who owned estates applied for credits by submitting to a bank a simple letter from their corps commander confirming that they were men of means and immediately received considerable amounts. The Emperor eventually paid for all of them and we were saved from any reprimands and admonitions.

[. . .] Horses were extremely expensive in Paris and those that usually cost about 200 francs now cost more than 1,000 francs. This price-rise was caused by Napoleon's requisitioning of all serviceable horses in Paris for the needs of his artillery. Colonel A. who had lost vast amounts in [card games] resorted to a desperate enterprise to pay off his debts: he sold twenty horses from his squadron and received an enormous sum of money for them. To escape a terrible responsibility [for this crime], he begged Grand Duke Constantine Pavlovich to allow him to join the expedition against the still fighting Marshal [August] Marmont. The colonel's squadron, where I was assigned, moved some 30 verstas [32km] from Paris before it had a small skirmish with an enemy outpost. In the aftermath, Pavel Burtsev and I accepted the surrender of twenty-five French cavalrymen and brought them to Colonel A, who profusely thanked us. He thus removed the shortage of horses in his squadron and returned to Paris with plenty of cash in his pockets. This swindle made him a profit of more than 40,000 francs. [From the Russian text in N. Kovalskii, *Iz zapisok* . . .]

Louis-Victor-Léon de Rochechouart

On 31 March I mounted my horse early to return to headquarters at Bondy. On my way I learned that the Emperor was already near the barriers. Turning in that direction I met Colonel Brozin, who had told me of Rapatel's death at Fère-Champenoise. He exclaimed: 'Where the hell have you been hiding? They are looking for you everywhere.' 'What for?' I asked. 'You are appointed Commandant of Paris, and General Sacken – Governor. Make haste; they are waiting for you.' Before I had recovered from my astonishment I heard General Sacken himself calling me: 'I was despairing of finding you, but we have no time to lose. I am glad the Emperor has chosen you because you are a Frenchman, and it will show the Parisians that he wishes them well. As for me, I rejoice to have near me, working with me, the brother of one who was for two years my Chief of Staff, and whose death I greatly mourn. You will take the command of three battalions of Russian Guards. They are drawn up near here; I have added two cannon. You will go to the Hôtel de Ville, and take possession of it in the name of the [Russian] Emperor. You will leave your cannon and two battalions there, and with the third battalion you will go to the Élysée, which is assigned as a residence for the Emperor of Russia, his staff and chancellery. Afterwards, you will consult with the Prefect of the Seine, and the Municipality of Paris, with regard to billets, rations, forage and accommodation for our sick and wounded at the hospitals. Two officers of the National Guard will be in attendance to guide and protect you, but act prudently and avoid any incidents. You will choose a suitable residence for me, and come and tell me where it is. Go, be prudent, and firm.'

Imagine my astonishment, delight and confusion! I was dumbfounded by this totally unexpected command. Beside myself with joy, that I should thus make my entry into this great city that I had left ten years before under such sad circumstances . . . But there was neither time nor possibility for reflection – I was carried along by the torrent of events.

I made my entry by the Rue du Faubourg-Saint-Martin. I chose Montpezet as aide-de-camp, and M. de Zasse as major de la place . . . Just as I was about to give the word of command to my battalions 'Forward! March!,' one of the officers of the National Guard referred to by General Sacken came forward to escort me. Imagine our mutual surprise when I recognised Albert de Brancas, the future Duc de Cerest, and he found an intimate friend in the Russian officer charged to take possession of the Hôtel de Ville in the name of the [Russian] Emperor . . . We greeted one another most cordially; then M. de Brancas, turning to the crowd around us, said: 'Parisians! The Emperor of Russia gives you a pledge of his goodwill towards this great city. He has just appointed this officer, his aide-de-camp, as Commandant. He is a fellow-countryman, a native of Paris, a friend whom I have found again, and I present him to you as a friend of yours.' A murmur of approval greeted these words; my name flew from mouth to mouth, and as we were quite close to the barrier, and the street, Rochechouart, the effect was complete. The other officer of the National Guard was the handsome Count Albert d'Orsay, also a good friend of mine; he had just been thrown from his horse on the pavement of the Faubourg Saint-Martin, and was being carried home on a stretcher. I pressed his hand as he passed.

I reached the Hôtel de Ville without opposition; I drew up my troops in battle formation on the Place de Grève, and went up to the rooms of the Prefect, the Comte de Chabrol. He received me very coldly, and resisted everything I asked. I therefore felt obliged to speak harshly with him. I repeated that I was responsible for taking possession of the Hôtel de Ville with two battalions of Russian Guards and two artillery pieces, and for securing the Place de Grève and the palace on behalf of the Emperor of Russia and the Allied sovereigns, and I intended to carry out these orders at once: 'Therefore, monsieur,' I told him. 'I have not come to ask you. I am here to give you orders and demand that you to obey all requests that I consider necessary for the Allied army. To give you an idea of the good intentions of His Majesty Emperor Alexander and his benevolence for France, the city of Paris and for the [French] people, he chose me, Count

Rochechouart, your compatriot, to discuss with you all the details of the occupation of the capital by an army of 150,000 men. So it is with me, monsieur, that you have to decide these serious issues.' M. de Chabrol at once adopted a different tone, and assured me that he was entirely at my service. I asked him to assemble the twelve mayors of Paris, while I went to carry out the orders of the Governor, General Sacken.

I left M. de Zasse at the Hôtel de Ville, with the two battalions, to arrange billets and rations, and with my third battalion I took possession of the Élysée. I installed the Emperor's military household in this palace, I chose the residence of General Hulin, the late Governor of Paris, on the Place Vendôme, for my staff and myself, and finding nothing suitable for General Sacken near the Élysée, I selected for him the house of M. Roy on the rue de la Chaussée d'Antin. All these arrangements being completed, I rejoined the Emperor and the King of Prussia on the Place Louis XV. The Generalissimo Prince Schwarzenberg was parading the Allied army before Their Majesties. Napoleon's latest reports had represented this army as exhausted, disorganised and reduced to inefficiency. Instead of this, the Parisians, who gathered in great crowds, watched for three hours the Russian Guards, in splendid uniform, marching past; the Prussian Royal Guards, less numerous, but equally fine troops; the entire corps of Hungarian grenadiers in martial array; at least 20,000 Cossacks or Kalmyks, and another 35,000 cavalrymen from three nations, followed by 400 cannon with all their trains. This display of overwhelming force seemed to make a great impression on the Parisians. The most numerous and brilliant staff ever assembled completed the picture. Add to this, an electrified crowd, shouts from more than a hundred thousand voices, 'Long live the Emperor Alexander! Long live the King of Prussia! Long live the King! Long live the Allies! Long live our Liberators,' mingled with words of command in Russian and German, the sound of carriages, horses and marching infantry. The scene was truly indescribable . . .

After informing General Sacken about arrangements for lodgings, I was about to withdraw when he told me of a decision that had just been taken by the Allied sovereigns. The Russian General, Count Sacken, was retained as Governor of Paris and three Commandants – Russian, Austrian and Prussian – had been each given four arrondissements under their orders, in which they should billet the officers of their nation. The commands of the twelve districts of Paris were distributed as follows:

The first, second, third and fourth were under the command of Colonel Count Rochechouart, Aide-de-Camp to the Emperor of Russia.

The fifth, sixth, seventh and eighth districts were under the command of the Austrian Major-General Hertzogenberg, who was an émigré whose French name was Comte de Pecadeuc; in Breton, his name meant 'duke's mountain' and it was literally translated into German as 'Hertzogenberg'.

The ninth, tenth, eleventh and twelfth districts were under the command of Prussian Major-General Count von Goltz, who replaced another general who refused this commission.

The headquarters of the Russian Emperor was installed at the Élysée while the palace was prepared, Alexander agreed to enjoy for several days hospitality of Prince Talleyrand's house at 2 rue Saint-Florentin, which before the Revolution was owned by the Duc de l'Infantado.

The headquarters of the King of Prussia was set up in the house of Prince Eugene de Beauharnais at the rue de Bourbon. Prussia bought this building to house its embassy.

We placed at the disposal of the Emperor of Austria and his suite the house of Prince de Wagram [Alexander Berthier] at the Boulevard des Capucines, which later became the Ministry of Foreign Affairs.

Due to the lack of space in Paris, the palace of Saint-Cloud was assigned to Prince Schwarzenberg and his numerous staff officers. The wide array of Russian, English, Austrian, Swedish, Prussian and German uniforms had caused confusion, so to avoid future incidents, all Allied officers were ordered to wear a white armband on their right arm. We hoped that this colour was chosen to demonstrate our favour for the Bourbons, but that was not true. White was simply selected because it could be easily identified at all times, day or night. The Royalists of Paris, however, attached great importance to the colour of this armband, even though it was just a coincidence . . . [From the French in Rochechouart, *Souvenirs*]

Eduard von Löwenstern

The whole army was occupied with their personal hygiene; and in the morning at eight o'clock. Count Pahlen with his entire cavalry was standing in front of Porte-du-Trone. The barriers were still closed. I and Taube were curious enough to slip in the suburb of St. Antoine. The people here, so famous in the annals of the Revolution, also put fear and terror into me – for we had barely gone a couple of hundred paces when we saw ourselves surrounded by a mass of people whose angry, twisted faces and expressions accompanied by swearing and threats unsettled me.

Since I saw how unfortunate my situation was, I, appearing quiet, continued on my way and went into an open store as if I had come to buy something. The shop was immediately surrounded and only with difficulty could the merchant prevent the angry half-naked fellows from coming in. I played the calm one and walked firmly into the middle of the crowd of people. All of them stared at me, only an old stinking woman smelling of brandy and garlic put her fist under my nose and screeched in my face: '*Qu'est-ce-que tu veux, bougre de cosaque, no, veux-tu casaquer!*' I spat and this brave deed caused the loud laughter to increase, since I also laughed heartily. Taube was standing in the meantime in the shop. Nearby National Guardmen came very *à propos* to help us. The old fury was shoved aside. These people put us in their middle and led us out of the barrier without our being seen by Pahlen. Soon afterwards, the barrier was opened and Count Pahlen entered the city at the head of his light cavalry. White cloths were waving from all of the windows. The people screamed and pushed toward us. All of the windows, doors, and roofs were full of people. Only with difficulty did we force our way through the crowd with drawn sabres. Our corps was designated to follow the enemy [toward Fontainebleau]. So [Taube and I] went along Faubourg-St.-Antoine, over the square where the Bastille had stood earlier, over the Austerlitz Bridge, and past the Jardin-des-Plantes through the boulevard to the street from Fontainebleau. I took leave of the Count for an hour. Since we could not see anything in such a short time, we decided at least to get something to eat. We entered a bad inn in the outskirt St. Charneaux. Immediately a crowd gathered to look at our people and give them wine and bread. When we wanted to leave again, two of our hussars were so drunk that they could barely hold themselves on their horses. In Rungis that belonged to a woman dancer at the opera, we found the Count. Our Hussars had taken 700–800 *traineurs* [stragglers] prisoner on the *chaussée* to Fontainebleau; and at Chevilly, we came upon the [French] rearguard. We spent the night here.

Toward noon, we saw the enemy in the Ballee-de-Montmorency. Pahlen stopped at Bourgneuf. Through deserters, we learned that Napoleon himself had been in Ivisy [Ivry?] in the night and had spent the night in the postal inn *Cour de France* [Court of France]. I immediately had to mount up to bring the news to the Emperor as quickly as possible in Paris. An acquaintance gave me five ducats; and thus I galloped off toward the imperial city, my loyal Isyumov behind me. I rode as fast as my horse could go in order to reach Paris by evening. It was already beginning to turn dark when I rode into the Barriere. At the Jardin-des-Plantes on the Austerlitz Quay, I went into a pub, the *Cheval Rouge* [Red Horse], left my Cossack and horse and climbed into a bad cab that took me to the *Élysée Napoleon* where Emperor Alexander was residing. The adjutant on duty took my dispatch and took it to the Emperor. Soon I was handed a letter from him to Schwarzenberg, to whom I, accompanied by a military policeman, was to go and hand it to myself. Schwarzenberg was living in his own hotel. I found him just wanting to sit down to eat surrounded by a large number of generals. I gave him the Emperor's letter and Pahlen's dispatches. Since I had absolutely no desire immediately to be sent head over heels to the advance-guard, I hid behind the broad back of a Bavarian general and softly snuck out the door again. I heard my name being called; but with three jumps, I was down the stairs, jumped into a fiacre and drove off before they could catch me.

Now I was free as a bird. But where was I supposed to stay? That was an important question which despite considering this and that I could not answer. My whole wealth consisted of five ducats. My fiacre had already cost me one. In *Cheval Rouge,* I had had to pay for my Cossacks and horses; thus I had much too little to take quarters in a hotel. I also did not want to bivouac in the middle of a street in Paris.

For better or worse, I had to go into some house. But before acting upon this desperate decision, I wanted to try to find Woldemar and Georges, who certainly were in Paris. It was no easy matter to find them in the turmoil. I thought of a trick with which I was exceedingly successful. The first Frenchman whom I caught I asked in which hotel can you dine the best and not only that, the most expensive. The man seemed surprised at my question since my rather shabby Hussar skin and my entire clothing did not look like an exceedingly well-filled purse. He named the *Beauvilliers, Bery, Les Trois-Frères-provinciaux* in the *Palais-Royal, Nicole, Hardy* on the Boulevard-des-Italiens, in short, a lot of the best restaurants. I however remained persistent. He should tell me the one where one paid the most: 'Good' said he, 'if your money is burning such a hole in your pocket, then go to *Rober-au-Salon-des-Etrangers.* There you will indeed pay for every little thing a couple of *Napoleonsdors* more than in the rest of Paris.' Otherwise, he did not know one that was more expensive. Oho! I thought *Robert* is my man. Where it is the most expensive that is where I will certainly find Woldemar. I thanked the man who gave me a surprised look, shrugged his shoulders, and probably thought me insane.

As I entered the room at *Robert*'s the first thing I saw were both of my gentlemen brothers and Count Modene sitting at an imperially-set table. You can imagine their astonishment how and with what means I was able to find them in Paris. [My brother] Woldemar almost made himself sick from laughing at the means I had used. After lunch, we drove to the Theatre-Français where *Pizarro* [by August von Kotzebue] was playing. In the evening, we dined splendidly in the *Palais-Royal.* Then I went to the *Grand-Hotel-Richelieu* vis-à-vis *La-Chaussée-d'Autin,* where I lived together with both of my brothers. We drank coffee at home; then it was off to breakfast in *Rocher-de-Cancale* where we drank oysters in champagne. At noon, we dined at *Robert*'s or *Beauvillier*'s; to the opera or a theatre, in the evening, we dined at *Berry*'s in *Palais-Royal.* Thus we spent several days in the lap of luxury; and by doing nothing, we had no time to see the curiosities of the imperial city. After dining once more at noon with my brothers at *Nicole* in the Boulevard-des-Italians, I hired a fiacre and went to the *Cheval-Rouge,* where I found my Cossack felt completely at home. He had so ingratiated himself during his stay with the innkeeper and had been so useful during the tumult that he, out of gratefulness, had made the bill for him and my horse as small as possible. Thus, I left Paris for the first time without having seen anything but the city itself. I had not been in either the *Musée Napoleon,* or in the *Pantheon,* or *au pêtit Augustin,* or in the *Louvre,* or *aux Invalides* or the *Tuileries*; in short, I had done nothing else in Paris but eaten, drunk, kissed pretty girls, visited almost all of the theatres and gawked at the houses and streets. I had been with Georges in the *Jardin-des-Plantes* where I saw the bears that had just devoured a veteran who had fallen into them. Several Tivoli balls entertained me royally. Among others a French officer with one foot and a crutch danced all of the contra dances. *Robert* and *Beauvilliers* replaced for me the *Musee Napoleon*. The happy girls in *Palais-Royal* or the crowds waving back and forth on the Boulevard-des-Italiens interested me more than the limping one-eyed invalids *aux Invalides*. I had visited all of the theatres except for *a-la-Porte-St. Martin*.

After paying for my Cossack Isyumov, I galloped in a good mood to the *Barriere*. After looking for a long time, I found Count Pahlen with his numerous main headquarters in the Valle-de-Montmorency in Château Fleury. At first the Count made a sour face that I had stayed away for so long without permission; but what was I to do. You do not come to Paris every day. None of the gentlemen had been in Paris yet. I therefore had to tell about it until my chops were foaming. Everything on and about me was admired. Mr. Armand had cut my hair. I'd had my trousers tailored. I played the Parisian dandy *en merveille* and amused the whole audience with fact and fancy.

In Fleury another joy awaited me. I received the Order of St. Anne around the neck for the battle of Brienne, was transferred for the battle of Paris as Captain of Cavalry to the [Russian] Imperial Guard Hussar Regiment and received the Prussian Order *Pour le merité* for the of La-Fère-Champenoise. Therefore I was now Lieutenant of the Army, thus already not an unimportant person in the nation. I was only twenty-three years old, decorated with several great orders. You can imagine my joy and pride to be more than my older comrades. I had served as Captain of Cavalry for only six months and twenty-two days. If this continues, I inevitably would have had to become at least a general in a couple of years. We lived merrily and blithely in the marvellous Fleury. Everything seemed united in providing us with a pleasant stay here, the mild pleasant time of year, the beautiful palace, our apartment, my room in the library, the large gardens next to their romantic surroundings, what could be more heavenly. Turnau and Schilling quarrelled because of a chair at table. As always in such cases, I was both of their seconds. They duelled in the garden, and an insignificant hit on Schilling's cheek ended the fight without the spilling of a large amount of blood.

Peace was signed in Paris on 18 May between King Louis XVIII and the Allied monarchs. Hurrahs rang out in all of the bivouacs, and everyone gave into to his joy. Champagne and burgundy bubbled in the goblets and flowed into the wide throats of the heroes. Anyone with two ducats in his pocket went to Paris. Château Fleury was soon emptied of guests; and after a couple of days, I, poor devil, remained without credit, without money, totally alone there. As beautiful as the palace, the garden, and the surroundings at Fleury were, I soon knew that I am no Arcadian shepherd only living from nature's beauty; but that

I could very comfortably starve to death in the midst of the beautiful rooms or green arbours. Therefore, I left Château Fleury and moved to Courcoronne where Taube was stationed with the Imperial [First] Squadron.

I rode to Corbeil every day. Here I settled on the bridge and let the French marshals and generals riding from Fontainebleau to Paris file past me. In Corbeil our Cossacks together with the French *Chasseurs* held the advance-guard positions. Every one riding past had to stop and produce his permit. Thus, I had time enough to learn their names and even get to know them. Here I saw Marshals Ney, Lefebvre, Marmont, Mortier, Macdonald, Augereau, Oudinot, the Generals Lefebvre-Desnouettes, Petit, Gérard, and several others. I stayed in Courcornne for the Easter holidays. Ilovaiski XII gave the village inhabitants several *fêtes champetres*. There was dancing and drinking, and we were fishing in muddy waters.

When the Sumy Regiment received orders to march, I went with it. My memories of this march have remained so pleasant. We went through an earthly paradise made more beautiful by the glorious time of year. During the war, I had not been able to see the joyful national character of the French. With peace it now totally revealed itself to me. Everywhere you saw friendly, happy faces. Everywhere joy and song reigned. Young girls played in the streets *volant* or *jeu de diable*. Our Corps stayed in Beauvais. Pahlen's main headquarters went to Marseille-en-Picardie. Since no good quarters could be found in the small town, we went to Château Achy, a lieue [4km] from Marseille-en- Picardie. The palace was spacious and offered all of us the greatest comfort. The owner of Château Achy was Count Clermont Tonnerre, who was in Paris. Only a little infamous *Abbe* acted as host in his absence. Achy is in a charming area of Picardie, but lacking totally in society for us. Pahlen and most of our gentlemen were absent or in Paris.

Since I did not have even a heller of capital, I had to stay in Achy even as boring as it was. Taube was staying in Gremonvilliers in an old knightly palace and Nicholas Read in La Fontaine. I visited both of them very often. The peasant girls in La Fontaine sang complete ballads in a monotone for us that became quite boring, since the singers were anything but pretty. The Sumy Regiment was stationed in Songent, a charming little city. General [Alexander] Seslavin was living in the palace. The Songent family was home and often put on little gatherings for us in the palace. Evenings we danced with the daughters to music provided by our officers. The youngest, Mlle. Songent, a quite pretty, shapely girl, had by a strange accident lost all of her teeth at the age of sixteen. You can imagine how this disfigured her. That is why she seldom spoke with anyone and always withdrew. By happenstance in the city, I had found a sweetheart, a fat little Fleming, who with her mother was living here, where they had bought a house and were living very well from their rents. I had made their acquaintance through Captain of Cavalry Tamilov, who was living in a wing of the house. The little one was very good to me; and before I could even dream of it, I had a love affair with her that gave me a great deal of pleasure. Toward evening, I always rode in from Achy that was three lieues [12km] from Songent, left my horse with the regiment's adjutant, and in the garden of the city's preacher, she granted me a rendezvous. I climbed over the wall and she had used another entrance that was hidden behind a rose hedge.

The little Abbot in Achy, through his stinginess and his scheming pushed us so far that we in all seriousness wanted to thrash him. Even I had grabbed him one time by the scruff of the neck, and woe betide him if Pahlen had not just arrived from Paris at that moment. Thus, I let the little rogue go in order to avoid any unpleasantness. This lesson nevertheless improved the Abbot, who had more respect for me and had better wine served at meals. Gradually, the gentlemen of our headquarters gathered. The Count also left Paris and move to Château Achy. Nice billiards, thousands of little games, and an exquisite library were available to us and letting us spend our time pleasantly. We drank tea outside, went for walks until dinnertime; and only late at night did everyone look for his bed. Gradually, the Count let his numerous main headquarters scatter. Lützow, Berg, and Tiesenhausen went to Paris. Budberg followed his brother who commanded an [Russian] Imperial Guard Cuirassier Regiment. Turnau and Babst on the Count's recommendation transferred to the [Russian] Imperial Guard Light Infantry Regiment that Potapov was forming in Versailles. Schilling returned to the Bavarian mission. Kavtereov disappeared. One of Korssakov's adjutants was chased out of Fleury for cheating at gambling. Around the person of the Count only I, Kolatshevski, Novossilzev, and Macdonald remained. Soon we also received orders and the march route to Russia.

General Order to the Army, 2 April 1814

The capture of Paris was a culmination of a two-year-long struggle by the Russian army. It was appropriate then to remind the Russian troops of their accomplishments and celebrate victory.

Soldiers !

Your perseverance and bravery have delivered the French Nation, oppressed by a Tyrant who acted only for himself, and who forgot what he owed to an esteemed and generous people. The French Nation has declared itself for us; our cause has become theirs and our magnanimous Monarchs have promised them protection and support. From this moment the French are our friends: let your arms destroy the small number of unfortunates who still surround the ambitious Napoleon; but let the cultivator and peaceable inhabitant be treated with consideration and friendship, as allies united by the same interests.

Barclay de Tolly

Given at headquarters, Paris, April 2, 1814.

[From *The Gentleman's Magazine, and Historical Chronicle*, 1814]

Sergei Mayevskii

Mayevskii commanded the 13th Jager Regiment.

To describe Paris is akin to attempting to build new pyramids of Egypt. I must note that I found widespread kindness among the Parisians, which is to their great honour, and even more importantly, this people never attempted any treacherous violence against us. A Frenchman who tainted himself with the murder of an unarmed man, would have been denounced as a rogue, ceased to have an honourable name and been shunned by society. The Parisian passion is for news, levity and entertainment. Their streets and squares resemble waves as crowds of people moved around and supplant each other. But the rabble is rabble everywhere and it follows its base instincts and is as equally capable of attempting ridiculous and great. The very day of our entry into the city, the rabble wanted to tear down Napoleon's bronze statue [at the Place Vendôme] but soon came to its senses . . .

The Palais-Royal is what the bourse is in England. At seven o'clock in the evening both a marquis with his wife and his filthy stoker with his grimy spouse (wearing wooden shoes) rush to the Palais-Royal. Men walk hand in hand with their women. Despite the presence of numerous people, I witnessed commotion and noise only on two occasions, and even then they lasted but a moment. Both the marquis and stoker give each other just enough space so as not to touch each other with shoulders. This is quite unlike us who, just like Turks, like to push and shove each other which caused daily fist-fights on Corfu. Our famed mathematician Rakhmanov could not tolerate that the Germans did not let him pass and did not even remove their hats in front of him. To the great credit of the French nation, everyone here is preoccupied with himself and does not resort to that contemptuous smile that distinctly reveals one's status and appearance. . .

Around eleven o'clock in the evening the Parisian sirens came out of their lairs and lure the pleasure seekers. Knowing that Russians are generous and prone to sin, they almost forcefully dragged our young officers into their dens. I remarked about this to one old Frenchman, who replied, 'Everyone is given various means by nature. There is nothing surprising if they are peddling what comprises their main offering.' But even here one can see a certain [French] trait: a woman who lured you into her lair, home or attic, would never try to rob you. In fact, on the contrary, she is anxious to maintain the reputation of her house and would even give you a [business] card so you can easily find her in the future. The proprietor and physician are responsible for her health, although in this regard one cannot trust them.

In Paris, there are five or six different entertainments at every step. In one place you might see one magician demonstrating birds taking a fortress by assault while another shows fleas dragging, loading and firing a cannon. Just then a third one appears in between them shouting as loudly as he can, 'Come here, I will show you what you have never seen before!' The crowd rushes to him and he, having fleeced the people of their money, makes some sharp joke that makes people laugh and ready for another 'miracle'. Thus Paris spends its days and nights. While some are entertained by magicians, others go underground where they are treated to cheap popular theatres but many of them are so good that [I prefer] them to many of our festival performances. These theatres feature deaf and mute [actors] but you will not be able to distinguish them from healthy actors . . . Visitors pay nothing to enter and the proprietor's main income is from the sale of drinks. If I had authority I would have made it a state policy to reduce fees for public entertainment, including theatres, so as to make it more accessible and change public mores and educate the entire nation. [In Paris] all of these entertainments and pleasures are enjoyed by the rabble and the middle class. People of more refined sensibilities have numerous superb theatres and the Grand Opera that has no rival in all of Europe.

In Paris, the spirit of entertainment and levity is so widespread that everyone, from the highest officials to the lowest odd-jobber, has his own hours for walking, resting and entertainment in one of numerous public spaces. If you go the Tuileries Garden on any given day, you will find numerous people strolling around and further away you might observe crowds dancing that sometimes involve hundreds of people. The Palais-Royal is filled with people twenty-four hours a day: in the gardens, taverns, shops and cafés, in short everywhere, there are crowds of people. The Champs Élyssee is usually crowded on holidays and it must be noted that it offers nothing but an impressive name. A small grove, a small house and sands – this is what people call the Champs Élyssee . . .

Parisians have a passion for news that is so powerful that there is not a single place, not even a tavern, that does not have its own placards and broadsheets. All around myself I saw people deeply immersed in reading and conversing about the world! [From the Russian text in S. Mayevskii, 'Moi vek, ili Istoriya. . .']

Alexander Chertkov

An officer in the elite Life Guard Horse Regiment.

On 18 [30] March, a short but fierce battle took place near the village of Belleville, at the gates of Paris. . . We entered Paris through the gates of St. Martin and then proceeded by boulevards towards the Place de Louis XV (also known as Place de la Concorde or Place de la Révolution), the Champs Élysées, Pont d'Iena. Champ de Mars and finally reached the École Militaire, which was assigned to us, the Prussian guardsmen, [and] the [Life Guard] Izmailovskii and Finlyandskii regiments. Several days later the Chevalier

Guard [Regiment] and the Prussians were moved to Versailles while our regiment and the Life Guard Cossack Regiment stayed at the École Militaire. The officers had quarters in the city and Tatishev and I received apartments in the house of Margueré at Rue St. André-des-Arts No. 35; one month later we were moved to another apartment at Rue des Grands Augustins No. 5. Officers, who wanted to stay in barracks, received 5 francs per day for food allowance while staff officers got 10 francs.

The cost of renting a carriage for an entire year is some 6,000 francs but, in general, only those having an annual income of over 90,000 francs can afford a carriage. At Palais-Royal, merchants, restaurant owners and others pay 3,000 francs for a place in the arcade. No. 113 at the Palais-Royal: the third floor is a gathering of prostitutes; the second floor is for roulette, the entresol is occupied by a moneylender and the ground floor is a weapons shop. This house is a precise and true picture of what the revelry of the passions can lead to. Descending into a basement at Piat (Palais-Royal) one can order a lunch of six dishes and pay a modest price of 1 franc and 50 centimes. It is said that between 4,000 and 5,000 rag pickers [staryevshik] reside here.

The Hôtel des Invalides shelters, feeds and clothes some 4,000 veterans, most of them lacking a leg, hand and almost all of them bearing the scars of glory. When entering the church [Saint-Louis-des-Invalides], you can see Turenne's tomb on the right-hand side and on the left, across from it, the tomb of Vauban. The former was built under Louis XIV while the latter was built under Bonaparte. Inside the church, on the left-hand side there is a capella draped in black – it was here that the former emperor ordered to be placed three coffins with the remains of [Marshal] Bessières, Duroc and Laribossières before their final resting-places at the Pantheon were completed. Franconi was displaying a white horse that was so well trained that on his voice command she could pick up a handkerchief, gloves, spurs, whip, etc. She accomplished all orders at once, picking things up with her teeth and bringing them to him.

All day long eight theatres are staging plays: 1. Le Théâtre Français; 2. Le Grand Opéra, which stages opulent operas and ballets; 3. L'Odéon, also known as Théâtre de l'Impératrice, where Italians, and occasionally the French, are playing; 4. Le Vaudeville, where only vaudevilles are shown; 5. Les Variétés, where Potier and Brunet shine in operettas and comedies; four plays are usually staged every day; 6. L'Opéra Comique, also known as Théâtre Faudeau, where, as the name implies, comedies are shown; 7. Le Théâtre de la Gaïeté; 8. and finally, l'Ambigu Comique; the last two theatres show melodramas and short plays (the theatre near the St. Martin gates is closed).

These theatres are so packed in the evenings that if you are only half an hour late, there will be no seats left for you. Such is the Parisians' passion for theatre. An enormous crowd of people gathers before the ticket booths open and waits in theatre vestibules. But if a new play or one on a current issue is staged or if a king or other august person attends it, then one has to come to the theatre three or four hours before the curtain is raised. Just imagine that after experiencing all these difficulties, you finally enter the hall and find your seat only to spend next three or four hours sitting constrained by your neighbours' elbows, suffocating from unbearable heat, and forced to give up your space three or four times (especially if you are in front seats) to women who are in habit of coming late; in Paris politeness requires you to pay respects even to grisettes. Even if the curtain has finally been raised and you think that everything will be fine now and you will at last enjoy performances of the best French actors, your hopes will be soon dashed: aside from deafening applause which will always distract you at the most interesting moments, if nature calls and you have to leave the hall for a few minutes or if, during the entr'acte, you want some fresh air, then you must be assured that upon returning back you will find your hat thrown on the floor and your place occupied. Then you have to choose one from two solutions: you either challenge the man who took your seat, which will inevitably end with an appointment in the Bois de Boulogne (which happened to many our officers) or you decide to leave the hall, which is more prudent since, in the end, does a human life mean so little so as to have yourself killed over a seat in a theatre? [. . .] Here are prices for the best seats in various theatres: at le Théâtre Français – about 5 francs; at Les Variétés – 3 ½ francs; at l'Odéon and le Vaudeville – . . . francs; at l'Opéra Comique – 5 francs; at Le Théâtre de la Gaïeté and l'Ambigu Comique – . . . francs.

Beside these theatres, there are other places of entertainment, such as:

Franconi's Cirque Olympique – art of horse riding, acrobatics on horseback [*voltage*], and a peculiar ballet pantomime.
Olivier's Cabinet – card tricks, phantasmagoria, etc.
Lebretin's Cabinet de physique – demonstration of various physical and psychological experiments, summoning of spirits, etc.
Mr. Pierre's Cabinet mécanique which organises very interesting chiaroscuro shows.
Les Ombres Chinoises.
Les Cosmoramas.
Les Panoramas – there are currently four of them: of Naples, Boulogne-sur-Mer, Léopoldsberg and Amsterdam; the latter town is beautifully shown in wintertime, with all streets, roofs and trees covered with snow.
Les Panstéoramas, which are relief models of various cities.

Franconi's Cirque occupies the same place where the Convent of the Capucins existed before the Revolution. Monks had been living here twenty years ago but now the church has been turned into stables. Autres temps, autres moeurs! The old church on Rue des Grands Augustins, whose dome has been demolished, is now a market where meat, poultry and other goods are sold.

M. Fontin has been selling cheap apples (just 3 sous for apple) in one of Palais-Royal's passages but still managed to give his daughter a 60,000-franc dowry. The owner of the Salon de la Paix (in Palais-Royal), where they clean footwear, pays 3,000 francs a year in rent. One must note that some 60,000 shoes must pass through these cleaners' hands to cover the rent alone, not to mention the pay for 5–6 artisans [artistes-décrotteurs], subscription to three newspapers as well as various shoe colours that are applied to brushes. The most skilled masters are paid 12 francs per service.

[. . .] The claqueurs and the siffleurs from the parterre often incite fights during performances. It is said that blood was shed during the first staging of *Colombine*.

[. . .] Some streets in Paris are so narrow that four people cannot pass in them. In others, if two carriages encounter each other, one must move back and allow the other to pass. Most streets are extremely dirty and dark because of the seven- and eight-storey houses that stand above them. But there are very beautiful streets as well, for example all the boulevards and streets built under Napoleon. Near Palais-Royal, there is a house in which I counted nine storeys, not counting attic and basement.

One Frenchman, while conversing with me, frankly admitted that most of French clergymen cannot write and that his wife's record of baptism [éxtrait baptistaire] reads, 'Marie, fils d'un tel,' instead of 'Marie, fille d'un tel.'

The French never eat bread with soup made of vegetables or vermicelli, and laugh at us every time we eat it with bread.

Police regulations require payment of 1½ francs for a trip in a fiacre and 1 franc for a cabriolet. We usually paid 25–30 francs to hire a fiacre for an entire day and about the same amount for a cabriolet, which is, without a doubt, a more preferable carriage since it always has a better horse and, therefore, moves faster. Because, if walking fast, one can arrive before a fiacre or at least at the same time with it; these fiacres are harnessed with poor horses. . .

L'Hôtel-Dieu is a hospital where free treatment is provided to people of both sexes. It is located on the bank of the Seine River, which makes it the most healthy of the city hospitals, you will never contract a disease called hospital fever [fièvre d'hôpital] there. Its wards are spacious and, most of them, high-ceilinged; the sisters of the Order of St. Augustin look after the patients. In each ward, patients are cared for by one nun and two novices, who are assisted by many servants [servants et domestiques]. Novices wear white clothing while nuns cover their heads with black cloths; on Sundays, all of them wear black. They entered the monastery and the hospital serves as that monastery. There are eight physicians who treat patients. The building itself is ancient and it is said that it is 700–800 years old; at first sight, it is not eye-catching. Looking from the Seine, it blocks and conceals the riverbanks from two sides. There is even a gallery built over the river that can serve as a bridge connecting the Île de la Cité with the Faubourg St. Germain. The entrance is from the square or parvis of the Notre Dame Cathedral. The hospital can receive over 3,000 patients of both sexes. It is said that the Parisian hospitals and shelters cost the government about 7–8 million francs a year.

Along the embankments, one can by very good books quite cheaply from bouquinistes. I bought Brisson's three-volume *Dictionnaire de Physique* for ten francs, and *Médailes du reigne de Louis XV* for 1 franc.

[. . .]

During our stay in Paris, a young man was guillotined for producing counterfeit coins. This is the easiest death one can imagine for criminals: they probably do not suffer at all since as soon as the executioner pulls the lever, the criminal's head falls off. Executions are usually performed on the Place de Grève where scaffolds are built on such occasions. We paid 2½ francs per person to watch this execution from a window of a nearby house. [From the French text in A. Chertkov, 'Mon Itinéraire . . .']

S. Khomutov

A staff officer in the Russian imperial headquarters.

20 March [1 April, Friday]

We remained in Paris and I spent the entire day moving around the city in cabriolet, fiacre, on horse and on foot and visited the Pantheon, Louvre, Tuilleries. But one day is just not enough to see everything worthy of attention in this great, sophisticated and glorious city. The Parisians desire to see the Bourbons on the throne and they all wear white cockades. The Senate announced that Napoleon had ceased to govern, and it established a provisional government. It appears that Bonaparte has been for ever deprived of the throne which he had seized through terrible crimes and the blood of many of his unfortunate victims. He is approaching [Paris] with his army, but no one is afraid of him anymore and a large part of the [French] army abandoned him.

In the evening I went to the opera. At first the play *Trajan*, appropriate for current circumstances, was supposed to be staged. But the Emperor [Alexander] was unwilling to accept such a flattering expression of the Parisians' devotion and requested to change the play. The hall was already full of spectators when one of the actors came out on the stage and announced that the play *Vestal Virgin* would be offered instead. This announcement was met by a universal disapproval and a terrible clamour arouse, people banged their feet, hands, and canes and yelled '*Trajan, Trajan!*' The same actor then announced that the play was changed on the request of Emperor Alexander and the commotion immediately ceased. [Instead,] a loud and joyous roar began at the appearance of the Russian Emperor and the Prussian. People demanded the removal of an eagle emblazoned on Napoleon's box. Enthusiasm increased with every passing minute. People keenly welcomed the old song 'Henri IV' and wept, calling for the restoration of the Bourbons to the throne [of France].

21 March [2 April, Saturday]
The main headquarters of Prince Schwarzenberg moved to Chevilly, two miles from Paris. I travelled there and found nice quarters for the General [Toll] and myself.

22 March [3 April, Sunday]
Today is Palm Sunday. We prayed in a Catholic church. I am not as sad about leaving Paris as I am about not being able to hear our mass during the Week of Passion.

23 March [4 April, Monday]
We remained at Chevilly and the Week of Passion began, Count Apraksin invited me to a lenten breakfast which consisted of caviar and horseradish. From our conversation with Novosiltsev (General Seslavin's adjutant who ate breakfast with us), we learned that Prince Schwarzenberg went to visit our outposts and met with Marshals Marmont, Ney and Macdonald, who agreed to abandon Napoleon and accept the Bourbons, whom the French people unanimously desire on the throne. Since we had no precise news, General Toll sent me to the outposts to verify the information. Arriving at the château where the meeting [between Schwarzenberg and the Marshals] was held and asked Count Radetzky about it. He confirmed that the Marshals had forsaken Napoleon and sent a messenger to our Emperor asking for an audience. I returned to General Toll with this news around 1 a.m.

24 March [5 April, Tuesday]
We learned that Prince Schwarzenberg had returned to Paris. General Toll decided to go back as well and sent me to get new quarters. It is so much better to be in Paris than in that small village. Now it seems we can expect peace very soon since Napoleon had formally abdicated his throne. I chose for the General the same apartment where he stayed before while I myself settled at M. Tercy, my previous host, who very kindly received me. Having arranged everything, I went to see Prince Volkonsky, meet my friend and gaze at crowds that surrounded the palace and eagerly awaited the Emperor [Alexander]. He

soon travelled to a church and I followed him. At lunch, General Toll told me that Count Kankrin promised to distribute our pay. This news thrilled me and I rushed to share it with my friends. We ate at the Palais-Royal and then returned to the palace for all-night prayer.

25 March [6 April, Wednesday]

At the mass [held today], there was a large crowd and our entire guard cavalry since the Annunciation is their regimental holiday. We spent the entire day in our quarters and gathered at the church in the evening. After a night mass, the Emperor went to confession, asking forgiveness from all of us with an immense and touching humility. He was followed by the Grand Duke [Constantine], all the generals and then us.

26 March [7 April, Thursday]

The church was again full today. When a communion hymn [prichastnyj stix] was sung, the Emperor approached the altar, kissed icons, bowed to everyone and received Holy Communion with such trepidation and tender faith that his face seemed even more beautiful; happiness and heavenly joy sparkled in his eyes while humility and kindness, reflecting on his features, turned his face, his entire persona, into an unearthly apparition. When we approached the Cross, His Majesty congratulated us. After having lunch with my friends at Palais-Royal, I went to see M. Decre, my former tutor at boarding school. He was thrilled to see me and reminisced with me about happy years of my childhood. Leaving him I went to the palace church to listen to twelve Gospels.

27 March [8 April, Friday]

The vespers was held at 4 p.m. There were many French men and women. After the vespers, the Emperor took off his sword and gave it to his duty adjutant-general, made several deep bows, kissed the shroud and waited until everyone else had completed this holy ritual.

28 March [9 April, Saturday]

After mass I walked in the Tuilleries Gardens with Ofrosimov and Vishnyakov, visited the Invalides, and then watched as the statue of Bonaparte was removed from the Vendôme Column. The Place Vendôme was packed with people, and great efforts were made [to remove the statue]. However, the statue was firmly fixed to the column, so it was removed only with great difficulty. Napoleon signed his abdication, all of his Marshals abandoned him and his entire army left him as well. Praise the Lord! Peace has returned to Europe and Europe owes its wellbeing to our Emperor. What glory for Alexander I, what glory for Russia! I cannot thank the Heavens enough for being able to participate in this war which future generations will marvel about.

29 March [10 April, Sunday] Holy Day of Christ's Resurrection
At 12 a.m. I went with my General to the church. Everyone was waiting for Emperor, who appeared with the King of Prussia, the Crown Prince of Württemberg, Prince Schwarzenberg and General Wrede. They were followed by numerous generals from all nations who came to bow to Resurrected Christ. It seems that the faith has united all peoples on this exultant and joyous day. Mass was served with particular pageantry. The Emperor prayed fervently. His Majesty was unwilling to accept congratulations in usual time and after the mass everyone went home. But a small number of participants went to the palace, and I was among them. We congratulated the Emperor and he kissed us three times [khristosovatsya] and invited us to share a meal [razgovetsya] of the Holy Easter. The Emperor told that that the nominations submitted by Prince Volkonsky and General Toll have been all signed. I was promoted to a staff-captain and thanked the Lord for this royal benevolence. At noon, a large parade was held and the troops marched in front of the Emperor, halted on the Place de Louis XV or Concorde in the middle of which an ambon was erected on the very spot where the unfortunate Louis XVI ended his life. A liturgy for the resent victories, capture of Paris and the Bourbon restoration was served on this ambon. Guns fired one hundred and one times and joyous shouts of 'Vive Alexander I! Vive Louis XVIII!' could be heard from all directions. All participants had tears in their eyes and all kneeled in front of the compassionate God, who is the sole source of all good! After the mass the Emperor embraced the French marshals, telling them that on this day the Russians always kiss thrice [khristovatsya] with their friends

30 March [11 April, Monday]
The church was once again packed with the French curious to see the Emperor [Alexander]. Anyone desiring to attend service inside the church was allowed to get tickets from Rochechouart. I was busy preparing reports all day long and finally submitted them to General Toll in the evening.

31 March [12 April, Tuesday]
I went with Voyeikov to the Notre Dame Cathedral, where the Comte d'Artois, the brother of Louis XVIII, was expected. He arrived at 3 p.m. and the people greeted him with great joy. As he entered, loud exclamations filled the church where the service was underway. During the mass the Comte d'Artois knelt and prayed eagerly. He is not a young man [anymore] but is still fresh and his face radiated kindness,

2 [14 April, Thursday]
I visited the Gobelins Manufactory and the Zoological garden today. In the evening I went to the theatre. It was so crowded with people that I could barely move inside, but still managed to get a good seat. The Emperor [Alexander]

was expected to attend but did not arrive. The King of Prussia and his sons sat in a closed box. [People in the] parterre were yelling 'Long Live Emperor Alexander! Long Live King of Prussia! Long Live Louis XVIII, Count d'Artois, even Sacken', who also attended the play. That day the theatre staged *The Hunt of Henry IV* and I liked this play, particularly in light of current circumstances. The entire parterre was singing the song of Henry IV and everyone cried with joy. At the conclusion of the play, the actor Michot sang several couplets about the glorious events of recent past which thrilled the audience and caused thunderous applause.

4 [16 April, Saturday]
General Toll informed me that he was returning to Russia and that we will be assigned to Count Diebitsch. I was rather upset by this news since I feared that the Count will sent us to some forsaken corps. I spent the entire day thinking how I could resolve this and finally decided to ask for a furlough.

5 [17 April, Sunday]
Today I went to our General [Toll] with a furlough request. He, as usual, was very kind to me and promised to talk to Prince Volkonskii. In the afternoon he told me that my request was granted and I can return to Russia.

6–7 [18–19 April, Monday-Tuesday]
I was busy with reports and other official papers. General Toll is departing soon so I have to organise everything very soon. Orlovskii is travelling with me to Russia.

8 [20 April, Wednesday]
General Toll left today! I was distraught to say good-bye to him. It is quite heartrending to depart with such a kind superior, to whom I owe so much and with whom I spent so much time.

16 [28 April, Thursday]
The Return of Ulysses was staged today. I did not like the play, although it is written in beautiful lyrics and is played by the best actors. Talma played Ulysses.

19 [April, 1 May, Sunday]
Despite my haste, I was late for mass. The Emperor left for Compiègne to meet the King [Louis XVIII] and so the mass was held earlier than usual.

21 [April, 3 May, Tuesday]
King Louis XVIII entered his capital. In the morning I went to the Notre Dame Cathedral to wait for him but it was so hot and crowded inside it that

I returned home. At noon the gun fire announced the King's arrival to the church. I then went to the Tuilleries Garden, fought my way through the crowd and saw the parade of the French troops. The troops were poorly dressed, poorly deployed and, overall, seemed pathetic. The King did not appear for a long time so I went to the Palais-Royal, where I took a stroll with my acquaintances. I soon heard joyous exclamations and run to the street, where I witnessed the entire ceremony. Numerous well-decorated carriages preceded the golden carriages which carried Louis with the Duchess of Angoulême, the Duc de Conde and the Duc of Bourbon. The King is very fat and, people say, he cannot even walk because he suffers from gout. Military music and people's exclamations followed the King all the way to the Tuilleries Palace, where he stayed. At 9 p.m. the city was illuminated and I went with Neledinskii to watch the illuminations, then visited Prince Volkonskii's gallery to see fireworks which were quite poor. I found the illumination rather pitiable as well – what a difference compared to the one that blinds us every year at Peterhof. [From the Russian text in S. Khomutov, *Iz dnevnika svitskago ofitsera*]

Nikolai Golitsyn

An officer of the Kievskii Dragoon Regiment.

On 20 March [1 April] I received permission to travel to Paris, which I had never seen before. If I were asked what I found the most amazing, I would have replied, as a certain Venetian doge once did, by saying that I am here as a victor. Indeed, there was a dramatic contrast with all the Kalmyks and Bashkirs roaming in the stylish streets of Paris . . . That day I visited everything I could – the Tuilleries, Palais-Royale, the Opera, where the humility of our Emperor did not allow for the staging of the *Triumph of Trajan*. The play *Vestal Virgin* was staged and the public compelled the actor Lays, a diehard republican, to sing 'Vive Henri IV' against his will. To honour of our Emperor the French had already composed poems that began with 'Vive Alexandre, Vive ce Roi des Rois!' and which were greeted with deafening applause. After the play, just as our Emperor left the theatre, the crowd rushed into Napoleon's box and ripped apart the Imperial eagle, thus destroying an idol that it so adored not long time ago. A scene so worthy of the Parisians! The same fate befell on the colossal statue [of Napoleon] erected on top of the column at the Place Vendôme. [Some Parisians] threw a noose over it to bring it crashing down but the statue was made of bronze and resisted the efforts of these newly minted enthusiasts. Shortly afterwards we took measures to contain this Parisian hot air. Looking at this column, Emperor Alexander made a profound observation, 'I would have become dizzy if I were standing so high.'

Alas, my campaigning was not over as yet and I only managed some brief sight-seeing in Paris. At least I got an impression on this vast capital, the old sinner that had been abandoned by God and that for years had enjoyed an almost exclusive privilege of pestering Europe with wars and revolutions. I rejoined my general at Arpajon. We soon received order to continue military operations in the direction of Fontainebleau because the Allied sovereigns were unwilling to repeat Napoleon's mistake of idling in Moscow that cost him so dearly. As long as he was still standing on his feet, we could not afford relaxing. So we marched through Montlhéry, Limours and encountered the enemy near the town of La Ferté Allais, about 16 verstas [17km] from Fontainebleau, on 28 March [9 April]. We fired several rounds at the enemy and was startled to see that our attack caused incredible disorder in the enemy camp. Soon an enemy messenger arrived protesting what he called a violation of international law since Napoleon had already abdicated and the warring sides had concluded an armistice. This was the first we had heard about this and since we were not supposed receive such important news from a French envoy, we replied that we did not have any instructions for such an occasion and could only allow the enemy general to fall back peacefully but the town had to be surrendered. We thus seized this town but later that evening we also received a letter from General Vasilchikov, who had by now become our commander, informing us of the cessation of military operations and instructing us to halt wherever this letter found us. As the result of these new orders, which confirmed the French envoy's statements, General Emmanuel sent word to the enemy general that he had been ordered to end hostilities and was therefore ready to hand over the town of La Ferté Allais back to him. The French general naturally received the news of the armistice before us because his forces were located close to Fontainebleau where Napoleon signed the abdication document; we, meanwhile, had received our orders from Paris. However, the enemy general chose to ignore this and demanded that, in light of yesterday's events, he desired to have a hostage to ensure the safety of his troops. There was no point arguing about this and so I was sent to serve as a hostage to the French until a formal delimitation was established.

I travelled to the French camp which was commanded by General Piquet and consisted of only cavalry from the Garde d'Honneur that belonged to General Bordesoult's corps. I spent three days in the company of French officers and living with their general. They adored their Emperor and expressed extreme frustration at the misfortunes that had befallen him. They said that only bad luck forced him to abdicate his throne at a time when he had so many resources to continue fighting. They listed all these resources and argued that Napoleon could have retreated with his forces to the Département des Vosges, where, surrounded by impregnable fortresses, he could gather the remaining troops, call up the Italian Vice-Roy (Eugene) with his army, and get Davout's corps out of Hamburg, which would have given him an army of some 150,000 men. He should have then published an appeal to all of France, declaring 'la patrie en danger', abolishing the decrees of the Senate and condemning its members as traitors. This is what Napoleon should have done, these officers argued, but, alas, bad luck prevented him from doing it. I responded that the [Russian] army was still unaware of what this 'bad luck' was and instead believed in divine Providence. Among these bubblers was Pigault-Lebrun, the son of the author of somewhat libertine novels, who particularly stood out with his fascinating chatter. I was curious to meet those same cavalry officers who fought us at Reims and I was pleased to hear them describe that action as a veritable trap because they were suddenly showered with bullets from the rear. They of course referred to the attack that Colonel Skobelev launched with the Ryazanskii Regiment which routed the enemy. So our conversations were quite lively and engaging.

Among the officers visiting General Piquet I also observed a certain colonel who commanded the 10th Hussar regiment, a man with a grim appearance who always looked at me askance and never spoke a word to me. There was something revolting in his appearance. He was swarthy, balding and his face looked like a skull. General Piquet once took me aside and told me that the Colonel was incessantly pestering him with claims that next night the Allies were intended to suddenly attack and that I was sent to tempt some people to desert. Upon hearing this surprising confession, I asked General Piquet, 'Do you really believe this delirium?' Startled by my question and the brusque tone in which I made it, Piquet replied that he personally could not suppose that there would people in the Russian army capable of such dishonourable conduct, and that I must excuse the colonel's mistrust because his regiment had lost many deserters and that our attack after the armistice had been concluded provided plenty of support to deep suspicions in a man who had been burdened with so many hardships. As for a nocturnal attack, this information was based on the words of local villagers who came to the camp. 'In such a case,' I replied with a certain animation, 'I must inform you that being the sole representative of the Russian army I cannot lower myself to disapproving rumours dreamt up by the colonel of the 10th Hussar Regiment. I tell you that he must bear in mind our gallant conduct just three days ago when we caught you unprepared and, by all the rules of war, could simply have annihilated you but instead, upon your request, chose to let you leave peacefully unwilling to fight the enemy who was not prepared for the battle. Allow me, also, to add that if there anyone who can complain about the violation of international law, then it is certainly me for I have been sent as a flag-bearer to Reims but was greeted with an artillery round.' Unwilling to continue this conversation, I bowed to the general and left without waiting for his answer. For the rest of the day we treated each other coldly, not because there was some aloofness on the part of general but rather because I could no longer enjoy frank conversation after I had been subjected to such unfounded suspicions. This conversation reminded me that earlier that morning I played billiards with an officer at the general's apartment and when we were left alone, this officer furtively approached me and confided that he wanted to desert to our army and asked my help to do it. I gave a strong look [of disapproval] so he could clearly see how I received his request and then offered to finish our game. I had forgotten about this incident but my conversation with the general reminded me of it and I guessed that this officer was sent on purpose by the hussar colonel, especially since he was from the same regiment. Meanwhile this ever mistrustful colonel continued to bustle and fuss about. I later learned that he shot himself in an act of desperation after the battle of Waterloo that put an end to Napoleon's power.

Early in the morning I got up from my bed and went to the guest room of General Piquet, where I was surprised to see numerous officers, except for the colonel. They were all in full uniform and seemed to have spent a sleepless night. The General approached me and shook my hand warmly, saying, 'We want to apologise for offending you with our suspicion that there will be an attack tonight. The colonel of the 10th Hussar regiment assured all of us that he was completely certain in his information and threatened to hold me responsible [for any setbacks]. So I was forced to take necessary measures to prevent an unexpected attack. That is why we built barricades at all the town entrances and spent the night manning them.' – 'I am very sorry that you had such an eventful night,' I replied. 'I myself had a excellent night and slept well. I do hope that you will be now grateful to me for not reproaching you even though I have every right to do so. You are men of honour and are, without a doubt, regretful yourselves so I am not going to increase your misery any further.'

At ten o'clock in the morning General Emmanuel arrived to negotiate the final delimitation of areas. With these [French] officers in attendance, I naturally did not tell him what a marvellous opinion these gentlemen had of us. My position was too advantageous [to lose it] and besides, one must forgive people in misfortune.

The war thus ended. I spent several more days as the commandant of the town of Etampes before asking for permission to return to Paris, where I arrived in [late] April. Emperor Alexander's name was praised all around and his benevolence had touched everyone's hearts. I learned that Napoleon had been exiled to the island of Elba and in this incredible end to remarkable events that I had witnessed over the last twenty months I saw a perfect punishment for his invasion of Russia and defilement of our sacred altars. I envisioned the struggle between Alexander and Napoleon as the conflict between the spirits of Good and Evil in which the former could not but be victorious.

The Bourbons were soon restored in France. I watched as Comte d'Artois entered Paris and never before had I thought that popular enthusiasm could reach such levels of insanity as it did among the Parisians upon the sight of this prince. People praised him to the heavens, kissed his clothing and wept openly

– it was an indescribable public ecstasy. People all around tore white ribbons that [d'Artois] threw to the public from each other's hands, and immediately put them into their buttonholes. I was very touched by this scene. [From the Russian text in N. Golitsyn, *Ofitserskie zapiski* . . .]

Pavel Pushin

Pushin commanded a battalion of the elite Life Guard Semeyonovskii Regiment.

19 [31] March. [Thursday]. Triumphant Entry into Paris
Excitement prevented us from sleeping; we were ready [to march] much earlier than we were required. Our columns were deployed long before the Emperor arrived to lead the troops. We entered the city [of Paris] exactly at noon. We marched in the following order: [Our] sovereign's flügel-adjutants; [Our] Sovereign, the King of Prussia, princes, field marshals, commander-in-chief and others; 3rd Army Corps; Austrian grenadiers; 2nd Russian Guard Division; Prussian Guard Infantry; 1st Guard Division and all of the cavalry; [followed by the] artillery.

We entered through Faubourg Saint Martin. Crowds of onlookers increased as we advanced into the city and all of them expressed genuine happiness, shouting 'Vive Alexander! Vive King of Prussia! Vive Bourbons!' But can we really believe in any of this? Just yesterday these same people were yelling 'Vive Napoleon'. Reaching the boulevards, we marched along them to Grand Meuble and then crossed the Place de la Revolution to enter the Champs-Elysèes. Here the monarchs stopped and, as [Parisians] mobbed them, we marched in front of Their Majesties.

The Parisians were truly stunned by this spectacle. They were assured that only a small blundering column of our troops was marching on Paris, but now they saw a powerful army of splendid appearance in front of them. Passing by Their Majesties, our regiment halted in the Widow Alley, where we remained till 8 p.m. The regiment was then sent to barracks to spend the night. The Preobrazhenskii Regiment was assigned to guard the Emperor, who settled in the Hôtel de Talleyrand; one battalion of the Preobrazhenskii Regiment surrounded the Hotel while two others occupied the Champs-Elysèes.

Meantime, we, drunk with happiness, found the owner of a meagre tavern not far from our barracks and he delivered to us a rather paltry dinner, which we, nevertheless, immediately devoured as a consequence of an arduous day.

20 March [1 April]. Friday
[Today], our regiment guarded the Emperor. It was deployed in battle formation on the Place de la Revolution and our music [band] played as we waited for

the arrival of His Majesty. The famous hymn of Henry IV* made a profound impression on numerous onlookers who, as expected, gathered around us. Many of them already wear white bands on their left arms as do we. As both monarchs [Alexander and Frederick William] appeared in front of our ranks, the crowd's excitement increased and the same shouts, as the day before, began to be heard again. We made a parade march, the 1st Battalion then proceeded to the Hôtel de Talleyrand while two other battalions remained on the Champs-Elysèes; the third battalion bivouacked on the right side while the second on the left. This time we had a glorious dinner but, being unwilling to risk moving too far from our positions, we were unable to explore the streets. In the evening, however, I still managed to walk a bit in the Palais-Royal.

21 March [2 April]. Saturday
Our regiment woke up early in the morning. Officers received billets in the city, the soldiers were moved into Imperial barracks on the Quai Malaquar. I was given the apartment of M. Bourdeau on the Rue Croix de Petit Champs. Taking advantage of this first free day, I immediately went to see the Hôtel des Invalides. I visited the new bridge, the Arc de Triomphe separating the Tuileries Palace on the Place du Carrousel and the Notre Dame Cathedral. The Provisional government announced the toppling of Napoleon and declared his subjects to be [under the authority of] the Bourbons from now on.

22 March [3 April]. Sunday
Today I went to see the Pantheon, which Napoleon had not yet completed. Still, under its arches, one could already see the tombs of Voltaire, Rousseau and other great men of France. The New Pantheon is located very close from Saint-Geneviève, the most ancient church in Paris, built during the reign of King Clovis I. I then went to the Botanical Garden [*Jardin des Plantes*], where I saw a zoo that contains virtually all known species of animals. I was unable to get into a zoological cabinet because it is usually open only three times a week.

Leaving the Botanical Gardens, I crossed the Pont d'Austerlitz and, following the boulevards, I walked throughout the city. This long stroll did not tire me at all. [Later in the day] I even walked for a bit more in the garden of the Tuileries Palace, where numerous people congregated. I returned home around 6 p.m. and dined with my hosts, whose care towards me I cannot praise enough. The family consisted of old mother Madam Bourdeau, who occupied the second floor and rarely came down, M. Berten, his wife and their sons Alexis, Henri and daughter Adelie, and finally M. Berten's brother, Alexander Berten, who had spent considerable time as an émigré in Germany.

---

* Pushin refers to 'Marche Henri IV' or 'Vive Henri IV' which served as the nominal anthem of the Bourbon dynasty during the *ancien régime*. During the Revolutionary and Napoleonic Era, the song became a rallying cry for the Royalists.

After dinner I left the dining room to go to the Theatre Français. Both comedies were perfectly played. The Emperor attended the play and, expressing his approval of the actors, he compelled the public to applaud, to which Paris is rather susceptible. Particularly thundery and widespread applause began during the entr'acte when the lowered stage curtain revealed an ancient French coat of arms, the fleurs-de-lis painted on a sheet of paper. The shouts 'Vive Alexander, our saviour! Vive le Roi' could be heard from every direction and hats with white cockades quickly became vogue. The Senate, the guardian of laws, officially declared that it no longer acknowledges Napoleon [as a ruler of France].

23 March [4 April]. Monday
I went to see the Louvre and the Museum. Both owe so much to Napoleon. The architecture of the Louvre will forever serve as a monument for this unordinary man. The works of art gathered here from all countries of Europe during last few years represent everything that is breathtaking in this world. I saw here the statues of Apollo Belvedere, Venus de Milo, Laocoön, Raphael's *Resurrection of Christ* and many others. I took pleasure in the newest works of art and would have happily spent entire day in looking at all of these marvels if only several of my friends had not distracted me from my diversion and dragged me to the Palais-Royal, a more simply and marvellous place, and no less interesting as well. In the evening I went to the *Theatre des Varietes* and must acknowledge that Brenot's [?] sharp wit brought me great pleasure.

Napoleon, and the remnants of his army, arrived at Fontainebleau. Despite all the advantages of our situation, he still caused some concern and we were ordered to prepare for battle.

24 March [5 April]. Tuesday
The French Marshals Ney, Macdonald, Mortier and Marmont, as well as Caulaincourt, visited the Emperor today and informed him that Napoleon agreed to abdicate his throne but only in favour of his son.

26 March [7 April]. Thursday
Today I was at the Longchamp [Abbey] but it is unimpressive. Maybe it is because of the turbulent times.* The famous festival here usually starts on Wednesday after the Easter and continues for three days.

29 March [10 April]. Easter Sunday
A large mass was held on the Place de la Concord, also known as the Place de la Revolution. The entire Guard was under arms, made a parade march in front

---

* The Longchamp Abbey was almost completely destroyed during the French Revolution.

of the Emperor and then deployed in closed battalion columns around the prie-dieu* erected at the very spot where the French once beheaded the unfortunate Louis XVI. Now this same spot saw prayers reaching to the heavens to thank the Lord for a fortune turn of events that led to the accession of Louis XVIII to the French throne. Napoleon's marshals were present as well and had to kneel when [the accession] was announced to the thunder of Russian guns.

31 March [12 April]. Tuesday
The Comte d'Artois† made his entry into Paris. Large crowds greeted him, indescribable joy. After escorting Madam Berten to the boulevards, I could stay with her to wait for the prince's arrival because I had to dine with all colonels of the Russian and Prussian guards at the Emperor's place. At 6 p.m. the Comte d'Artois, who was declared lieutenant du Roi, appeared in front of the Emperor [Alexander]. Napoleon's abdication, signed by him the day before at Fontainebleau,‡ was publicly announced today.

1 [13] April. Wednesday
M. Berten owned an estate at Rueil where he invited me to visit them. We covered the three-mile trip between breakfast and lunch. Also near Rueil there is the small Châteu de Malmaison, the last refuge of Empress Josephine. Although this place is not spacious enough for an empress, it is, nevertheless, very beautiful, particularly a small statue, famous for its antiquity, which Napoleon brought with him from Egypt. Some people assure that it is over 4,000 years old. After lunch, for which I was invited by my hosts in Paris, I travelled to the Luxembourg Garden but because the garden is usually open until 7 p.m., I was not able to get inside and instead enjoyed the exquisite architecture of Saint Sulpice Church and then returned home crossing the Pont des Arts.

2 [14] April. Thursday
Yearning to visit the Luxembourg Palace at any cost, I went there immediately after breakfast. It was wonderful but was visited by fewer people than the Tulleries Garden. I did not enter the palace. Returning home, I went to the Saint Sulpice Church. This enormous building is decorated with marvellous columns and very beautiful murals.

3 [15] April. Friday
The Austrian emperor made a triumphal entry into Paris today. On account of this, we all were put under arms, and showed no particular excitement

---

* Pushin uses a Russian term 'analoi' to refer to the prie-dieu.
† Charles, Comte d'Artois, was the brother of Louis XVI and Louis XVIII, and the future king of France.
‡ Napoleon signed his unconditional abdication on 11 April.

about it. During the entire French campaign the Austrians contributed very little to our successes. As we entered France, a large number of the Austrian troops and Emperor Francis himself proceeded to Lyons, where they had no combat with the enemy. Still, the French admonished the Austrian emperor that he contributed to the misfortune of his own son-in-law.

[. . .]

9 [21] April. Thursday

The Duc de Berry, the son of the Comte d'Artois and nephew of the king, entered Paris today. He was greeted quite cheerfully and, when he entered the Tuilleries, the crowd rushed into the garden demanding that the prince appear on a balcony. He finally appeared with his father, who kissed him lovingly which caused general excitement and applause. My attention was drawn to an old lady, who kept grabbing my hand with tears streaming from her eyes and continually yelling, 'These caring princes, these precious princes.' I later learned that this was a certain Madam Auverne, who once was a court lady but lost everything during the Revolution; she came here with the crowd to praise the princes whom she knew quite well and who have returned to their ancestors' palace as a result of extraordinary events.

11 [23] April. Saturday

After lunch I went to see the former Augustine monastery, which is now a warehouse of various remarkable items gathered after the Revolution. The monastery is divided into the halls of the thirteenth, fourteenth, fifteenth and sixteenth centuries, and each hall is decorated in the style of that century. The halls of the sixteenth and seventheenth centuries have red glassworks, which are very beautiful. They largely show various stories, for example the story of Eros and Psyche, etc. There is no other place where you can observe the successive development of arts over 500 years. Furthermore, each hall contains monuments to famous people of that century. The gardens also feature several monuments as well as the tombs of Abelard and Heloise, Molière, [Nicolas] Boileau [Despréaux] and others.

Leaving Saint Augustine, I went to Notre Dame [Cathedral] where I climbed one of the towers to enjoy the panorama of Paris. Despite the tower's height, the city's narrow streets and tall buildings still did not allow me to observe these interesting environs and instead had to satisfy myself with a view of piled-up stones. I then went again to the Luxembourg Gardens but this time I got inside the palace and was able to see its art gallery. One can find views of all the port towns of France here.

12 [24] April. Sunday

I finally received letters from Madam B. After the parade I went to mass at the Saint Sulpice and, since I tried looking on Paris from above, I decided to climb one of the towers of this church as well. Although this tower is higher than that of Notre Dame, the panorama was even less interesting. The same sight of piled stones, and you cannot even see the Seine and its harbours from here.

In the evening, as usual, I went to the theatre. Today I was at the Vaudeville. The last of three plays – *Tyrant Women* [by Blansini] was highly inappropriate and outraged the audience. People whistled fervently, while the play's author, enraged by such a reception, insulted one of the whistlers which led to a dreadful scene which subsided only after the author was arrested. Such incidents are common occurrences in Parisian theatres.

15 [27] April. Wednesday
We were introduced to Grand Dukes Nicholai [the future Emperor Nicholas I] and Mikhail, who had recently arrived at Paris. They have grown up a lot.

19 April [1 May]. Sunday
On the occasion of the restoration of the Bourbon dynasty, all theatres offer free passes today so one can imagine enormous crowds that besieged theatre entrances from 1 p.m. Since decent people could not get inside the theatre, I took advantage of the free time to walk with Madam Berten and her family along the boulevards. We first went to the boulevard du Temple, visiting the Turkish Garden and the Princes' Garden.* They were bursting with people and illuminated which allowed bystanders to watch dancing artistes on ropes.

20 April [2 May]. Monday
The French King Louis XVIII made a jubilant entry into Paris. There were enormous crowds of people. I was with Madam Berten and other ladies in a house near Pont Neuf and watched the procession. The town was illuminated in the evening. The Tuilleries Garden was magnificently illuminated but the fireworks, displayed on the Pont de Revolution, was rather meagre.

22 April [4 May]. Wednesday
We held a review after which we marched in parade formation before the King. He can no longer sit on a horse so he was standing at one of the palace windows.

23 April [5 May]. Thursday
Both the Bertens and their uncle Alexander offered me to travel to St. Cloud after lunch. We took one of those carriages, known as a coucou, that always wait near the Tuilleries. They have one horse, are on two wheels and you

---

* The Jardin Turc and Jardin des Princes were famous and very popular cafés and gardens in the Marais district of Paris.

have to sit in front. Four people easily fit inside but usually more people sit in them. So, travelling in such carriage we covered the one mile that separates Paris from St. Cloud. Unfortunately we arrived too late to see everything that was interesting since dusk was expected soon. But while Alexander and Alexis Bertens went to see a horse which they wanted to buy, Henri Berten and I took a stroll in a park. The landscape is marvellous here but the château is quite small. I heard that it is magnificently decorated inside. The entire village, located on a hill on the Seine riverbank, was an enthralling sight. The same can be said about everything found on the road from Paris to St. Cloud. The road runs through the Bois de Boulogne, the village of the same name and streaks along the Seine River. We returned to Paris at 10 p.m. We were thoroughly searched at the gates to ensure that we were not transporting contraband. Contraband is handled rather strictly here and people are not allowed to transport even two bottles of wine inside Paris without paying a fee for them.

27 April [9 May]. Monday
During breakfast M. Berten (the father) got the idea to travel to Versailles. I naturally eagerly agreed to accompany and so the three of us – M. Berten, M. Portier and I, went. M. Portier, a jovial, merry fellow, made us laugh the entire trip. We could not stop to see the famous porcelain factory at Sevres since we were hurrying to Versailles, where we, despite all our haste, arrived only at 3 p.m. Versailles is a very beautiful town. The façade of the palace, facing the road from Paris, is very handsome, and the stables built in a semi-circle greatly adorn it. As soon as we stopped, a certain person, very courteous, appeared and offered to show us everything noteworthy in Versailles. We accepted his offer and here is what I deduced from the Versailles sight-seeing.

The library, beside the books that embellish it, contains several idols brought from the Americas, models of various ships, a skeleton of a small creature which closely resembles a human one, except for its skull. The Versailles Park is seven miles (about 28 verstas [29.8km]) in circumference and is magnificent, although it is monotonously planned. The palace façade from the park is fabulous and was refurbished by Napoleon. Thus edifice, built by Louis XIV, is enormous and its opulence cannot be compared to anything else. Here even the superb bronze and marble statues by great masters seem rather casual and ordinary creations.

The palace itself is located on a hill, the slope of which descends into a garden with numerous fountains which, however, cannot operate all day but only for a few hours because the famous mechanism,* which supplies

---

* Pushin refers to the famous Machine de Marly, a French engineering marvel built by Arnold de Ville and Rennequin Sualem in 1684 to supply water to Versailles and its

water from Marly two miles away, cannot provide enough water. I came to the conclusion that our Peterhof garden* is incomparably better. The Grand and Petit Trianon are two small palaces inside the park. Their architecture and interior are scrupulously maintained. Napoleon lived in the former at one time. The art gallery and malachite vases were given by Emperor Alexander as gifts to the French emperor when they were still on good terms. The interior of the main Versailles palace has been neglected since the years of the Revolution. Gilded decorations attracted attention as remnants of the opulence which once adorned this palace. Nevertheless, the palace theatre and church are still in good condition and deserve attention.

After completing sight-seeing we went to eat at a tavern and since M. Berten had several acquaintances in Versailles, we visited them before returning to Paris at 10 p.m. If I ever have a chance, I will certainly return to Versailles to see it more casually and not as hurriedly as we did it today.

7 [19] May. Thursday
Twice a week, a festivity is held in the Tivoli Gardens† situated on the outskirts of Paris. Usually, these festivals are held on Thursdays and Sundays. Today the fête was declared an exceptional one, so how could I miss it? Shortly before 8 p.m, I took a carriage and went to Tivoli. Going through a long, lighted alley I came to the entrance. Here people were asked to leave their canes, swords, etc. so I did as requested, bought a ticket, which, because of the exceptional nature of this particular festivity, cost 5 francs, when it is usually 3 francs. The whole garden was illuminated and full of people. The first thing that struck me was this round grove which contained, both on the left and right, cosmoramas [illuminated pictures]. They depicted the sights of Italy: on one side – a volcanic eruption, on the other – a valley. Very pleasant music calmed our mood. Further on, mothers entertained their children with puppets, which also drew the attention of adults because they were indeed very entertaining. Moving on, I heard pleasant voices singing to the accompaniment of two violins and two harps so I stopped to listen to them. When this little concert was over, I continued my way but soon heard the sound of a quadrille,‡ performed by a large orchestra, so I stopped to watch the pretty dancers. A few steps away – swings, shooting galleries, and

---

fountains. The machine consisted of fourteen gigantic water wheels, each about 36ft wide, that moved dozens of pumps to bring water up a hillside from the Seine.
* Pushin refers to the Peterhof Palace founded by Peter the Great and completed by Empress Elizabeth in the mid-eighteenth century.
† Jardin de Tivoli, Paris, a garden and park open between 1766 and 1842, created to resemble the gardens of the Villa d'Este in Tivoli, Italy.
‡ The quadrille is an historic dance performed by four couples in a square formation, a precursor to traditional square dancing.

thousands of other entertainments that all caught my attention. Finally, two jugglers in different places completely befuddled me and I did not know where to go and what to see first. In conclusion, this beautifully illuminated garden presented a magnificent sight and I did not notice how time passed before 9 o'clock. Artists on a tightrope also held my attention. After 10 p.m. magnificent fireworks were on display. I walked around until midnight, and I confess that 5 francs is a very small fee compared to the pleasure that one gets at this outdoor celebration in Tivoli.

11 [23] May. Monday
Finding no place in the theatre 'Variety', I went to Mr. Pierre's *Cabinet mécanique*. This place is the height of perfection: it showed the island of Corfu, with its ports and vessels sailing in and out; Windsor Castle, traffic on the Thames, the movement of vehicles and pedestrians; valley of Montmorency, the famous place of residence of J.-J. Rousseau; the port of Brest; a storm, etc. The whole mechanism is so simple that if not for the small dimensions that highlighted the lack of living people, one could just fall into the error [of believing it was real].

14 [26] May. Thursday
Today, at 4 p.m., I witnessed a very grisly scene – the execution of a counterfeiter carried out in the Place de Grève. Usually, the guillotine is set up for a few hours before the execution and removed immediately after it is dome. The unfortunate was brought in by a gendarme in a cart. He did not mount the scaffold but was instead carried up on to it because he was unconscious.

19 [31] May. Tuesday
I wanted to visit Bagatelle, an English garden in the Bois de Boulogne, but the Duc de Berry, who visits it almost daily, has prohibited letting anyone in except on Mondays and Fridays; besides, a ticket was required to get in. So I, being on horseback, travelled around its walls and looked into the garden over them, unable to get inside. However, from what I had seen I found Bagatelle to be a mere trifle, which I did not hope to see because a daily order announced our impending departure on Friday.

21 May [2 June]. Thursday
Emperor Alexander has left Paris.

22 May [3 June]. Friday
We left Paris in pouring rain at 9 a.m. King of Prussia was present at our departure. The corps headquarters went to St. Germain, while my battalion halted at Noisy, a few miles from St. Germain, at 6 p.m. We passed through Marly and saw the famous [water wheel] machine [delivering water to

Versailles] that seemed rather worn out which is hardly surprising since it has been around since the time of Louis XIV. My host at Noisy is not particularly polite, but his house, and his garden in particular, is very beautiful.

23 May [4 June]. Saturday

Today, I went to spend the day in Paris. I had to travel six verstas [6.4km], passing through Saint-Cloud. You cannot describe the joy of the Bertin family when I arrived. I could not refuse their lunch and I spent the rest of the time on shopping until it was time to go to the theatre. I was at Fabo, and since it was too late to return to Noisy, I stayed the night in Paris and asked permission to spend the night at Mademoiselle Louise Chatelet, Rue Valois. She was my kept woman, so I was accepted with open arms and spent a fun time. [From the Russian text in P. Pushin, *Dnevnik, 1812–1814*]

A. Baranovich

After more than a month in Paris, the Russian troops began to gradually leave the French capital and return home. But some Russian troops enjoyed France so much that they decided to stay.

[In 1814], following the peace with the French, our artillery company was ordered to stop at Epernay [on the Marne], in a region famous for its champagne. During our six-week stay here, our soldiers became known to the locals for their honesty and service and the latter began to employ them in vineyards, field work, and at home; oftentimes, when the owners left for work, they trusted their property to our soldiers, later treating them to plenty of champagne, which however had no effect on Russian minds, only making soldiers go red in the face. After a six-week respite, we received orders to prepare to march back to Russia. On the scheduled day, all the rank-and-file gathered at the camp, where local residents and their families bid farewell to us, treating us to various foods and wishing us a safe journey back home. Some locals even decided to accompany [our soldiers] to our next bivouac some 17 verstas [18km] away. There they again treated [us] with great delight and then bid us farewell once more. The following day, as we prepared to march, we discovered that seventeen soldiers were missing – they had fled to the locals who promised to take care of them and even marry their daughters to them. When we reached the borders of Russia, we heard that some 40,000 [Russian] soldiers had deserted and stayed behind in France. Emperor Alexander requested their return from King Louis XVIII and promised that those who returned on their own to their unit or family would not be punished and their travel costs would be covered by the Emperor himself. But the [French] king was unable to satisfy the Emperor's request because the French people had hidden our runaways and none of them [ever] returned. It was easy for our soldiers, who are skilled for any work, to find a shelter [with locals] but our officers with their meagre edification . . . would have found no place to stay and no piece of bread to eat so no one heard of any Russian officer abandoning his post. [From the Russian in A. Baranovich, 'Russkie soldaty vo Frantsii . . .']

Eduard von Löwenstern

A junior officer in the Sumskii Hussar Regiment which was attached to the Russian 6th Corps.

Soon we also received orders and the march route to Russia. Our cavalry set in motion. I barely had time to ride to Songent to take leave of my fat Fleming. I could not resist the pleasure of giving the little Abbot a good flick on the nose from my horse. Thus, we left Achy and marched to Beauvais. In this large and beautiful city, I was given quarters at a widow's house. The woman was not yet old but never since then has such an evil fiend crossed my path as this one. I had just ridden into the courtyard when she, blue with rage, grabbed my horse by the reins, throwing thousands of swearwords at me and becoming so angry that she got cramps when I stayed calm amidst all the noise. The neighbours collected, laughing at the very comic scene and tore the crazy woman who had bitten my horse off me. In order to have peace, I rode to an inn where the *diligence* from Boulogne was coming in. Here I found a happy group, mostly English, who were taking advantage of the peace to travel to Paris. We treated each other to champagne, and I enjoyed myself immensely the whole evening, especially since a *diligence* from Paris greatly increased the size of our party. I had to leave my bay with the Sumy Regiment. The horse had a damaged hoof and afterwards, like all of my other things, was lost.

In Clermont, I billeted with a notary in the outskirts. Pahlen left the corps behind and travelled on ahead. I had earnestly to think about paying all of the little debts I had here and there with members of the Regiment. That was no little task to pay a quite considerable amount without money. I did not sleep the whole night, my thoughts going in every direction; and since I could not think of anything intelligent to do about it, I took the Extra-post before sunrise and went to Compiègne. My creditors were all still sound asleep. I think that they could not have been completely satisfied with me, but what was to be done. I was gone and the gentlemen had to have patience. The sun was just coming up when I reached beautiful Compiègne. I was breathing more freely because I had Clermont with all of my creditors behind me. The palace and garden of Compiègne were most charming. The Count came riding after me at noon. He laughed when I explained why I had not paid in Clermont. He thought that had been the wisest thing. Count Pahlen was travelling with his own horses. He and his younger brother Ivan were sitting in a two-seater,

Kolatshevski and Novossilzev were using the Count's droshky,* Macdonald his little carriage; and I was sailing out in front with the post carriage in order to find quarters and forage for the gentlemen.

In St. Quentin, I had an argument with Macdonald because of the quarters. He complained that he always got the worst ones. In order to have peace and quiet, I sent him to the major in the office for quarters and took care of the matter that way, since the doctors were usually quartered with ones of their craft or with apothecaries. Since these were not always the richest people in the city, Macdonald was not completely wrong to complain.

In Guise I climbed the old ruins of the ancestral palace of the Dukes of Guise, who had caused the Kings of France many a sour hour. Here I housed with a rich jeweller on the market who took me in. After resting for several hours, we went to friendly La Chapelle in the night. We passed through Girson and stayed in Maubert-Fontaine. Even though my landlord went around in *sarrau* and *sabots,* he was no simple peasant. He spoke French like a Parisian and talked intelligently about France's present situation that it was a pleasure to listen to him until late at night. As a young boy, he had been in Paris during the Revolution and related many an interesting story about the time of the Terror. The meal he set before me was small but tasty, the wine of the best. His only daughter seldom came into the room. She busied herself with something. If she stayed too long, he gave her a nod that she should leave. We parted in the morning as good friends since our opinions of the Bourbons and Napoleon agreed completely.

The French garrison did not let us enter Fort Rocroy. We had to detour by way of Glacis, and the heavy fog prevented me from seeing the fort. The swampy poor area of Rocroy contrasts unpleasantly with the marvellous area along the shores of the Meuse we could not admire enough. In Fumay, we rented a boat and took a pleasant trip on the Meuse. Count Pahlen, as he admitted later, had a happy intrigue with his landlord's daughter. At Vieuz Mollin, we crossed the Meuse. The impenetrable Fort of Charlemont and the city of Givet close beneath Charlemont still had a French garrison. We were immediately surrounded by a detachment of National Guard that hurriedly moved us through the fort. These people did not even give us enough time to enjoy a refreshing glass of wine. I was riding in a little carriage pulled by two horses; and since I wanted to get to Dinant early to assure quarters would be ready, I encouraged my driver to go fast. A command of French gendarmes came toward me. My peasant complained about me and the commander gave the peasant a loaded pistol with orders to shot me dead like a dog if I wanted to force him to drive faster. I acted as if I did not understand French and happily arrived in Dinant. The area around Dinant is enchanting. I had to drive through a natural gate in Mont-

---

* A droshky or drozhki was a type of light four-wheeled carriage used in Russia,

Bayard to reach Dinant. Since it was not yet late, we drove to Namur for the night where Pahlen wanted to rest for several days.

In Namur I billeted with President Dupres. I really liked Aline, his pretty, cheerful daughter, a sixteen-year-old girl. The Russian powder depot there had exploded due to carelessness a few days before, taking several dozen houses nearby with it. I accompanied Monsieur Dupres and Aline on a walk to the powder depot and watched that lovely girl distribute over twenty ducats to the recently wounded. It is hardly possible to wish for something better than I had it in Namur. The old President loved a good drink and found in me a brave drinking partner who regularly drank him under the table every evening.

Old Madame Dupres was a kind, somewhat sensitive woman. In me, pretty Aline found a tender suitor since I was really in love with her. After a stay of several days, I left Namur with a heavy heart. Aline tenderly shock my hands in parting since she too had not been totally indifferent. Young Dupres' governess, a girl about twenty years old, cried her eyes out. I finally had to promise to satisfy all of them that I would leave the Count in Cologne and return to Namur to spend several months with them. I promised them all of this in order to prove to them how much I liked them all and how difficult it was for me to leave them. After the Count's departure, I stayed in Namur for two more days. I count those two days to the happiest in my life. The Dupres family did not know what they should do with me to make my stay as pleasant as possible. After several sacred assurances that I would return, after tender hugs of old and young, I left my very beloved Namur.

In Huy, I only changed horses and caught up with the Count in Liège. Liège, or Lüttich, has 45,000 inhabitants and is by far larger and better built than Namur, but I could not get to like Liège. My heart and all of my thoughts were in Namur with amiable Aline Dupres. We wandered around Liège; and in the evening, I let Macdonald entice me to admire the pretty girls who were there in unbelievable numbers. We travelled through Herve to Aix-la-Chapelle. The marvellous bathing season in Aachen had begun. The streets and squares teemed with arriving bathing guests. You heard music all over. A theatre troop had arrived. Tightrope walkers, virtuosi and comics with dogs were drifting around by the dozen. The newly-finished promenade teemed with finely decked-out gentlemen and ladies; in short, the jubilation was great. Unfortunately for me there was gambling in the baths. I went there and at first only observed, risked and lost not only all the money the Count had borrowed with difficulty but also the silver off my hussar uniform; in short, anything that I had of any value. All of this bad luck did not prevent me from visiting the oldest Christian church, Charlemagne's grave, and the other sights that Aix-la-Chapelle, as one of the oldest royal residences and spas, offered visitors.

The order that no Russian officer should be billeted militarily in the spas drove me, so short of money like so many others, out of the temple. After staying ten days, Count Pahlen left Aachen and I followed him. My position was desperate without any of money, and without clothing in which I could be seen in polite society. I travelled from one place to the next. I nevertheless never lost my good mood; and I felt quite happy seeing something new every day, and travelling was my passion. In Julich a Prussian garrison was stationed. We ate at noon here, changed horses in Bergheim; and late in the night, we arrived in Cologne. Cologne lies on the beautiful Rhine that here, not like at Fort Louis, loses somewhat on width and breath because of lots of islands and curves. After staying the first night in an inn, the Mayor of Justice, whom I had got to know at the quarters' office, took me in. Novossilzev billeted together with me. We stayed in the noble old city for about two weeks. The city streets are like a labyrinth thrown together helter-skelter. Even though from boredom, I ran around the city the whole time, I was never able not to get lost, not be able to find either my own or the Count's quarters. My finances got better here with a thousand rubles pay; but to my disappointment, I gambled this last resource in drunken audacity to a dozen amicable infantry officers.

From anger always being unlucky at gambling, I drowned my worries in several bottles of old Rhine wine. I have got used to being without money, that no one should really see if I am poor or rich. I know many who feel unhappy as soon as their purse is empty. Quiet and introverted, like shadows of the dammed, they skulk around. Every sound, a somewhat wild party is horror. Every inn frightens them. The tiniest incident causes despair. I am definitely the opposite: if I have money, I am restless. The golden pieces burn holes in my purse. Thousands of plans fill my head and rob me of sleep and appetite. If I have no money, I am quiet, live from one day to the next without worrying much about the morning. Only debts are burdensome and can take away my good mood.

Novossilzev and Kolatshevski left the Count in Cologne and since they had money; travelled to Aix-la-Chapelle where they intended to spend the bathing season. They made several other travel plans which they later were not to carry out because of a considerable loss in *rouge et noir*. I remained alone with the Count at his request in order to accompany him to Karlsbad. Macdonald had also stayed. Several days later Woldemar came to Cologne from Paris, but he soon left again to go to Frankfurt am Main to get money. Woldemar gave me, when he heard that I had been transferred to the Imperial Hussars, a black horse that he had bought from Count O'Rourke for 120 *Napoleondor*. That horse was one of the most beautiful in the Army. I left it with the Sumy Regiment, where it was sold for a measly five hundred rubles to Count Keller. The trip to Carlsbad cost me since I had to hand over all of my things to different people in the Regiment. Out of all of my riding and reserve horses, I did not get a one of them returned to me. My bay became ill and had to be shot. They rode my Tscherkesse to death. My Mustapha was thus lost, and the black they sold for a trifling sum. [From the German text in E. Löwenstern, *Denkwürdigkeiten*]

Bibliography

Rossiiskii Gosudarstvennii Voenno-Istoricheskii arkhiv (RGVIA) [Russian State Military Historical Archive]

Fond No. 846 (Voenno-Uchebnii Arkhiv; VUA), *opis* No. 16

Delo 3376/2: Sergei Mayevskii's letter of 29 April 1835 to Alexander Mikhailovskii-Danilevskii, accompanied with his memoir on the battle of Craonne.

Delo 3376/2: General George Emmanuel's letter of 13 July 1835 to Alexander Mikhailovskii-Danilevskii, accompanied with a journal of his military operations in 1814.

Delo 3376/2: Colonel Moisei Karpenko's letter of 15 November 1839 to Alexander Mikhailovskii-Danilevskii, accompanied with his comments on the 1813–14 Campaigns.

Delo 4120/1: Dossier on Military Operations in France from 1 January to 1 April 1814.

Delo 4120/2: Dossier on Military Operations in France from 1 April to 31 December 1814.

Delo 4122: Dossier containing various opinions and observations on military operations

Delo 4134: Dossier with Mikhail Orlov's memoir on the capture of Paris in 1814.

Delo 4135: Dossier with printed proclamations and orders.

Published Material

Alison, Archibald, *Travels in France, during the years 1814-15: Comprising a residence at Paris during the stay of the allied armies, and at Aix, at the period of the landing of Bonaparte* (Edinburgh: printed for Macredie, Skelly, and Muckersy [et al.], 1816).

'Aperçu des transactions politiques du Cabinet de Russie. III Epoque: Depuis la rupture avec la France jusqu'a la 1-ére paix de Paris, 1813-1814', in *Sbornik Imperatorskogo Russkago Istoricheskago Obschestva*, XXXI (1880), pp. 278–416.

Baranovich, A, 'Russkie soldaty vo Frantsii, 1813-1814 gg. (iz zapisok)', *Golos minuvshego*, 5/6 (1916), pp. 153–6.

Bronevskii, Nikolai, 'Iz vospominanii generala Nikolaya Bogdanovicha Bronevskogo', *Golos minuvshego*, 3 (1914), pp. 226–38.

Chertkov, Alexander, 'Mon Itinéraire our Journal de Route,' in *1812-1814. Iz sobraniya Gosudarstvennogo Istoricheskogo muzeya* (Moscow: Terra, 1992), pp. 402–51.

Divov, N., 'Po povodu rasskaza M.F. Orlova o vzyatii Parizha,' in *Russkii arkhiv*, 1 (1878), pp. 127–8.

Glinka, Fedor, *Pis'ma russkogo ofitsera o Pol'she, Avstriiskikh vladeniyakh, Prusii i Frantsii, s podrobnym opisaniem Otechestvennoi i zagranichnoi voiny s 1812 po 1814 god* (Moscow: [n.p], 1870).

Golitsyn, Nikolai, *Ofitserskie zapiski ili vospominaniya o pokhodakh 1812, 1813, i 1814 godov* (Moscow: Tip. Augusta Semena, 1838).

Kakhovskii, Mikhail, 'Zapiski generala Kakhovskogo o pokhode vo Frantsiyu v 1814 godu', *Russkaya starina*, 2 (1914), pp. 444–62; 3 (1914), pp. 676–85.

Karpov, Aleksei, *Zapiski polkovnika Karpova, 1807-1837* (Vitebsk: tip. M.B. Neimana, 1910).

Kazakov, Ivan, 'Pokhod vo Frantsiyu 1812 g. Po neizdannym zapiskam praporshika leib-gvardii Semeyonovskogo polka Ivana Mikhailovicha Kazakova', *Russkaya starina*, 3 (1908), pp. 522–44; 5 (1908), pp. 351–68.

Khomutov, S., 'Iz dnevnika svitskogo ofitsera, 1813-1814', *Russkii arkhiv*, 7 (1869), pp. 219–303; 1 (1870), pp. 161–74.

Kovalskii, Nikifor, 'Iz zapisok pokoinago general-maiora N.P. Kovalskago', *Russkii vestnik*, 1(1871), pp. 104–17.

Langeron, Alexandre Louis Andrault, *Mémoires de Langeron, général d'infanterie dans l'armée russe. Campagnes de 1812, 1813, 1814* (Paris: A. Picard et fils, 1902).

Lazhechnikov, I., *Pokhodnye zapiski russkogo ofitsera* (Moscow: tip. N. Stepanova, 1836).

Liprandi, Ivan, 'kak byl vzyat gorod Soissoins 2/14 fevralya 1814 goda', *Russkii arkhiv* (1869), pp. 903–25.

Lorer, Nikolai, *Zapiski dekabrista, ed. Militsa Nechkina* (Irkutsk: Vostochno-Sibirskoe knizhnoe izd-vo, 1984).

Löwenstern, Eduard von, *Mit Graf Pahlens Reiterei gegen Napoleon: Denkwürdigkeiten des russischen Generals Eduard von Löwenstern, 1790-1837* (Berlin: E. S. Mittler, 1910). English text from *With Count Pahlen's Cavalry against Napoleon: memoirs of the Russian General Eduard von Löwenstern (1790-1837)*, translated by Victoria Joan Moessner with Stephen Summerfield (Huntingdon UK: Ken Trotman, 2010).

Mayevskii, Sergei, 'Moi vek, ili Istoriya generala Mayevskogo', *Russkaya starina*, 9 (1873), pp. 253–305.

Meshetich, Gavriil, 'Istoricheskie zapiski voiny rossiyan s frantsuzami i dvadtsatyu plemenami 1812, 1813, 1814 i 1815 godov', *1812 god. Vospominaniya voinov russkoi armii* (Moscow: Mysl, 1991), pp. 25–103.

Mikhailovskii-Danilevskii, Alexander, *Zapiski 1814 i 1815* (St. Petersburg: Tip. sjtaba otdelnogo Korpusa vnutrenneu strazhi, 1841).

—— *Opisaniye pokhoda vo Frantsii v 1814 godu* (St. Petersburg: [s.n.], 1845).

—— 'Sluchai, predshestvovavshie vkhodu v Parizh rossiiskikh voisk v 1814 godu', *Syn Otechestva*, 12 (1816), pp. 215–27.

—— 'Vkhod rossiiskoi armii v Parizh marta 19-go 1814 goda', *Syn Otechestva*, 48 (1816), pp. 81–92.

—— 'O prebyvanii russkikh v Parizhe v 1814 godu', *Russkii vestnik*, 9 (1819): 5-44.

—— *Memuary 1814-1815* (St. Petersburg: Russian National Library, 2001).

Mirkovich, Alexander, 'Vyderzhki iz zapisok Aleksandra Yakovlevicha Mirkovicha o pokhode 1814 goda i o prebyvanii v Parizhe', *Fedor Yakovlevich Mirkovich, 1789-1866* (St. Petersburg, 1889).

Muromtsev, Matvei, 'Vospominaniya Matveya Matveevicha Muromtseva', *Russkii arkhiv*, 1 (1890), pp. 366–94.

Ortenberg, Ivan, 'Voennye vospominaniya starykh vremen', *Biblioteka dlya chteniya*, 7 (1857), pp. 18–23.

Otroshenko, Jacob (Yakov), *Zapiski generala Otroshenko (1800-1830)* (Moscow: Bratin, 2006).

Petrov, Mikhail, 'Rasskazy sluzhivshego v pervom Egerskom polku polkovnika Mikhaila Petrova o voennoi sluzhbe i zhizni svoei i trekh rodnykh bratyev ego, zachavsheisya s 1789 goda', *1812 god. Vospominaniya voinov russkoi armii* (Moscow: Mysl, 1991), pp. 105–355.

Pushin, Pavel, *Dnevnik, 1812-1814* (Leningrad: University of Leningrad Press, 1987). English translation from *Diaries of the 1812-1814 Campaigns*, translated by Alexander Mikaberidze (Tbilisi: Napoleonic Society of Georgia, 2011).

Radozhitskii, Ilya, *Pokhodnye zapiski artillerista s 1812 po 1816 god* (Moscow: tip. Lazarevykh Instituta vostochnykh yazykov, 1835), Vol. 3.

Rochechouart, Louis-Victor-Léon de, *Souvenirs sur la révolution, l'empire et la restauration* (Paris: E. Plon, Nourrit et cie, 1889).

Skobelev, Ivan, *Rasskazy russkogo invalida: 'Ryazanskii pekhotnyi polk pri Reimse 28 fevralya, 1-e i 2-e marta 1814 goda'* (St. Petersburg, 1844).

Volkonskii, Sergei, *Zapiski Sergeya Grigorievicha Volkonskago (dekabrista)* (St. Petersburg: Sinodal'naia tipografiya, 1902).

Wellesley, Arthur, Duke of Wellington, *Supplementary despatches and memoranda of Field Marshal Arthur, duke of Wellington* (London: J. Murray, 1861), Vol. 8.

Wittgenstein, Peter, *Lettres du Feld-Marechal Prince de Sayn-Wittgenstein-Berlebourg a sa femme pendant les Guerres Napoléoniennes, 1804-1814* (Lausanne: Payot et Cie, 1905).

Zhirkevich, Ivan, 'Zapiski Ivana Stepanovicha Zhirkevicha', *Russkaya starina*, 11 (1874), pp. 411–50; 12 (1874), pp. 642–64.

Periodicals

Cobbett's Political Register, 1814.

The Examiner, 1814.

The Gentleman's Magazine, and Historical Chronicle, 1814–1816.

Le Moniteur, 1814.

Index